LE

FRO

095

19

LEOPARD III

FRONTIERS

Edited by
Christopher MacLehose

HARVILL
An Imprint of HarperCollins*Publishers*

First published in 1994 by
Harvill
An Imprint of HarperCollins *Publishers*
77/85 Fulham Palace Road,
Hammersmith, London W6 8JB

1 3 5 7 9 8 6 4 2

A CIP catalogue record for this title is
available from the British Library

ISBN 0 00 271403 5

Photoset in Linotron Galliard
by Rowland Phototypesetting Ltd, Bury St Edmunds, Suffolk
Printed and bound by
Redwood Books, Trowbridge, Wiltshire

CONTENTS

POETRY

FICTION

ACKNOWLEDGMENTS

The Publisher would like to thank all those who gave permission for the inclusion of the following material in this anthology:

Giuseppe Tomasi di Lampedusa: *Izaak Walton* and *Doctor Johnson* from *Letteratura inglese*. First published by Arnoldo Mondadori Editore, Milan, 1990 © Arnoldo Mondadori Editore S.p.A. 1990, English translation by David Gilmour © HarperCollins*Publishers* 1994.

Claudio Magris: *Who Is on the Other Side?* © Claudio Magris, 1991, 1992, English translation by Guido Waldman © Harper Collins*Publishers* 1994. This essay takes up certain themes developed in the Berliner Lektion on 1 September 1991, at the Carrefour Littéraire, Strasbourg, 9 November 1991, at the Freud-Gesellschaft, Vienna, April 1992 and at the University of Salzburg, July 1992.

Malachi O'Doherty: *It Was One Damn Good Car*. First published in the *Independent*, London, 1993 © *Independent* 1993.

Andrew O'Hagan: *Bad Bastardness*. First published in the *London Review of Books*, 1993 © *London Review of Books* 1993.

Jonathan Raban: *Julia's City* © Jonathan Raban 1994.

Dermot Healy: *Within an Ass's Roar*. First published by Harvill, 1994 © Dermot Healy 1994.

Sven Lindqvist: *To Ain Sefra* from *Ökendykare*. First published by Albert Bonniers Förlag AB, Stockholm, 1990 © Sven Lindqvist 1990, English translation by Joan Tate © HarperCollins*Publishers* 1994.

Cees Nooteboom: *Gateway to China* © First published in *Voorbije passages* by Uitgeverij de Arbeiderspers, Amsterdam, 1981 © Cees Nooteboom 1981, English translation by Ina Rilke ©HarperCollins*Publishers* 1994.

Jean-Paul Sartre: *Walking in Venice* from *La reine Albemarle ou Le dernier touriste*. First published by Editions Gallimard, Paris, 1991 © Editions Gallimard 1991, English translation by Barbara Bray © HarperCollins*Publishers* 1994.

Dermot Healy: "Prayer". First published in *The Bally Connell Colours* by Gallery Press, Co. Meath, 1992 © Dermot Healy 1992

Jaan Kaplinski: "The East-West Border" and "Once I Got a Postcard" from *The Wandering Border*. First published in the USA by Copper Canyon Press, 1987 and in Great Britain by Harvill, 1992 © Jaan Kaplinski 1987, English translation © Jaan Kaplinski 1987.

Benno Barnard: *An Autumn Day in Bohemia* from *Het gat in de*

Leopard acknowledges with gratitude the financial support of the Foundation for the Production and Translation of Dutch Literature, Amsterdam.

EDITOR'S PREFACE

Claudio Magris's essay *Who is on the Other Side?* was the keel on which this edition of *Leopard* was laid. "Literature," he says, "is intrinsically a frontier and an expedition in search of new frontiers, to shift them and define them." Not a few of the ribs are obedient to the theme, notably and enjoyably Harry Mulisch's story *The Boundary* and the poems of Jaan Kaplinski and Dermot Healy's picture of life on the edge of the Atlantic. There are stowaways, of course, as on all the best voyages: Paola Capriolo's two stories, which must be read together, and three very different visions of childhood (in Belfast and Glasgow and Holland) by Malachi O'Doherty, Andrew O' Hagan and Frans Pointl. But a *Leopard* which sails with Jonathan Raban in the American North-West, with Cees Nooteboom in the Far East, with Sartre in Venice, with Ma Yuan in Tibet, with Sven Lindqvist in North Africa, with Benno Barnard in Bohemia, with a story by Peter Høeg, a story by Zinovy Zinik, a story by José Saramago, and extracts from novels by Jean Rouaud and Boris Pekić, with a play by Zbigniew Herbert and brief essays by Giuseppe Tomasi di Lampedusa on Samuel Johnson and Izaak Walton, is a *Leopard* which conforms to its determination to publish extracts from the best work we can find in the world.

All of the editors at Harvill have contributed to this edition of *Leopard* and the lion's share has been done by Robina Pelham Burn. We are very grateful to all of the authors and to all of the translators*, invariably our counsellors and pilots.

CCML

---

*There are notes on the authors and translators at the end of the book

GIUSEPPE TOMASI DI LAMPEDUSA

Izaak Walton *and* Doctor Johnson

From *English Literature*

The Prince of Lampedusa's acute interest in English literature, nurtured on very wide reading and on extended visits to Great Britain, bore remarkable fruit in a series of informal seminars to a circle of students in Palermo. The charm of these short essays resides particularly in the appreciation brought by a great Continental writer to the English national character, to the English sense of humour; his view of what constitutes "Englishness" tends to be most perceptive.

IZAAK WALTON

In London there is a street, St James's, which is almost entirely occupied by luxury shops for men. Ties, shoes, polo sticks and golf clubs adorn the windows of minute shops in which the quality of the articles for sale has been examined with the scrupulous care of a poet examining the lyrics which might adorn his collection. The finest shotguns for every sort of quarry from a thrush to an elephant; every type of cartridge from the lightest for killing a bird without damaging its plumage to the most powerful for shooting dead a furious rhinoceros charging at you. Tobacco of every kind and from every country, from our own coarse "Tuscan" to certain cigars from the Philippines which smell of pineapples, Turkish cigarettes as well as Egyptian, Armenian, Afghan, Russian, Indochinese, Peruvian and Australian; cigarettes whose tobacco has soaked in the oil of roses, and cigarettes which after manufacture have lain for a year in the same vaults as dried cod; cigarettes with saffron, with cinnamon and with incense; cigarettes red, black and yellow; cigarettes flavoured with whisky, and cigarettes flavoured with patchouli. Briar pipes, meerschaum pipes, pipes of amber and ivory, old and new, smooth and carved, rounded, cubic, in the shape of a tomato or a pyramid, straight pipes, pipes curving downwards and pipes curving up, mouthpieces of every variety from those of Manila leaf which make the smoke cold to those dug from bones of the dead which make the soul frozen. Cigarette lighters working on petrol, gas, electricity and now, I suppose, nuclear energy; lighters made of gold, silver, platinum, steel, jade and wood, functioning by means of springs, rollers, pistons and levers – plus flint from Tibet; lighters that do not go out unless there's a gale of 125km an hour, lighters with clocks and lighters with compasses, lighters which emit a dull rumbling in your pocket to warn you that the fuel is nearly exhausted. And the different types of fuel! Colourless, red, green, amaranth and yellow. Quick-lighting fuels and others with a delaying action, fuels scented with oregano, with *peau d'Espagne* and Chanel 22; and other fuels as well, particularly evil-smelling, which are useful for getting rid of bores.

There are wine shops, shops for walking-sticks and shops for dogs. All with a tone of refined elegance. Even the most self-possessed of men are bemused. The prices are in guineas.

But there are also shops for fishing tackle, for the noble and combative sport of angling (even tunny fish are caught this way) much practised in the seas, rivers, lakes, streams and brooks of England. These shops are overflowing inside with hooks, rods, bait, lines, barrels and whatever man has ever designed for deceiving and destroying these innocent creatures. But the window, chastely draped with ivory-coloured velvet, exhibits only one book, a slender little volume bound in green leather: *The Compleat Angler* by Izaak Walton (finally we have reached it).

Izaak Walton (1593–1683) is at the same time one of the most solid "classic" writers in English literature and one of those still read in our own times. In his ninety years he produced only two slim books, about six hundred pages all told; but he owes his fame and constant popularity to the fact that he is the most English of the English: the model Englishman. (Besides being an excellent stylist.)

First of all he was "a scholar and a sportsman": one of his books is about fishing, the other is made up of nine brief biographies of famous men whom he knew (what he meant by "knowing" people we will see shortly). A duplicity of talents which is an indispensable requirement in England, a country in which a student, let's say from Cambridge, who excels in the composition of Greek verse is morally disqualified if, to these humanistic exploits, he does not add equivalent feats of rowing and boxing.

Walton has great talent in both fields. (Over Milton hangs an unexpressed, perhaps unconscious shadow, because to his repeated academic triumphs in ancient languages there was no corresponding success in "games".)

Apart from this, *The Compleat Angler* is a book full of flavour and humour. With the most detailed instructions on the ways of preparing bait and shortening rods are mixed the most delightful descriptions of rivers and lakes; types of amateur and professional fishermen are delineated with the most good-humoured benevolence; the ample drinking in welcoming taverns after the fishing is narrated with a humour not unworthy of Shakespeare or Dickens; and the wisest (let us also say the most high-minded) advice about "fair play", of fair-mindedness towards rival anglers and towards the fish themselves (who must be allowed to "struggle" at their leisure) – all this is dispensed with an unexpected solemnity which makes one understand how close these things are to the good Walton's heart. This subject matter has produced the most delightful, most "Anglican" style that one can imagine: everything in "understatement", in half-tones, like a watercolour by Rowley. One needs to have a well-trained palate to appreciate how many subtle ingredients have been put into this sauce which complements that taste for shade shared by the trout and salmon of the lakes.

Very similar is the attitude Walton adopts in his *Lives*. Instead of tench and carp he is dealing with men, truly illustrious men such as Donne and Herbert. But that is of no importance to Walton. For him they are not great poets but "gentlemen and friends" which is much more important. The biography of Donne discusses only his ecclesiastical life and his sermons; the fact that he was one of the greatest English lyric poets is not even mentioned. The life of Herbert describes at fascinating length how he helped a carter drag his cart out of the mud and how many pairs of shoes he distributed to the poor in his parish. Walton does not know (or pretends not to know) that Herbert was one of the greatest religious poets of his time.

In short, Walton is the anti-Plutarch. Delightful Englishism, faithful mirror of that extraordinary country in which one can spend weeks in daily contact with an old gentleman before realizing that he is an illustrious admiral or an ex-viceroy of India (in fact, a similar thing happened to me with Lord Haldane).

Walton, one must understand, is not Shakespeare nor Donne nor

Milton. There is nothing one can compare (in intensity) with Dickens or Browning. But if one wishes to know "the Englishman" in a pure state it is better to know him and ignore the others.

(Neither Hitler nor Mussolini had read him.)

DOCTOR JOHNSON

I have entitled this part of the course the "Age of Johnson". This is not a title which I myself have invented but the one which is generally given to this period. Now I must explain to you why Johnson deserves this honour, and that is not easy. Like many things in England, the country least governed by logic, it has to be perceived by intuition. Every civilized Englishman has known it, one might say, from birth, I have succeeded in understanding it only after much effort, and I hope I can succeed in making you understand it as well. I will begin by saying that the definition is correct, doubly correct and perhaps triply so. The first reason is intrinsic to Johnson himself; the other two are extrinsic and I will explain them afterwards. I will add that it is important to understand the reasons for Johnson's great fame because *Johnson is England* and to understand him is to take a short cut to understanding his country.

Johnson was a man of the highest learning, of that degree of learning that in any other country would have forced him to espouse a philosophy. Johnson's philosophy does not exist. He was a pure empiricist. First point.

Johnson's learning was exclusively classical or English. Other countries did not exist for him, not because of any nationalist zeal (it was he who proclaimed that "patriotism is the last refuge of a scoundrel") but because of his absolute and innate inability to comprehend anything other than the English style. Second point.

He did not belong to any particular sect and had not set foot in a church "since my mother dragged me there by my ear". Yet every evening before going to sleep and every morning he knelt in his nightshirt beside his bed and said his prayers. And he used to justify his behaviour by referring to such and such a passage from the Bible. Johnson was a religious man. Third point.

He was full of humour, a choleric, uncompromising, sometimes coarse humour, like Swift. Fourth point.

Johnson was born in Lichfield, a grim industrial town in the Midlands, and lived for fifty years in Cheapside, right in the centre of the

City of London, which in his time was the heart of the already immense capital. But each Sunday he took himself out into the country, had a picnic on the grass and returned home with a bunch of wild flowers. Every Englishman, like him, is a countryman in exile, even if he lives in the middle of square kilometres of buildings. Fifth point.

When he was working for a publisher on his *Lives of the Poets*, he refused to return the proofs (preferring instead to pay a heavy forfeit) before receiving from the provinces some insignificant information about the life of an obscure poet. Another time he got up in the middle of the night to go to the printing-press to correct the punctuation of an article. The scruples not so much of righteousness but of a man who cares about his profession. Sixth point.

Each morning at five o'clock Johnson had a cold bath and he also changed his shirt every day. But his shoes were seldom polished and he often had dirty nails: the content is more important than the appearance. Seventh point.

One evening he was assaulted by thieves who robbed him and beat him up to such an extent that he lost three teeth and had two ribs broken. To the friends who visited him he said he was surprised by so much concern because all that had happened was a lively exchange of opinions. (Any one of us [Sicilians] would have cried, "they have killed me!") On another occasion he was received by the King, who in recognition of his talents gave him a snuffbox studded with diamonds. At the coffee-house the following morning he said that the King had been very kind: "He has given me the means to take snuff." *Understatement*. Eighth point.

I could continue but it would be pointless. It is the fusion, the mutual animation of these and many other English characteristics that formed the character of Johnson. One example, ten examples, a hundred examples are not enough unless one grasps the astonishing fact that these national peculiarities all met in one man who was, for other reasons, so remarkable. Dante, to give a different case, was a good example of "the Italian". He possessed many of the characteristics that we all have: the cult of form, figurative language, the factiousness, the poverty, the sense of political exile. Imagine that we now knew for certain that he had also been a gossip, a womanizer and a "double-crosser": he would no longer be Signor Dante Alighieri, he would be Italy. Similarly, our man of letters is no longer Dr Samuel Johnson but Mr John Bull.

Many people before him had possessed two or three or ten of these

English peculiarities. No one either before or after has possessed all of them, or at least no one that we know of. And here we arrive at an extrinsic reason for Johnson's fame. Living in England at that time was James Boswell, a strange type of Scotsman, partly a man of letters and partly one of that extraordinary regiment of adventurers which invaded Europe at the end of the eighteenth century (and to which Italy contributed with its Goranis, Casanovas and Cagliostros). This curious fellow regarded Johnson with limitless devotion. He saw him every day for several hours; on leaving, he noted down in great detail what Johnson had said and done. And after his death, Boswell published his biography, an enormous work, part monumental pyramid and part washerwoman's gossip, which combine to make it the finest biography ever written. I feel justified in calling it a pyramid because inside Johnson is guarded like one of those Egyptian mummies to which people wanted to grant all the gifts of life.

Boswell himself stands aside and gives us the pleasure of hearing Johnson's voice as if it were a gramophone recording, of understanding his sarcasm, of appreciating the wisdom of his judgments. And around him is the picturesque crowd of contemporary writers, some haughty, others voracious, all subjected to the scowl of the Master. This is the "pyramidal side". On the "laundry side" we are told about the subject's personal habits, his whims, his gastronomic tastes and his clothes with such a mass of detail that his living presence becomes almost overpowering. Boswell's *Life of Johnson* is one of the key books in English literature. Johnson had the extraordinary good fortune not only to incarnate his own country but also to be the "least . . . dead" of men.

To this should be added the second extrinsic reason: the admirable portrait painted by Reynolds which shows him alive and pulsating in all his ugliness, with his warts and those serious eyes of his that resemble an intelligent dog's.

Recently Boswell's diaries, written before he met Johnson, have been discovered and published. These are also of total sincerity and give us in a couple of volumes a picture of the epoch that otherwise one could obtain only through studying hundreds of documents. It used to be said that Boswell without Johnson would have been nothing. Perhaps it was true. In any case Johnson without Boswell would have been very much less than he is now.

"But," you will say, "what has this blessed man written to deserve such authority in his lifetime and such a reputation after his death? We had never heard of him before."

He wrote a good deal: little of great value, though several things are useful. Above all he excelled in the type of criticism which was in those days the most immediate and effective: spoken criticism. Socrates never wrote a thing. But he talked, he taught and he influenced a restricted circle of people which contained the seeds of the human future.

His principal works are *A Dictionary of the English Language* (1755) and *Lives of the Poets*. Although compiled a hundred years before them, the *Dictionary* is the equivalent of our Tommaseo or the French Littré, and was the first to use passages from great writers to clarify the meaning of words. In it he demonstrates that he was not only a great philologist but also a skilled writer, capable of grasping different nuances in the meaning of words. Naturally, since then the English language has changed a good deal, but for those words that were contemporary or preceded him, Johnson remains valuable.

Lives of the Poets is an enormous work in more than a hundred volumes in which each collection of poems from every single author is accompanied by an account of his life. I unearthed a set in a second-hand bookshop in Turin, bought at a high price and totally destroyed in the bombing [of the Palazzo Lampedusa in 1943]. Johnson's honesty shines through every page: his judgments are always just, except in the case of Milton whom he detested for political reasons. There is a minor poet, Edmund Allen, of whose life Johnson admits that there is very little to record; "But since I do not wish his shadow to disappear without a little fame lighting the dark way, I want to draw attention to this sonnet as homage to his solitary soul." [NB This is a translation of a translation, not the original quote.]

Apart from these two colossal works, Johnson wrote an account of a visit to Scotland, numerous fine essays and a sort of philosophical novella which has as its setting Abyssinia (for which he always had a curious esteem), *Rasselas*, which is delightful and which I still have. He also wrote some verses in the manner of Boileau: a satirical poem "London" and the moralistic "The Vanity of Human Wishes", which are not bad. He wrote, too, a great many critical works, among the most notable of which are a defence of the old English drama and an attack on Aristotelian unity, which was plagiarized by French Romantics (a euphemism so as not to mention Victor Hugo) when, sixty years later, they wished to create "the new theatre".

Translated from the Italian by David Gilmour

CLAUDIO MAGRIS

Who Is on the Other Side?

Considerations about Frontiers

In his best-known book, Danube, *Professor Magris succeeded in lucidly marking out the basic cultural identities of each people through whose lands his journey took him. He was forever crossing frontiers, and in this essay he develops the question that remains all too relevant at the present time in the Balkan lands: Borders divide and encourage mutual distrust; but people need boundaries within which to define their own collective identities. Borders might well be swept away – but would that make for a more peaceable world?*

A Polish writer, Lec, relates how, finding himself once upon a time at Pančevo, on the left bank of the Danube, and looking across to the opposite bank and Belgrade, he felt that he was still in his own land, at home, because this bank on which he stood had once formed the border of the old Austro-Hungarian monarchy which, even many years after its collapse, he continued to consider as his world, while beyond the river a different world began. For him what lay beyond the river was "the other side". Another Polish writer, Andrej Kuśniewicz, comments on this page of Lec to observe that he fully recognized this feeling; for him, too, that lost frontier marked the confines of his world. In both their minds Belgrade was "the other side".

In both cases the writer seems to recognize perfectly well where it is he belongs, behind which frontier he feels at home. On other and more frequent occasions, such identification does not seem so simple.

Once when I was a student living at Freiburg in the Black Forest, in one of those inns which serve as nothing less than a university of knowledge and life for a young man, I went with some friends to Strasbourg, which I had never visited. It was the winter of 1962–63. For our guide we had a gentleman who was a good deal older than us, a fellow-guest at the *Goldener Anker* or Golden Anchor. He was a German from the Black Forest like all the others, but he had traced very much his own path. A few years after the Nazis came to power he had left Germany, impelled not by necessity, for he belonged to the Führer's beloved Aryan race, but simply for political reasons, or better, ethical ones. His loyalty to human kind had not displaced his love for his German homeland, and assuredly was never to dull the pain of the ensuing German catastrophe, the destruction and dismemberment of his country. When he had crossed the border between Germany and France, he had not the smallest intention of forgetting his German homeland or of turning his back on it; what he did feel was that, at that moment, and for so long as the Nazi regime endured, his authentic homeland, or better his proper place, was on the other side.

A border has two sides to it, it's ambiguous: at one moment it is a bridge on which to meet, at another, a barrier of rejection. Often it is an obsessive need to situate a person or thing as being on the other side; I take the view that literature is, among other things, a journey towards discrediting this myth of the other side, towards grasping that everyone finds himself now on this side now on the other – that Everyman, as in a medieval mystery play, is the Other. The writer who invented the literary landscape of Trieste, Scipio Slataper, begins *Il mio Carso* by seeking to identify himself, and discovers that, in order to establish his basic identity, he needs must invent it and claim to be another, born elsewhere, in some part of the Slav world that finds itself in conflict with all in Trieste that is Italian, even while it remains an element in Trieste's civilization.

In Trieste I was born and lived until I was eighteen; when I was a small boy, it was not merely a frontier town, it seemed to be a frontier in its own right, made up of all those borders that intersected within it, boundaries that sometimes crossed inside the persons and lives of the town's inhabitants. Borderlines are also lines which cross and dissect a body, they mark it like scars or wrinkles, they sunder a person not only from his neighbour but also from himself.

The Triestine frontier, moreover, is and in particular was a frontier with the East; what I used to see quite concretely before me when I'd go to play on the Carso with my friends was the Iron Curtain, the frontier which in those days cut the whole world in two and ran just a few kilometres from my house. Beyond lay the vast, unknown and threatening world which was Stalin's empire, a world more or less inaccessible, at least until the beginning of the 1950s. But at the same time those lands beyond the border, which belonged to the "other" Europe, had been Italian until not many years previously, until the end of the war, when they were occupied and annexed by Yugoslavia; these were lands I had seen and known as a child, they formed an integral part of the Triestine cosmos, of my own reality – and they continue to do so.

Beyond the frontier, therefore, resided at the same time the known and the unknown; there was an unknown that needed rediscovering. Since my childhood I had more than an inkling that if I was to grow, if I was to form my own identity in such a way as to avoid a total split, I should have to cross that border – and not only in a physical sense with a visa on a passport, but most of all on an inner journey to rediscover the world that lay beyond the border and to integrate it into my reality.

Beyond that border began the other Europe – this adjective "other" derived principally, of course, from the area's forming a part of Stalin's universe, but it also displayed Western ignorance. As a child I too believed that Prague lay to the east of Vienna, and I was not a little amazed when the school atlas put me right. This widespread ignorance was and is often tinged with scorn, whether intended or not. What lies to the East tends to look obscure, alarming, promiscuous, undignified; there is a tendency to equate East with Negative. Prince Metternich used to say of Vienna, that beyond the Rennweg, the great artery crossing the Austrian capital, began the Balkans, and he used the term to mean something vague and indistinct, something pejorative; today, at Ulm, several kilometres west of Vienna, they say that at Neu-Ulm across the Danube (which runs through the city) the Balkans begin, and here too the term is by no means complimentary.

The frontier is bridge or barrier; it stimulates dialogue or stifles it. My sentimental education has been marked by the odyssey of frontiers, arbitrary and inevitable as they are. Hence the definition of Trieste, for instance, which was very prevalent in those years, as "little Berlin": the Iron Curtain was very close and, at least until half-way through the 1950s, separated the city from its hinterland and therefore from itself, sundering our lives. One occasionally had the sense of not merely living on a frontier but of being a frontier. The comparison with Berlin applied in fact far better to Gorizia, a city literally split in two. "Just like Berlin," Doctor Krainer (a Gorizian notary of Austrian origin) would smugly remark as he opened his windows which gave on to the Transalpine Station and pointed to the barbed wire a few metres beyond.

Some cities are located on borders, others contain borders and are defined by them. These are cities denied a part of their reality by the vicissitudes of politics, denied their hinterland, for instance, the strong bond with the rest of the national territory; history serves to open the wound and turn them into a world-stage, i.e. a theatre of the absurd. It is in these cities that the ambiguity, the positive and negative aspect of the frontier, is most intensely experienced; frontiers open and closed, rigid and flexible, anachronistic and obsolete, protective and destructive.

In Trieste all this tended to produce a feeling of uncertainty, of alienation and estrangement, a sense of living at once at the centre and on the periphery. The city, which until 1954 was a free territory administered by the Americans and British, was and was not a part of Italy; it was easier there than elsewhere to question the possibility of a future, there was no knowing who and what one was, and this provoked continual rehearsals of one's own identity. The collective consciousness felt itself smothered by boundaries on all sides, but it kept desperately surrounding itself with new borders to avoid all clear-cut attribution and create an identity by virtue of this exaggerated otherness. Here was an Italian city which had lived to the full a life of nationalist zeal, a city whose patriots often had names of German or Slav origin, not unlike Prague, where you had German nationalists with Czech surnames and vice versa. Or like those Croat irredentist leaders in Dalmatia, who in the last century met at the Café Muljačić at Spalato to formulate, in Italian, programmes urging the most inflammatory Croatian demands. A city that felt itself Italian in so unique a fashion, it was inclined to consider itself misunderstood by the rest of the nation and to see in itself Italy at its most authentic – as if beyond the Isonzo (another crucial boundary on the geopolitical and imaginary map) lay the official and therefore less genuine Italy.

A city at once proud of and mistrustful of its multinational components – as, among others, the German or Austro-German, the Greek, Serb, Armenian – and above all the Slovene, a sort of secret Double, expunged by the former and underlined by the latter. Sometimes as I walked about the city I would ask myself precisely where, with which paving-stone – as the Nationalists emphatically pro-pounded – Slav territory began, a realm that stretched for thousands of miles all the way to Asia. Perhaps during its cultural and economic heyday at the beginning of the century Trieste was already at a dead end; here Joyce rediscovered Dublin and Ireland, the unendurable, unforgettable homeland, so obsessively vital to the exile and to the poet: a maternal bosom from which to escape and yet which was not to be left behind, a city that one must forever disparage, but never by any means stop discussing.

One physiognomy that stands out among the many faces of Trieste is the Jewish one. The Jews played a decisive role in the cultural, economic and political development of the city; they identified themselves with it and with the Italian option. In a short story, *Music Lessons*, I described an incident, reworked in the context of the fictitious main plot; it was a real incident which testifies almost ludicrously to this link. At the end of the 1920s a Polish businessman, an orthodox Jew, set up a branch of his business in Trieste and moved his family there. The little Polish town where they had lived was heavily anti-Semitic in atmosphere. Italy was already fascist at the end of the 1920s, but not yet the slightest anti-Semitic, least of all in Trieste, with the result that the family integrated quickly and painlessly, and the Polish-Jewish businessman's son (who was later to tell me the story and who was then a little boy) became a Balilla, that is, he joined the fascist youth movement and wore its vaguely military black uniform.

A few months later his father arrived in Trieste with his kaftan and his ringlets and was delighted to find such a congenial atmosphere, in which for the first time being a Jew did not pose a problem for his family. Speaking Yiddish with his wife and son, he would observe that this Moischale (i.e. Mussolini) was really putting himself out for the Jews. Above all he was proud that his son had been accepted into the Balilla and was wearing that uniform, a military honour that would have been unthinkable for a young Jewish boy in the small Polish town from which they came. So the father in his kaftan was constantly making his son put on his Balilla uniform and stroll with him through the streets of Trieste in the hope of meeting some fascist bigwig. And when they ran into one, the father hastily urged his son to give the fascist salute: *"Hejb' die Hand, meschugge!"* (Salute, idiot!)

Barely arrived in Trieste, this man had crossed the border which had enclosed him hitherto within the walls of a Polish provincial ghetto. A few years later, when Moischale-Mussolini introduced the racial laws in Italy, in order to imitate his German ally however amateurishly, the border closed about him once again. Trieste became a ghetto, from whose walls he managed to escape in the nick of time to Palestine. *Hejb' die Hand, meschugge!*

At Trieste even the boundaries of time were somehow different: they shifted, advanced, withdrew. When I was studying at Turin and returned periodically to Trieste, I had each time the impression of returning within a different time-frame. Time shrank, expanded, contracted, curdled into clots one could almost touch; it melted as into drifts of fog which dissolved totally. It was as if time ran on several tracks, which crossed only to diverge again, heading in different and opposite directions. In 1948, during that fateful election campaign that pitted communism against anticommunism in a decisive encounter, the year 1918, which saw the end of the First World War and Trieste's adherence to Italy, seemed an age ago, a part of history – indeed a chapter of history that was over and done with and beyond provoking debate or entrenched positions. A few years after that, this past history suddenly became topical again, it meshed into the present, into the political realities of the moment, and became somehow intrinsic to the present.

Those who had suffered these tangled skeins fell victim to a precocious disillusionment, a disabused scepticism regarding any sort of trust in history as a straight progression. It was here, in that cul-de-sac on the Adriatic, where the sea casts ashore every disenchantment, that so many illusions about real socialism came to grief before they did so elsewhere; between '45 and '48 all manner of things came to light which elsewhere were not to betray themselves until '56 or '68, and perhaps even an inkling of that friability of communism which took almost everyone by surprise in 1989. Still, that precocious disenchantment provided an early warning against a subsequent illusion, according to which the fall of communism would resolve every problem, and it has saved some of us from the ignominy of aiming a kick at communism when it was down. When we saw the tangled skeins of 1914 break the surface just as they ever had been, albeit gangrenous and congealed with the passage of the years, we were perhaps not quite so surprised; we realized that communism did leave behind a considerable inheritance, not in the answers it gave, but in the questions it posed.

Borders get displaced, they vanish and suddenly reappear; with them the concept of what we call *Heimat*, our homeland, changes shape in a somewhat erratic fashion. Cities and individuals often find that they have become an "ex", and this experience of displacement, of the loss of a world, is not confined to political geography, it embraces life in general. I have my character Stadelmann observe that everyone is an ex in some capacity, even if he is unaware of being so.

Perhaps for me the experience which first turned me to writing, to making the connection between writing and the misconstructions of life and history, goes back to a grotesque and distressing relocation of boundaries which I happened to witness as a child. In the winter of 1944-45, when I was five or six, I chanced to be with my mother at Udine, where my father was in hospital. The city was occupied by the Germans and by Krasnov's Cossacks, with their strange, makeshift uniforms, their horses, their families, their goods and chattels – a small-scale tribal migration. When the Nazis fished them out of prison and exile, they had promised them a homeland, a *Kosakenland*, which was originally to have been situated in Russia but which, as the fortunes of war gradually forced the troops of the Third Reich to retreat, was constantly moved westwards on the map, until it was installed just a few kilometres from Trieste, in Carnia, that rugged, mountainous part of Friuli, whence the Pasolini family originates.

In this terrain the Cossacks had transferred not only their tents but also their roots; they had transplanted their past and their steppes into this region, of whose existence, until a short while before, they had not heard the slightest mention. The Friulian villages, which my peasant-grandfather had left at thirteen to go and work in Trieste, had suddenly assumed strange foreign names, they had become villages of the Don, of the Donetz and the Kuban. Seeing this army, which was so different from all the others, I began to understand that every invasion is also an escape, and that the betrayer is not infrequently the betrayed as well. In this case the people were Cossacks who, in the conviction that they were fighting for freedom, had placed themselves at the service of the starkest tyranny. In the name of a homeland for which they were seeking, and in their anxiety to secure their own focal point, their own stable and peaceful borders, they robbed another people of their homeland, of their borders. This homeland of theirs, which they had sought with true devotion, was a product of violence, it was grotesque and artificial. Dazzled by their destiny, they were in effect living a lie, and their quest was in consequence a painful and senseless tragedy.

We know how they ended up: on the gibbets of the Soviet Union or in the Drava, into which many of them plunged together with their horses when the British were about to hand them over to the

Russians. Krasnov too was hanged in Moscow, for all that people long nursed the belief, however unlikely, that the old man had been killed by the partisans near Rio San Michele, in Carnia, during the retreat, while he was dressed in a private's uniform. I too, to my own surprise, wanted somehow to go on believing in the historically false and unconvincing version of Krasnov's death. And it is precisely this attempt to understand what truth, poetic and human, lay concealed behind this earnest desire to believe in a historically inaccurate version that gave rise, many years later, not only to a long narrative (*Inferences from a Sabre*), but perhaps, more generally, to my desire (or better, my need) to become a writer. Perhaps it was this lost Cossack odyssey which revealed to me the ambiguous nature of history and of life, the short circuit between fidelity and treason, between the authentic and the artificial, the dispersal of frontiers and the destructive force this entails.

This Cossack story shows how the boundary running between truth and falsehood is often indeterminate, even if it's up to us to be forever seeking to stabilize it. Truth in its outward manifestation has a way of being turned on its head, it will assume a mask and become a lie; here too is an instance where a boundary is overstepped or blurred without anybody noticing. At Katyn there is a monument erected by the Soviets in memory of the victims of the massacre of the civilian population perpetrated there by the Nazis in March 1943; that monument stated – and states – a tremendous truth and at the same time it until but lately camouflaged and covered up a truth no less horrible, that is, the graves and corpses of the Polish officers massacred on that very spot by the Soviets in April 1940; this crime was denied and concealed. Here we have the perfect symbol of the frontier, in this tragic representation, wherein denunciation and concealment meshed together like the recto and the verso of a page; here the Soviet Union showed up with the two faces of Janus, its grandeur and its infamy. In this case the frontier is that between truth and falsehood, between which there runs a clear line of demarcation, like the yea and the nay in the Gospel – a line which nonetheless is often blotted out, blurred or displaced by history and ideology.

My sentimental education has been marked by much experience of frontiers lost or sought, reconstructed on the ground and in the heart. After the experience of the phantom Cossack state, for me the other seminal experience in this sense has concerned the exodus of three hundred thousand Italians who left Istria at the end of the Second

World War. Once Tito's Yugoslavia had won its freedom with its remarkable war of resistance, it not only reclaimed Slav lands but also annexed Italian ones – Istria and Fiume. Prior to this there had been the fascist oppression of the Slavs, when even many Italians who were not overtly fascist but nationalist set little store by their rights. The Yugoslav response, under the auspices of a totalitarian regime, was violent and indiscriminate. In those years marked by terror, by intimidation and crime, some three hundred thousand Italians left their lands and homes at various times to wander the earth and live, even for many years, in refugee camps. These people, who had lost everything, were often misunderstood and cold-shouldered in their plight, and consequently would tend to shut themselves away behind other frontiers, established within their hearts, frontiers of bitterness and resentment which isolated these exiles not only from their lost homeland but not infrequently from the land into which they had intruded and which ignored them or made them feel more or less like aliens.

Other yet more complex frontiers came to be created around those outcasts who, while victims of exile and of the incomprehension shown them by the Italian state, and while accepting no truck with the Slav nationalist violence that was driving them out, refused to espouse Italy's nationalist sentiments and the indiscriminate rejection of the Slavs that these entailed, but persisted in looking to the dialogue between Italians and Slavs for their own most assured identity. They persisted in considering their world, the world of Istria and the Adriatic, to be a mixed and composite world, not just Italian, not just Slav, but both Italian and Slav; thus they incurred the hatred of both the Slav and the Italian nationalists, and found themselves in a sort of spiritual no man's land surrounded by another lot of frontiers.

That eastern border of Italy has been the theatre of another migration, far more modest in numbers, but far worse neglected and more tragic, which I evoked in *A Different Sea*. In 1947, just as the Italian refugees were leaving Istria and the other lands which had become Yugoslav and were on their way to Italy, about two thousand Italian workers from Monfalcone, a town near Trieste, were heading in the opposite direction: for political and ideological reasons they were on their way to Yugoslavia because, as convinced communists, they wanted to live in a communist country and contribute to the building of communism. Many of them had known fascist prisons or even the German concentration camps, and they too were leaving everything behind.

When, a short while later, Tito broke with Stalin, a political act for which world history owes him an eternal debt of gratitude, they protested openly against the Yugoslav regime which, in their eyes, was betraying Stalin or (as they saw it) the world revolution, and Tito, fearing attempted coups d'état, deported them to a pair of small islands in the upper Adriatic, Goli Otok (Bare Island), and Sveti Grgur (Saint Gregory); here the Titoist regime had established two gulags similar to those of Stalin, for the persecution of the Stalinists. In these two islands the "Monfalconesi", as they came to be called, were subjected to all manner of persecution and ill-treatment, while everyone turned a blind eye: Yugoslavia naturally remained silent about their fate, the Soviet Union disparaged the Titoist heresy in every way but had not a word to say about the gulags because they had so many in their own backyard, Italy as usual noticed nothing, and the Allies did not want to undermine Tito in his fight with Stalin.

In that inferno the Monfalconesi resisted – as they had resisted the other persecutions – in the name of Stalin who, had he proved victorious, would have turned the entire world into a gulag similar to those in which they themselves were incarcerated. When, years later, they were set free and returned to Italy, some of them found their homes occupied by Italian refugees who had also lost everything in Istria – bitter symbol of a two-fold exile that intersected, of a border twice crossed, twice lost. But they were persecuted especially by the Italian police for being communists, and shunned by the Communist Party, in whose name they had sacrificed their lives, because the Party preferred not to know all that much about them: they were inconvenient witnesses and reminders of the anti-Titoist and pro-Stalinist policies embraced by the Italian communists who were now trying to sweep all this under the carpet. They found themselves, once again, on the other side, on the wrong side at the wrong moment, surrounded by the most uncompromising of frontiers.

Without this experience of the frontier many books which I have written would never have been born. *Danube* is in its entirety a book of the frontier, a journey towards overcoming and transcending borders, not only national borders but cultural, linguistic, psychological ones; borders in the external world, but also boundaries within an individual, frontiers that partition the hidden and obscure zones of the personality and which also need to be crossed if one is to recognize and accept even the most disturbing and difficult components of the archipelago that makes a person's identity.

We are talking, of course, about a difficult voyage, one that may be attended by landfalls, but also by shipwreck and failure; the Danubian traveller will sometimes succeed in surmounting the frontier, in mastering the fear and rejection directed at Them – which underlie the violence meted out against Them – and in going out to meet Them, but on other occasions he is unable to make this step and shuts himself in on himself, the victim of his own prejudices, of his own phobias and insecurity.

Every boundary has to do with insecurity, with the need for security of some sort. A border is a necessity, because in the absence of a border, of distinctions, there is no identity, there is no form, there is no individuality, there is not even any authentic existence, for this is absorbed into all that is shapeless and indistinct. The border constitutes a reality, it provides contours and outlines, it constructs the individual character, be it personal or collective, existential or cultural. The frontier is form and thus it is also art. The Dionysian culture, which proclaims the dissolution of the self in a disorderly magma of impulses which ought to be liberating but is in fact an enslavement, deprives a person of all capacity to resist, to deride, it exposes him to violence and obliteration, it takes every embodiment of values and disperses it into powdery granules of mere turbulence. The self is like Baron Münchhausen, it needs to pluck itself out of the quicksands by tugging on its own pigtail. All it can count on is that little pigtail and on that awkward and contradictory situation, but it is in the irony of this situation that its strength lies. Irony dissolves borders that have been rigidly imposed, it makes for humane, flexible and enduring ones instead; irony stands up to every sort of woolly mysticism and to every muster of totalitarian coercion, because it makes distinctions, it articulates, adapts and self-adjusts. Irony is a running battle against windy bombast and postmodern minimalism; it is a virtue at once tender and strong.

The *Odyssey*, that romance of romances and book of books, is perhaps above all an epic about borders, about the individual who forms or defines his personality in relation to the indiscriminate, seductive and ruinous flow of Nature that seeks to dissolve it; the individual self is enriched by contrast with the diverse, it is neither blotted out nor absorbed by it. Dialogue brings together those who engage in it, but it rests on the assumption of a distinction made between them, and a tiny but irreducible and yet fruitful distance.

In the present day two models of odyssey might be proposed as feasible. On the one hand, the traditional, classical model that runs from Homer to Joyce, the odyssey as a circular voyage or as the progress of the individual who sets out, crosses the world and eventually returns to Ithaca, home again, enriched and assuredly changed by what he has experienced, but confirmed in his identity. He arrives, that is, at a deeper identity, as he constructs secure boundaries for his own personality, neither obsessively shut off from the world nor dissolved in chaos, in total loss of definition.

On the other hand there is the rectilinear odyssey as narrated, for instance, by Musil, wherein the individual does not return home but proceeds in a straight line towards the infinite or towards nothingness, getting lost on the way, and radically altering his own physiognomy, becoming another, destroying every frontier of his own identity. What Musil describes is the explosion of a person's individuality and the consequent abandonment of those pivotal points which give it form and limits. This applies especially to two characters in *The Man Without Qualities*, Moosbrugger and Clarisse: they are no longer individuals but rather bundles of compulsions, collective dreams or dizzy identifications of the self with reality – here the self overflows and goes astray without establishing a border between itself and the world.

Behind all this literature we find, explicit or implicit, the great lesson of Nietzsche, who explored and exploded every fictitious individual identity, dissolving it into an "anarchy of atoms"; here the traditional and age-old structure of the individual self, which has from time immemorial laboriously established its own frontiers, appears on the point of dissolution, of losing its own confines and merging into a plurality that still awaits precise definition, as into a new anthropological stage. So much of the greatest modern and contemporary literature is characterized by a two-pronged relationship between the self and its own frontiers, with their dissolution (linguistic to boot) and ossification, both equally lethal.

What is needed is an identity informed by irony, capable of cutting free from the obsession to give itself shape and also from that of making itself redundant. The writer of the frontier often finds himself between Scylla and Charybdis, between the rhetoric of a compact identity and that of an elusive one. We all recognize and scorn the former, the writers who appoint themselves the austere guardians of the frontier – of Italianism, Slovenism, Germanism. But the latter, too, those who fight them from positions so much more elevated, are often the victims of a different rhetoric of the border, bent on denying every border at all costs, on placing themselves invariably on the other side, on feeling themselves – in Trieste for instance – Italian among the Slovenes or Slovene among the Italians, or – in the Tyrol – German with the *carabinieri* and Italian with the *Schützen*.

This position will often be politically commendable in a climate of savage ethnic conflicts, but it risks becoming a cliché, a convenient literary alibi, and of relapsing, in its turn, into that mind-set of the border-to-be-wished-away, into that obsessive self-questioning which comes out in the complacent assertion that one refuses to admit to any precise identity. Even a passionate and controversial literature of the border can, under the impulse of the claim that we take no sides, turn into a repertory of tired commonplaces, like those old rhyming books with a rhyme for every purpose. Bitterly criticizing the land of one's birth may be better than a mawkish eulogy, but it all too easily generates threadbare catch-phrases: Triestine writers who satirize Trieste, those Prague folk who rail against Prague, those Viennese who scorn Vienna and those Piedmontese anxious to shake the dust of Piedmont off their feet, are often teetering between authentic detachment and conventional prejudice.

The best way to emancipate oneself from an obsession with identity is to accept it in its ever-precarious approximation and live it spontaneously, or forget all about it, just as one lives without thinking the whole time about which sex one belongs to, one's marital status and one's family; in fact it's better to live life without thinking too much about it. It's as well to accept one's own boundaries, so long as one recognizes that they are all relative, just as one accepts those of one's home.

Accommodating one's boundaries in such a way, with simplicity and affection, they serve to develop one's character. Writers and intellectuals especially, grist as they are to the mill of the culture industry with its surface glamour which turns out to be all a tedious chore, these are threatened with a loss of boundaries, a pseudo-cosmopolitanism – which does not mean that they're past the need for borders, merely that they've dropped out of the real world. The habit of being forever on the move, sleeping in four different countries in a single week and of returning home for a couple of days to change one's linen and prepare the lecture and readings for the next symposium, entails losing touch with the world. In the end all one knows of a foreign country is its airport, one or two good restaurants and the conference centre, standardized and interchangeable with that of any other country, the more so because one meets more or less the same faces and the same people; meanwhile one loses the continuity of a shared life, the adventure of day-to-day living, the creativity of free invention and of serene labour, one's home, the pub, one's children, one's friends. Dante used to say that our homeland is the world, as the sea is for fish, but by dint of drinking the water of the Arno he had learnt an intense love for Florence. Those two waters, which meet and mingle without effacing the boundary, are complementary. The one without the other is false: forgo the sense of belonging to that sea and the attachment to the Arno becomes a reactionary constriction; forgo the tangible love for one's native stream and harking back to the sea becomes an empty abstraction.

It has perhaps fallen above all to the Jewish civilization of the Diaspora to combine rootedness and distance in a symbiotic blood-tie, love of home and nomadic flight which finds a provisional dwelling only in some anonymous hotel room, in a station concourse, a run-down café, stages in exile and in the journey towards the Promised Land and therefore concrete albeit fleeting boundaries of a true homeland.

There's an oriental-Jewish story, which gave me the title for a book on exile, about a Jew in some town of Eastern Europe, who meets another on his way to the station with several suitcases and asks him where he's off to. South America, replies the other. "Ah," says the first, "what a long way to go!" The other gives him a puzzled look and asks: "A long way from where?" In this tale, the oriental Jew has no homeland, he has no fixed point by reference to which he might consider himself near or distant and is therefore far from everything and from everyone, he has no homeland, historical or political and therefore no frontiers. At the same time, however, he has his homeland within himself, in the law and the tradition in which he is rooted and which are rooted in him, and therefore he is never far from home, he is always within his own boundaries, which thus become a bridge giving access to the world.

But the frontier is an idol when it is experienced as a barrier of rejection. The obsession with one's own identity hems itself in with ever more boundaries in measure as it pursues the retrograde and indeed unattainable goal of its own purity, and leads to violence, of which the horrendous and pointless war in what was Yugoslavia is today's most flagrant example, although by no means the only one in Europe. Like every idol, the frontier often requires a tribute in blood, and in recent times the renewed fixation with borders, the parish-pump mentality with the furious jealousies this unleashes as it turns its back on the world to idolize its own peculiar genius and reject all contact with Outside – herein lies the recipe for savage struggles. Differences which are rediscovered and justly appreciated as variations in what is universally human may be turned into absolutes, in which case they become merely negative and destructive. This fetishism needs to be parried with the words of Nietzsche, misguided if taken at face value, but still luminous metaphors of truth: *"Wozu sich in hässliche Sprachen verlieben, weil unsere Mütter sie sprachen? Warum dem Nachbar gram sein, wenn an mir und an meinen Vätern so wenig zu lieben ist?"**

Boundaries between states and nations, established by international treaties or by force, are not the only kind. The pen that scribbles on from day to day, as Svevo says, traces boundaries, moves, dissolves and restores them; it is like the spear of Achilles, which both wounds and heals. Literature is intrinsically a frontier and an expedition in search of new frontiers, to shift them and define them. Every literary form and expression is a threshold, a zone at the edge of countless different elements, tensions and movements, a shifting of the semantic borders and grammatical structures, a perpetual dismantling and reassembly of the world, its frames and its pictures; it is like a theatre in which the scenery and the perspective of the real world is being constantly rearranged. Every writer is a frontiersman willy-nilly; it is along the frontier that he moves, as he does away with values and meanings or denies them or proposes new ones, articulates and dis-articulates the sense of the world with a ceaseless motion that is a continual slippage of frontiers.

Writing is working at the boundaries and at their point of drift, at their moment of fading and dying. Moral commitment, the good fight which is fought daily and which permeates literature as well, places on us the responsibility to keep setting up borders and defending them; to knock down those that look factitious and to establish new ones, to block off the road to evil. A world without frontiers, without distinctions, would be the ghastly no-holds-barred world of a Dostoyevskian nightmare, a world subject to all manner

---

* Why should we be enamoured of a plain tongue simply because it is our mother tongue? Why should we be at odds with our neighbour simply because we find so little to love in our paternal inheritance?

of violence and tyranny. In this sense the fight is against borders, but in order to set up new ones.

On the other hand, there is the fascination of the moment when one thing passes into another, the ceaseless metamorphosis of the world which is the very essence of life: life indeed consists in a perpetual supersession of borders. I have always been fascinated by the boundaries between colours and the delicate way they wash each other out as they reach their term; often a change of hue, especially where water is involved, becomes the very symbol of the sense of life and of poetry which seeks to capture it. Travel too, a narrative structure whose attraction I find so persistent, unfolds according to a rhythm which is that of a continual passing on, fading out and discolouration of borders. It is no accident that travel takes place so often by water: along rivers, in lagoons, at the point where the river meets the sea, in the noonday shimmer over the ocean that symbolizes at once the seduction and the destructiveness that lie at the heart of a boundless Absolute.

The persistent image of the line at which the water of the river meets that of the sea may stand as a sign of this fascination with changes of hue. And yet every narrative gives a form to life and thus establishes a frontier; the fascination in the merging of colours will make sense only if, even in the dizzy moment of change, one tries to fix, be it for but an instant, some image that rescues it from the merely indeterminate. Literature in addition analyses the passage of sentiments and passions, that continuous and ambivalent process whereby a sentiment will shade off into an adjacent one, sometimes to the point of turning into its very opposite – in this case, too, a frontier is being crossed, the discovery is being made of both the necessity and the fragility of borders.

Literature teaches us to cross boundaries; and yet tracing boundaries is what literature is about, for without them the very tension needed to overcome them would be unable to exert itself, in order to arrive at something more exalted and more humane. The borders present in contemporary history do not, alas, fall exclusively within the realm of literature, they relate to an altogether more violent and immediate situation. What is happening at present in Yugoslavia reveals the terrible weight of the past and of history, the lethal power of frontiers established centuries ago, frontiers of hatred and division. After the great emancipations of 1989, which created the possibility of knocking down walls and frontiers and building a new European unity, here we are witnessing the construction of new borders and new ramparts – ethnic, chauvinist, particularist. Furthermore, looking ahead, we can see the spectre of countless migrants, racked by hunger and driven beyond endurance, who will most likely forsake their roots and their borders; this will give rise to hatred and fear with the result that new barriers will be raised. The response to these population movements has to be quite exempt from hatred and gut reactions that please the crowd – it is on the quality of this response that the existence or at least the dignity of Europe will depend in the not too distant future.

Like Biagio Marin, the poet from Grado who in 1915 was an Italian irredentist, and flaunted before the Rector of Vienna University his desire that Italy should make war on the Habsburg Empire and destroy it – whereupon, barely enlisted in the Italian army, he bridled at the insolence of a captain saying that "we Austrians" were unaccustomed to his sort of conduct; or like that distant acquaintance of mine from Freiburg, one would need to be capable of feeling oneself as belonging on the other side, of crossing to the other side. What is needed is for everyone to be ashamed of his country's chauvinism, a factor for which everyone is always a bit to blame.

Yugoslavia is but a striking example of a mortal illness which slips in everywhere. In Italy the movements towards national disintegration belong to the same group of symptoms. Two years ago, when I saw the border between Slovenia and Croatia being staked out with such pride and enthusiasm, I was reminded of a story told me by some Estonian and Latvian friends. In 1929 or 1930 some Latvian students entered Estonia, climbed up the Suur-Munamäki, the highest hill in the Baltic, at 317 metres, four metres higher than Latvia's highest summit, and shovelled away those four metres to deprive the Estonians of their eminence. The Estonians made it good straightaway, at all events, piling those four metres of earth back on to the summit and topping it off with a tower. There are vertical boundaries too. We should be capable of seeing them – even when they surge up proudly like the Berlin wall only a short while ago – as piles of rubble, like every border, and of knowing that it is our duty to sweep away those ruins and heap them up where they do the least damage, just as the famous Berlin *Trümmerfrauen* did in 1945.

The image of a woman like this with her broom, sweeping up rubble and crumbling walls, could be the very symbol of the angel of the frontier. But hers is an unlikely image – the one looming on our horizon is rather the sniper clutching his rifle and lurking behind borders that tower ever higher, like so many towers of Babel. As the world becomes ever more unreal, it is ever more difficult to answer Nietzsche's question: *"Wo darf ich heimisch sein?"**

Translated from the Italian by Guido Waldman

* Where might home be for me?

MALACHI O'DOHERTY

It Was One Damn Good Car

*A man I'll call Jay says he kneecapped his first joyrider in 1972. "This wee
lad was driving right into town, and he couldn't see over the top of the
steering wheel. It was that cheeky. We didn't really kneecap him. We shot
him in the arms and legs."*

*Jay insists that no personal feelings were involved. "I still see him the
odd time," he says. "He gives me a wave."*

*Joyriders in English cities risk arrest and, when they lose control of their
stolen cars, injury or death. Belfast joyriders, mostly Catholic, mostly from
West Belfast, run added risks. They may be killed in encounters with armed
police and soldiers: most of the casualties have died at the hands of the
security forces or from crashes as they sped from them (two young joyriders
died last week in a crash on the Falls Road). But Belfast joyriders also have
to reckon with the IRA. Last year the IRA kneecapped 59 people, more
than in any other year for a decade. Most were joyriders. More bullets went
into the knees, ankles and elbows of teenage Catholic tearaways in West
Belfast than into British soldiers, policemen, or loyalists. And this is something the joyriders accept as inevitable. One joyrider shot recently says he
knows the man – a neighbour – who tucked a revolver in the hinge of his
leg and pulled the trigger. "I wouldn't pass him," he says. That means: I
wouldn't pass him without saying hello. "He was only doing what he had
to do."*

*"They are the law," says another. "And there's no point in arguing or
complaining." A dozen others say the same thing. They tend to reserve their
hostility for the people who report them to the IRA rather than the men
sent out to shoot them.*

*Republicans say they are fighting a war. By doing what they do joyriders
are seen to be making a mockery of that war, fooling about on the battlefield.
Joyriders know this. For them, bucking the establishment is bucking the
IRA. Joyriders have been known to seek out the IRA, to rev up their cars
under the bedroom windows of IRA men in the middle of the night. "We
would beep the horns at them," says one joyrider, "and give them the
finger."*

Joyriding started in Belfast in the early Seventies. As the phenomenon has intensified, so too has the IRA war against it. Like their other war, it is elegantly rationalized. Ask Republicans why they get involved in this squabble on the street – why they put all this energy into protecting Opel Mantas and BMWs – and they will give one clear answer: they are responding to a demand from the community to come down hard on what they call "anti-social elements". It is a policy whose alleged aim is to foster community support. But it is also designed to embarrass Sinn Fein's chief political rival, the SDLP, making it seem soft on crime and supportive of the RUC.

The police are perceived as neglecting the joyriding problem. Offenders say that when they are caught they are frequently offered money and encouraged to serve as informants. Complaints to the police about stolen cars are often met with a hesitant response, for fear they are part of an IRA lure. In its turn, the IRA has never stopped the joyriders, although it has occasionally terrorized them into laying off for a few weeks at a time. Teenagers are visited in their homes by Sinn Fein workers and ordered to observe an after-dark curfew. Some manage to stick to it for a few days, then they are back on the streets. The appeal of fast cars is irresistibly greater than the fear of losing their legs – and their lives.

Johnny McGivern was motivated by a love of cars. Born in July 1971, he went to St Colm's secondary school in Twinbrook, a Catholic housing estate on the edge of Belfast. He was expelled at fifteen. According to his family, he was joyriding at sixteen. They tried to keep him away from temptation. Twice they sent him to relatives in Canada.

In January 1989, aged seventeen, he was kneecapped by the IRA. Eight months later, the night before he and his family were to move to Canada, he came off a mountain road in a stolen car, chased by police. He suffered brain damage. He lived in a coma for three months and died on 28 December.

While in hospital recovering from the kneecapping, McGivern was given a jotter pad. He started writing, signing himself Johnny T Brook. These are his words:

I got home that Friday night at about two o'clock and just as I was about to head into the house I stood at the path, well staggered really, and I thought of what a night it was. Most of the night was good at the club. The disco was brilliant and the bouncers didn't even come near our table all night, which was strange because we were making a load of noise, giving the girls stick walking past until Burly was grabbed by a bouncer and he was carried out by at least eight of them because he couldn't walk, but it turned out to be a good move because he had £15 in his pocket and that paid for the next round.

So I went into the house and there was nobody up except the damned budgie. Somebody forgot to put something over the cage and every time it sees me it goes crackers, well anyway, I went on up to bed.

The next morning, I awoke to the sound of banging at our front door. It was about 9.30 at this time, and I thought it would be a strange time for the cops to come, and at that moment I remembered the night before and my head just went into a spin and it hurt like mad but the bedroom door burst open and this man came in with a CB [radio] in his hands. I noticed he was wearing gloves and he was mostly dressed in black.

Then he left the room but shortly came in again and said he was from the Provisional Irish Republican Army and that he was along with the Belfast Brigade cleaning up Twinbrook and Poleglass of hoods, and that he wanted me and some of my mates for questioning, but he promised me and my parents that I wouldn't be harmed, and that I would be home within the hour. And then he said: "Get dressed quick and don't try anything stupid."

As soon as he went downstairs, I forgot about the hangover and I went into a state of shock. I looked out the backroom window and I noticed a car parked over by the fence with a lot of men in it. So that was no way out. But then I thought what they wanted to question me about.

Surely they weren't really interested in a joyrider, but I remembered what happened to Harry. He got his arms and legs broke, plus tar and feathered, and he was only a joyrider, and all sorts of things raced through my mind and I thought of the amnesty I had signed a month before, and suddenly I got this rotten feeling in my stomach that it was this amnesty that had got me in this position because I had admitted stealing over a hundred cars and they made me sign a statement that if I joyrided again I would be dealt with by the Republican movement, but I did. I was in a car on Thursday night and I was seen getting out of it at the entrance of Twinbrook, so this is what it was all about.

To be honest, I would, at all times, wish it was the cops at the door, but I had to bring myself back to reality and face it. I thought: "God, I wish I went a week from now and seen what had happened."

At that moment my mother and father came into the room and I noticed they were both crying, but I told them I had done nothing and that I would be all right and back soon, so that calmed them down a bit. I left the house with the man and another man. Both were dressed the same but there was another man at the end of the street and he had a big black bin-liner with something long in it, and he was wearing a balaclava and he kept his distance, plus he was leading us around towards the shops where we met my mate Quinn with two more men. There was three car loads of people and the thought went to my head that they must be going to make an example of us.

The man that was walking in front of us came over and said if we didn't do as he said we would be two sorry people. So he and the other men brought us over to the corner of the shops and the wall so that it was like a V-shape and the place was absolutely stinking. The men started to form an arc around me and my mate and then they said: "Lay face down."

They told us to put our arms behind our back, and then they Sellotaped our mouths. When they done that, me and my mate looked at each other and I bet if anybody had seen the fright in our eyes it would scare the hell out of them.

We lay there for about five minutes and one of the men said something in Irish. The man with the bag pulled out a baseball bat and a leg of a table, and as I seen them I got uneasy and started to turn around, but the men kept kicking me and punching me, shouting to keep face down. But when the blows started I couldn't take it and I pulled the tape off and rolled round. But the man wouldn't stop. With all the shouting going on all the neighbours were out, and they were calling the men everything, so I kept kicking and finally I kicked the stick out of the man's hand. The man was a skinny-looking creep but there was too many Provies there. The man swapped over with the other man with the baseball bat and he started laying the blows in, but by now there was a crowd gathering and I think the IRA thought it was too risky, and they started to move away and get into their cars. As they did this everybody was shouting abuse after them, so I felt the urge to shout as well but I hadn't got the strength. I turned round to my mate, but he didn't move so I shouted to the crowd to get an ambulance and something to drink. My Da came

round and he was shouting so I told him to shut up because he was
making it worse.

The ambulance came shortly after that, and I gave out a great sigh
of relief. I thought I wasn't hurt that much because I was able to
move my legs, but my arms felt broke. I could get up and, to be
honest, I could walk into the ambulance. But when I got into it I just
flopped down on to the bed and my mate was carried into the other.
He looked very bad so I felt sorry for him because he wasn't really
all that bad and these men thought they were big lads and beat up
two sixteen-year-olds with baseball bats and that really made me think
there was no good in Northern Ireland left.

When the ambulance arrived at the BCH [Belfast City Hospital],
I felt a bit better, because the gas was sort of calming me and my
mate down. We were separated when we got our X-rays, and thank
God all I got was very bad bruising and the two of us never suffered
anything broke, so that sort of made us feel better and we were let
out a couple of hours later. All my mates came round with drink,
sweets and it really cheered me up, and all the neighbours comforted
my parents, but I will always remember that Saturday.

The Manta was metallic black and two-tone grey and it had a sunroof
and alloy wheels with bucket seats. In other words it was one damn
good car. The name was a 1.8S Berlinetta, which isn't top of the
range, but about £10,000-worth.

I walked up the street, just about to go round the corner, and my
heart was beating faster thinking of being behind the wheel. I had
seen bandsmen about, all wearing red, white and blue, but I didn't
think much of it.

But I seen a car with five in it and they were all staring at me. I
could feel their beady eyes on me and I was wondering what they
were thinking, but then I got scared, so I quickened my pace to get
to the Manta. I turned the corner and to my delight there she was,
just as we had left her, so I scanned for police, in case it was a set-up.
But there was none.

I went to the driver's door, just to put the screwdriver in the lock,
when suddenly I spied a man coming out of the house directly facing
me. The stare he gave me would make your blood curdle, but I
thought it's too late now, get in quick and get away fast. I opened
the door and pulled the casing off and started the car and left with

wheels burning rubber the whole way down the street and round the bend that takes me to the road to Twinbrook.

But to my horror, you'll never believe what was there. A whole damn parade with police and UDR all standing up and down the road and directing traffic. I thought they wouldn't have the car reported yet, so I just stopped in the line of traffic, trying to get by and the peeler waved me on and the butterflies were running all over me.

But I could never get near Twinbrook that way because there was a checkpoint on the road to my left that takes me home, so I had to go down Dunmurry, but that was risky because every other time I went down there I got chased, but there was no other way, so I drove on and to my amazement there wasn't one peeler to be seen. I hit Twinbrook in about five minutes and right away I started to throw the car about doing handbrake turns and spinning round corners so fast that there was times I didn't think I would survive. It went along like that for half an hour and there was this big crowd out, and the other stolen car was flying about too. It was an Astra GL. But the Manta I had was much, much faster. I wasn't deliberately running the Astra down. It was just that the Manta was so fast.

I got bored staying there so I went to Glasvey, which is the other side of Twinbrook, a much quieter place, and I livened that place up a bit, and I was sure someone would call the peelers soon, so I decided to get out of there fast, but it was too late.

I had seen the patrol on my left. It was two police jeeps and one army jeep, and as soon as they seen me they gave chase. They were no match for the Manta. It blew them off, but the thing I was worried about was if the last jeep went round the other way and blocked me off, because the way Twinbrook's made, there's only three ways out, and one was away over the other side, and I had already missed the other.

I tried to get down to the third one and I looked in the rear-view mirror and noticed they had split up, but I wasn't really too worried because I could go out round Milltown. While I was driving down that road, I seen Mally and he tried to wave me down, and he was calling me everything for taking the car without him, but when he seen the peelers coming, he ran.

As soon as I went round the roundabout I remembered there was a checkpoint out there so I doubled back and drove down a grass verge with a jeep right behind me. I went into a cul-de-sac and got out and ran. I got to my mates just in time, because the other police jeep found the Manta. But it didn't do anything, so when they left we went up to look at it. I knew the cops were watching it so I didn't take it till I thought it was safe.

But when I finally did go near it again the man in the house beside it threw a brick and he cracked the passenger side of the windscreen. But it was still all right for me to drive away.

As soon as I got the car out of the cul-de-sac, I was chased by a jeep, and while I was driving about sixty miles an hour, I seen another jeep going down the library hill, and the way it was going, I thought it was going to hit me, and sure enough it rammed straight into the driver's door and I felt the inner panels almost touching the right-hand side of my body, and the car went out of control, going left and right up and down kerbs, and I fought to control it again. Finally I did, just when it was about to crash into another car.

As I was desperately trying to get away from these jeeps I headed out towards Milltown because there was no other way. I thought that if I drove fast enough before the peelers were behind me, I could let on that I was just another normal car and then accelerate as I came within yards of it, but the jeep must have radioed to them because they were coming at the car as if to shoot, so I done a handbrake turn ready to dodge the other jeeps, but I conked the engine dead and the police officers were all round the car trying to trail me out.

The passenger door was locked and my driver door was squashed in and I was trying to find the screwdriver, which I did find under the seat, and when I started up they all ran behind their jeeps and I was on the run once more. I thought they were going to shoot at me, but no. They didn't shoot, and while I was escaping those jeeps I seen another going straight towards me, and it was playing chicken with me.

At the last moment it went to the left and, to be honest, I was going to go straight into it. But it chickened out. Behind it there was two army Land Rovers and a police jeep coming behind me, and I wasn't going to chance that, so I tugged right and slammed on the brakes and went down a grass verge, but to my horror I heard an army helicopter overhead, and it came right down and wouldn't go away. I had lost the jeeps but there was no way I was going to get away from the helicopter, so I thought I should get out. I drove into the shops, got out and ran. But the army stopped and got out, and one took aim at me and shouted, "Stop or I'll shoot".

But I wasn't stopping. Later on, I heard that if it wasn't for a policeman telling the Brit to stop, he would have shot me.

As I was running I took my coat off, but it was still no use. The helicopter was still there. So I ran down to the school, and I was trying to make my way to the forest, but the helicopter knew what I was trying to do, so it was directing the jeeps to block me off. They did, two at the front and one behind.

They all got out of the jeeps and came at me, punching and kicking and trailed me into the back of a jeep. I thought, Johnny, this is going to be hell now. Because they had to chase me for nearly half an hour, wrecked one jeep, and they had to use a helicopter, and if it wasn't for that chopper I'd have been free.

But then I was thinking of the beatings and shouting I would get when I got home.

As they drove into Woodburn police-army barracks, the peelers were all laughing, saying I was in for a hiding and that they were throwing the owner of the car into the cell with me. But I was more interested in what my parents were going to say.

When I got into the place, and my property was taken off me and lodged in the big red book, as everybody says, they led me down to the galleys, which is another phrase of speech everybody says.

I was lying on the hard plastic mattress in the corner when the two detectives came in, and they said was I going to co-operate, and I said yes. So they left. As I was lying there thinking, I thought that I could get off with this if I never owned up to it, and they could only keep me for forty-eight hours and send me home if they couldn't prove it was me.

But when they started asking questions, they laughed and said there was witnesses and fingerprints and a film from the helicopter. But still I never said I done it.

So they threw me back in the cell and I heard these enormous bangs, and the whole place started to shudder. And the next minute a loud buzz was sounding all over the place. But I didn't know what to think.

Then I came to the conclusion that the barracks were being bombed and I was locked in this small room, and I could be trapped any second. A soldier let me out and told me my mother and aunt was waiting and I was going home, and I was so happy, but on one condition, that I came back tomorrow to admit everything that happened that night.

So I said yes, just to get out, but I also asked him what was the noise and he said the place was being mortar-bombed, and everybody was to get out.

So we ran out across the road to get into my aunt's car, and I seen hundreds of soldiers all over the place, and then smack and then another. It was my Ma hitting me shouting: "Are you pleased you've disgraced yourself, you good for-nothing b***."

Then I knew I was in for a really hard time, and that was one day to remember.

It was 7 January, and it was about 6.30 at night. I was sitting bored in the house waiting to go out and get my carryout on a Saturday night, which I thought was going to be a good night.

I walked out of the house, not thinking, not even suspecting what was going to happen to me later that night. I was walking up Gardenmore Road, as usual, when a car was coming up behind me but I didn't think much of it until I was walking along by the boxing club when the car stopped, and two men got out of the back of the car. I've seen that car about and the person who drives it does private taxiing, so I thought they were just somebody that got a lift until one of the men asked me if I knew the name of the flats. The name is right plain to see and the two men were starting to walk towards me, also I noticed the car was staying there, so I thought best get out of here and be safe, when the two men grabbed me. We were fighting in the car park for a couple of minutes before they overpowered me and they pulled me over to the car. I tried to get away again, but it was no use.

They kept on asking me my name, so I told them my cousin's name thinking they wouldn't know because I had never seen them before, but they brought me over to the driver, and he asked me: "What's your name and don't give me no shit or I'll put a bullet in your back." I told him the wrong name again and he said throw him in the back of the car.

When they got me in the back they punched and kicked me trying to find out my name, so I told them my real name and I asked why I was being taken away, but they kept saying shut up and keep my head down. I panicked and told them I was only out of Hydebank [a young offenders' centre] a couple of weeks before this and I hadn't done anything. But he turned round and said, "Where were you last night?" so I told them I got a carryout and was in Danso McCabe's house, and I kept on saying I hadn't done anything, but he turned round and said: "For fuck's sake shut up moaning. We're only going to talk to you, so calm down." I knew that wasn't much of an assurance because you couldn't believe a word they said. They said they only wanted me for questioning the last time and they ended up beating me and my mate with sticks, so it didn't really calm me down. It made me worse.

Then I felt the car moving off and they kept telling me to keep my head down. The car drove for about three minutes, but it felt ages to me, and when it stopped at the shops I knew something was wrong, because that's where I got beat up.

The car stopped and they opened the door, and they pulled me out keeping my head down, but I could see more men, possibly three, and they were wearing balaclavas. So they were walking me towards the flats and there was another two men in there and they pulled me over to the corner, pushed me down on my stomach first and one of them sat to on my back, making sure I didn't turn round, but I wanted to know what was wrong and to find out what this was for, but they kept punching and kicking me so I gave up and just lay there.

You should have seen the thoughts that went through my mind, and I didn't care about the pain in my legs and the whole of my body. Then one man came in and said that the other one wasn't in, so I thought they were after another wee lad, but he wasn't there.

I was lying there for about twenty minutes or half an hour when two men came in, pulled me to my feet and were walking me outside. I prayed to God in Heaven to make the next couple of minutes a blank for me.

They brought me round to the wall where the bushes were, and one of them said "Lay face down." My heart sank to my feet. I pleaded with them: "Please, please, leave me alone. I didn't do anything."

But no.

While I was lying there I kept turning round but they kept kicking me to turn round. I looked quickly and spotted a man standing there with a handgun, and I knew that I was getting kneecapped or done really bad, and to tell you the truth I would have cried if it would have helped, but I couldn't bring myself to cry. I done some begging and when I felt the gun at the back of my leg I just froze.

But the gun didn't work and that made it worse, so I started kicking my legs. They tried to hold them but to no avail. I was in such a panic nobody would have been able to hold them. While the gun kept jamming and me kicking, one of the men said: "Just stick one in his back." But another one said: "Look son, it's only going to make it harder on yourself." So I kept my legs straight and I heard the thud of the gun and a split second later my right leg jerked and I knew it was shot, but it never sank in that "Look Johnny, you've been shot", and I never really felt pain in that leg. Then I panicked and shouted: "Fuck off, that's enough." And then the thuds sounded again, but the left leg wasn't the same as the right one. I felt it buckle and bend, and I could feel the leg really messed up inside, and the pain and the shock, and all the thoughts that went through my head, and my leg was bending and I couldn't bring myself to cry. I looked up and seen all the men running away and I felt like shouting something after them, but one of the men stayed for a split second and I looked into his eyes and he stared at me for what seemed ages, and then he ran.

A couple of minutes shouting for an ambulance brought some people round, and the look on their faces was like something out of a horror movie. I asked one of them to get me a drink of water or run to the shop for a tin of Coke, and while he was getting that, I asked to be moved on to my side but they made me sit upright against the wall and the legs went jelly, especially the left one. It didn't feel right, so I asked to lay down again and somebody asked would I want my parents round, and I said yes, because I wanted all the comfort I could get.

The Coke came and I thanked him and took an endless drink but couldn't get enough. The thirst was like fire in my throat and I couldn't drench the burning going through my whole body.

I seen everybody making way and I knew it must be my Ma or Da and then I seen my Ma. I told her I was all right but she was in shock and I had to tell her to stop shouting because she was nearly taking it out on the people helping me. Then I heard the squeal of tyres and the sound of our car, then the shouts of my Da when he came round the corner. Almost immediately I held my hands out and said, "Hold me, Daddy, hold me Daddy", and he held my hands and the grip in his hands helped me take my mind off it a bit.

Then I heard people saying, "There's an ambulance" and I felt relieved a bit but the pain in my leg was driving me crazy. When the two men came round they looked at the legs and I showed them where the wounds were. So they cut the jeans, and I said I had only got them jeans today and everybody started laughing. But it wasn't funny. Then they tried to lift me by my ankles and arms, and I cracked up and couldn't take the pain.

It was like the whole left leg was being crushed, so I started to shout at them, and they didn't look too pleased, so my Da and Joe Corr asked for a hammock sort of thing to carry over to the stretcher. They did that and it was a lot easier than what the ambulance men were doing, but when I was being carried out I seen my brother Gareth's face and I seen the shock and horror in his face and I told someone to get him away, but I looked round and seen everybody looking at me. There was a big crowd.

Looking back now, I wish I never shouted as much, but it's all over now, after two operations lying here in my seventh week in the Belfast City Hospital and another couple of months to go. And if it wasn't for the support of my family and friends, I would go insane and this fucking TINGLING IN MY FOOT IS DRIVING ME CRAZY. My mother and brother are in Canada now and they are trying to get their troubles over, so good luck – and maybe soon, I know someday, my whole family will be together and happy, someday. *Ye ha!*

ANDREW O'HAGAN

Bad Bastardness

On the afternoon of 2 March 1993, Jon Venables and Robbie Thompson, two ten-year-old boys, abducted a toddler from a Liverpool shopping mall. After dragging and kicking the baby, James Bulger, on a journey lasting over two hours, they murdered him on top of a railway track. Once caught, the killers were demonized and reviled, at home and abroad, and after several weeks in court – during which the boys stood on a custom-built platform inside the dock, each of them by turns bored and upset – they were found guilty of the crime and ordered by the judge to be confined "at Her Majesty's pleasure".

Watching those boys on camera brought into my head a flurry of pictures from my own boyhood. At that age, we were brimming with nastiness. I grew up on a scheme in the last of Scotland's New Town developments. There were lots of children, lots of dogs and lots of building sites. Torture among our kind was fairly commonplace. I remember two furious old teachers driving me and my six-year-old girlfriend Heather Watt home early one morning. In recent weeks, we had been walking the mile to school in the company of a boy, smaller and younger than ourselves, a fragile boy with ginger hair called David. I think we thought of him as "our boy". We bossed him. Occasionally, when he didn't walk straight or carry our bags or speak when we wanted him to, we'd slap him or hit his hands with a ruler. We had to pass through fields to get to school, with diggers going and "workies" taking little notice of us, though from time to time they'd bring over empty lemonade bottles which we could exchange for money or sweets at the chip shop. We must have looked innocent enough, holding hands, Heather and I, walking the younger boy to school.

Over time, we started to hit the boy hard. Our way to the school was dotted with new trees, freshly planted and bound to supporting stalks with rubber belts. We got into the habit of removing belts every day: we began to punish David with them whenever we thought he'd "been bad". Just a few hits at first on top of his shorts, not so's you'd notice. It got worse, though, and on the last morning, when we were caught by the two old lady teachers, we were beating his bare legs with the coiled up straps. Though we'd set out on time that morning we were late, having spent the best part of half an hour on top of an out-of-the-way railway bridge practically skinning the screaming boy's legs.

That incident caused a scandal in our square. My mother was employed as a cleaner in another local primary school with David's mother and — although I remember crying and being confused and not quite knowing what we'd done wrong — I could see that we'd caused a lot of embarrassment. Up until the age of ten, I'd both taken part in and witnessed many such incidents. My three elder brothers had reputations for being a bit mad; other boys said they'd "do any-thing". I watched them do any number of crazy things to other kids around the squares, and I watched the other kids do some crazy things in return. Early in the Seventies, on Halloween Night, a scarlet-faced man appeared at the door, shouting the odds and holding up a torn frock. My eldest brother and his pals had been ripping at the man's daughter's clothes "for a laugh" and, as usual, it had got out of hand: they'd torn her dress to shreds and then taunted the girl, leaving her distraught. My mother and the rest of us sat in the kitchen biting our nails and covering our ears as my father, upstairs, gave Michael the beating of his life for that.

Another time, the whole family had to sit in front of a children's panel. That's what happens in Scotland if a child under sixteen com-mits an offence: the social work department calls in the whole family in an effort to assess what the real problem is and decide whether the child should be in care — which in my brother's case would have meant a residential List "D" school. In the event that didn't happen, but it took a long time for the community — especially our teachers — to forget what he did. With a friend, he'd burnt down a wing of our local Catholic secondary school.

It's not that any of us were evil; even the more bookish and shy among us were given to a bit of destructive boredom and stupid imagining. Now and then it got out of hand. The boys I hung around with in my pre-teen years were always losing the head. During the good weather, the light nights, what started off as a game of rounders or crazy golf would end up as a game of clubbing the neighbour's cat

to death. A night of camping on the playing fields could usually be
turned into an opportunity for the wrecking of vegetable gardens, or
the killing of frogs and people's pet rabbits. Mindless stuff. Yet now
and again people would get into things that you sensed were about
to go over the edge, or were already over it. My memory tells me
that that point was much more difficult to judge than I'd now like to
think.

My friend Moggie began taking accordion lessons at the house of
a rather anti-social woman who lived in the corner of our square. She
started going out when she was supposed to be teaching him, leaving
him to baby-sit her child, who was not yet a year old. Moggie would
have been about seven or eight. One day I was in with him, bashing
uselessly on her old piano, when he shouted me to the front of the
living room.

"I'm biting the baby," he said. "D'you want to?"

The baby was lying on a white towelling nappy and Moggie was
bent over her, biting her arms and then her legs and then the cheeks
of her face. He said he did it all the time and that the baby liked it.
He said it was like tickling. I didn't want to do it but said I'd stay
and watch. Another game he played was to put on a record, hoist the
baby on to her legs and shake her in time to the music. She obviously
wasn't walking yet, but he would jostle her and jam her legs on the
carpet. Her head would jerk about and she would cry. Some time
later, the bite marks were discovered and Moggie was barred from
the house, although everyone – including the baby's parents – said
that she had been bitten by the dog. I got to stay, since the woman
reckoned I was sensible. Another boy who came to that house used
to swallow handfuls of the woman's pills (she always had a great
variety lying around, so much so that her daughter was eventually
rushed to hospital after eating a load). Moggie joined the Navy and
the pill-swallower was on the fringe of a mob of boys who killed
someone at a local Cashline ten years later. In the years that I hung
around it, that house (and there were many others like it) had been
the site of a large number of life-threatening games, solvent-abuses
and youthful experiments gone wrong.

Something happened when we all got together, even when we
were that young. We were competitive, deluded and full of our own
small powers. And, of course, we spoke our own language. We even
had our own way of walking – which wasn't unlike that of the two
boys on the video – dragging our feet, hands in our pockets, heads

always lolling towards the shoulder. That culpable tilt gave the full measure of our arrogant, untelling ways. As only dependants can be, we were full of our own independence. The approval that really mattered was that of the wee Moggies and Bennas and Caesars we ran around with. There were times when I'm sure we could've led each other into just about anything.

Just William-type adventures – earning pocket-money or looking for fun – would more often than not end in nastiness or threats to each other or danger to other people, especially to girls our own age and younger boys. There was badness in it, a form of delinquency that most of us left behind. The girls with whom I read books and coloured-in, with whom I regularly played offices, were the victims of verbal taunting, harassment and gang violence when I ran around with boys. We all carried sticks and were all of us baby-arsonists who could never get enough matches. We stole them from our houses, stole money out of our mothers' purses with which to buy them and begged them from construction workers. I can remember pleading with my mother to buy me a Little-Big-Man action doll from Woolworth's and then burning it in a field with my pals. Most of our games, when I think of it, were predicated on someone else's humiliation or eventual pain. It made us feel strong and untouchable.

If all of this sounds uncommonly horrific, then I can only say that it did not seem so then; it was the main way that most of the boys I knew used up their spare time. There was no steady regression towards the juvenile barbarism famously characterized in *Lord of the Flies*. We lived two lives at once: while most of the stuff detailed above went on, we all made our First Communions, sang in the school choir, did our homework, became altar-boys and some went to matches or played brilliantly at football. We didn't stop to think, nor did our parents, that something dire might result from the darker of our extra-curricular activities. Except when that murky side took over, and your bad-bastardness became obvious to everyone.

Bullies who had no aptitude for classwork – who always got "easily distracted" scribbled in red ink on report cards that never made it home – had unbelievable concentration when it came to torturing minors in the playground, or on the way home. For many of the pupils bullying was a serious game. It involved strategies, points scored for and against, and not a little detailed planning. It was scary, competitive and brought out the very worst in those who had anything to do with it. Kids who were targeted over a long period we thought deviant

in some way, by which I mean that they were in some way out of it
– maybe serious, bright, quiet, keeping themselves to themselves.
When I was nine, there was a particular boy who lived two squares
up. For years I'd listened to boys telling of how they'd love to do
him in. I sort of liked him but, even so, I joined in the chase when
we pursued him in and out of the scheme and across fields. This stood
high in our repertoire of time-fillers. "Where's Broon?" – the boy's
name was Alan Brown – took its place in a list of nasty games that
included snipes (skinning each other's knuckles with cards after each
lost game), kiss-cuddle-and-torture (with girls), Blue-Murder (the
same, but sorer) and that kind of thing. If anyone came to the door
when these games had gone too far, our mothers and fathers went
ape. Belted and sent to bed, many of us would get up after dark and
stare out the window, over the square, into each other's bedrooms.
We grinned and flashed our torches, trying to pass messages. The
message, I remember, was always quite clear: it meant see you
tomorrow.

Even the youths who came from happy homes enjoyed the childish
ritual of running away. When parents, sick with anxiety, came to the
door or to school looking for their children, we'd never let on. We'd
help eleven-year-old absconders get together the bus fare to a bigger
place, all of us filling a bag with stolen tins and chipping in coppers
for some hero's running-away fund. Of course, they'd always be
caught and brought back, but not before we'd enjoyed the parental
worry and the police presence in the classroom while the drama lasted.
In Jeff Torrington's novel *Swing Hammer Swing!* a similar pleasure is
taken by the boy Jason after the book's hero, Thomas Clay, takes him
to the Kelvingrove Art Gallery. We hear of it in an exchange between
Clay and the boy's mother:

> "Dammit, how long was he missing for?"
> "I've told you – two min–"
> "You're a liar! Ten minutes, Jason says."
> "What's a wee boy know aboot judging time?"
> "You damned eejit – that man could've been one of those
> perverts. Places like that hoach with'm. Come clean – how long
> did he have'm?"
> "Two minutes at the outside. Get a grip on yoursel. That
> guy'd been a perv, d'you think he'd've taken the boy to an
> attendant? C'mon, think about it. Another thing, the man

didnae lure Jason from me – Jason followed him because he was wearing the same clobber as me . . ."

Although I was fairly certain that the boy hadn't come to any physical harm – taken to a WC and interfered with, I mean – I didn't dig this being forced into lying complicity with my dress-alike. Jason, like most imaginative kids, hadn't been content to tell of the incident as was – he'd jived it up some, flung a few more squibs on the fire.

We all did that at times. We all took and assigned roles in cruel little dramas of our own devising. Our talk would be full of new and interesting ways to worry or harass our parents, especially our fathers, who we all hated. Stealing his fags or drink brought a great, often awesome, feeling of *quid pro quo*.

I found many girls to be the same in that respect: I had a twelve-year-old table-tennis friend Alison, who told us she'd been crushing old light bulbs in a bowl and sprinkling them into her father's porridge. We thought that was great. Some of us knew how to stop it, though, while others just kept it up. A couple of my boyhood friends assiduously built bridges between their mindless, childish venom – their bad-boyish misdemeanours – and adult crime.

Around the time of our cruelty to the boy David, the local news was full of the disappearance of another David – a three-year-old boy who'd last been seen playing on one of the town's many open construction sites. Guesses were that he'd either fallen into a pipe trench and been covered, or that he'd been abducted. He was never found. We thought about him, in class we prayed for him, and when we weren't out looking for something to get into, we tried to figure out what had happened to him.

Our mothers' warnings to stay clear of the dumps taught us that David's fate could easily have been our own. And in silent, instinctive ways I'm sure we understood something of David's other possible end, the one that wasn't an accident. We knew something of children's fearsome cruelty to children, and we lived with our own passion for misadventure. Though we knew it neither as cruelty nor as misadventure. No one believed that David was playing alone at the building site that day. We didn't know it then, but as many of us grew older we came to think it not inconceivable that David had come to grief at the hands of boys not a lot older than himself, playing in a makeshift sand-pit. All of these things have returned with the news of James

Bulger's murder. More than once this week, a single image has floated into my head: a grainy Strathclyde Police picture of a sandy-haired boy, with its caption "Have You Seen David?"

JONATHAN RABAN

Julia's City

I came to live in Seattle in 1990, when I was forty-seven. It was late – very late – in the day for a new start. Literally so. At the departure gate at Heathrow Airport, it was announced that the flight would be delayed for an hour while engineers fixed a minor problem with the instruments. One hour grew, announcement by announcement, into ten, and it was dark when the plane eventually took off and we flew into the longest night I've ever known. There was a faint blue glimmer around the edge of the Arctic Circle, but otherwise the world was black. Working in the dim cone of light shed by the lens in the overhead console, my watch set to Pacific time, eight hours short of what felt like reality, I scribbled in a notebook through the in-flight movies and the meal services. I wrote excitedly about the life I hadn't yet begun to lead: I wrote about the companion whom (as it seems now) I barely knew; I wrote about the house we had not yet found to rent; I wrote about the book I hadn't yet written.

By the time the captain's voice came over the loudspeaker system to say that we were passing the lights of Edmonton, this unlived life was in perfect order on the page. There was the room, furnished with books, overlooking the water; the boat tied to the dock, within view of the window; the chapter steadily unfolding on the typewriter; my companion, pecking away at her computer within earshot. The scene was framed by fir trees, rimmed with sea. It included a softly-lit restaurant, Italian, with the level in the bottle of Valpolicella sinking fast; the voices of friends, as yet unmet; the unbought car in which we scaled a logging track over the high Cascades; long sane days of reading and writing and talking; rain on the roof; a potbellied wood stove; love in the afternoons.

Looking back at the scribbler from a three-and-a-half-year distance, I see (of course) that he's a flying fool – a middle-aged man, inflated with unlikely hopes, trying to defy the force of life's ordinary gravity. Sailing over the wilds of Alberta at 38,000 feet, in time out of time, there's only one direction for him to move in and it's *down*. At best, he deserves to figure as the fall-guy hero of a comic novel.

Yet the West wasn't settled by realists. I think of James Gilchrist Swan, walking out of a deadly marriage in Boston in 1850, to take ship for California and the Washington Territory. In the same year, Dr David Maynard walked out on his wife and family in Ohio, set off on the Oregon Trail for Puget Sound, and became a founding father of Seattle, the city's first real-estate magnate. Swan was thirty-three, Maynard forty-two, at a time when those ages were a good deal older than they are now. The graveyards of the Pacific Northwest are packed with people like Swan and Maynard – last-chancers, who left their failed businesses and failed marriages back East, hoping, against all experience to the contrary, that things might yet work out differently for them.

Jolting clumsily from cloud to cloud, its engines working in disquieting bursts and hiccups, the plane lost an awful lot of height in no time at all, and suddenly we were there, swaying low over Seattle. Lake Union was a black hole encircled by light; a late ferry, like a jack-o'-lantern, hung suspended in the dark space between Elliott Bay and Bainbridge Island. We scraped over the tops of the banking and insurance towers of downtown, and as the aircraft steadied itself on its glide path, I felt a rush of dizzy panic at what I'd done.

We found a house on Queen Anne Hill and furnished it from yard sales, joining the Saturday morning drift of cars with out-of-state plates and people with out-of-state accents. The idea that my own move was a strikingly bold and original one was blown clean away at the yard sales, where everyone in sight was hastily patching together the ingredients of a new life. We were all chasing the same old things, hoping that their comfortable and well-used air would rub off on us and make us feel less keenly our own awkward novelty in the landscape. I bought a couch on which, I speculated, the sixteen-year-old Mary McCarthy might have been found necking with the painter Kenneth Callahan in 1928, when the precocious McCarthy was making her debut in the White Russian bohemia on the south slope of Queen Anne. Saturday by Saturday, the house filled with congenial bits and pieces, each one somewhat scratched, or stained, or tarnished, or in need of glue or reupholstering: within six weeks it looked as if we might have been living in Seattle all our lives.

I was a newcomer in a city of newcomers, where the corner grocer came from Seoul, the landlord from Horta in the Azores, the woman at the supermarket checkout from Los Angeles, the neighbour from Kansas City, the mailman from South Dakota. Every so often I would meet someone close to my own age who was born in Seattle – but it nearly always turned out that their parents had moved here during the Boeing boom of the early 1940s. It is comfortingly hard to feel a misfit in a society where no one you know exactly fits; but to live, rootlessly, among so many other uprooted people does tend to make you feel like a guest at some large, well appointed but impersonal hotel. Seattle manners seemed like hotel manners: civil, in the chilly fashion of strangers keeping other strangers at arm's length.

There was another city, seen in rare glimpses and at a distance. Down by the Ship Canal, along Ewing Street, in the atmospheric tangle of cranes, ships, sheds and floating docks, I eavesdropped on an older Seattle. The tug captains from Foss Maritime, boat builders, marine engineers and sea-entrepreneurs had a language of their own. They talked in gruff laconic wisecracks and were masters of the sly obliquity that takes the indirect route to the heart of the matter. Unable to contribute, I was happy to offer myself up as a sacrificial stooge in return for being able to listen. The talk was knowing, intimate, affectionate and malicious by turns – closely akin to the London gossip that I'd left behind me. These people remembered each others' parents and grandparents; they could speak allusively, confident of being understood; their city was an intricate closed circuit, built on a deep reservoir of shared memories and shared labour in the shipping and timber industries. To an outsider, it looked like a far happier city than the Seattle I saw most of – the Seattle of the lone Greenlake joggers, the transplants, the anxious liberals in REI outdoor gear and Volkswagen Cabriolets.

The society of the Ship Canal made me feel homesick and threw my own situation here into sharp relief. Lacking a usable past, we newcomers were like amputees. Without a shared past, we were short of humour, short of intimacy, short of allusions and cross-references – short of that essential common stock of experience that makes a society tick. It was no wonder that living in Seattle sometimes seemed like perpetual breakfast-time at some airport Sheraton.

At the Seattle Public Library I was struck by the busy prominence of the genealogy section. I'd always thought that digging up one's ancestors was an eccentric hobby, and that people who went in for it – Mormons, rescuing their dead relations for Judgment Day; English snobs, claiming descendence from the belted earls of Loamshire – were to be given a wide berth. But in Seattle, suddenly hungry for history, I saw the point of trying to patch through a connection between oneself and the articulate and meaningful past. This was a place where everyone felt in need of a family tree.

Having no ancestors of my own in the Pacific Northwest, I bought some at a Queen Anne yard sale. They came in a job-lot in a Red Delicious Washington Apple box and cost me $15. The early birds had been picking at the contents of the box, but there were still more than 100 sepia photographs left, some going back to before the Civil War. The early birds had missed a little book of portrait miniatures, taken by a Philadelphia photographer, showing an extended family, including four men in Union army uniforms and a platoon of grim-visaged aunts in mobcaps and crepe. Some photographers came from Maine; some from Albert Lea and Austin in Minnesota; but the bulk of the collection had been taken by J. Foseide, Artistic Photographer, of Buckley, Washington, and Pautske, Artist, of Auburn.

The name McNish was written in pencil on the back of a picture of a waterside lumber mill, its employees posing stiffly in line in the foreground. Sorting through the heap on the floor of my study, I found the ghost, at least, of a story. There was a Buckley man, moustached and pomaded, in wing collar and white tie. Though his nose was on the large side and his eyes seemed a little shallow, he looked handsome and self-assured, like a successful door-to-door salesman. From Austin, Minnesota, came a plump girl of high-school age, sweet and pudgy, first found garlanded with flowers in a tableau depicting the Three Graces. Soon the man and the girl were in the same picture. Here they were with a baby. And another. And another. The first of the amateur snapshots showed the couple on a rowboat outing, with a son of ten, or thereabouts. The woman grew, photograph by photograph, from plump to stout. She put her hair up in a not-too-tidy bun and in the course of a decade or less she lost her meek smile and took on an expression of exhausted resignation. Meanwhile the man's moustache went grey: he began to wear steel-framed specs and an Odd Fellows pin; at sixty or so he sat behind a great desk piled with ledgers, his hair still exuberantly full, though nearly white now.

Someone had scribbled "Uncle Alonso and Aunt Ottie" on the back of one of the husband-and-wife pictures, but there was little else in the way of clues.

I drove to Buckley, an engaging town, its 1890s Main Street still largely intact, and plodded up and down the rows of tombstones in the cemetery, hunting for names and dates. I called up Murray Morgan, the Edward Gibbon of Washington State. In the newspaper archive of the University of Washington I scrolled through the *Buckley Banner* on microfilm. Bit by bit, I came to know the family in the cardboard box – and to anyone without ancestors in Western Washington, I commend Alonso and Ottie Bryant as the perfect proxy-forebears.

Alonso had grown up in Machias, Maine, where he was born in 1855. His grandfather had fought in the War of Independence and was proud of having once caused a British sloop to founder on a sand spit by putting out the light in the Machiasport lighthouse and erecting a decoy a few hundred yards south of the harbour. Alonso himself was a boy during the Civil War, and would later remember carrying letters to the post office for the wives and girlfriends of Union soldiers.

In the first half of the nineteenth century, Machias had been an important port in the timber trade, but as the loggers moved westwards, the towns on the Maine coast drifted into recession. When he left school, Alonso Bryant worked as a casual labourer in the construction industry, but the jobs were few and far between. He went west – finding well-paid and dangerous work building bridges for the Northern Pacific Railroad as it crossed the Rockies and followed the Columbia River to Portland, Oregon. I've seen those huge black timber trestles on which the trains creep over the gorges, and imagine Alonso, aloft, guiding a swinging beam into its slot in the cross-hatching.

By the time the railroad reached Portland, he'd saved enough to set himself up in business as a builder and contractor – though not for long, because he evidently saw that the people who were making most out of the construction industry were the suppliers and merchants, not the builders themselves. What he wanted was a rapidly building town and a hardware store. He found Buckley.

He arrived in 1892. He was thirty-seven; a big, tough man with a dandy's taste in tiepins and starched collars, the points of his moustache oiled and twisted, his glossy hair trimmed close around the sides of his head. He swaggers through his pictures, and looks as if he knows that he can still turn the heads of girls.

Buckley, on the White River, south of Auburn, had been incorporated in 1890 — a brand-new mill town standing in the middle of a desolate acreage of logged stumps. It had a brick main street, a newspaper, an opera house. It had great expectations. Picket fences enclosed dozens of swanky wooden villas in every phase of construction. Buckley was prime hardware-store territory.

Four years after Bryant's arrival, in the early summer of 1896, William L. McNish brought his wife and daughter to Buckley from Austin, Minnesota. (They weren't the first McNishes in town; a labourer, W. S. McNish, was reported by the *Banner* to have lost his tool chest in a fire at the sash and door factory in 1892.) Ottie McNish — the garlanded Euphrosyne — was seventeen, and not the most likely match for the forty-one-year-old owner of Bryant's Hardware.

Between 1896 and their eventual marriage in 1903, I've followed Ottie and Alonso through the social columns of the *Banner*, where Alonso makes a big splash and Ottie a few shy appearances. By now, Alonso was a Justice of the Peace, active in the Republican Party, a bachelor bigwig in great demand. Ottie's claim to public attention was her singing voice. She joined the Presbyterian choir and graduated to singing solos, as when she took a leading part in the oratorio *Under the Palms* at the Presbyterian church.

I see Ottie in the hardware store, dithering in the fastenings section, and Alonso, self-important, avuncular, thumbs in his buttonholes, setting her to rights. He smells of patchouli oil and cigars. (I know about the cigars because I now keep my business cards in a scuffed black-leather wallet, made for the purpose, that once belonged to him. It is lettered in gold-leaf: *Compliments of Julius Ellinger & Co. Havana Cigar M'frs Tampa Fla. and New York*.)

For a muddy frontier town — and perhaps *because* it was a muddy frontier town — Buckley had an intense social calendar. Newcomers were immediately enrolled by the clubs, church groups and Masonic lodges. In winter there were several musical evenings in private houses. Both Ottie and Alonso attended one at the home of Mr and Mrs J. F. Jones, where Miss Elisabeth Jones "rendered several choice selections in rich contralto". There were organized trips to Tacoma for Christmas shopping and to see the Ringling Bros Circus. The town turned out for a demonstration of mental telepathy at the Opera House by Keller the Hypnotist. At the Women's Club, the mayor's wife, Mrs McNeely, read a paper on Sappho and Mrs Browning. The Buckley Dramatic Club mounted regular entertainments, including one of which I have a photograph (Alonso appears in it, resplendent in eighteenth-century wig and stockings).

In September 1903, the Bryant–McNish wedding merited seven paragraphs in the *Banner*:

WEDDING BELLS

At the residence of Mr and Mrs Wm. L. McNish, in Buckley, on Saturday, Sept. 19, at 7 o'clock P.M. occurred the wedding of their daughter, Miss Ottie R. McNish, to our well-known townsman, Mr Alonso M. Bryant.

The wedding was a quiet one, only the near relatives of the bride and the wife of the officiating minister, Rev. O. E. Cornwell, witnessing the ceremony.

After a delicious wedding supper the bride and groom departed on the evening train for a brief bridal tour to Victoria, BC, and other points down the Sound.

A goodly number of friends gathered about them at the station, with congratulations and showers of rice. Their friends who are many wish them a very happy journey together through life.

They will soon be at home to their friends at their new residence on East Main Street, Buckley.

The bride is a young woman of reserved habits and is held in high esteem by all who know her. She has been a resident of Buckley for a number of years and her friends are not a few.

The groom is one of our hardware merchants and has been here for a period of eight or nine years. In that time he has built up a good business and is highly respected by all who know him.

THE BANNER joins the host of friends in wishing them many years of unalloyed pleasure.

Ottie was twenty-five, Alonso forty-eight. Though in the pictures of the couple one might mistake Ottie for the older of the two, she is so ample and matronly, Alonso so spruce (I suspect him of dyeing his hair – or, possibly, of persuading J. Foseide, Artistic Photographer, to work some darkroom magic on it).

Ottie had babies – three sons and a daughter. Alonso went into local politics. He was on the school board and the town council. He was town treasurer and later mayor of Buckley. In 1913 he was elected to serve as a state congressman at Olympia. In the young and fluid society of western Washington, this rolling stone from the East Coast had become a fixed pillar of the community. In the portrait that I've propped beside the typewriter he is looking up from his papers in the state house at Olympia: his eyes swim behind his glasses; his broad mouth is set in a downturned arc; he exudes that air of sombre rectitude that might gain him election to high fiscal office. He looks too refined for his large practical hands, which he keeps closed, as if they embarrassed him.

Ottie's health broke in her fifties and she died in 1935, aged fifty-eight, but Alonso continued to run the hardware store in Buckley, which spawned an offshoot, Bryant Hardware in Kirkland, managed by Alonso's and Ottie's son, Mariner Bryant. When the United States entered World War II after Pearl Harbor, Alonso – who could remember his grandfather talking about the War of Independence, and who had himself lived through the Civil War – was still in business. He was eighty-seven, going on eighty-eight, when he died at his daughter's home in Seattle on 19 July. I was then five weeks old – old enough, by a whisker, to count this pioneer of the Pacific Northwest as living in my own lifetime.

The newcomer here should at least be able to feel that he or she is in the historical swim of things, for the history of the Pacific Northwest since 1792 has been a history of newcoming and newcomers, a braid of interwoven Alonso-and-Ottie stories. The stories are all around us – in the fabric of the houses we live in, in the names of places and streets; they go begging at yard sales and can be fished out of dumpsters.

My own house (built in 1906 in the wake of the Alaskan gold rush, a creaky timber warren of rooms with sloping floors and doorways that have twisted out of true – a relic of another wave of newcomers to the region) stands just below Mount Pleasant Cemetery on Queen Anne Hill. I like to walk among the tombstones there, where so many of the dead are buried thousands of miles from where they were born.

Carl Ewald, born near Marienwerder, Prussia, 12 June 1817, died at Seattle, Washington . . . Isabella Blair Ormston, native of East Lothian, Haddington-Shire, Scotland . . . William Dickson, native of Belfast, Ireland . . . Anna Lloyd Tinkham, born 28 May 1849, Wales, England (sic), *died 9 Feb. 1908, Seattle, Wash.* One inscription pleases me particularly: *Sylvester S. Bower, born Newfield, NY, April 1854, came to Wash. 1889, died July 12, 1936.* That the date of his arrival in the Pacific Northwest should be commemorated as one of the three salient facts of Mr Bower's life seems exactly right. That's how it feels to me, and how I want it on my own tombstone, please: . . . *came to Wash. 1990* . . .

You can't look out of the window here without seeing that you are in an uprooted and homesick land. Seattle's domestic architecture pines for a world elsewhere. The old German Club on Ninth Avenue, with its tall and narrow second-floor windows, harks back to some tree-planted *Strasse* in nineteenth-century Hamburg or Cologne; the well-to-do English who settled around St Mark's Cathedral on Capitol Hill had their own mullioned and half-timbered enclave of replica manor houses, their details copied from Chamberlain's *Tudor Homes of England*, the great architectural source book of American mock-Tudor. Close by the English quarter, a greystone Russian *dacha* glooms over a lordly view of Interstate 5 and Lake Union. Down in the International District, the glum brick buildings with balconied shrines set high over the street are homesick for Shanghai, while the "classical" terracotta friezes of downtown, with their gargoyles and cartouches and anthemions, are homesick for history itself – anybody's history, and the older and grander the better. Stand near the corner of Third Avenue and Madison Street, and look up at the wild and dizzy conflation of Ancient Greek, Ancient Roman, English Gothic, Art Deco Egyptian, French Empire, Italian Renaissance, all handsomely moulded in Green River mud. Out in the countryside, there is a Bavarian mountain town, a Norwegian fishing village and, in the Skagit valley to the west of Mount Vernon, an entire landscape that even a Dutchman (with a slight case of astigmatism) might plausibly mistake for the flat farms and poplar-fringed villages of Friesland.

What is true of the architecture and the landscape is even truer of people's domestic interiors here. When I first visited Seattle, to research a chapter of a book, I got used to the oddity of parking my car outside a ranch-style bungalow in a street of more or less identical ranch-style bungalows, then, inside the door, taking off my shoes and entering the cross-legged-on-the-floor life of the immigrant Korean family, with its rugs and carved chests. Outside lay Greenwood, or Ballard, or Phinney Ridge: inside, we were half-way back, at least, to Seoul or Inchon. When I came to live here, I found that half the houses I visited in Seattle were like this – nostalgic reconstructions of another time, another place. A ground-floor apartment turned out to be a Greenwich Village loft, the plaster on the walls hacked off to expose bare brick, the ceiling strung with decorative, non-functional plumbing. I'm writing this with a mild hangover, incurred at a party last night in the Madrona neighbourhood: the American owners of the house were Anglophile enthusiasts of Early Music, and as one stepped through their front door one entered a sort of legendary Merrie England of shawms and sackbuts and psalteries, of morris men and maypoles. The pictures on their walls were watercolours of the great Elizabethan piles, like Moreton and Hardwick Halls; the books on their shelves had the sort of bindings that you rarely see outside the set of "Masterpiece Theatre"; the books themselves were described to me by an awed friend who had checked out the library in the downstairs bathroom as "works of medieval feminism". I like to think that the next-door neighbours were passionate Arabists whose living room was a faithful reconstruction of a merchant's *diwan* in a house deep in the Aleppo souk; or maybe tribal-Africa buffs, with a houseful of spears, blankets and goatskin drums.

For Seattle tends to slop about in time and space. In New York, you're rarely in doubt that this is New York and the time is the present, but there's less here-and-now in Seattle than in any city I've ever known. Its woody plots and inward-looking houses, screened from their neighbours by thick tangles of greenery, allow people to live in private bubble-worlds of their own construction. My neighbour's Seattle isn't mine – or yours. There are days when the city seems to me to be dangerously like an old-fashioned lunatic asylum: here's the lady who believes herself to be Anastasia Romanov; and here's Napoleon; and this gentleman is Alexander the Great; and here's a teapot . . . Seattle does not insist – as both bigger cities and smaller towns do – on its own overbearing reality: it is unusually indulgent to those of its citizens who prefer to live in dreams and memories. If you want to bury yourself in a cottage in the trees, pretending that you are living inside a nineteenth-century French novel, or that you're back home in another decade and another country, Seattle will do astonishingly little to disturb your illusion.

My Seattle is a city of émigrés and migrants, and inevitably I see deracination as part of the basic fabric of the place. But I've planted a much deeper root here. My companion of the first paragraph of this piece became my wife, and we have a child, now a year old. My American daughter – a Washington Native, as they say on the bumper stickers.

Even now, I see our two cities diverging.

For Julia, the word "tree" already means the shaggy cypress and the drooping fir, whose inky green will never convey to her the alien and depressive associations that they have for me. To my English eye, the Douglas Fir has a sort of grim splendour, but it seems to me a congenitally unhappy vegetable. To Julia's Pacific Northwestern eye, it's the most homely tree she knows; it's where the squirrels live and where the little pine siskins fuss and flutter.

So, too, the word "water" is coming to mean the deep and dusty stuff of Puget Sound, on which she has already been afloat. To me this water, which drops to more than a hundred fathoms just a few yards out from the shore, is uncannily, shiveringly deep, and queer things live in its ice-cold profundity, like *architeuthis*, the giant squid, and the brainy, jet-propelled *octopus dofleini*. I grew up in a country where wild things were rabbits and foxes; she is coming into possession of a world where killer whales live in the watery suburbs of her native city, where real bears raid trashcans on the outskirts of Everett and mountain lions are sometimes spotted in Gig Harbor. God knows what she'll make of the wild exciting world of Beatrix Potter's Lake District animals – Peter Rabbit and Jeremy Fisher.

Growing up in the mock-antique, mock-heroic architecture of Seattle, Julia won't be amused by its comedy or touched by its pathos, as I am: it'll just be old to her – as real Tudor and Jacobean architecture is old to me – and dull, in the way that merely old things are. When she gets to see Florence, and tires of the long hot hike around the Uffizi and Bargello, she may be fleetingly reminded of Seattle; as when she visits her English grandparents in Leicestershire, she may notice some battered, down-at-heel versions of buildings that are in a fine state of upkeep back home.

As children of migrants to the West must do, she'll grow up with a sense of distances unlike anything that either her New Yorker mother or I knew as children. Her maternal grandfather lives on the Upper West Side of Manhattan, her English grandparents in Market Harborough, and Julia has been born into a house where the phrases "back East" and "in England" are constant, almost daily references –

points where two shadowy worlds-elsewhere hover in the middle distance behind the world she lives in.

That is such a standard feature of West Coast life that I bet Julia will share it with half the children at her school. I've heard people born in this region talk of it as "out here", as if to be a Westerner was to be in some sense, however faint and ancestral, in exile from the warm centre of the world. I hope my daughter doesn't grow up to speak of her birthplace as "out here", and doubt that she will: if the present tilt of the world economy continues, if there's even a grain of truth in all the boosterish talk about the Pacific Century, then Seattle will be, and perhaps already is, a good deal closer to the centre of things than are New York and London.

This is her city in a way that it can never be mine; and as newcomers must take their cues from the natives, I now have to learn about Seattle from Julia.

I'm making a beginning. I'm relearning the meaning of the word "tree", and a whole enormous syllabus looms ahead. But I am – in my daughter's American English – a quick study. I'll get to figure it out.

DERMOT HEALY

Within An Ass's Roar

Once we took a wrong turning in northwest Sligo and found ourselves on a rocky beach overlooked by a stone white-washed three-roomed cottage that sat on a cliff with its back to the sea.

There were fossils in the stones of the gable wall. The roofless ruins of the sheds behind were filled with fishing nets, small glass buoys, old mud thatch and black turf. Sea thrift grew in wild clumps everywhere. It was a small homely place by a big spilling ocean. We walked the beach in different directions, thinking our separate thoughts. Maybe a year later I unknowingly bought the same house by candlelight.

Tom Carraway, the owner, drove me up there in the dark. He struck a match, unlocked the door and lit the butt of a candle.

"Is there a draw in that chimney?" I asked.

"Is there a draw!" he said, offended.

He stuffed newspapers in the grate, lit them and the fire took with a whoosh. There was an old iron bed in the far room, just as it had been when Joe Donlon died. Two pairs of black shoes were placed neatly beneath it. There was a black suit and a battered suitcase in the homemade yellow wardrobe. The middle room – the kitchen – was painted canary yellow, battleship grey and chocolate brown. The third room was filled with tins of Andrew's Liver Salts and baking soda. Joe must have had a bad stomach. Holy pictures lined the walls. A wooden box was filled with nails, a hammer, a levelling rod made of string and a stone weight, a measuring tape, one massive wooden plane and an old saw.

"The Donlons," said Tom, "were all craftsmen. They were great masons."

"What's the weather like here?" I asked.

"Ah, we get the odd storm."

"I'll take it," I said on my way back in the car.

The next day I drove Helen my companion out to see what I'd bought
but I couldn't find the cottage. All the sea-roads in Maugherow look
the same.

"Donlon's?" a man said on the road. "You want Donlon's. What
Donlon's?"

"Joe Donlon's," I said, "of Dooneel."

"Sure that place," he said, "is falling into the sea. There hasn't
been a soul in that house for years. You don't want to be going up
there."

"He just bought it," said Helen.

"Oh Holy God," he said backing away.

When at last we found it, we discovered it was the same cottage
we'd seen the previous year.

The first night we stayed there we slept on the floor in a drastic storm.
It was freezing and ghostly and alarming. I stood on the cliff and saw
feathery lights on the night sky over the Atlantic. They were snapping
like fireworks. Then the sky turned a deep blue. It went quiet. A
wedge-shaped cloud appeared on the horizon. The hurricane was
coming from America.

I ran down in a bitter wind. The dog was distraught as the hail
battered his eyes. Then the house seemed to charge forward. We heard
gunshots and the sounds of car doors slamming. Aeroplanes landed.
Juggernauts struggled uphill. When we lay down, the floor under the
mattress was thumping. The dog reared up with a mournful cry.
Ghosts slipped from room to room. The candle flames leaped wildly.

"I don't know about this," said Helen.

The next morning I stepped out to find it was blowing salt like
rain. The air was smoking. The entire stones on the beach had shifted.
Spumes of spray forty foot high blew over the bar. Waves the height
of the cliff were crashing beyond the north gable.

"Do you think are you wise?" asked Helen.

The cottage I'd bought was on an eroding cliff on an alt called
Dooneel. Seven brothers and two sisters were reared in its three
rooms. We lived for the first two years there by candlelight. Came
home at night and walked into each other in the dark. Washed by a
tap outdoors and did our toilet down the field.

I bought a Shetland pit pony called Wally off a neighbour's child who'd won him in a Christmas draw, and installed him in the back field. The iron bed in the gap was down the next morning and he was gone. I found him back in McSweeney's. I led him home. That meant covering about ten yards of the road every five minutes. That pit pony was stubborn and strong and very uncivilized.

Over the next few weeks he kept disappearing.

"What that fellow needs is a companion," said Helen.

A few weeks later I tried wild, bearded, rheumy-eyed mountain goats, who arrived in a van that was spilling their urine. The minute they were released they were walking the walls and the roof of the cottage. Helen was not having that.

"What you need up here," said Jack Donlon, a neighbour, "is an ass. Try Mickey Foran. He's your man."

I bought two asses, or donkeys if you like, in a local pub. The man who sold them to me said they'd be the right job, and in time I might buy a cart and harness.

"And if ever you want to sell them back to me," he said, "remember that's all right too. We're always at that sort of business in Maugherow."

When I left Ellen's bar that night I saw myself as a small farmer, doing deals and keeping livestock. The £60 cheque I'd handed over for a cart-trained mare ass in foal and a six-month-old stallion foal seemed a fair enough price. Instead of lugging up rocks from the beach one by one by hand to build walls, myself and the she-ass would bring them up by the cartful.

The next day Mickey Foran arrived with the grey beasts – the mother in a rope harness and the foal trotting behind. They cut a lovely pair. When Wally saw them he grew ecstatic. We drove them in to join the pit pony in the back field. I put the old cast-iron bed back in place as a gate and went to the creamery for horse nuts. On my way home I met the three animals on the road. They were trotting towards McSweeney's. We walked back through the heady days of June. The sun was up. The wind a creamy southern. Every few yards I dropped a handful of nuts and they followed me home.

The asses strolled the moist salty grass while Wally looked towards America. We had the mother's hooves done by a man from Raughley Island. His German lady held the ass's head while he pared. Peggy stared with disdain at Wally. The stallion ass – Jimmy – bit at his mother's left hind leg. We dug up floors. Roofed two of the sheds and had a toilet installed. In September the seas came higher. Then in November the first huge winds struck. I put pallets in the gaps. The beasts were a sad sight as they stood out of the wind behind the low stone walls.

Helen deplored the fact that the animals had no shelter.

"To think," she'd say, "that they're out there and we're in here; it's shameful."

Over the next few months I got to know Maugherow well. That came from following the animals round the parish. In a bid for freedom Wally began knocking down walls. He led the two asses everywhere. He'd go down to McSweeney's with the two asses in his wake. He'd bring them off round The Bent towards the sweet grass. Some times we'd find them in The Long Squares, fields divided by the Land Commissions into strips. They broke down fences and tormented bulls.

Once I heard they were above asleep at the back of Ellen's bar.

We were getting a bad name. And I was getting queer looks in the bar.

It was all Wally's doing. Then Helen began to worry about when the mare ass was due to foal.

"Think," she said, "what would happen if she gave birth in a neighbour's field."

I fed them bales of hay and rich horse food to keep them at home. Peggy at feeding time would dunt Wally with her rear end to get him out of the way. They'd bare their teeth at each other. They ate with a fierce hunger as the wind lashed them. Jimmy would suddenly dart under his mother's legs to get at her teats. Peggy did not like that. Neither did Helen.

"That she-ass," said Helen, "is having a terrible time."

By December you could not walk outside the door. Winds veered from north to west. The key in the door swung like crazy. The car had a coat of rust. Cats sailed by the window. The trees I'd set perished. In the dark afternoons I wrote and in the breaks in the wind moved stones. For the few days after Christmas there was an extraordinary swell on the sea yet no wind.

Something was happening away out there. The wash was powerful and green. The sun shone. On Stephen's Day a trawler from Killybegs fishing port went down just beyond the bar. All were saved.

Waves, thirty to forty foot high, broke on Ardbollan rock.

"If a storm comes," said Jack Donlon, "you'll be in trouble."

It came on 8 January, with winds going west-southwest. Gusts of 90mph were promised. It was the night of the full moon. The highest tide of the year was due at six in the morning. Everything was set for catastrophe. That evening, on the advice of a fisherman from Raughley, we tucked the car inland by a neighbour's house. We walked home through a powerful blast of wind and hail, lit the oil lamps and lay down.

The bed boomed beneath us. The lights on the mainland went out. I kept remembering what Jack Donlon had said — "The worst seas are before the dawn."

"I think we are in trouble," said Helen the next morning at six-thirty when she looked out the window. We were on an island. All the walls I'd built were gone. The road to the house had been lifted by a raging undertow. The front fields were covered in over ten foot of churning sea. The bank that I'd had built with a JCB was torn to shreds.

We phoned the County Council, but they said they could not help us. At low tide people came to see were we all right. "The 'say' has done a murder," said Jack Donlon. That afternoon the sea closed in round us again. It hoked at the cliff. Huge rocks were lifted and thrown on to our land. All day we watched the elements. That night we saw cars on the mainland with their full headlights switched on. Locals were driving out to watch the waves rising 'to the left of the cottage.

And the beasts. They crouched together behind the ruins. The foal, who was coated like an Afghan hound, stood by his mother with his tresses streeling. Peggy gave me a baleful eye. The pit pony nudged the rocks in the wall with his head. The hay I threw them blew away.

The storm lasted five days.

"I can't sleep," said Helen, "with the thought of poor Peggy out there."

When the storm was over I had a machine come in to unblock the drains and release the sea. When the road had been rebuilt Helen sent me up to Ellen's bar to sell the mother ass back to Mickey Foran.

"Mickey," I said, "I think the weather is too bad to keep the mother above. I'll sell her back to you and keep Jimmy the foal."

"Good enough," he said.

"What will you give me for her?"

"What are you asking?"

"Well," I said all business-like, "I gave you £40 for her and £20 for the foal in the first place."

"I think you did," he said thoughtfully.

"And I've had her for nigh on six months. So wait till I see – how about £50?"

"You must be joking," he said and turned aside.

"£45?" I asked tentatively.

"Go away out of that!"

"£40 then," I replied, "and we'll call it quits."

"No," said Mickey Foran. "I'll give you £30."

"But £40 was what I paid you."

"That was then. This is now."

"But she's in foal."

"Who told you that?"

"You did."

"Well, I wouldn't believe all I hear if I was you."

I was astounded.

"£35?" I asked lamely.

"No," he said, "£30. I'll give you £30. And a luck-penny."

He gave me £30 and a £3 as a luck-penny. We shook hands. It was a lesson in dealing. He peeled off three tenners, three punts and bought me a pint.

"You're a hard man," I said.

"I am," he declared proudly.

He led the she-ass back to his place the following evening. The foal tried to follow her then stood bewildered by the iron bedstead. But Wally roared madly as Peggy was led down the newly constructed road. He stood by the wall snorting, went up on his back legs and whinnied. His eyes were black and crazy. He followed her every movement till she was out of sight.

Then he raced in circles round the field followed by the foal. He stopped. The foal stopped. Wally looked towards where Peggy had gone and raced off again. Jimmy stood perplexed. He turned and for the first time in his life tried a proper ass's roar. It came out all wrong. It was an eerie nose-chugging wail. It frightened him, this crunching sound that had suddenly issued from his lips. The foal's screech drove Wally demented.

He head-butted the wall and broke free.

A few weeks later I sold Wally. Then only Jimmy remained.

Two years on we have electricity and Jimmy the ass is still with us. He trumpets his call for breakfast each morning like a rooster. He bellows a welcome when Helen's car comes home. His roar is now the full male-ass's roar. If you walk the back field he slants his ears, puts his head down and snaps at your left leg like he used to do to his mother.

Mickey Foran is selling us a cart sometime. He's coming up to train Jimmy on the beach. But first we'll have to have the vet in to de-man the ass. The cats have been done, so has the dog. He was shot for wandering and his testicles were blown off. Jimmy is next in line but at least his doctoring will be gentle. Soon all the animals in this part of the world will be eunuchs. As for the others, I see Wally now and then going the roads in a rubber-wheeled trap. Peggy in blinkers can be found drawing a cart in Cloonagh. The computer gave up in the damp air from the sea. A start-of-day disc throws it into a frenzy. So I'm back to the pen.

Helen, who used to dread being in the cottage alone, now loves the solitude there.

But the truth is, I've seen her cast an envious eye round the living rooms of people we might visit in Sligo town. And I've caught myself stopping at an estate agent's window to look at a new batch of houses for sale. I have a longing sometimes for a place where trees can grow. The thought of the eroding cliff to the side of the cottage can be painful. I watched with alarm that hotel slip into the sea off a cliff in the North of England. But any talk of erosion is banned in the house. I'm superstitious. If you talk of something it's bound to happen. Even thinking about it can bring it to pass.

That's why we never discuss selling the cottage on the alt at Dooneel. That would be the most blasphemous thought of all. So we don't mention it. We keep warm in the storms and do a little to the house every year. Set spuds. Spread seaweed. Roof the sheds. But nothing that's too ostentatious. Just enough to keep it ticking over.

Whenever I have to stop inland I find there's something missing. For a while I can't place it. I think it's the usual disorientation. Then

I remember when I lie down in bed. It's that sound. The gunshots. The slamming doors. The thumping. The boom on the lava rock. The powerful traffic that never stops.

SVEN LINDQVIST

To Ain Sada

The following is a chapter from The Desert Divers *(1990), a combination
of travelogue and literary analysis discussing the desert experiences of André
Gide, Antoine de Saint-Exupéry, Isabelle Eberhardt and other divers into
the Saharan desert.*

I drive westwards from Laghouat. The road follows the Atlas Mountains: empty grandstands facing the endless football pitches of the
desert. Signposts indicate direction and give distances straight out
into the gravel – but I see no other way apart from the one I am
taking.

"Long hours of emptiness, nourished by silence", to use the words
of Isabelle Eberhardt.

In Sweden, when trying to imagine the desert, I thought of sandy
beaches which never reach the water. But it is fairly rare to see beaches
in the desert, which resembles more an endless schoolyard, a vast,
hard-packed desolation extending without end towards the horizon.

Some rocks are left behind, alone on the bare ground. They were
too heavy. The light ones have gone. Everything that can fly has fled.

Fromentin's success with *A Summer in the Sahara* has tempted many
writers to follow in his footsteps. Daudet, Gautier, Maupassant, even
Flaubert, all travelled in Africa and had a relationship with the desert.

But the universal heir to Fromentin's desert romanticism is Pierre
Loti.

They both came from the French Atlantic coast – Fromentin from
La Rochelle, Loti from Rochefort. Between these two towns lies a
water-logged marshy area sliced through by brim-full ditches and
canals, the ebb-tide exposing muddy river beds. The oyster beds over-
flow like Chinese rice paddies. The farmland is sticky, the water
flourishing and stagnating in the pools.

A landscape totally opposite to the desert. In addition, Loti was a naval officer, the sea his profession. He had the desert within him.

In Fromentin's life, the desert was more or less chance. In Laghouat, he found out by chance things he never dared tell and shrouded them all in mystery, which attracted the great general public. Success created a demand for his desert images, and they kept him busy, earning him a living for the rest of his life.

Loti's desert romance is no chance. It is part of a mendacity running far deeper and embracing his whole personality.

A small boy was once given a miniature landscape by his elder brother. All through his childhood he continued to add on to this wonderful landscape, which extended into a whole little world in which every stone and every butterfly was charged with fantasies.

When the boy left his childhood home, he locked up his museum and sealed the door, locking in his childhood. Time was not to be allowed in there.

By then disaster had already struck the family. First his beloved elder brother died. Then his father was charged with embezzlement, lost his job and crept like a rat along the walls of the houses in Rochefort. The money for which the father had been responsible had to be repaid, the family sank into poverty, the childhood home was sold, the father died and the only son took on the debt.

That is how he became a writer. That is how he came to adopt the pseudonym of Pierre Loti.

Fifteen years later, when the debt has been paid off, he asks the ship's watch to wake him *once an hour* to tell him he is free of debt.

When his success as an author has made him rich, he buys back the parental home and turns it into a museum of fantasy, into a world in miniature. The façade remains untouched, but the interior he rebuilds according to his exotic dreams. The old quarter is filled like a honeycomb of the different rooms of his writing: the Turkish room, the Gothic, the Renaissance salon, the Japanese room, the Chinese, the Egyptian . . .

One room alone is left untouched. It is the smallest of them all and lies squeezed between the mummy room and the Turkish room. It is bare, but not like the bedroom, seeking effect in a calculating way. It is simply an ordinary little French study with a black chair and a black desk.

This is where Loti worked. Here he wrote a great many of his forty books, at the same desk at which his father once did his accounts.

All round this sober little room rose the scenery of his life. Few authors have had such a need as he had to enter into his dreams and inhabit them. To write a book set among Basque smugglers, he does not just live with them: he takes his Basque clothes and weapons home with him, has the back of the compound equipped as two Basque rooms and sends for an unknown Basque woman who bears him two Basque children. After work every day, he goes and plays with them for a little while.

But his existing wives, both the one at the front of the compound and the one at the back, mean less to him than the heroine in his first novel, *Aziyadé*. Every evening he retreats into his private mosque and spends several hours dreaming and weeping at her tombstone. The dead increasingly fill his existence – parents, relatives, favourite animals, all of them buried beneath the courtyard of his childhood home, incorporated into the museum of his life. His museum of death.

It all started when he locked away his childhood. Then he locked everything else away bit by bit. He wanted to preserve, perpetuate, to prevent every change.

No wonder Loti loved the desert. In the desert all changes have already occurred. Nothing grows, nothing dies. nothing decays. Everything has gone. Only eternity remains.

The flatter the desert, the more you become imprisoned and locked in by the horizon. You welcome every movement that elevates you and provides a view. You welcome every interruption: hills with hard peaks like the cap on the neck of a broken bottle, great movable yellow boulders which should really be called "immovable boulders", or quite simply distant heights coloured milky white or pale blue by the distance.

This morning I saw a *marabout*, the sepulchre of a holy man, the white walls reflecting the light like a beacon at a distance of several kilometres.

It takes about an hour to climb to the stillness and solitude up there. There is nothing there.

Nothing but a few lizard tracks in the sand.

Nothing but a few unglazed, cracked and crumbling jars, the tombstones of the poor.

Nothing but a few large split palm trunks, grey with age, their timber resembling pressed straw.

And then the *marabout*'s door glowing acid green and sulphur yellow in the morning sun.

Far down below, a man is hacking away in the dry river bed. Some dark men are spreading out their dark, moist dates to dry beyond a low mud wall.

I go down to them. Down there, it is already hot in the sun. But when they greet you, the men's hands are still cool, almost cold − as if the night had remained behind in their bodies.

The only language we had in common was our hands.

All his life, Pierre Loti has himself photographed in ever more handsome costumes. He holds his head thrown back, thrusting out one leg in order to appear taller than he is.

That is when you see how small he is. And how that tormented him.

He walks on tiptoe in high-heeled shoes. His wives are made to measure, to be smaller than he is himself. To be on the safe side, his mistresses are of "lower" race.

As a child, he read with thumping heart the letters from his admired older brother, Gustav, a ship's doctor who took a "wife" in Tahiti. On his first trip abroad, Loti goes to Tahiti and looks up his dead brother's woman. The love of his brother, as the little brother dreamt of back at home, becomes the constantly recurring paradigm in his life and his art.

Again and again he writes the same novel. It is about a white man, often a naval officer, who has a romantic relationship with a woman of alien race or culture. She looks up to him as to a higher being. The love is estrangement, passion, departure. They part with pain, doomed to eternal longing for their lost paradise.

Once only, he falls in love with a Frenchwoman. He proposes and is turned down.

In the diary he kept all his life with a book-keeper's thoroughness these are the only pages missing.

That is when he becomes a bodybuilder. He can't change his height, but he can build up his muscles. He becomes an athlete and appears in a circus in close-fitting tricot.

"With a certain satisfaction, I regard the body I have created with

my exercises. The muscles stand out in relief in the close-fitting costume. An old juggler elevates the effect by lightly shading in the
contours of my muscles with a pencil. This strange anatomical toilet
takes twenty minutes."

Even in his nakedness he has to disguise himself. On the photographs of him naked are some small telling wrinkles showing him
pressing up his chest muscles with his folded arms to make them seem
larger than they are.

Over the years, he redoubles his efforts. He dyes his moustache
and rouges his cheeks; he sits in the French Academy made up like
an old whore − hoping no one will see how small he is.

He loves his way through the world, conquering it in the form of
women. Asia, Africa, the South Seas and the Atlantic, the deserts of
Sahara, Sinai and Persia − he has been everywhere, he has loved and
deserted everywhere, he has skimmed the romanticism of existence
and taken it back with him to his art and his home.

In his doll's house, at last the world is given its correct proportions.
Inside it, he is large.

A moon-pale and determined young woman has been given an assign-
ment by the French Academy to free Pierre Loti from his enchanted
house. The Academy Action Group arrives in a helicopter and those
most immortal climb down rope ladders on to the roof of the mosque.
They search through the house without finding Loti. "Search
thoroughly," says Isabelle. "He's always in disguise." But they find
nothing but a little dog which she takes in her arms as she climbs up
into the roaring helicopter, its rotor blades making the roof tiles jump.
The dog is a little black and white Scottie with bristly moustache and
yearning eyes. One of its hind legs is rather stiff from almost always
being raised. It also carries its nose very high.

"You can see it's Pierre Loti's dog," says Isabelle. Then the disguise
suddenly falls away and little Loti is standing there with his nose in
the air − without his dog-mask, but all the same strangely dog-like.

More people drown in the desert than in the sea. They drown from
lack of imagination. They simply cannot imagine so much water in
which it is possible to drown.

An *oued* is a dried-out river channel. But it can be thousands of years since any river flowed there. So it is more correct to say that an *oued* is the track left by torrents that have passed by. The desert is full of tracks of that kind, and you can live a whole life without ever seeing them filled with water. It is like living by the main line south without ever seeing a single train. Gradually you begin to think none can come. And if the whole landscape is a shunting-yard full of similar railway lines where no trains run, either – well, then you finally feel utterly safe.

When the express train comes thundering along one night according to some unknown timetable, you are not prepared. The torrent suddenly roars past and drowns everything in its way.

It came to Ain Sefra on the night of 21 October 1904.

I admit it is with fairly rapid steps I cross the *oued* in Ain Sefra. I can see bits of skeleton in the sand on the other side. And further up, whole corpses of sheep, goats and cattle – swept down by a tidal wave? Or a kind of animal cemetery?

I come into a forest planted to bind the dunes. There is a shepherd reading a book there.

"Sidi Bou Djema?" I say, in monosyllables.

He points at a wall faintly outlined up on top of the dune and replies equally monosyllabically:

"Sidi Bou Djema!"

But when you get up there, there is nothing but the wall round a small garden where a lone man and his dog grow chick-peas and onions.

He is a very friendly man and he speaks beautiful French. He knows perfectly well where the tomb is and is pleased to take me there.

It is his garden. He has laid it out himself. He has dug the well himself, eleven metres deep. He has fired the clay bricks for the wall himself. It would have been ready by now if it hadn't rained the other day. His semi-fired bricks have run out into the ground – look at this! Now he has to start all over again from the beginning. He is used to that. He was a guest-worker in France for eight years and has worked in Marseilles and Lyons. He has even been to Paris. Now he has come back, has a wife and six children, five of them boys, and he is looking forward to a secure old age when he no longer needs to work, other than to potter around in his garden.

As he is telling me this, we have got as far as the burial ground of

Sidi Bou Djema. It lies with dunes and mountains behind it and a view over the *oued* where it happened.

A few spindly stems of grass grow in the sand after the rain. But all the same, it is a very desolate place. The desolation seems to be concentrated on the absurd buckled aluminium saucepan hanging at the back of the tombstone. On the front it says in European letters:

ISABELLE EBERHARDT

"The act of departure is the bravest and most beautiful of all actions. A selfish happiness perhaps, but it is a happiness – for him who knows how to appreciate it. To be alone, to have no needs, to be unknown, a stranger and at home everywhere and to march, solitary and great, to the conquest of the world . . ."

That is what Isabelle Eberhardt writes in a piece sometimes called *The Road*, sometimes *Notes in Pencil*.

Departure is a tradition in her family. Her surname comes from a German mother, Fräulein Eberhardt, who has left her country to live with a Russian Jew.

Her mother has married an old Russian general, but leaves him and goes to Geneva with the children's young tutor – a handsome, intellectual Armenian, Tolstoy's apprentice, Bakunin's friend. He has been a priest, he is married and now leaves his wife and children to live with his beloved in exile.

He teaches Isabelle six languages: French, Russian, German, Latin, Greek and Arabic. But he never admits to her face that he is her father.

She grows up among exiled anarchists in a chaotic milieu in which catastrophe is the norm.

When she is eight, her brother Nicholas joins the Foreign Legion.

When she is nine, her sister Olga runs away and marries against the will of her family.

When she is seventeen, her favourite brother Augustin joins the Foreign Legion.

When she is twenty, she goes with her mother to Algiers. They both convert to Islam. The mother dies and is buried in Annaba.

When she is twenty-one her brother Vladimir commits suicide.

When she is twenty-two, she gives her father, who is dying of cancer, an overdose of a pain-killing drug which, intentionally or not, ends his life.

She is alone in the world. At the turn of the century in 1900 she writes in her diary:

> To be a nomad in the great deserts of life in which I shall never be anything but an outsider – such is the only form of bliss, however bitter, the Mectoub will ever grant me.

In secret, my sister Isabelle winds wet cotton bandages round her chest. She wears these bandages under her clothes and does not betray with the slightest sign what is going on. Only I know about it and I cannot stop her. She winds the wet bandages tightly, tightly round her chest. When they dry and shrink, they slowly crush her chest and suffocate her heart. No one can save her.

"Where have I got this sickly longing for infertile ground and dry desolation from?" Isabelle Eberhardt asks.

As early as in her teens she was charmed by the melancholy escapism in Loti's first novel *Aziyadé* and he became her favourite author. When his *Le Desert* came out in 1895, she was eighteen years old. Two years later she set out into the desert on her own for the first time. Loti was the only one she always took with her on her journeys, the only person she looked up to as forerunner and example.

She thought she had found her soulmate. He had a beloved older brother who had gone to sea, she has a beloved older brother who became a legionnaire. Her life, like his, is shrouded in departure and loss. Both live in disguise. And both love the desert, where they see their emptiness and their longing for death take shape.

Michel Vieuchange set off into the desert disguised as a woman. Isabelle sets off into the desert disguised as a man.

To her it is not just a disguise. The French language mercilessly reveals whether the writer considers him- or herself to be man or woman. Even in her diary, Isabelle uses the masculine gender about herself.

Pierre Loti disguised himself as an Arab, but also as a Chinese, a Turk and a Basque. In every harbour, in every book, he takes on a new disguise. He became a cut-out doll for ever new costumes, a cultural chameleon melting into every environment and lacking authenticity wherever he went.

The disguise goes deeper in Isabelle. When she returns to Africa, she wants to free herself from her past and take on a new and Arab identity. She becomes the Tunisian author Si Mahmoud Essadi.

Dressed in male Arab clothes, she sets off into the desert. She has been waiting for this moment all her life. She rides between the oases with a few native cavalrymen, with a group of legionnaires, with a *chaamba* caravan, with an African on his way home to his village to get a divorce. She writes:

> Now I am a nomad – with no other homeland but Islam, with no family, no one in whom to confide, alone, alone for ever in the proud and darkly sweet solitude of my own heart.

She soon finds a real confidant in her Arab lover. Slimene Ehni is a sergeant in the native cavalry. She meets him in El Oued and through him becomes a member of a Sufi fraternity, which is secretly opposed to French rule.

She is subject to a murder attempt by another Arab fraternity closer to the French. A stretched washing line softens the blow and saves her life.

The French army banish her and she ends up in Marseilles, where she supports herself for a while by writing letters in Arabic for the guest-workers.

Slimene also goes there, and on 17 October 1901, they marry. By marrying an Arab in the service of France, she becomes a French citizen and can return to the Sahara.

With Slimene she rents a small house in Ain Sefra, which is the headquarters of the French troops during the "pacification" of the border with Morocco.

Even as Madame Ehni, she wears men's clothes and continues her previous androgynous life round campfires and in soldiers' brothels. Only the male role provides her with the freedom to ride around on reporting assignments for the newspaper *l'Akbar* in the Sahara which the French army is just conquering. Only the male role gives her the freedom to make love with anyone, to drink anisette with the legionnaires and smoke kif in the cafés, where she shocks listeners with her expositions on the pleasures of brutality and the voluptuousness of subjection.

I push my way through a thick dark desert of trees which is called "forest". I am in a hurry and must not come too late. In the end the forest opens up into a clearing. I see a figure hanging from its feet from a branch and I rush over. It is Isabelle! Her otherwise moon-pale face is blue-black, cracked and deformed. I cut her down and carefully put the dead body to rights on the ground.

The Globe is transformed from a landing hot-air balloon to a diving-bell. Isabelle and I are sluiced out into the water, spouting cascades of pearly bubbles from our oxygen tubes. But very soon we are forced to go back as if into a womb. We have been born into an element that is not ours, in which we do not belong, in which we cannot live – except for short moments with the piece of bitumen between our teeth.

"The thought of death has long since been familiar to me," wrote Isabelle towards the end of her life. "Who knows? Perhaps I shall soon let myself slip into it one day in the very near future, voluptuously and without the slightest worry. With time I have learnt not to look for anything in life but the ecstasy offered by oblivion."

Pierre Loti lived with his death-wish until he was seventy-three. Isabelle Eberhardt only lived to twenty-seven. By then she had no teeth, no breasts, no menstruation, was as thin as a well-diver, and was almost always depressed. "If this foray of mine into the darkness does not stop, what will be its terrifying outcome?"

The life she lived was an extended suicide. With increasing regularity she took refuge in drugs, alcohol and a brutal, self-destructive sexuality with almost anyone. She suffered from innumerable illnesses, among them malaria and probably syphilis.

At her own urgent request, she was discharged from the hospital in Ain Sefra on 21 October and returned to her house by the *oued*.

The torrent that drowned her came that night.

When Isabelle died, her first novel, *Vagabond*, was just being published as a serial in *l'Akbar*. Her sketches and short stories had often been included in Algerian newspapers. A large number of manuscripts was saved from the flood.

The editor-in-chief of *l'Akbar*, Victor Barrucand, published a selection in 1906. Quite well-meaningly, he had first prettied up her texts.

She wrote: "Everyone laughed." He added: "People laughed at his rusticity; his gesture belonged to a shepherd."

She wrote: "Freedom was the only happiness accessible to my nature." That sounded too simple. He improved on it: "Freedom was the only happiness that was necessary for my eager, impatient and yet proud nature."

Despite the revisions, the book was a success and Barrucand continued to publish Isabelle's manuscripts in 1908, 1920 and 1922, by then with greater respect for the integrity of her writing. The diaries and other writings she left were published in 1923, 1925 and 1944 by R-L. Doyon. Grasset began to publish her collected writings in 1988. Most of these editions also contain short biographies. More extensive biographies have been published in France, Algeria, England, and in the USA in 1930, 1934, 1939, 1951, 1952, 1954, 1961, 1968, 1977, 1983, 1985 and 1988.

What is it about Isabelle Eberhardt that goes on fascinating generation after generation?

I have plenty of time to think about that as I drive on through the desert.

She did not write nearly so much as her master, Pierre Loti. As a rule, nor did she write so well. And yet she is the one to survive. Why?

"One does not seek happiness," she writes. "One meets it always on the way and coming in the opposite direction."

There is a great deal of sparkling use of words in her work. It is not the average that counts. It is the highlights.

It is not the quantity that counts, it is the totality. And not only does the language belong to that, but also body language. The gesture of life.

Isabelle dressed in male clothes and dived into the wells of the Sahara Arab world. At the same time, Jack London was putting on working clothes and letting himself sink into *People of the Abyss* (1903).

He was making a social experiment. He wanted to experience with his own body what wretchedness entails for the truly poor.

Isabelle was doing the same. But with no secret gold coins sewn into her waistband. She dived without any safety rope. She was a Wallraff with no return.

She not only crossed a social boundary, but also the race boundary. A white woman in the American South openly preferring black men as lovers and marrying one of them as she continues her unbridled life – if one considers it in that way, one understands what forces Isabelle challenged.

The French Empire in North Africa rested ultimately on the myth of the superiority of the white race. Her whole way of life questioned that myth.

It also questioned the myth of male superiority. If a female trans-vestite could penetrate the man's world and acquire his freedoms, vices and privileges, then the gender roles were made to rock. Unclear sexual identity aroused anxiety and aggression. Isabelle put herself outside all categories.

Even that might possibly have been forgiven, as her fate verified all prejudices, apparently confirming that anyone who defies the con-ventions sinks into the dregs. So far, so good. But Isabelle had the insolence in all her degeneration to maintain a sense of moral superior-ity. That was unforgivable.

In that way she belongs in a totally different family from Loti. She belongs in the long line of French literature running from Villon via Baudelaire and Rimbaud to Céline and Genet. Perhaps she is actually the only woman in that company.

Translated from the Swedish by Joan Tate

CEES NOOTEBOOM

Gateway to China

It's a mistake to think of a peninsula as a virtual island, especially when you ought to know better. You may find yourself wandering into the biggest country in the world, by mistake. This sounds like a riddle, and so it was.

It is morning, October, and Tokyo. But before it is morning, October and Tokyo, someone who will turn out to share my name is in the unconscious domain of middle sleep, from whose depths the soul is loath to return. But return it must: there is evil in the air, the shrill, enervating ring of an old-fashioned bell between the stone walls of a cell. A Japanese voice barks out of the bakelite telephone: holding the receiver aloft I am slowly transformed into a character from the nineteen thirties, and I remember where I am, in my room at the Asia Centre, two beds wide, one-and-a-half long. I get out of bed and it is as if I am rising up out of my own body which remains inert on the mattress. I am already going down the corridor to the washroom where I shave in the weathered mirror, standing next to a dark figure winding long strips of white cloth round his head. It's five in the morning; the yellow taxi driving through empty streets, the silent trip, all this still belongs to the domain of sleep. Two hours before check-in time the bus leaves from the city terminal to the airport 120 kilometres away. Next to me in the bus sits a Pakistani laden with electronic equipment, prizes to take home. The sun has come up in a part of the sky I think of as the West. Orange-tinted streaks, I write the words and think: so this is my vocation in life, to be a girl writing in her diary. The sheer *mass* of Tokyo lies beneath me, we are coasting along one of those merciless elevated highways which dwarf and darken the life under them. Every few minutes we hear the same tape, *cling*, *cling*, and an impassive lily voice announces that we are on the way to the airport, what will happen there, and that Japan Airlines wishes us all the best. That's what I wish too: all the best, and a safe flight as well. She can intone her message thirty more times, and so she does.

School children in uniform wait for a bus, someone potters about in a back garden, the Coca Cola plant is still shut, the driver is wearing white knitted gloves, a small aquatic bird perches on a mud-flat in a small river. Birds, a tenacious species: searching for food, sleeping, mating, laying eggs in the midst of sixteen million people, and meanwhile not forgetting how to fly, all those mysterious tricks with wind directions, air pockets, descending and alighting.

A month of pent-up Japanese frustration is released in a little cameo performance for two actors. The passport control officer says I haven't written my signature clearly enough and I say I'm not going to write it a second time. I have already gone half-way past his booth and he directs me to the front again with a stern wave of the hand. The difference is half a metre, but to take a step back means re-entering Japan, and I want to get out. A battle of looks. The amorphous sleepy head of the European face to face with the inscrutable mask of authority. I realize that he can send me back, can keep me there, but an unpleasant person inside me – me, in other words – declares with conviction "No way, Mr Slit-eye." His riposte is without doubt of the same order. Four hours later it is still morning, but by then I have flown over Tiananmen Square, the Gang of Four and a hundred million Chinese, and have landed in the midst of an excrescence of skyscrapers lying like a disease in the dun-coloured hills. Hong Kong. The horrendous discipline of Japan has given way to a welcome disorder, it's the relief of crossing into Mexico after infallible America. I feel at home again.

A Chinese officer in colonial-style shorts tells me where to catch the ferry to Macau, and wreathed in the indecent heat swirling into the ramshackle taxi I am driven to Fisherman's Wharf. It's the weekend, the Chinese are on their way to gamble in the casino at Macau, the ferries are chock-a-block, but I slip someone a bribe and am allowed on.

How long ago is it that I first read Slauerhoff?* Perhaps thirty years, I don't know. It must have been then that the word Macau first

---

* Jan Jacob Slauerhoff (1898–1936): Dutch poet and novelist who went to sea as a ship's doctor; his restlessness and contemptuous dislike of Holland are prominent themes throughout his work. His novel *Het Verboden Rijk* ("The Forbidden Realm") was inspired by the life of the Portuguese poet Camões.

entered my consciousness. For Slauerhoff everything to do with Portugal is associated with melancholy, listlessness, tarnished glory. It appealed to me. Perhaps the reason why is clearer to me now than it was then, but the sentiment behind it was the same, and there was some kind of contradiction there. Spaniards weren't melancholy, they tended to be hard, but *they* had lost all their colonies, while the gentle, fado-singing Portuguese with their sensual, lilting language in their decaying corner of Europe were still masters of their ridiculous empire. I first went to Lisbon in 1954. Men with tired eyes strolled arm in arm along the Tagus, wearing *white* shoes. It made an indelible impression on me. Nowadays even Dutchmen wear white shoes, but then I felt as if I had wandered into a long-forgotten opera by an unknown composer, and at the same time I knew that of course that was how one ought to live, somewhat plaintively and self-indulgently, a spent hero in the last act. And yet there was that weird contradiction: the very same people had explored half the globe, and if you looked on the world map you could see, in addition to the great swathes of Portuguese territory in Africa, also those slivers of land, enclaves, leftover forts on the West African coast where the Portuguese flag was still raised every morning at daybreak to the accompaniment of a "dull cannon salute"; and then there was also their half of Timor, and that absurd spot of Goa that India hadn't yet managed to reclaim, and the strangest thing of all, there right next to the mammoth shape of never-ending China, so tiny on the map as to be obscured by its own name: Macau, followed by (Port.), and I would imagine the last of the Portuguese having to live out their lives there like exiles, exiles not only from their country but also from their time, colonial fossils. The *nonsense* of it pleased me, the irrationality, so far away from Europe and still keeping up faded appearances. Perhaps it resembled fiction more than anything else, some writer had invented it all, and now the whole story had to be lived, too. That the Portuguese elsewhere in the world stood guard over their frayed empire not with white shoes but with guns, and that the Chinese only tolerated Macau (and Hong Kong) because it was (and still is) in their interest to do so, I could understand, but all that was irrelevant: the absurd spot at the end of the world still existed, Portuguese was spoken there on the rim of mainland China as it had been spoken for the last four hundred years, the *Governador* still resided there in a pink palace, and drifters and outcasts gambled away their money in casinos. In short, I would have to go there sometime.

Now that time has come. The ferry bobbing on the brownish-yellow waves of Hong Kong harbour is a hydrofoil called *Flying Ibis*. The Union Jack flies over the quayside, the sea is choppy, Slauerhoff's beloved ships are waiting in the roadstead. Tugs, flaky coasters, junks and sampans. The sunlight is sharp and white, it shoots through the heaving waves like a shuttle, almost blinding me. With some difficulty I make out the names of the gleaming or blistered ships riding at anchor: the *New Sea Pioneer*, the *Kotan Mari*, the *Pacific Courier*, the *Oriental Express*. We sail along the coast past the Hong Kong United Dockyards, the ground is steep and stony, a bedraggled green like the hide of an ancient animal. The ferry gathers speed, the brown water foams against the windows, and after a while I lose sight of the land; all I can see are gulls diving blackly into silver and dissolving in the waves. Around me Chinese is spoken. I listen drowsily to the blurred fricatives of that secret language until I catch a word I recognize: Macau. It had never been a Portuguese name, of course, but it is only now, pronounced like this, that I realize it's Chinese.

These hydrofoils have no decks, so I can't watch the island loom up on the horizon as I had hoped, but beyond the brown veils I can make out a hazy streak, then trees, hills, that must be Macau. We disembark on a wooden jetty and shuffle in single file to the customs office, my third that day, but now the forms I have to fill in are in Portuguese. Emerging from customs, the heat slaps me in the face. Friends have told me I should stay at the Bela Vista Hotel, and the inevitable ancient taxi takes me there. Chinese voices on the radio, Portuguese street names: Avenida da Amizade, Rua da Praia Grande, Rua da Praia do Bom Parto. Hills, crumbling mansions, elm trees, junks with sails like dragon fins, everything is as it should be. The hotel too has seen better days, it is plastered with paint like an old actress. The lobby has the usual sprawling dimensions of the tropics, a rattling fan stirs the heat around, my name is written in pencil in a big ledger in which it will be inscribed for ever, a silent young man takes me to my room, a dingy cubicle still inhabited by the evil dreams of previous guests. Stains, cracks, tears, the tap which starts growling suddenly like a guard dog before disgorging rusty water, and the same mirror as the one this morning in Tokyo, covered in a mottled, disfiguring skin cancer through which a bewildered stranger looks at me.

From the window of the grey bathroom I look out over the brown sea and the Praia Grande, and it's all there:

de tuinen
Waar dwars door 't gebloemte vervallen
Paleizen hun praal in puinen

Storten, tot waar beneden
Bekoorlijk de Praia Grande
Blank omarmt de verzande
Voorgoed verlaten reede . . .*

The only other room on my corridor has something to do with the Red Cross, there's a basket containing dirty linen in front of the door, the unmistakable acrid smell of urine wafts from the lavatory, and somehow I know that this is as it should be. Nonsense, of course, but it all happens to fit in with how I imagined it. Out in the street I notice that scaffolding has been put up around half the hotel, just as I later discover that half of Macau is being demolished: in ten years' time this place will be a sterile Singapore with banks and tax-free shops. Decay, too, is transient.

But we haven't reached that point yet, and I don't want to think about such things just now. They haven't got a map of Macau for me at the hotel. I pick a direction at random and go down a long, mossy flight of steps, my covetous eye recognizes the small Portuguese cobbles, reads shop signs, spies a garden rampant with hydrangeas, the ear registers the voices of Chinese children singing, I walk past the Deutsche Asiatische Trading Company and the office of Porfirio Azevedo Gomes, *Advogado*, and Dr Yhyp Bum, *Médico Veterinário*, and lose my way in the labyrinth of downtown. There is no point in asking directions, I wouldn't know what to ask for. But then I catch sight of the Livraria São Paolo next to the Teatro Diocesano (*Snoopy Come Home* is playing tonight). I buy the only newspaper I can find, *O Clarim*, a fortnightly Catholic journal, published by the See of Macau for God and the Fatherland. The headline reads, appropriately, "Camões and the Nature of Things", and with this version of the world news tucked under my arm I ask a snow-white nun for a map of Macau. She rummages around for a

---

* " – the gardens / where surrounded by blossoms crumbling / palaces shed their opulence / casting it down to where / the Praia Grande charmingly / puts its white arm around / the silted-up, for ever deserted roadstead . . ."

long time and then produces what looks like a mimeographed sheet on which the maze is depicted in heavy black lines. I stand there staring at it, can't see how it works because this map doesn't show the sea as blue and the parks as green, and then suddenly my eyes are drawn to the small picture, in red, of a gate, just above the centre where the vast expanse of white begins. Beyond the gate there is nothing, so where can it lead? The waxwork nun eyes me with some suspicion.

"To China," she says, "that's the gateway to China."

So I am not on an island, I am at the far end of an isthmus, and I arrived here after crossing the bay from Hong Kong.

The nuns deliberate in Portuguese.

"Do you want to go there?"

"To China?"

"No, that is not possible. To the gate?"

The ensuing conversation is one between the deaf and the blind. I am already thinking in Chinese terms, of interminable bus trips. They know better.

"So how far is it?"

"If you hurry you can be there in twenty minutes. But you must go now, because it gets dark quickly."

And so it does. An ashen dusk begins to trickle down the houses, scattered lights start twinkling, soon I can't see enough to read the words on the primitive map; I pass peeling houses, broken-down villas, the heavy tropical fragrance of extinguished flowers. The streets grow narrower, the houses more modest. I go past a night market lit by acetylene lamps and discover that I am still walking in more or less the right direction. Then things get darker still, the dwellings are wooden now, small fires flicker here and there, little girls are spinning by hand in a workshop, this has nothing to do with Portugal any more, this is an older China – much hooting, ringing, teeming, tea-drinking under family portraits. I am struck by my own strangeness, by the fact that I am walking about in this different life, that the same person who got out of bed this morning in Tokyo is now hurrying to the gateway to China, striding over roads that are no longer paved in this part of the city. Singapore used to be like this once, before progress came along and razed the flotsam of little houses, then raked up the seething mass and redistributed it over stone blocks more than ten storeys high.

"So you'd rather they went on living their old picturesque lives for ever, would you?" asks the inner voice that represents the New World, production figures and per capita incomes, but just as the ever-present other voice is about to hit back with arguments of human happiness and rising suicide statistics the voices fall silent because the alley suddenly widens into an open space. I am standing under tall trees and it is so quiet that I can hear the leaves softly rustling. Further away, in what is now the black of night, I make out the dark shape of an old gateway, imposing and wide. The space in front is empty, but as I approach the gate eagerly a hazy figure suddenly steps forward out of the black void: a Chinese soldier in a Portuguese uniform.

"Stay there," he says in English.

I stand still. He gives me an earnest but not unfriendly look. He watches over the Portuguese Empire, all on his own. Short and slight, he stands there with his gun, his back to the sombre mass of the gate, blackened by the darkness of Asia, and I am reminded that, for more than four centuries, Portuguese soldiers have stood guard here. It has been a long vigil. Somewhere between me and the gate, or between the gate and whatever lies behind it, runs an invisible line, as tenuous as a thought. Exactly above that line there is nothing, neither Portuguese nor Chinese: it would be possible to erect a gossamer screen there to reach up into the highest sky. On one side of the screen the invisible air is ruled by Lisbon, on the other by Beijing. One could conceivably stand exactly on that line, and one's body would be in two countries at once.

Frontiers are mysterious, they are both invisible and visible, they are described in books, they actually exist. It is the *notion* of a frontier that is being guarded by the slender figure before me and that I am not permitted to cross, this is where Portugal and China meet, the king and the emperor have gone, their realms are still intact. But this is also where capitalism borders on communism, it is in this precise spot that the world is divided in two, and since the world is round I have seen the same division twice. Just as I am standing here now I stood years ago at the top of a wooden watchtower overlooking the Berlin Wall, thinking *it goes on like this all the way to the end of China*, and so it does, I can see it before me now even though I see nothing, and it does go right up to the other side of this shrouded gateway, and all this is just imaginary, and still it is all true.

The next day I will get a better look at the weather-beaten mossy
gate, the green-and-red flag with the gold emblem raised high and
on the far side that other, so much redder flag. Long grasses are
growing out of one of the walls and in two medallions carved in stone
I can distinguish the navigators' anchor and the crossed cannon of
the conquerors. HONRAI A PATRIA QUE A PATRIA VOS CON-
TEMPLA, [Honour the Fatherland for the Fatherland is Looking at
You] reads the inscription along the top, and in a flash I see the
pink-and-white languor of Lisbon on the Tagus. How long ago was
that? I was twenty-three, and I had signed on as a sailor on the *Gran
Rio*, we were on our way to Surinam in South America. Our ship lay
at anchor in the middle of the Tagus, dusk had fallen, an autumn
evening as it is now. I saw the lights of the city, beckoning, seductive.
Not until late did we receive permission to go ashore. Once on the
quay I had separated from the others, this was something I wanted
to experience on my own. I roamed through dark streets and alleys
and heard music somewhere and a raw, hoarse male voice singing an
infinitely sad song. So that had to be the fado. I went inside. The
singer was standing in the middle of the tavern. In my memory it is
like a scene from before the war. The reek of strong cigarettes, yellowish light. He was small, a bit shabby, perhaps slightly drunk, and with
his hands in his pockets and eyes fixed on the floor, he sang
unashamedly about sorrow and loneliness. Wherever in the world
people sing like that poetry is safe from laboratory experiments. No
Dutch poet has understood the essence of the fado better than
Slauerhoff:

> *Ben ik traag omdat ik droef ben,*
> *Alles vergeefsch vind en veil,*
> *Op aarde geen hoogre behoefte ken*
> *Dan wat schaduw onder een zonnezeil?*

> *Of ben ik droef omdat ik traag ben,*
> *Nooit de wijde wereld inga,*
> *Alleen Lisboa van bij de Taag ken*
> *En ook daar voor niemand besta?**

---

* "Am I slow because I am sad / and find everything pointless and vain / and know
no higher need on earth / than some shade under an awning? / Or am I sad because
I am slow / and never venture into the wide world / and only know Lisbon by the
Tagus / and there too exist for no one?"

I asked the waiter the name of the singer. Alfredo Marceneiro. Most of the lyrics of his song I could not understand, only the occasional phrase and that singular, ever-recurring word *saudade*, just as untranslatable as *spleen*, a special Portuguese province of melancholy in which a Northerner would die from over-exposure. Plaintive, that's what it was, what was being lamented didn't matter – a lover had been abandoned, a Cadillac stolen, a brother killed, a tyre punctured, a life ruined – the small space was filled with one great lament encapsulating the whole of existence. In later years I bought all Marceneiro's records, the pure essence of sorrow flows through that hoarse voice, and now, walking back to town, I think of myself walking back then, to embark in the very same place where Slauerhoff, in his novel *Het Verboden Rijk* ("The Forbidden Empire"), makes his alter ego Camões embark never to return, and the same atmosphere hangs in the tropical dusk with its concealed, vanished shapes: sorrow over everything, the things that belong to the past, poets and seafarers sinking into the mud of all-devouring time.

And yet – the insidious *and yet* of history – things had seemed different once, powerful and durable, everlasting, even. The year was 1513, and the first European had sailed up the estuary of Canton. Jorge Alvares. He had come in the name of the King of Portugal, which at that time had a population of barely one million, and encountered men with long pigtails and silk coats, representatives of the hundred million inhabitants of China under the Ming dynasty. More ships followed, envoys were dispatched and warmly received by the Emperor's officials, but another group of Portuguese led by Simão de Andrade behaved in a dastardly fashion, and in 1522 all foreigners were barred from entering China. The Portuguese took little notice of the ban and tried, unsuccessfully as it happens, to go ashore in northern China. Eventually, in about 1555, they gained a foothold in Macau. They called their bastion "City of the Name of God", but the goddess of the local fishermen already had her temple there (Ma Kok Miu), she was not so easily ousted, and the name Macau remained. In his novel Slauerhoff takes liberties with historical fact in his effort to fuse the ill-fated poet Camões, in whom he must have recognized himself, with a nameless, self-destructive twentieth-century ship's radio operator who likewise displays the wounded traits of the author. Some people doubt whether Camões ever went to Macau.

If he did, he presumably served in a lowly but highly poetic rank: "Commissioner for the Dead and Absent in China". However that may be, in Slauerhoff's book he does visit Macau (and he therefore *is* in Macau, for the reality of books is just as valid as reality itself), he has the most dreadful experiences there, is consumed by one of those passionate, doomed love affairs for which the Frisian author himself had a reputation, too, and there writes part of his masterpiece, *Os Lusiadas*, in a cave.

The life of Camões may have been tragic, but his merchant compatriots did very well for themselves. In 1557 the Portuguese were permitted to establish their trading post in Macau. Both parties were pleased. The ships from the West were invincible on the seas and assisted the Chinese authorities in suppressing piracy and in putting down a local mutiny of the coastal garrison in Canton in 1563. In 1573 China erected a wall to seal off the peninsula. Macau was allowed to continue to exist as a colony and was governed for a term of one year at a time by a Captain-Major of the Japan Trade, who was accountable to the Viceroy of India. During his stay in Macau this grandee was the absolute ruler of the colony. Once a year he would set sail from Goa in a heavily armed ship with a mixed cargo for Macau, where he purchased silver, gold and porcelain. After a couple of months he would sail on to Japan. There everything was sold at a high profit and on the return trip he would call at Macau again to buy silk. A Senate was established there in 1585 to appoint civil servants and judges, and in 1586 an *Ouvidor* was instated to govern Macau directly as a colony. The Church did not fail to contribute: Pope Gregory XIII appointed a bishop for "the entire province of China in addition to the islands of Japan, Macau and what lies nearby", and the Jesuit priests who were to play a prominent role in the exchange of knowledge between Europe and Asia appeared on the scene.

Names, titles, dates, memories. Street names, the flag, the governor's residence, the Senate, the lone soldier on guard, that's all that is left. Around me I hear only Chinese. I hail a taxi and the driver speaks neither English nor Portuguese. I tell him I want to go to a Portuguese restaurant, but I might just as well ask to be taken to heaven or the cemetery, his smile never leaves his face. Finally I find what I am looking for, a dark restaurant where old Portuguese gentlemen gather and consume their nostalgia in the form of *bacalhau à brasa, vinho do porto, vinho verde, cafézinho, aguardente.* After a month of America and another month of Asia the familiar food makes me feel close to home, the alcohol finds its way effortlessly to my feet. They have walked a considerable distance already today, but they too seem to find the way to the casino effortlessly, almost without touching the ground.

A hall as big as a cathedral, and circling above all those heads only one thought: money! I listen to the chips rattle and slide, see someone win on my number before I have even had the chance to change my money, a bad omen. I exchange my Patacas and Hong Kong dollars for multicoloured plastic and soon my money too slides into the green jowls of the great predatory dragon, away with it! Once, a long time ago, I was a true gambler, a casino fanatic, but I have mended my ways because it brings one nothing but misery. Since then I still regularly enter a gambling house to undergo the ritual of loss, a little masochistic séance. After that I am free to look at the other players, and there is plenty to look at here. A priestess dressed in purple towers above all the rest of us, she supervises, if I see correctly, the supervisors supervising the croupiers. I look at the hundreds of Asian faces that betray no trace of loss or gain. Chemin de fer, roulette, blackjack, grandfathers in navy suits, grandmothers in black, fortunes dance to and fro across the tables and everyone follows the money with their eyes, but what are they thinking? I know from experience that as soon as the gambler enters a game he transfers his private fate to that chip-shaped matter moving away from him or towards him, stacks shrink, stacks grow, the ball spins in the wheel, jumps, bounces, searches and nestles itself in the predestined number, the fatal card is turned up on the oblong palmwood tray, hands holding chips hesitate above numbers, it has to be twenty-three, or five, or à cheval, it will be the carré, or red, or black, they are absolutely certain and yet they are not, thin Chinese voices distribute luck and misfortune with the authority of a last judgment, the spectral white-haired grandfather loses his fortune, the pearly claw of the young woman encrusted with gold and diamonds closes over a pile of the biggest-size chips. On the wall there is a glass sign that can be illuminated: AVISO DE TUFÃO, Warning! Typhoon! and in my imagination the notice lights up in red and everyone gets up and flees, clutching treasures of gold, into the raging dark where the storm lashes the elms. Then I feel how the powerful soporific of liquor combined with a much too long day takes me by stealth. I go outside. A rickshaw waits in a pool of dead neon light. The sinewy Charon on the saddle points commandingly at the vacant seat behind him. The rise and fall of his muscular calves has a hypnotic effect, and for the second time that day I ride along the Rua da Praia Grande as far as the steep side-road up to the hotel; I don't want him to pedal uphill. He doesn't understand but I am past caring, I am dreaming and I hear my own footsteps.

The next morning I am woken by the relentless yelping of dogs. It is light in the room, there is scarcely a curtain to speak of. I go over to the window and look out at the sea, the distant hills of the Chinese mainland, a few junks, the sagging buildings. Last night I made a sort of little altar with my copy of Slauerhoff and a photograph of my father, which his last surviving sister gave me on the spur of the moment just before my departure. My father was killed in the war, I hardly knew him, I don't have the feeling I ever really *talked* to him. He was born the same year as Slauerhoff, he didn't live to be as old as I am now, and in the photograph he is, I suppose, in his early twenties. People who have seen that photograph think it's a picture of me when I was a young man. It was taken on board a mail boat sailing to the Dutch East Indies, but still in Europe, because the two men in the picture have not changed into their colonial outfits yet. No one seems to know who the other person is; he looks like a member of Al Capone's gang, this Mr Chicago, wearing a black hat and a handkerchief in his breast pocket and leaning heavily on my father's slim shoulders – but how can that youth be my father? He has the air of a dandy: trenchcoat, tweed cap, spats, bow-tie, a cigarette in his right hand, his left hand nonchalantly in his pocket, a light, ironical smile, the feet comfortably apart, a traveller. What he did in the Indies or why he went there in the first place no one can tell me. I stand there in that drab room staring somewhat vacantly at the book and the photograph. Slauerhoff has left the scorch-marks of his restless life on Dutch literature for ever, my father has left nothing but a few amateurish sketches, there isn't even a grave, but I remember thinking when I first set eyes on that photograph of *his* outward-bound passage and looked into his sardonic face: it's your fault that I have to wheel over the world like a madman all the time, you sowed the seed of that restlessness in me.

But photographs don't answer back, and he goes on smiling, on his way to the same Asia where I now find myself, a passerby who preserves his passage in words, until they too are blown off the table.

I can stay here a week, a month, a day; at this slow rate everything will remain the same. Decay is visible, the process of decaying is not. The slow disintegration has been going on for centuries, but from now on things will speed up. Foundation trenches leer at you everywhere in the low neighbourhoods, and wherever you look there are menacing billboards repeating the same meaningless names of construction companies. I want to go to the Camões Museum, but it is closed for repairs. The green-and-red flag flutters on top of the old fortress, antique cannons point their idle mouths to the unassailable sea. The hollow façade of the cathedral is still standing high above the crumbling steps, the church behind it dynamited, blown away. It's a great sail of stone, that façade, erected between nothing and nothing, with griffins, lions, gargoyles and bizarre spheres, and the windows like empty eye-sockets. Gone, all gone. "The Port is reached, the sails are furled," reads the inscription on a gravestone in the Protestant cemetery. I say the names of the dead aloud, and they look up briefly from their shadowy realm:

> *Capleia Christian IPLAND von Apenrade*
> *die Witwe sandt diesen Stein aus Deutschland*
> *aus Furcht der Erste wurde bald verfallen*
> *Nun ruhen beiden Christian Iplands tod*
> *im fernen Land.*

A Chinese gardener rakes the paths, trims the bushes, waters the flowers, pretends not to notice me or does not notice me.

> *John P. Williams, of Utica NY*
> *died 1857, 31 years old.*
> *He assisted in setting up the first*
> *magnetic telegraph in Japan, 1854.*

I write down the names and dates like a belated auditor of death until a church bell peals in the distance and the heat and hunger drive me back into the din of the city. Towards evening, on the tiny roof of the *Flying Condor*, I watch the hills and towers of Macau melting into the gargantuan bulk of mainland China. Then that vision too drowns in the night or in the sea and all that lies behind me is obliterated.

Translated from the Dutch by Ina Rilke

JEAN-PAUL SARTRE

Walking in Venice: Femininity and Loss of Momentum

From *Queen Albemarle, or The Last Tourist*

The last tourist of the season? – the Italian journey Sartre is writing about in 1951 took place, in the company of a woman friend, in the autumn. The last tourist to make a grand tour *of the old Europe in the old way, now that the world was overshadowed by the atomic bomb? Sartre himself compared this unfinished work, half analytical essay, half journal, to his novel* La Nausée *(1938), and it does indeed show him taking a kind of existential holiday. He had almost finished his lengthy work on Genet, and after this brief interlude would soon – in the spring of 1952 – have to "engage" himself once more in the defence of the Communist Party.*

A tourist in Venice wakes from his first night in the city to find he's become an amphibian: he's grown fins, and at the same time recovered the use of his legs. This is a place where walking is restored to its original nobility; where walking is sacrosanct. And so, this morning, I'm walking. At a gait that may be either Sumerian or Doric but is certainly of an age both pastoral and ancient, I stroll through *calli*, cross bridges, come out into *campi*, lose my way, find I'm in a blind alley, retrace my steps, go across other bridges – sometimes, almost without noticing, passing through the same *calli* and *campi* as before. No matter: Venice is Venice all over. I don't know any other city that's always so obstinately itself, nor where the poorer districts are so like the wealthy ones. Feeling ancient and solemn myself, I wander about amongst miniatures with but one object in mind: to enjoy my primitive status as a walker in the only city with a population of over four hundred thousand that still treats a pedestrian as someone of consequence.

I once met a St John the Baptist. It was in the Hoggar region of

Algeria, a couple of kilometres from Tamanrasset and the oasis. He was walking barefoot, his brown shanks powdered with all the sand of the desert. He wasn't a Tuareg (his face wasn't covered), but he wasn't a Negro either. He carried a staff and wore a short mantle, rather like a toga, tied in at the waist with string. He mumbled to himself as he went along, but that wasn't what made him seem odd. Nor was it his fine but distraught eyes, rolling around wildly in a countenance almost all beard. No – what was so surprising was that here, in a desert habitually crossed by Tuareg on camels and by Europeans in Dodges, he *was travelling on foot*. That in itself was intriguing enough to make you wonder where he could be from, where he was going, and how he endured the heat of the desert. Here was a genuine "foreigner" or outsider, someone from elsewhere, nobler than a warrior on horseback simply because his way of getting about was the mode of locomotion proper to man, though we increasingly relegate it to performing animals. He proclaimed the dignity of humanity with his own calves and thighs, making his way as the worm on a mulberry tree makes silk or a bee makes honey, his feet weaving a long ribbon in the form of the track he left behind him. You may say I was walking too. But no. I was merely trotting around. Which of us really does walk nowadays, apart from fashion models or hikers out for the day from Marseilles? I myself am like a hermit crab: my soft belly clings for protection to the insides of shells – cars, buses, tubes, trains, planes. Even that day in the Hoggar I was only dragging my torso over the sand in search of a new carapace.

Admittedly, some people do still walk. In Europe, at least. But they do so usually for reasons of health, and sometimes even furtively: it's an activity no longer very highly thought of. The virtue went out of it when it ceased to be used to mark out routes. Nowadays we trail along in the ruts left by tanks, or between steel rails, in the path of speed gone cold. In a universe criss-crossed with missiles, our own journeys are puny, trivial and brief. Once we built roads; now we merely follow them. The trouble is that you out there, you tourists, are no longer at home even in your own cities, which have become mere stop-overs for the traffic of Europe. Flattened like grass by heavy lorries, the towns stretch after them in vain, trying to keep up but bound to be left behind. Your streets are really highways in disguise, reaching out into time and space, and no matter how many blocks of flats you put up alongside them, no matter how deep you cover them in tarmac, you can never conceal the fact that they're on the way to somewhere else. Other people have used them before you: feet from the north have worn them down; they sweep towards you from foreign borders, and sweep away towards other frontiers still. The whole world hurtles past between your walls. If you take the family out for a stroll on Sunday, you step on to a moving pavement and are hustled forward by the force of others, your legs driven along by an impetus rushing down from north to south and up from south to north. You're just an immobile object; if you move at all it's because you're propelled from outside. Going along a road that would really like to be an autostrada buzzing with cars, you progress at a merely human rate, getting a kilometre closer either to Lille or to Marseilles, moving cautiously, conscious of not being at home. And by the time you get to the Place Edmond-Rostand, the motorcycle that overtook you in the Place Saint-Michel has already passed through the Porte d'Orléans. You are slowcoaches in your own cities.

But the Venetians *are* at home in Venice. And a mild sky like this morning's, with the light so sweet and smiling, is enough to make even a tourist feel less like a visitor and more like a Venetian. In other places he's washed up like flotsam and deposited in the city by a road that also sweeps him away again. But here roads don't exist. Venice was built to fend off the great continental migrations, out of the path of barbarian invasion. It might serve as a destination, or more often as a home port or point of departure – but never as a transit point. It doesn't move itself, and no motion is imparted to it from outside: all earthly powers expire in the surrounding waters before they can reach it. Venetians have travelled the world, but the world has never passed through Venice. Roads may trundle or speed along on the mainland twenty leagues away, but Venice just stands where it is, creating its own measures, distances and speeds. Its *calli* are purely local: none begins or ends outside the city. And they're genuinely native and "home-made", each belonging to its own neighbourhood and bounded by other streets just like it, or different only in that they end in a cul-de-sac or a *rio* without a bridge. They don't seem meant to go from one place to another; they don't "lead" anywhere. And when you start walking along one of them you can never be sure you won't have to give up and turn back. None of them is designated in the usual way: in Venice, no one would dream of wondering whether he was going north or south. Venice has coordinates of its own: St Mark's Square, the lagoon, the Fondamenta Nuove – it knows nothing of the points of the compass. I was wrong just now when I

said Venice invented its own speeds: inside the city there's no such
thing as speed. Its streets stand still. If they were straight you might
at least be able to detect some bearing, but they never *are* straight. If
you do give them credit for an aim, they promptly contradict you by
making a right-about turn. In Venice, space has nothing to do with
direction – it's undifferentiated and neutral. Much more than the
narrow gorges of Naples, the slender, winding *calli* of Venice seem
the work of artifice. Their shadowiness, their pointless complexity,
their obvious impracticability, all lend them an air of sophistication.
Yet in spite of or perhaps because of this, their rose-coloured walls
enclose the indifference of deserts and of the sea. So drowsy and still
are they, they look like strips cut from the earth's crust before motor-
way networks were ever thought of. My footsteps are more my own
here; as I said earlier, in other places one follows a certain direction,
whereas here one makes one's own way. My steps make sounds on
these dead flagstones; my feet draw a line. As I go along I gather up
and form into a whole an infinite divisibility that will soon lie scattered
again behind me in all its disparateness; then suddenly I come out
into another desert, into a *campo*. Back home, in France, two or three
roads occasionally collide at full tilt and merge in a maelstrom of legs
and wheels. Then we smartly sow some grass at the still centre of the
vortex and call the scene of the accident a square. On that analogy a
campo isn't a square, because it wasn't called into existence by a disaster. Far from being the cause of the *campi*, the alleys leading into
these stone spaces arise out of them. It would be absurd to see or
think of one of these narrow streets as the prolongation of another.
Not that it occurs to many of Venice's *calli* to end anywhere near
where another begins. Some careful plan has seen to it that they're
all slightly out of alignment. No line either straight or curved runs
through them; they're simply stretches or marshes of stagnant stone.
And they're all alike, each with its white flagstones, walled well and
Counter-Reformation church. More often than not a café sets out a
dozen or so chairs in a kind of "terrasse", looking rather lost in that
abstract space without any road or kerb to serve as a boundary – like
the chairs you sometimes see roaming about in an Italian cathedral.
But the chairs in the *campi* don't stray, even though there's nothing
to stop them: they huddle against the walls as if scared by so much
emptiness. Perhaps that's what makes a *campo* remind one of the nave
of a church with its red hat blown off. Be that as it may, the great
roofless room seems under-furnished, and once again I have a feeling

of emptiness. Something is missing. But what? A lot of people pray-
ing? A fair? Or is it that the city hasn't finished moving in yet? I'm
inclined to think the *campo* hankers after the same giddy whirl of cars
and motorbikes as that which so amply fills the Place de l'Etoile. In
such glades, such bald patches as these, the slightest movement is like
a sudden spark, spreading out like wildfire over the whole of the *campo*
and then as suddenly dying. And the mover himself is responsible for
it all. I'm proud to think that, for a *campo*, my passing through constitutes an event. Yet at the same time I feel rather scared, as if I were
obliged to speak out loud in a cathedral. Amid such stillness, walking
is as incongruous as a shout amid silence. And the people sitting
outside the café or leaning against the coping of the well give me odd
looks as I go by, as if for them walking is simultaneously sacrosanct
and sacrilegious.

And yet, as usual, my pleasure soon palls. I can't help thinking of
yesterday's unemployed. This is the city for them: I can just see them,
men with no one waiting for them and nowhere to go, walking on
and on through streets that don't lead anywhere and tiny deserts
where nothing stirs. Like tourists, they walk for walking's sake and
aren't allowed to stop and sit down.

. . . No line, straight or curved, runs through the *campo* I've just
walked into. It's a space as vague and classical as an atrium of tragedy:
you could perform Act IV of *Robert the Devil** here, complete with
doomed nuns, or *The Removal of St Mark's Body*,† including the thunder and lightning and the heathen fleeing in terror. Or even, more
obviously, given this morning's grey sky, the scene where the Horatii
swear their oath.

I feel guilty without knowing why, tired with a weariness that has
nothing to do with my legs; as if I'd eaten too heartily of Venice. Is
it because I keep seeing the same thing? No – I still derive pleasure
from the mere sensation of novelty. But there's no future in it. Instead,
I have a strange feeling of finiteness. It's as if one of those ancient
sensualists, expert, bland, and wandering the earth like a ghost, had
descended on and possessed me. That's how I imagine them. I once
heard a mulatto woman speak of a kind of surfeited sadness, pleasant

* Opera in five acts by Meyerbeer, with libretto by Scribe (1831).
† Painting by Tintoretto, in the Accademia gallery in Venice.

yet tinged with apprehension and impossible to communicate: she explained it as being "like when you've made love too often without friendship". That's just it – I love Venice, but without friendship. Why? And why is it that, in Venice, one can't deal with one's pleasures more simply?

There I go – delving into things again. How I wish I could convey my pleasures to you lightly, without emphasis and above all without explanation – almost without words. But I can't help it. I must just be made that way. The age I live in is the same. And in an age when you're expected to account for everything, how can you simply say "I was happy," like Stendhal? I don't know anyone who does that now-adays. And if somebody *is* far enough behind the times to risk it, his happiness sounds strained. He's happy to be *against* something. Happy to bear witness that happiness is possible. Happy on the left wing, happy on the right . . . A man who's happy these days is so unusual he's obliged to explain his feelings. But it's like someone trying to explain colours to the blind. Eventually the glad day will come when it will be possible to speak of happiness without having to spell it out. But we'll be dead and buried by then, and if anyone still reads our books they'll probably laugh at them. "To think they called *that* happiness!" they'll say. All the time I'm walking, all the time I'm looking at things, I'm keeping watch on myself – as if I were afraid of being carried away by this forgotten pleasure. At once a prisoner falsely pleading innocent, *and* the court that tries him – that's me.

Ah yes, I felt more light-hearted in Rome. Not so guilty. Rome can be delightful too, and you never feel you've had too much of it. Here's one of my last memories of Rome: I was in the Via Cristoforo Colombo, looking at the ramparts. The dusty white road was dazzling, imparting a pleasure dazzling but harsh. A cuttle-bone. Why? There was I standing in the middle of the road, and a car drove straight at me, then another. I had to jump into the ditch. That's how it is: Rome gives itself in snatches. A glance at the ivy-covered ruins, and a Vespa misses me by a hair's-breadth; a look at a Roman gate with its dark purple bricks, and an urchin yells at me and runs away.

I walk along a shady alley and in the distance, through the gloom, I glimpse a plain yet attractive palace; but suddenly the scene changes completely and the alley pitches me out into a sunny square and abandons me there. The palace vanishes, the god Ra half blinds me with his red-hot knives. From morn till night I'm the target of

pin-pricks: the reel of my perceptions unrolls in fits and starts, like a
film on a faulty projector. But such tiny upsets are necessary to our
normal equilibrium. It seems there are some charming societies where
the young males are pampered and stuffed with food. Later on they
act like affectionate sisters towards their wives, and when they sleep
with them their lovemaking is like the lascivious toying of the harem.
But there are other societies, and not poorer ones either, where the
children are left to cry for their food: these nestlings, having shrieked
themselves hoarse when young, grow up into magnificent vultures. I
probably belong among the vultures myself. I didn't have to screech
for my own beakful, but I've heard so many others doing so around
me it comes to the same thing. Everyone's an activist nowadays – it's
become the general rule. I've seen the most broken-down old nags
sign on for another ten years to fight for Art for Art's sake and against
"committed" Art. You have to be either a militant or a member of a
militia or a military man. And no member of such a militant society
can do without the small but constant stimuli, the superficial irritants
that serve to keep him in a permanent state of bad temper tinged
with cheerfulness. A tough and brilliant woman married a youth and
promptly presented him with a male child. But the little boy's
behaviour soon gave cause for alarm: he was modest and shy, and at
ten years old was still playing with dolls. Asked what he wanted to
do when he grew up, he'd say, "I want to be like Mother and have a
baby." He'd obviously been born into the wrong society. A friend of
the family who fancied himself as a psychoanalyst summed up the
general misgivings: "If he doesn't hate his father by now," he asked,
"how on earth is he ever going to acquire any aggression?" But, thank
God, the father is to be found everywhere: in Versailles, Madrid and
Naples the vestiges of absolute monarchy still have the power to vex
us. Then the middle-class democrat feels ill at ease, and turns into an
aggressive son.

But where can you find a father to hate in Venice? The insidious
feminine power of the élite has castrated the doges; the pink spider
of the Adriatic has devoured her male partner. Nowhere will you
come across the grim edifices – the towers, keeps, prisons, police
stations and government offices like palaces – that remind us of the
severity of our fathers and awaken our sleeping super-egos. Of course,
there are the Leads. But they're not so very awful. A Don Juan with
piles escaped from them across the rooftops. As for the lovely bridge
that links the prison to the palace, its name suggests the yearning of

lovers rather than captives' groans. The fatherless tourist strays through mucus membranes reminiscent of the mother, reviving dark but pleasant memories of magic caverns. The city hides me. I've lost my visibility, the dread that held me upright in the crossfire of other people's eyes. These alleys enfold me; I'm camouflaged by the play of light and darkness. And who is there to see me, anyway? Sometimes I hear footsteps, but when I turn round . . . nobody. And what's left of a person when nobody sees him? Just his own smell. Perhaps it's my own smell I'm sated with? As tourists we regress to our earliest childhood, before we were weaned; to that silent infancy without either carapace or corset, shield or constriction, when we lived with our mothers in a damp and fleshly fusion in which we weren't yet an object for anyone. Venice doesn't keep us at a respectful distance, as most cities do; it comes close to and brushes against us with feminine scents and maternal intimacy. Everything's much too easy: the body becomes less alert, even the source of one's energy flags – the little latent anger that's usually kindled into flame by continual acts of aggression from without. For the usual townscape is full of shocks: children spit on you from balconies overhanging the street; beams and ledges hit you on the head; gutters drench and roof-tiles fall on you. But Venice's surfaces are flat: if this city adds anything to a façade it adds only holes. Aristocratic caution has planed away all excrescences: there are no pitched roofs, only vertical surfaces laid horizontal. In Venice my eyes, after nearly half a century of scraping painfully over cornices, spikes, bosses and ridges, can glide over walls without let or hindrance. Perhaps if my personal radar occasionally hit on an obstacle warning me of danger, I'd wake from this hypnotic slumber. Or if my gaze were able to forge straight ahead, as it can in New York, until it broke under its own weight. But no – in Venice the world is at once finite and boundless, like Einstein's universe. The eye encounters no limit: at the end of each narrow street a shadow beckons slyly, leaving a chink for it to enter, slow down, then come to a gentle halt of its own accord. Such considerate treatment's surprising, when you come to think of it. After all, Venice isn't *our* mother. And there *is* a certain coolness in its solicitude. What's really happening is that things have stripped themselves of their contrariness. Yes, as a matter of fact it was like that even yesterday. But yesterday, on the canals, I was only dreaming, and today I'm walking, I'm conscious – yet even so the hostility of the universe is less keen than usual. What's really worrying me is my own lack of concern: my only cause for anxiety is that there's nothing for me to be anxious about. I wish I could worry but I can't: I'm filled with the pernicious yet soothing mildness of everything. In my chequered youth there were a couple of years, the period just before I became an adult, when life was one long terror. And yet even then I was sometimes visited by simple happiness: it was a fine day, I was on my way to meet a friend, my work had been going well. I'd yield to the feeling for a moment, then suddenly a jet of poison would spurt up out of the satisfaction itself, and I'd think: "It's not natural to be so happy. There must be a snag somewhere – something not quite right." Then I'd look for the snag, and of course I'd find it. Even now such sudden accesses of happiness still make me look for a catch: I'm being lulled into a false sense of security, I'm being led up the garden. Why? Surely I can find *some* little thing to worry about, even in Venice? But I can't: the place is completely innocuous.

And yet the way Venice limits your view – that *does* bother me. I can't see any further than the end of my nose. And that irks me, because a person's field of vision is his immediate future: what he sees there is always to a certain extent prophetic. My field of vision tells me, a few minutes in advance, what's going to happen to me. Sometimes you can see as much as an hour and a half of the future lying ahead of you, as when you set sail for Capri on a calm day with the island already visible in the distance. But in Venice my future shrinks like Balzac's *peau de chagrin*, and the minutes are meted out to me one by one. In sixty seconds exactly I'll be standing in front of the plaster Virgin. But my gaze reaches as far as her and no further. Here I am, I'm touching her, blue in her plaster niche. And now I'm being given another ration of future, reaching as far as that strange coat of arms set into the brickwork. But there's no reason why I should ask for more. Why should I be told an hour in advance what's waiting for me around the next corner, when I know from experience there's nothing waiting for me, neither temptation nor danger? No Vespa to run me over, no thief to rob me. All I need do is simply trust in the city. I imagine that's how the common people used to receive their future at the hands of the ruling patricians: piecemeal, a bit every day. And the people, well-nourished and amply supplied with entertainment, asked nothing better: they knew it was "for their own good". And here am I infected with their shortsightedness: it's incredible. I know the citizens of our modern democracies are kept just as much in the dark: one day they're told war's at the gates, and the next that it's moved on to Korea or Malaysia. And what do I know about it myself – the war? Just that it won't take place tomorrow, that's all. It's true we moderns do have our illusions: the press, the mass media, telecommunications. But ever since I was a child my own mystified gaze has scanned a vast plain and never seen anything coming. All it can see is a dusty road leading to the Caucasus and a green plain stretching out towards Denmark. Meanwhile, whatever's about to happen comes and hits me in the back of the neck. But what does that matter? Democrats are supposed to be broadminded and far-sighted. They can cope very well with kicks up the behind. What they, what *I* can't bear is what's just happened to me – coming upon a Jesuit church without any warning, without even enough room to look at it properly from a distance. I call that downright rude.

And yet no offence was intended. It's just that I'm walking about in a very ancient patch of time that's probably been here since the fall of the Venetian empire. When Algiers was ten days from Marseilles and the coast of Spain two months from Constantinople; when, if a merchant in Paris wrote to a banker in Venice on the first of the month, he received a reply by the twenty-sixth;* when the space covered by the whole world economy could be crossed in seventy days – well, *then* the dilapidated old time that still survives within the walls of this city was simply *normal* time. When the swiftest courier could travel no more than ninety kilometres in twenty-four hours, no external event could ever hit an aristocrat at more than four kilometres an hour. The battle of Lepanto hung in the balance for some time; the ships involved fought at fifteen kilometres an hour; and it took eleven days for news of the outcome to reach Venice. The future travelled overland at the pace of a walking horse, and at sea at the speed of a thirty-ton boat; it was by boat or on horseback that you either fled it or went out to meet it. History happened slowly. A Venetian who chanced to go and look at the Lido or the Guidecca could see around him a space-time continuum measuring half an hour. Why should he care if in the streets of the city it measured only two or three minutes? What could happen to him in a couple of minutes – apart from being shot – that he couldn't avoid if he wanted to? If at the end of the street he saw some enemies of his, carrying weapons, he could escape down a side alley before they had time to catch up with him. How shall I put it? Space and time had a different

---

* i.e., travelling about 2,200km in 25 days. [Author's note]

consistency then. A day used to mean ninety kilometres; now it means six thousand. In the broad boulevards of my own age, my future bears down on me at ninety kilometres an hour; a distance of three kilometres represents two minutes of my future. It takes a month to travel through the space occupied by the world economy, conterminous now with the world itself. The news of a battle fought in Korea can reach me with the speed of light, causing a world war complete with bombers heading in my direction at nearly a thousand kilometres an hour. My anxiety takes the form of always wanting to see further ahead, and to see more. Perhaps that's what makes New York, so forbidding in many other respects, seem reassuring: when you're there you can see at a hundred kilometres an hour. So what kind of madness makes me, still vibrating with the speed at which I've hurtled from Nice to Rome by plane and from Rome to Venice by train, come to this maze designed for snails, where the measures and speeds are still those of the sixteenth century? Every so often I get exasperated and see myself as I was: in a car whizzing along at top speed, emerging from one alley so fast I've already nearly reached the end of the next. I clutch at the steering wheel, afraid I'm going to crash into the walls, then gradually feel myself slowing down: this anxiety at not being able to see ahead is really that of someone on a train or a plane. So I calm down and go more slowly, adapting myself to local time. Then my former disquiet is succeeded by another. Sometimes a train will stop in the middle of nowhere for no apparent reason, and the passenger feels as if something is flowing out of him, as if he's suffering from a sort of invisible haemorrhage. The fact is, he's losing momentum: the icy chill of immobility is creeping up from his feet to his navel in a kind of minor death. A typhoid patient lying in sweat-drenched sheets, a man with a bad temper forcing himself to smile, a passenger in a halted express train – all feel the same contradiction in their very bones. And I feel this slowing down in the whole of my being. I've lost so much momentum I'm exhausted. I'm an almost stationary tourist in Venice, where time itself stands still amidst the fields of the sea.

Translated from the French by Barbara Bray

DERMOT HEALY

Prayer

To pray is to wish another well
FRANCES MOLLOY

Sometimes I am bewildered
By all this foolish energy
Battering away
Miles from people.

I envy those
Who live upriver
At the quiet source.
Here we are forever

Stepping between
The incoming roar
Of life, and the tides
That carry death out.

They are right
Who had long ago
The sense to collect
In great numbers

In sea-cities
To protect themselves.
Men should put miles
Between themselves

And the sea
From which they spring.
You should not stay too long
In your mother's house.

Mourn
From some place inland.
Praise her
To a new woman

Raised the midlands
Whose birds and trees
Keep autumn and spring.
What wakes us here at night

Is not something
We've imagined.
It's the real thing.
The parent ocean

Giving birth,
And the sound of all who ever existed
Surfacing and striking
For shore

Into the dreams
Of sea-folk in their beds.
The first tractor rises
On the stones of a path,

And smoke rears
From a chimney.
Winds harry the cliffs.
This is the new day.

I search the words for it
And would break out
Into prayer,
If I could.

Or if I knew
One prayer to the sea
I'd say it. Instead
I remember

Your definition
Of prayer –
To wish another well.
This is all we can do.

JAAN KAPLINSKI

The East-West Border

The East-West border is always wandering,
sometimes eastward, sometimes west,
and we do not know exactly where it is just now:
in Gaugamela, in the Urals, or maybe in ourselves,
so that one ear, one eye, one nostril, one hand, one foot,
one lung and one testicle or one ovary
is on the one, another on the other side. Only the heart,
only the heart is always on one side:
if we are looking northward, in the West;
if we are looking southward, in the East;
and the mouth doesn't know on behalf of which or both
it has to speak.

Translated from the Estonian by
Jaan Kaplinski with Sam Hamill
and Riina Tamm

JAAN KAPLINSKI

Once I Got a Postcard

Once I got a postcard from the Fiji Islands
with a picture of sugar cane harvest. Then I realized
that nothing at all is exotic in itself.
There is no difference between digging potatoes
                              in our Mutiku garden
and sugar cane harvesting in Viti Levu.
Everything that is very ordinary
or, rather, neither ordinary nor strange.
Far-off lands and foreign peoples are a dream,
a dreaming with open eyes
somebody does not wake from.
It's the same with poetry – seen from afar
it's something special, mysterious, festive.
No, poetry is even less
special than a sugar cane plantation or potato field.
Poetry is like sawdust coming from under the saw
or soft yellowish shavings from a plane.
Poetry is washing hands in the evening
or a clean handkerchief that my late aunt
never forgot to put in my pocket.

Translated from the Estonian by
Jaan Kaplinski with Sam Hamill
and Riina Tamm

BENNO BARNARD

An Autumn Day in Bohemia

From *The Hole in the World*

The Hole in the World, *a semi-autobiographical novel, recounts Benno Barnard's stint as a guest lecturer at Austin University and his travels, often back in time, in Eastern Europe. In this extract he visits Mariánské Lázne, once the fashionable spa of Marienbad, with his father.*

PEPPI AND US

On the journey back, one week before socialism's death knell began to sound, the train stopped in what had once been Marienbad, the most famous spa town in what was formerly Kakania.* My father and I were the only passengers to get out and be left behind, standing amongst our suitcases, at an altitude of 697m. That was shortly after midnight. We cast one more glance westwards along the Pilzen-Cheb line at our express, which was disappearing through the dancing snow and into the forest's white-dusted firs, and then, when the vehicle of our desire had been fully engulfed by the night, turned around and found that the desire itself was also gone. Herr Klat? No one, we were alone, with our feet planted firmly on the ground of a *fait accompli*: a deserted platform. Our fingers tingled, a dog howled somewhere in the surrounding darkness, neither moon nor stars, only the pale dial of the station clock, which seemed to be running backwards, because it indicated shortly before twelve, yesterday. . . . Romantic Marienbad! We, who wished to see something which both existed and did not exist, had, in analogy to that desire, both arrived and not arrived. And it was he, Klat, who had to deliver us from this twilight, this misunderstanding, this Escher-like no man's land.

---

* Kakania is the nickname Robert Musil introduced for the old dual monarchy Austria-Hungary (which also included what later became Czechoslovakia), the dream realm of the Central European bourgeoisie.

The population of Mariánské Lázně was a good 15,000 but this number clearly did not include any porters on night shift. Further along, on the Pilzen side, there was a pile of crates next to the entrance of a refreshment bar. I opened the door and stared into a blocked toilet bowl. This is how the city teased us, members of the newly prosperous middle class making a brief stopover in history, with the small provincial inconveniences which seemed to be the provisional achievements attained here by the Glorious February of 1948. "Don't forget how ridiculous you are in my eyes," it called out from under the platform roof. "Without that nitwit Klat you haven't got a ghost of a chance with me!" Its taunts made our coat-tails flap, dishevelled our hair, made us hastily seek another entrance. Where was the ticket hall, the logical way out?

Then a door squeaked in the wind, right under that demented clock, and inside we found the ubiquitous naked light bulb, the one that illuminated all of Eastern Europe, swinging in the draught on a bare wire above two back-to-back seats. Both of them were empty. This then was the waiting room – style flaking Franz Josef I, furnishings late Bolshevist – or, conversely, the antechamber of this ambiguous city. Of two cities, to be more exact, two Marienbads. And as soon as this got through to me the miserable room underwent an instantaneous metamorphosis: fresh pink plaster flowed over the walls, a chandelier blossomed around the light bulb, a divan grew out of the coarse furniture. And look! We too were subject to the transformation, suddenly we were dressed like the living dead, in the latest of nineteenth-century fashion. Kid gloves glided over our hands and the canine lament outside had been transformed into clearly audible whinnying. I was already reaching out for the cane and hat floating before me ... But in the same instant it all tarnished completely, a mad tyrant in me destroyed Habsburg; even worse, he immediately shaped the rubble into an antithetical world, an inverted Kakania: our cheerful antechamber, painted over in field grey, was full with young men in uniform, the ghosts of war heroes, delivered by train from hell to the field-hospital city of Marienbad to be once again made flesh and blood for the front. And, at the same time, in the one kaleidoscopic second, I knew, of course, that the wounded's heavy breathing was the wind, thank God, and the creaking of their stretchers the squeaking of dry hinges, thank God. Yes, this pitiable chimera dissolved just as quickly as that first blessed illusion and then reality imposed itself in its own way, with a bang. *Klat!* But it was only the door slamming shut.

We put our luggage down on the floor and sat down, one on each seat. "Sixty-nine is a fine age," said my father. "But unfortunately one unsuited to standing outside in the freezing cold." I said that the friend of our friend in Prague would definitely not be expecting him to do that. The light buzzed and my father closed his eyes. "Our mysterious Jozef Klat," he said. "He'll be here soon." After that I observed from a strange expression around his mouth that he had fallen asleep.

I flicked through a Čedok brochure we had brought with us from Prague in which Mariánské Lázně's development into a communist spa was described. It was the usual elegant bureaucratic prose, in a sensitive German translation, illustrated with photos of buildings painted in sickly-sweet colours, all kinds of fascinatingly arranged bottles, and the overjoyed faces of the bathing proletariat. The waters of the forty or so springs, rich in alkaline salt and iron, which had, in the days of the Kakanian double thesis, ameliorated the ailments of noble gastrointestinal tracts and contributed to the fight against royal obesity, now offered, after the deplorable but unavoidable anti-thesis of Nazism, responsible synthetic relaxation to workers, farmers and the *"arbeitende Intelligenz"* (from that last term one could conclude, humorously enough, that pig breeders and lathe-turners were industrious fools). It was all very simple. In this city, this dialectical Lourdes, history had followed a course of alternating hot and cold baths to emerge, in 1948, before an elated populace as a socialist-realist nymph with bone-dry hair and a stern bosom. "I was mistress to royalty," whispered Mariánské Lourdes. "Do you think I like playing concubine to the mob? Think of my sister Prague! She was Vienna's lover before she became Moscow's whore . . ."

Which special characteristics in Jozef Klat's face explained my intuitive certainty that it was a face I would never forget? He was leaning over me and I wasn't even shocked. Perhaps it was just that our remarkable situation had made me all the more receptive to reality's first impression, the first undistorted image after rising up from sleep's submarine world, after ascending through the deformed apparitions and fleeting remnants of the day: a diver who rediscovers the sun, the light bulb beneath which Klat's white hair flamed – and, inside that metaphysical halo, his face with it. But no, that was sillier than a dream, the silver around his head turned him into Joseph, spreading rays of light like on an old-fashioned holy card, whereas the real Klat bore as little resemblance to a saint as to a devil. I sat up and he became who he was: a small man with rosy skin that was reminiscent of icing and eyes of some variable substance, liquid and yet solid, if such a thing exists. Blue in any case. Neither moustache nor beard, unbespectacled. A man without a mask, a newborn infant, the kind of creature I revere but could never become, not even if I took to wearing contact lenses and energetically shaved myself every morning. The same age or at least of the same generation as my father but, all the same, as many years my junior as my senior – though when I looked more closely I saw the cracks in the icing and the darkness mixed through the blue. The face I would remember was thoroughly his own.

In the inevitable Škoda we spluttered through his Marienbad which, grey from the snow, still had a few remaining hours of darkness to make itself up for us. It was half past twelve. "This car!" Sometimes the damned thing didn't want to start, he'd just spent an hour working on it. "And how are things with my good friend Slávek?" Speaking of friends, "Herr Klat" did not exist amongst them; his name was Peppi. Everyone called him that, Good Lord, they had done so since his childhood. And, by the way, if he, in his turn, were to address us as Herr Barnard it would be as if, by some stroke of magic, there were no longer two of us. "It's the truth, isn't it?" We laughed. Peppi then. Was that short for something? "*Du, mein Lieber!* It doesn't mean anything, just me."

He lived close to the centre of town, in a dingy yellow postwar bungalow, distinguishable from the adjacent Lego by the presence of the garage he'd built himself, his brick pride and joy: the Škoda was relatively better housed than its owner. Peppi's wife, Maria, welcomed us on the doorstep. Good Maria, a shapeless Bohemian guardian angel, as taciturn as her husband was talkative: despite her size her floral dress was almost invisible against the wallpaper in the living room where she dished up the soup and sat in an armchair waiting to see if there was anything else she could do for us – until our departure she was going to put on coffee and cook noodles as if her life depended on it. The overfilled, overheated living room, dominated by a complicated set of antlers above the fireplace and a loud sideboard, suffocating and pleasant, stifling and inviting . . . An unresolvable opposition ruled, the hostility between spirit and material that

overshadowed the whole country reduced to the proportions of one
house: hospitality versus ugliness, humour versus hunting trophy.
Was Peppi aware of our attempt to adopt an attitude? Did he feel
that we had been made insecure by the contrast with Slávek's world
in which someone whose worn-out furniture was overflowing with
books didn't have a crown left to buy himself a new second-hand
bookcase? Is that why he performed his theatre piece, doubtlessly
routine, but so puzzling and simple that only a child could have
plumbed its depths?

Through the back window we could see an untidy yard, bordered
by pines. When asked what he used the ground for, Peppi pointed
out his vegetable garden, Maria's chicken run, and a few scrawny fruit
trees and then began, inside, to imitate the work he did outside.
Digging up the earth between the massive pieces of furniture, turning
manure on the carpet, picking apples off the lamp, cautiously col-
lecting eggs in the name of Frau Klat, whose size made bending over
difficult: he actually convinced us. He mimicked the gestures with
grotesque precision, indeed, he became in turn Peppi and an apple,
man and thing, a spade, corpulence, a chicken, a clod of earth – until
finally he became a grimacing egg and broke himself. Then he stood
up, brushed off his clothes and bowed solemnly. We applauded,
stunned, enthusiastic and also, in a miraculous way, riveted: we had
forgotten that we were *watching*. I, at least, intent on Peppi's artistry,
carried away by his dance of subject and object, had forgotten it. And
now I had to tear myself away from his alternative world. For minutes
I'd been a balding child of thirty-five for whom the ponderousness of
facts had docilely allowed itself to be suspended. Oh, the gruff adult
in me would surely have been able to analyse the whole happening
as something else (for example, I could call that *something* the obliteration of Cartesian dogma), even if the accompanying verbal flood
would most probably have meant nothing to Peppi. But my analysis
would have clashed just as much with the nature of its object as the
teachings of the Viennese quack with Jozef Klat's soul.

The soup was finished, the show was over. We sat at the table
talking: Peppi served Austrian liqueurs in small goblets of Bohemian
glass which, after toasts to each other's health, he immediately refilled
with more disgusting sugar water. In exchange for a flattened Sparta
he took a Belga from my packet and smoked it down to the filter; he
laughed and coughed alternately. At three o'clock Maria showed us
the former scullery where there was a double bunk that had been used

by her sons; in the corner a tap dripped. My father stretched out on the lower bunk and fell asleep almost immediately. I brushed my sticky teeth in front of the broken mirror. Yesterday evening, Slávek had rung up to arrange for a place to stay with his connection in Mariánské Lázně, an old friend of his father's. He'd written the name and address down on a pad and now Jozef Klat had revealed himself to be Peppi. ("Are you a mime artist?" asked my father. "Sometimes," said Peppi. He smiled, a bit strangely, and I recognized that smile: it was the way my father twisted his mouth when he had to force himself to tell me something. "Actually, I'm a retired metal worker," he said. "And you?") He had initiated us into his magnificent naive art. Or had we, as an echo of that *sometimes*, merely observed an old worker's escapism? Nothing in this Bohemia was itself without being also something else. My father coughed. I rinsed my mouth and on both sides of the crack in the mirror I saw the democrat's face that had inherited so many characteristics from his.

THE SPRINGS

The wintry night was followed by an autumn day under a light blue sky: the sun made the snow crisp and the plasterwork on the front of the buildings creamy. This was how the city showed itself to us, nothing but fancy cake in melting old rose and mocha brown, shop windows in full-blown Biedermeier taste through which we wandered until we arrived at an imposing square. It was the place where all the streets came together and offered an unobstructed, panoramic view of the hills around the centre of the city with their grand hotels, eccentric villas, terraced gardens: the mausoleums, to put it in a nut-shell, of the lives led by self-satisfied Kakanian airheads. This unfolded before us and, at the same time, we were accompanied by someone whose one-second smile (which takes longer to write than it did to perform) will stay with me as a souvenir of the life he *had not* led.

But the square itself was more interesting than that breathtaking view. Its most inner part had been reshaped into a monstrous hole, discreetly surrounded with a hoarding of red-and-white painted planks which made it even deeper and all the more dizzying, as if one could secretly make the Habsburg hills vanish into it overnight. An absurd thought! But no more preposterous than the idea that the centre of Marienbad was a yawning abyss, dug by the diggers of a state with a predilection for dumping great chunks of history into a similar kind of hole, a mass grave for inconvenient facts: the Dubčeks carefully cut out of official group portraits twenty years before had descended like autumn leaves to the bottom of the pit and landed amongst Masaryk's charred papers and the testimonies of Stalinist deportations. "They're going to build a flash hotel here," said Peppi. "For German tourists and with German money, according to what I've heard. The Germans love visiting our Bohemia."

On the other side of the square was the pompous, crescent-shaped bathhouse where a dissipated plutocracy had been treated for their rolls of fat. Neoclassical style, garnished with a gallery of decorative iron station columns, the so-called Rudolf Colonnade, which gave the whole a certain frivolity after all. Fantastically restored. Isn't the collective memory an amusing thing? It can't possibly ever contain more than fifty or sixty years at once, more or less the trials and tribulations of one generation. "The Habsburg clique took an invigorating bath, you say, and then enthusiastically resumed their plotting and intriguing? Ah," smirked the Workers' and Farmers' State, "the odd drop of gonorrhoea here, an assassination there, maybe even a world war everywhere . . . Morally rotten through and through? That was the previous century in Marienbad which lasted, as is known, until 1918, let's say 1948, it depends somewhat on which perspective you take. You, as a bourgeois, do not, of course, understand that . . ."

But I understood it very well indeed. The State had, thank God, restored this building for its Peppis, its farmers and hard-currency-carrying Barnards, and the question whether or not the proletarian who bought the entrance ticket just before us got indigestion from carrying out his dictatorship was just as absurd as the question whether he might prefer to drink water instead of a liqueur.

November, the baths were closed. At the door of the museum wing a cleaner was busy polishing the last tiles of the parquet floor. We loomed up like dull spectres under her cleaning rag and with the following step could look down at ourselves. Because she'd rubbed the glass cases over with methylated spirits an old-fashioned smell hung in the air: nostalgia irritated my nose. But the exhibition! At the sight of it the eyes of the Austro-Hungarian eagle would have clouded over in both of its two heads. Those ridiculous bottles from my brochure, soldiers in rank, a glass parade. Next to them a regiment of life-size roentgenograms of clean-rinsed innards, neatly pinned up. One could study a plaster cross-section of the rock bed, out of which a battalion of scientifically justifiable pumps protruded. On a long panel it was written in adhesive letters that Mariánské Lázně was declared a public spa in 1818. There was an array of the requisite sterile water cans: during the season 40,000 were in use – filled with a few hectolitres of the local Radetzky water that must once have been enough to muffle the clap of all of Habsburg's camp followers. That they hadn't put all 40,000 out on display! The railway station was opened in 1872: in a photo that had been enlarged to Cyclopean proportions the first locomotive from Pilzen burst through the ribbon that had been stretched between platforms 1 and 2, to the cheers of a grainy human sea. It was understandable that Real Existing Socialism had no soul, since it didn't tolerate one in its servants. But why didn't it have any sparkle, any vision, a single grain of inventiveness? Why was it, at its best, nothing more than soporific?

On a third panel war broke out and Marienbad became a German military hospital: the insufficiently fallen were able to come to recuperate, provided they had attained a minimum rank of *Feldwebel* because, even as a spa in purgatory, Marienbad remained Marienbad. Forty years earlier it had effervesced with the decadent atmosphere of the top-heavy Dual Monarchy which had maintained a standing army of uniforms, a sitting army of bureaucrats, and a bent-over army of arse lickers – the mood was still just as bubbly as the champagne which fed it. Elegance, lightheartedness, a diet of tinsel and cocaine! Was the time bomb ticking? A *thé dansant*! Was the volcano rumbling? A last waltz, even if the lava was lapping at our boots! The young officers were now young managers, no great improvement that is, and for the rest it was all strongly reminiscent of the feelings of doom disguised as fashion which have cast a spell over my generation. Poor, foolish socialism which didn't want anything to do with eruptions, parties, explosions, swan songs. Poor? True enough, it did have exceptional success in aping those three armies. Is that why I, the mocking escapist, the sentimental Schweikian, had associated the complete lack of imagination surrounding us with military discipline, from the drilled bottles on?

In 1948 this spa, once one of Europe's most expensive health resorts, was opened to all layers of the socialist society's working population. Did this imply that the pensioners Peppi and Maria had had their chance at the quack cures? Were they perhaps now parasites on society, proliferating in its intestinal flora? But society, socialism's mystical body, could, of course, never take a bath as such. I started to get a headache.

Fortunately my father discovered another hall, or rather, a room. The door, which was behind one of the roller-mounted panels, had to be specially opened. The cleaner, who had been dozing off on a chair by the entrance, shuffled bad-temperedly over to us mumbling something toothlessly – there's nothing in there to interest the gentlemen, translated Peppi, just lots of old dust traps and she has her pride too. I took out my wallet and gave her a mark. The old witch: she pressed the coin to her lips, her face grotesque with bliss, and I was ashamed. Then she pulled a bunch of keys out of her dust coat and unlocked the door.

And so we passed from our world into another, through a hidden opening and, oh mystery, I felt as if this stuffy, darkened side room, this parallel world, immediately communicated with *another* other world, a reality I could not avoid thinking about: Rotterdam, the lower-middle-class world of my father's parents, disappeared for good these last fifty years, which I knew only from faded brown photos and infrequent stories, a family grave in words and images. Was I, too, being deluded by Marienbad? Something called up that world and made it suddenly contemporary to our own: perhaps my lack of sleep, the stale smell, the abrupt changeover from one environment to another. I descried two human silhouettes in the room and imagined that one was my grandfather, reclining on Crown Prince Rudolf's Turkish ottoman and brooding about the depression, and the other my grandmother, sitting stiffly at Empress Sissi's secretaire and doing the accounts. How farcical! Lost spirits and pieces of furniture spiritualistically drifting through the years from the Viennese Hofburg to an intermediary world, floating to Rotterbad . . . Then the cleaner flicked on the light, as if she wanted to capture this underlit dream with a flash. I blinked and saw a beautiful Empire sofa which had surely not belonged to Rudolf. And there was no one lying on it, only a dummy with clumsily painted staring eyes, wearing an *Oberstinhaber's* uniform and a kepi. There was also a bureau with a leaf, a maze of pigeonholes and drawers. But on the chair in front of it a second mannequin was sitting, in a garment with lots of pleats, neither my grandmother nor the ghost of Sissi. In addition there were armchairs with faded seats and backs, a table inlaid with light and dark diamonds which formed a continuous series of exploding cubes, a cabinet, a glass case . . . (but writing abut furniture does not appeal to me, it is there to be used). A screen had been pushed in front of the window. I looked at the wooden heads, which were clearly unable to bear direct sunlight, and suddenly realized that there was a photo of my grandparents in approximately these same positions.

The glass case held one object, a visitors' book. It was a great tome, open at pages 221 and 222, containing the names of all those who had visited this bathhouse in the fourth week of July, 1907: a random list of the prominent deceased, all written down in the same scholastically elegant clerical hand. Double column. Scribbled or grand, the guest's signature. The clerk himself was long dead: he had probably thought highly of all those whom coincidence had brought together on these pages. His respect, however, had been unable to alter the fact that he had unknowingly been keeping an obituary list – because what I read, from the very top left all the way down to the bottom right, was a passage from a book of the dead. Who had been there? Edward VII, with such an extensive retinue that it must have seemed as if the whole British court tended to dyspepsia. Aristocrats. Dignitaries. Mostly Kakanians but also French, Germans and Russians. A Thurn und Taxis. A von Metternich-Wolf. Names. And amongst them, *bien étonné*, a Belgian businessman, Louis van Cortenbroek of Brussels, who had spent the night of 27 July in the Hotel Esplanade. A faded, sturdy signature. He could have been a member of my grandparents' generation. A robust dash under *van Cortenbroek* that seemed to emphasize his solvency, his willpower, his life. "I'm chock-a-block with plans for the future," explained van Cortenbroek. He reached into his inside pocket for the postcard for his wife, *Marienbad – Rudolph-Colonnade: "Mon voyage est un très grand succès. Je passe le dernier jour à Marienbad . . ."* The clerk blotted his name and van Cortenbroek wandered off humming through the glass and through me, into balneology and oblivion, leaving me behind eighty-two years later asking myself why those transparent living creatures on the x-rays had annoyed me while on the other side a no less anonymous departed, called van Cortenbroek and nothing more, activated my imagination and, in a contrary way, even moved me. Possibly there was such a postcard, the memento of a forgotten man, waiting somewhere in a shoe box in Brussels for a new reader – just as he, in this hereafter of mock velvet and tinsel, this Kakanian cosmos in miniature, waited until someone invented a new life to go with his name.

"Strange," said Peppi outside. He stared up at the sky where leaden clouds were gathering and turned up the collar of his duffel coat.

"Snow clouds," he said. "With this climate you never know what's going to happen next." Was that really so strange? No, he meant something else. I looked at him. A shadow in his eyes was making them grey. He meant that in forty-four years in Marienbad he'd never been inside that museum. But that, of course, was not strange at all: nobody visits his own city, even if people from all over the world are bumping into their neighbours there, it's just as unlikely as someone buying souvenirs of their home town. Peppi had married in Marienbad, fathered two sons, worked himself up to relative prosperity. And now, half a life later, he suddenly found himself standing in the middle of the city, with his back turned to the red-and-white hoarding, surprised because he had never needed to remember anything special about Marienbad.

PEPPI AND THE PAST

Jozef Klat, who, as far back as he could remember, had always been called Peppi, was born in December 1918 in Vienna, less than a month after the armistice between the Entente and the Central Powers had been put into force: "I crept out of Austro-Hungary's carcass like a little maggot." For Jana and Jiři Klat the long, bewildered silence that had descended over Europe on 11 November was, in any case, drastically broken: the undernourished mother had no milk and the child cried constantly (imagine that, a little later, by means of an acoustic miracle, a sound hook-up was made between the Mirror Room in Versailles and the cradle of a half-starved German baby, then that accursed Treaty would . . . vain speculation). The father had connections in the country through whom he managed to obtain goat's milk, albeit in exchange for the last of their coal dust so that the temperature in the two-room flat hovered around freezing for weeks on end and the diluted milk could not be boiled. The circumstances in which Peppi came into the world were definitely Messianic; only the Kings were missing. But he survived, his star was a lucky one, at least in the fact that he lacked brothers or sisters with whom he would have been obliged to share the minimal amounts of food. He survived his war diet, the constant diarrhoea it caused, the cold, against which his mother protected him as far as she was able by swaddling him in his father's coarse uhlan's jacket, the horrible rash it caused, the Spanish flu epidemic, and the cholera bacilli in the unboiled water. In short, when Peppi was zero years old, he

miraculously survived the final death spasms of the thousand-year-old
Habsburg dragon – bitterly enough, he would, after this, not even
be granted enough time to attain his majority before being confronted
with the leviathan begot by the vindictiveness of the dragon-killer and
borne by Europe in the delivery room of Versailles.

Then came 1919 and, finally, 1989 too: the same Peppi, now in
the winter of his life, sat in a smoky Marienbad bar that was crowded
with young workers toasting the end of their working day, drank a
glass of Urquell with a foreign contemporary and his son, and talked
about his mother's stories which formed his indirect memories of the
earliest period of his life. Through the window I could see our
museum, a dark mass jutting out above the hoarding on the other
side of the square, *his* museum – I imagined Peppi's memory as a
grandfather clock whose mechanism had stopped years ago but had
suddenly been set in motion by the surprise he had just had and was
now ticking away with that monument as counterweight.

In the spring the epidemic was over, the ice flowers melted off the
windows and the former mounted lancer Jiři Klat was able to start
work in a brewery delivering full beer kegs to remote bars and col-
lecting empty ones. He used a handcart to transport them and in the
evenings he left it standing in the inner courtyard of their tenement
building in the Kohlengasse, a symbol of the status an honest job
meant in their social circle. The pay was niggardly but they no longer
suffered hunger even if "my parents must have implored God not to
send any more mouths to feed". And Peppi remained an only child.
His earliest conscious memory was of the arrival of an unknown
woman who had a cane suitcase with her and said, "Be quiet, *Liebchen*"
to his crying mother behind the bedroom door; this memory, combined with the memory of his mother spending the days after that in
bed, would much later give rise to the suspicion that the Superior
Being had received some assistance from the local abortionist.

"Much later" a mate in the factory made a daring plea for the
legalization of abortion in which he, with great feeling for realism,
described the contents of the tub between his lamenting fiancée's legs,
as if he had observed the climax of the operation through a film of red.
That, from that moment on, his own first memory was inseparably
associated with *blood* was something Peppi found worse than the forgivable murder of an unborn child. "What else could they do? They
were virtuous people. One morning . . ." That morning his father
found a half-frozen tramp in the straw that covered the bottom of his

cart: Peppi was dragged out of bed to slice bread while his mother sat the guest in a chair. Another morning his father appeared with a syphilitic whore whose teeth were chattering from her fever; when Peppi came home from school his bed was still warm. (Was he suggesting that the brother or sister who was never born hadn't missed out on much? I incline more to the point of view that he intended the anecdotes to prove his parents' virtue: they could not afford the luxury of an abstract respect for life but practised a kind of clear-headed love of their fellow man. Perhaps, an ironic misunderstanding, the former socialist in Peppi hoped posthumously to reconcile his parents with the former clergyman in my father.)

And mime, Peppi? He smiled and used his finger to trace over the circle his glass had left on the table. Mime. *"Ach, du lieber Gott . . ."* At every pause in his story the bustle around us swelled and, at the same time, crumbled into separate competing voices, each with its own story, the individuality of which once more dissolved into a background chorus as soon as Peppi recommenced talking – I had the feeling we were listening to a stammering antiphony of present and past and, also, that all the scraps of events had something inexplicable in common.

There was once a boy of ten or eleven who, as a very special treat, was allowed to go to the circus. Suddenly reluctant, he walked in under the awning and into the towering striped canvas tent: excited people, the fanfare, *Sehr verehrte Damen und Herren!* Every cliché was wonderfully new and would turn out to be unforgettable: for the first time in his life he saw *show,* experienced the sensation of pure splendour, form without content that wasn't hollow. And there, for the price of one and a half schillings begged out of his mother's apron, his fate revealed itself to him in the form of the lion tamer: he too, Peppi Klat, would one day appear in a wild animal act! After the show was over, he stuffed his pockets with dry horse dung from the field behind the tent which he later hid under his small steel bed in the expectation that this ersatz circus air would awaken the right dreams – but his taciturn father recognized the scent of memory as the stink of shit and gave the little Klat a thrashing. In a way, then, mime was beaten into him because, instead of dreaming, he started practising as a tamer. Due to a lack, in the Kohlengasse, of feline creatures more inspiring than the fish-head-eaters his mother threw the leftovers to every Friday, he began to tame himself.

A year passed and gradually his interest moved from the pseudo-lion to his real body, that of an adolescent who seemed unable to grow any taller than four foot eleven and, possibly for that very reason, imitated the girls for his classmates. He imitated all the well-known gestures and presumed rituals of those mysterious creatures with great success, which eased somewhat their unapproachability: as long as he played a girl, he didn't need one. Yes, he would become a mime artist, although he didn't yet know that word. But in 1933, after a youth of just fourteen years, he became an apprentice metal worker. Had we ever been in a foundry? The cacophony made any joke incomprehensible and so, in the expectation of half a century's galvanizing of sheet metal, he extended his mime repertoire bit by bit and entertained his workmates. In the midst of roaring furnaces and deafening flatting rolls he became the foreman, the clerk with the small spectacles and the pay packets, a tramp, a whore, oh, he was everyone . . .

". . . And then I heard about socialism for the first time and believed in it." In February 1934 the Austrian Marxists' uprising against Dolfuss's administration broke out and Peppi let himself be infected by the grim enthusiasm of the older workers: side by side with the young man whose fiancée had bled so much, he listened breathlessly to the impressive flood of words issuing from the mouth of Leopold Petznek, whose socially committed face under his cap bore a remarkable resemblance to Lenin's, even if the goatee was missing. Peppi understood precious little of all that rhetoric but was all the more impressed by it as a result – it was no coincidence that he himself excelled in playing dumb. One thing was, however, clear: the one thing that muffled, raspy voices make clear in every revolution: everything was going to be different. It didn't last long, just as it never lasts long. As far as that's concerned, successful and failed revolutions are copies and caricatures of each other. His father, the ex-uhlan from the Imperial Army, was hardly granted time enough to decry the socialists: Oh, old Austria, the Radetzky Realm, where the only red tolerated was the red fez on the heads of the Bosnian guards! Then silence descended anew over Vienna – until everything really did become different, terribly different.

Peppi was silent. "And what happened then, Peppi?" But we were silent too. His voice seemed, after the whole choral dance of words, to have been devoured by the hubbub, in which I could no longer distinguish separate sounds, only impersonal murmuring, as of the ocean.

A tall Bohemian about my age stood up at an adjacent table,

nodded to us and shook Peppi's hand. A four- or five-sentence conversation in Czech followed. He then shook hands with Peppi again, nodded once more, and walked to the door. Peppi watched him leave. Soft music slipped past him into the bar and was cut off by the closing door. He passed the window and disappeared round the corner of the hoarding. "He doesn't speak any German," said Peppi. "Otherwise he would have joined us. Maybe a little English. He's the son of an old workmate of mine. Milan. I know him from the war."

He took a watch without a strap out from under his jumper, peered at it, put it back. Then he drained his glass. All these old stories, he was just boring us. And Maria was waiting with dinner. He pushed his chair back and helped my father into his jacket. "*Danke*, Peppi." The shyness in his inflection. "*Servus*."

THE CROWN PRINCE

Rudolf of Habsburg came into the world in Vienna on 21 August 1859, and the first thing he heard, apart from his own cries and the firing of the usual salute, was music by Johan Strauss, the "Austrian Crown Prince March" which had been specially composed for that festive occasion. He died early in the morning of 30 January 1889, in the hunting lodge at Mayerling, not far from the capital. The last sound he heard in his life was the report of the revolver with which he, taking aim in a mirror, shot himself out of the world.

Rudolf's mother was Empress Sissi, the frigid shrew who would be reincarnated as the winsome, woman-child Romy Schneider – her good fortune, because that is how she lives on in the popular imagination. Once the real Sissi told her son that she had only become his mother "by accident", and with that "accident" she had definitely not meant a mathematical error. Her husband, Franz Josef, thought little more of the Crown Prince than that he was in the habit of uttering "twaddle": for example, the perceptive polemics the son wrote in opposition to his father's extremely reactionary pro-German politics. Rudolf's relationship with his parents was not too good.

When he was zero days old the Emperor-King appointed him *Oberstinhaber* of the 19th Infantry Regiment and at five the tiny Crown Prince was already being displayed in various repugnant little uniforms. His whole miserable youth in the depressing Hofburg, that ghost castle which lacked decent lighting and plumbing until well into the twentieth century, was organized according to the rigours of

Prussian military drill: in winter his tutor made a habit of taking him straight from his bed to character-forming exercises in the ice-cold inner courtyard. From the age of ten, if not before, Rudolf was ripe for psychiatry (at that time itself in its infancy): a bed-wetting, fainting neurasthenic, the product of a monstrous pedagogic vision and his parents' lovelessness, made unfit in perpetuity for life.

But his nervous system had not been all too ravaged because his mind remained clear and, for a scion of an ancient, venereally-undermined royal family, surprisingly intelligent. While still a teenager he developed into a free-thinker, an anti-cleric, a friend to the Jews, and a social-democrat – he revealed himself, in other words, as everything Habsburg was *not*. Characteristically enough, the German braggart Wilhelm, who had ascended the neighbours' throne with the necessary aplomb just before Mayerling, made Rudolf almost literally sick. To express his political ideas he began, around the age of twenty, feverishly writing. In all kinds of newspaper articles and pamphlets, for the greater part published under a pseudonym in France, he attacked virtually everything Habsburg was (as a satirist Rudolf could hold his head high: he rode like a sack of potatoes but wrote like a razor). And in the meantime, in contrast to all that, he pursued the notorious pleasures of his class with a passion, as if, in place of a Dual Monarchy, he would inherit a brothel. This possessed man, who himself provided the entry on Jewry for the Austro-Hungarian encyclopedia; this Rudolf, one big bundle of nerves with pen and penis as protuberances, antennae, apogees; along the way this case of self-hatred and thwarted love also married the "Belgian cow" Stephanie, the daughter of Leopold II, who gave him a daughter, Erzsi, in exchange for gonorrhoea (this Erzsi would share her father's leftist sympathies and end her life as the Widow Leopold Petznek: nothing is coincidental).

There is more that could be said about Rudolf but that is the essence of it. What followed was Mayerling, the blood wedding, which now, after fifty books and five films, has been covered with a veil of fraudulent Sissi romanticism. Rudolf's mistress at that time was Mary Vetsera, a seventeen-year-old baroness, whom he had got to know through the agency of his English fellow heir-to-the-throne, Edward. As is known, Rudolf murdered her first before shooting Rudolf-in-the-mirror dead. According to a less popular Mayerling school, he first tried, with the help of a candle and a catheter, single-handedly to perform an abortion on her; during this primitive operation the teenager bled to death, whereupon the despairing prince, and so on. Does it make any difference? So many books, so many versions, and still more. The only story about Mayerling that moves *me* is the one which relates that Rudolf spent the evening before his death playing chess with himself, thus, with a ghost as an opponent. Was he thinking of his father then? In any case he died, whichever version one wishes to believe: a brilliant flame that blew itself out.

Why did Rudolf really kill himself? Perhaps because he was ill. He not only had piles, sciatica, the clap and overstrained nerves (when one nerve was touched they all trembled) but also suffered from an incurable form of *Weltschmerz*, the nineteenth-century ailment par excellence. His name is bound equally with Mayerling as with Marienbad, suicide and health, blood and water.

A second assumption, which does not exclude the first, is that Rudolf had spent years trying to commit patricide through polemics. When that persistently failed, simply because the victim neglected to react, he finally committed suicide himself. If that theory is right, one of his last, desperate attempts at patricide was an *Open Letter* to his father, written under the pseudonym Julius Felix. Franz Josef's secret police presumably ensured that it reached its addressee. The Emperor must have felt as if the bullets were whizzing past his head when he glanced at that diatribe, because Rudolf pleaded for an alliance with France and Russia to erect a *cordon sanitaire* around his favourite enemy, Wilhelm II. A break with Germany! Alas, Franz Josef suffered from a completely different disease from his progeny, cerebral dualmonarchitis, an abnormality which so clouded his view of Kakania that he couldn't see the sun descending in that realm between the ends of his moustache. He would have laid that thing, *à la* Kafka's father, on his bedside table: yet more of Rudolf's typical twaddle. A future head of state as writer, the idea of it! His Apostolic Majesty yawned and devoted himself once more to the appetizing flesh of his mistress Anna Nahowski. (Was Franz Josef really as intellectually blinkered as the critical historians like to present him? One could equally justifiably claim that he was forced to play a role: he was *himself* the sun, the stationary centre of the Kakanian universe, in whom, therefore, nothing could possibly take place. And Rudolf? Because his father didn't want to listen to him, he made a date with eternity instead. Or was it because of the abortion after all? Whatever it was, it was pretty naive of him to think that a father like his would listen to his Copernican ideals which shone in the sunlight of democratic reason. But a hundred years after our death we are all naive.)

That brings us, therefore, to the twentieth century, without Rudolf. What was then still the future might yet have been the product of Rudolf's political genius – but he determinedly pointed the end of his barrel at it. *Bang!* Retrospectively it sounds like the starter's signal for our century, the century which, after all, ballistic clamour was to become the primary characteristic. Look, New Europe, born in 1889, whereas Old Europe died only in 1914, on the occasion of the blood wedding's silver anniversary. Humanity spent the intervening period in an indeterminate, twilight place, half-way between funeral chapel and delivery room, and I suspect that it never awaited its fate as unsuspectingly as then.

Turning it around, Rudolf was, of course, also a child of his times and, in 1989, it seems as if all of Vienna was, without wanting to know it, weary of life in 1889 (perhaps that's why Rudolf committed suicide: vicariously, as it were). Because what was Vienna? Vienna was the ballroom of the ineradicable Strauss family, where the nineteenth century was wound up in three-four time, and where a Kakanian parliamentarian had, in 1875, already declared: "The Vienna waltz is the expression of a positive feeling for life. When a woman has heard and danced the waltz she can long for death in peace and satisfaction." Vienna was Sissi's boudoir, shining in a bejewelled ostentation that cast its reflection as far as my prose about Habsburg, in the strass of falsely glittering adjectives and suggestive ends of sentences . . . But, as Kundera said, what is kitsch but a screen put up to hide away death, and which I now slide aside? Vienna was Freud's practice, the Jew who prepared himself for a voyage of discovery in the European subconscious, that sultry morass, inhabited by the anti-Semitic reptile and other extinction-spared saurians. Vienna was the extension with squares, boulevards, palaces, salons, coffee shops and Kohlengassen of Rudolf's nervous system, poor neurotic Rudolf, who cheered up the desk in his Ottoman study with a skull: I wonder how often he looked at the ornament and thought of his own head. Vienna was the laboratory where the powers which Franz Josef manipulated with such vitality contrived the destruction of humanity. The report from Mayerling rumbled around the Balkans for twenty-five years until a satisfactory echo was finally summoned up in Sarajevo – that second famous revolver shot announced the explosion which, during a fatal experiment with the pan-European death wish, blew the Kakanian laboratory sky-high. Another twenty-five years later, a ghost haunted Europe, an anti-Rudolf, the only spirit successfully summoned up by the spiritism that was so popular in Vienna's declining years, albeit somewhat delayed.

But after all those Baroque images of Habsburg, I still see just one simple image before me: Rudolf, photographed in his coffin, his shattered cranium held together by a bandage. No peace in that face, it's not "just like he's asleep". He needed thirty years and one second for his life – in that second he pressed his lips definitively together. Disappointment, anger, fear. If he wasn't dead, he'd be chewing on his moustache. So ended Rudolf's history and so began Rudolf's *non*-history, with an embittered stripe. Coincidence. A little further away in Austria, on the border with Germany, the wife of a *Kakanian* customs officer entered the seventh month of her pregnancy. The rest is that which I am unable to speak about.

"Do you hear the music?" asked Peppi. He let go of the bar's door handle and stuck his index finger in the air, his head bent upwards, as if the scales were descending from heaven. "It's close to the museum," he said. "We have to go that way anyway. Or would you prefer me to ring up my son? Peter, our oldest, is coming to dinner tonight. He can come and pick us up with the Škoda." But my father rapped on the pavement with his walking stick. He was, after all, two years younger than Peppi: "*Vorwärts!*" We walked round the hoarding; behind it, on a summer's evening in 1907, Louis van Cortenbroek had strolled through the middle of a group of future German tourists on his way to a hearty dinner in the Hotel Esplanade, whose window-panes were shining in the setting sun: it really was an idyllic location, half-way up the side of the hill, and it was not unthinkable that the faintly lit squares I could see above the bathhouse might be windows in that same building. Van Cortenbroek passed the stall where he'd bought his postcard, bent, picked up a newspaper from a pile and seized, at the same time, the opportunity to cast a glance full of cautious pleasure at the young women strolling by; did he catch a glimpse of a sweet face under a coquettishly twirled *en-tout-cas*? In the next instant it had already passed, a charming memory, which could now, at the most, become language, just as the outdated fashionable parasol.

The music became steadily clearer but I couldn't recognize either the melody or the instruments. And what was that colourful glimmer next to the Rudolf Colonnade? "It's a *son et lumière*," said Peppi. The authorities, ever keen on hard currency, had laid out a square and a fountain when they'd carried out the restoration a few years before and during the tourist season a show was presented. He was only surprised that some apparatchik or other had pressed the appropriate button now, in November.

We turned the last corner: in the extension of the colonnade which we, a little while before, had left on the opposite side, a small group of people had gathered round the fountain, which was spouting a fizzy rainbow. Milan's son was amongst them but didn't see us. "Listen," said Peppi. We stood still. Czech voices. Splashing. And, dominating everything, syrupy anonymous music. By the sound of it, vacuum-bottled by a synthesizer somewhere in America and squeezed into the air here by a water organ as acoustic propaganda for a system that slipped up on the time of year. I looked at Peppi. Did he like it? The colours glided across his cheeks and his expression gave nothing away. I looked at the row of columns. Peppi thought that this was the only monument dedicated to Crown Prince Rudolf in all of Bohemia. Who succeeded Rudolf? Franz Ferdinand. But actually Hitler. And the communists followed Hitler and Peppi's faded reality was the result, a reality which had just now been touched up by that organ. No one could have prevented the twentieth century, if only because it followed the nineteenth. But perhaps Rudolf could have spared us *this* twentieth century. Us? "Enjoy life!" cajoled the synthesizer. It began to snow blue, orange, yellow, red flakes. Maybe it would keep up and the digging machines would be stuck in their hole in the morning. "I'm sure you prefer to sleep in a decent hotel," snarled the apparatchik behind his switchboard. "Is the Hotel Esplanade perhaps good enough? Bour . . ."

The music broke off, in the middle of a beat, and the light dimmed. The fountain sputtered on for a second, then was quiet. Grey snow drifted down over us. Somebody suppressed a laugh. Someone else laughed and drowned out the first laugher. "Czech technology," said Peppi. A third shouted something and everyone laughed. "Maria's waiting," said my father. "Shouldn't we be going?" We turned round. All at once the snow hit us in the face. And while we walked towards Peppi's house the west wind lifted the mocking laughter and carried it up, to the roofs and then higher, as if it wanted to carry it with it, over the city, over the forests, over Pilzen, all the way to a future Prague, only there to sprinkle it over Wenceslaus Square, into the pealing of the bells and the calls of the people who had streamed there.

PEPPI AND WAITING

Maria dished up noodles and roast meat; Peter, his mother's taciturn
son, poured the beer. Peppi and my father talked to each other. I
listened, still lightheaded from the Urquell: the music and laughter
were still echoing in my ears, all the words became a drone, all that
German, in which I was suddenly unable to express myself. ". . . like
in East Germany?" My father's voice. "I don't know," said Peppi.
"There's no Wall here and we Bohemians have survived under different regimes for so long, the whole time except for Masaryk. We've
developed all kinds of ways to feel freer than we are, it's become
second nature to us. I don't even know if we've still got a first nature."
He pointed to the antlers above the fireplace. He'd shot that deer a
few winters before, somewhere deep in the ridged depths of the pine
forest behind his yard at a time when a halt in food shipments had
meant that there was almost no meat to be had. "Just as illegal," he
said, "as growing cabbage and potatoes." But whoever voluntarily
involved themselves with the bureaucracy here was either a fool or a
collaborator. Slávek had said the same: applying for an unnecessary
permit was sure evidence of a certain amount of obtuseness. "Then
Belgium and Bohemia have got something in common," I replied.
What an all-too-easy comparison! Because in this country every form
of anarchism, evasion, obstruction, no matter how slight, demanded
the readiness to have a mob of Moscow-inclined toadies declare you
a "parasite on the socialist society" or, at best, a "dissident" and that
required the necessary courage – a quality which the circumstances
might develop in people but which *I myself* had never needed and had
no idea if I possessed. That's what I thought and the thought was
clear enough. Only it seemed to have arisen in an air bubble: inside
of which vague music whined on and distant laughter tinkled, the
conversation penetrating contrapuntally. I didn't succeed in making
myself heard.

Maria served coffee, Peter got the sickly sweet liqueur out of the
sideboard; we presented cigarettes to each other and drank to our
health. It was a repetition of the previous evening but, at the same
time, it wasn't: a day had passed in the meantime and Peppi was
talking about different things, as if he needed finally to have told his
whole story before his listeners departed as strangers at midnight, to
cross the border to a *Drüben* where he could not follow.

After that second-rate show, the Anschluss, an operetta which the

Austrian people rewarded with a one-armed standing ovation, life in the Kohlengasse became more difficult by the day. Many ethnic Czechs moved to the fatherland, which had, after all, been allocated to them in 1918, but more than a hundred thousand lived on in Vienna where the brand-new Master Race treated them with the contempt appropriate to Slavs. Basically, the surname Hubálek or Zvěřina was now sufficient grounds for dismissal, no more valid reasons needed to be cited. In this way, the former Imperial and Royal lancer Jiři Klat found himself thrown out one morning, without knowing what he'd done. To be more exact: he stood in front of the brewery's gates, behind which he had been required to leave his handcart, and didn't know what to do. He, the twice-decorated war veteran, was in the position so many German Jews had occupied a few years earlier: grateful Germany let them know that they could take the Iron Cross they had worn on the collar of their morning coat, displayed on their desk or kept in the kitchen drawer and shove it. "He didn't even clench his fist," said Peppi. "He told me that later. 'You can go, Klat.' – 'But . . .' – 'Klat?' – '*Servus, Herr Direktor.*'" Perhaps that was a Bohemian disease, the inability to clench your fist. He stood in front of the gate, breathed in the smell of hops which always clung to his clothes and stared at a ship sailing past on the Danube. That was all. What else could he do? Go to Czechoslovakia? It was true that he'd been born in Bohemia and spoke the language fluently, but all he could remember were a few insignificant details of a Prague outer suburb. And anyway, thanks to Chamberlain's friendly conciliation of a month or so before, the Czech state was now nothing but a ball of paper in the Nazis' gigantic wastepaper basket. So he walked into the city and got drunk.

A Bohemian who can't go to Bohemia gets drunk, I thought inside my air bubble. A Bohemian who can't leave Bohemia gets drunk too. Bohemia is there where you're not.

"He came home and without saying a word marched to the bedroom. My mother followed him but he pushed her away, and that was something I'd never seen him do. His decorations hung above their bed, a Star and a Cross, on coloured ribbons with pins. As a little boy I was sometimes allowed to polish them on Sundays after Mass, very carefully. The pins were just stuck into the wallpaper, that old-fashioned wallpaper with brown flowers, under the holy-water font and the crucifix. He grabbed them from the wall, so roughly that the holy-water font fell on to the end of the bed. It broke, and my

mother started to cry. Then my father walked to the kitchen and
opened the window. And then he screamed: '*Scheisse an Österreich!*'
and hurled the Star into the courtyard. And then he screamed again:
'*Es gibt kein Österreich mehr!*' and then he threw the Cross out as well.
My mother ran down the stairs crying and picked up those stupid
bits of tin. She was naturally scared to death that one of the neighbours
would inform the police. She cried all evening. And my father just
sat in his chair and said nothing, as if he were somewhere else. He
didn't even say 'Quiet, *Liebchen*,' or something like that."

Silence. Something, perhaps a clump of soot that had come loose,
rattled through the stovepipe and plopped amongst the coals. Quiet.

"My father never shouted," said Peppi. "But he shouted all that
about Austria." He remembered the eight words syllable for syllable,
exactly as his father had called them out, including the intonation. Of
all his father's words they were the only ones Peppi had never forgotten – of all the visible and audible things that had made up his father's
life they were all that remained: he didn't even have any photos left
depicting a smiling or even a uniformed apparition of his begetter.
Peter didn't know what his grandfather had looked like and regretted
it. "Isn't that right, Peter?"

Peppi jumped up, tapped his temple with one clownish finger and
said: "*Entschuldige, Herr Oberstinhaber!*" We laughed at Schweik.
Peppi sat down again. More silence. My ears began throbbing painfully, as if the ridiculous air bubble were sucking the silence into it
to press against my eardrums with the full weight of the words no
one had spoken, the unbearable words, sorrow, fear, love, the *non-*
words. But I couldn't speak. I looked at Peppi, who was playing with
his empty liqueur glass and looking at the window, within which
there was nothing to see but another view of the room. I thought:
he's seeing the kitchen window his father threw open. Those words,
too, were painful.

"One of the decorations, the Cross, was embellished in the middle
with an enamel circle. Because of the fall it was all cracked and a flake
had chipped off. Strange that I can still see it so clearly. My father
died a year later. I came home from the foundry . . . We were producing tank components there by then, but I could be happy I hadn't
been fired, I was a Czech with socialist ideas . . . Of course I kept my
mouth shut at work, we needed the money much too much. Later I
was betrayed and then I was . . . But that's another story. *Ach, mein
Lieber*, so many stories! So, I came home from the foundry, and my

father was sitting dead in his chair. My mother had gone to do the shopping. And he was just sitting there dead in his chair, a dummy that couldn't talk any more. He hadn't even said goodbye. And a couple of weeks later the war broke out. But when I dream about him now he's always standing in front of the gate of the brewery, and his hands are hanging limply beside his body. But I never help him. I'm not there. Or else I'm sailing past on a ship."

What time was it? Peter filled my glass with the sweet muck that was sticking my lips together. Maria tidied up in the kitchen. Water ran from the tap, the kettle was put on the stove. My ears pounded.

"Sometimes," said my father in the distance. "Sometimes I dream of the house I grew up in. It was in Rotterdam. We had a shop. Then I see my mother putting on tea and I hear the bell ring. Or my father's wearing his good suit and smoking a cigar, so that I know in my dream that it's Sunday. Or I sit at the kitchen table playing chess with my uncle, on Saturday. That uncle was socialist as well; later he taught me not to vote for a Christian party. The weird thing is that in these dreams I'm always looking around suspiciously, making sure that everything's in its place, just as I remember it. Here my mother's bureau, there my father's easy chair, between the windows the Biedermeier cabinet, et cetera. Even though I'm aware of the fact that that cabinet, for example, is actually in the room I'm lying in dreaming. But nothing's changed, Peppi. No one's moved anything or thrown anything out. Only, it's turned brown or grey, our old interior. It looks as if all the pots of tea my mother ever made have been spilt over it, as if it had been rubbed with the ash from all the cigars my father ever smoked . . ." (Father, you never dreamt that. You're describing an internal pre-war photo. Everything you say is true but still you're making it up. You couldn't say the other words, nobody can say them now without falsifying everything even more. You don't want to be a minister. But Cartesian thinking, thinking that divides the world into egos and things, masters and objects, makes you want to puke. That's why you're a poet. Father! I love you, but I can't speak.)

"There's nothing left of my parents' house," said Peppi. "I never went back to Vienna. After the war my mother came to Marienbad, with one suitcase. That was all. With her clothes, a couple of bundles. I asked her if she hadn't brought any photos of my father with her. 'Yes,' she said, 'but the military police confiscated all the letters and photos. Otherwise I wasn't allowed to leave Austria. They have to

make sure I'm not a Brown Shirt's widow, and then they're going to
send it all on. That's what they promised.'" His dumb, trusting
mother. Later he bought a sideboard for her – the piece of furniture
which now graced his own living room: a little later he'd inherited it
through her from himself. "She thought it looked like her wedding
present. That marriage buffet was our showpiece at home and, as far
as I'm concerned, this colossus is like it only because she thought so."

No, his mother's family came from Prague too. But his friend
Milan Zvěřina came from Marienbad and together the two of them
had journeyed through Germany's smouldering ruins to Bohemia, on
foot and with rides hitched with Russian convoys. Thanks to Milan
he'd found work here, in the factory where Maria had cooked in the
canteen. And just like Milan he joined the Communist Party which,
in February 1948, through its mouthpiece Klement Gottwald, would
proclaim the new situation of compulsory happiness – everyone had
then eagerly taken their places in the folk dance of all workers, everyone was *young* because everyone was reborn as a child of the Revolution. But their mother couldn't wait to get started on her infamous
feast, devouring the children she herself had borne.

"And Slávek's father?" asked my father. "Slávek told me he'd been
a dentist in the Sudetenland." (Where did you learn German, Father?
Come now, don't screw up your face like that. In Germany, Son,
in that pleasant language lab called the *Arbeitseinsatz*, forced labour.
Strange, that I've never heard you speaking German before, Father.
You once said that Hitler had destroyed the language's sound and
idiom just as much as he'd destroyed Germany itself. You, who so
loved Hölderlin and Roth, were horrified by the word *Reiseführer*,
weren't you? You're right, Son. But I'm also speaking a different
language, a dead German, that I learnt even longer ago, at the Marnix
Grammar School in Rotterdam. The words from then are now
regaining their meaning. And with every old-fashioned turn of phrase
Jiři Klat smiles in heaven, that classless society where everyone speaks
Latin. He smiles at Rudolf and Rudolf smiles back. Father, dear
Father, you're getting sentimental in your old age! And you're still
so young, my son, you haven't experienced anything. Do you understand it better if I say that he, for an instant, one breath long, for the
length of a word, is amongst us?)

"We waited for the Russians together in Germany," said Peppi.
"Milan, Jan and I. Jan went back to his Sudetenland, with the same
expectations as us. We all believed in communism. All of us. And we

wanted to believe in it up till the day that Khrushchev made the first disclosures about Stalin. We *couldn't* believe it. Milan and I spent a whole night walking through the city, talking, discussing it, arguing, everything. We had no idea where we were going, we didn't care either. Finally it was morning. We sat in the grass, next to one of those villas behind the bathhouse. There was nothing unusual about that morning at all, an ordinary dawn, birds . . . Except that Stalin was dead."

There was once a machine made up of millions of inspired little wheels, springs, ratchets. One day two of those tiny components changed into individuals, betrayed, now-useless idiots. It wasn't true that Peppi hadn't needed to remember anything of Marienbad: he needed to remember *this* about Mariánské Lázně, the disastrous, liberating moment in which the waiting started anew.

I looked at his face, that human face full of cracks. His mouth trembled and became my father's mouth, distorted into the universal smile of disillusion – it became the mouth Slávek had shown us in Prague when, standing between our bags waiting for a taxi that wasn't coming, he turned to us and said: "That's my whole life. Waiting." It became my own mouth.

SOMEWHERE IN GERMANY

At Cheb station the Czechs got in, youths with spiky hair under crooked caps. They checked our passports but could just as well have shrugged their shoulders. We entered Germany. I lay in the upper couchette, my crumpled clothes by my feet, and listened to the cadence of the wheels which was occasionally disturbed by the points. And I thought about the untold, the hole in Peppi's story which consumed every human noise. What else could he have said other than that he was not entered in the gigantic Teutonic book of the dead? There was nothing else to say. Tomorrow I could go to the cinema and see convincingly made-up actors and hear stereophonic reproductions of groans of pain, but the essence of it would still be silence. I could read hundreds of books and watch dozens of TV programmes, all about that same subject. But it was no subject. It was that about which I had to keep silent.

Rain. Germany. Night.

Someone slid the door open, turned on the light and said: "*Papiere.*" Damn it. My father was asleep. Where's my passport? I felt amongst my clothes. "Papa, wake up, the Czech gave it back to you." – "Where is it then? Oh, here." I bent over the edge. The German looked at a photo. I couldn't see which one of us it was.

"*Holländer*?"

Forty-four years and one second passed.

"*Servus*," said my father.

Translated from the Dutch by David Colmer

PAOLA CAPRIOLO

The Giant

20 MAY

A long journey, but not tiring. Little Ottaviano slept the whole time, curled up on the seat of the coach, his head resting on Adele's knees.

We spoke quietly so as not to wake him. She seemed worried and kept questioning me about the prisoner, but all I remembered was the odd rumour I'd heard as a child – a jumble of rumours and veiled silences, which long nourished my childhood fantasy to create a blurred, terrifying picture.

The surrounding landscape was becoming more desolate, the villages few and far between. The placid geometry of the fields and vineyards gave way to moorland that clad the rolling countryside in a vesture of grey-green, interrupted here and there by the dusty purple of the heather. Mild spring sunshine, barely concealed by the odd cloud, played over the scene.

Then came the last of the moorland, and we found ourselves on the edge of a vast square area of beaten earth. At its centre stood the prison. We saw only its façade, a long blind wall of red brick, crowned at each end by a pair of guard towers.

A dark look from Adele: "He must have blackened himself with the most horrendous crimes to deserve such a punishment."

These words woke Ottaviano. He got straight up to kneel on the seat and look out of the window at the distant figures of the soldiers patrolling the area. I watched them, too, gratified by the almost mechanical precision of their movements, and considered that taking command of such well-trained men would be an easy task.

A mounted picket came to meet us and escorted us to the prison. We passed through the main entrance with its iron gates which closed at once behind us. Found ourselves in a sweeping rectangular courtyard.

Left our coach. The soldiers unloaded the few pieces of luggage we had brought with us and piled them in front of a door giving on to one of the short sides of the building, on the left as one looked at the façade. Noticed that the ground floor on the right-hand side was completely bricked up, while the windows of the floor above were closed with great iron bars, and had frosted panes to conceal the interior.

"Is that where he is?" I asked one of the soldiers.

"Yes, sir. Right opposite your quarters."

"So from some rooms we'll have a view of the prison."

"From every room, sir. The building has no windows looking outwards."

Adele laid a hand on my arm. Preceded by the soldier, we crossed the threshold on the left side, and went up a staircase leading to our quarters.

These consist of a series of rooms, including a big drawing room, connected along the back by an endless corridor. They all look on to the courtyard, as the soldier had said, exactly opposite the prisoner's windows.

Ottaviano ran happily from room to room, while Adele looked in dismay at the bareness of the place, with its forbidding architecture. Three camp-beds had been set up here, together with an old table and the odd non-matching chair.

"Don't worry," I told her. "When our furniture arrives, the place won't know itself."

She looked about her now with an alert, probing expression. "Here's where we'll put the piano, in the drawing room . . ."

Followed her as she passed the rooms in review. To me they seemed perfectly identical, but Adele, on the basis perhaps of recondite signs that none but she could recognize, established with absolute certainty which was to be my study, which the bedroom, which the guest-room, "for when cousin Teresa comes with her husband". And, the plans thus defined, those vivid pictures now being projected on our quarters by her own imagination contrived somehow or other to communicate themselves to me as well: I was now seeing everything as if each element was in place, and what had been so bare and alien gradually turned into the cosiest of domestic interiors.

At sundown Adele and Ottaviano went to bed, exhausted, and I stayed alone in the drawing room. A tenuous glow emanated from the windows opposite.

Rang the bell; after a moment a soldier appeared, a timid-looking lad; there was something incongruous about the pink peasant face atop that uniform.

Told him to bring me paper and pen, and on his return I sat at the old table and wrote a short note to greet the prisoner and advise him that as from today he was entrusted to my custody. I gave it to the soldier to deliver.

Have just received the answer, if such it may be called. Just a single line, no signature, written in large characters by a feeble hand: "Is there still a world, out there?"

25 MAY

Have made a tour of the entire building, or of as much of it as may be seen. The offices, kitchens and soldiers' quarters are at the front, while the ground floor opposite houses the stables. A staircase leads up to the first floor, a row of twelve empty rooms, each one with an iron door secured on the outside by a great bolt. The last door gives on to the prison proper, and is sealed shut. Beside it there's a turntable, the kind used in convents, and the soldiers use it to pass food, water and whatever else he needs to the prisoner. It seems no one has ever heard his voice.

The prison windows are the same as our own, long rectangles, each one surmounted by a half-moon transom, but unlike ours they cannot be opened, and they don't permit us to look in, nor the prisoner to look out. To change the air, or during the dog-days, he can open the transoms with the aid of a long pole capped with a hook. He's been living that way for decades, the invisible man, secluded in those rooms.

The cart has not yet arrived, and Adele's missing her things, not least the piano. She has to run the household single-handed, without Angelica to help, and doesn't take kindly to this unaccustomed labour. She says not a word, doesn't complain, but there's often a hint of dejection in her look. Not surprising: without any furniture there's nothing home-like about our quarters – they look more like the depressing dormitories where the men lodge. Outside there's nothing but the dreary view of the courtyard, crossed at intervals by the regular step of the soldiers, or the no less regular clip-clop of horses' hooves. Nothing to soften the austere lines of the building or to mitigate its rigorous symmetry. And I haven't the time, as I'd wish, to take Adele out on walks beyond the esplanade, along the paths that furrow the moors, or into one of the neighbouring villages which seemed to me so close at hand as we arrived.

Sometimes at night I wake with a start and see Adele sitting up in bed, her eyes staring into the darkness. She smiles at me, I smile back, and I remember the prisoner's words: "Is there still a world, out there?"

28 MAY

On Monday the wagon finally arrived, bringing us the furniture and, with it, our sturdy Angelica.

The horses had not yet come to a stop before she leapt to the ground and ran to her mistress. "Ah, ma'am," said she, grasping her hands, "are we really to live here, with that demon? Weren't we better off where we were?"

Adele smiled and tried to reassure her, but all to no purpose: the maid seemed quite petrified at the notion of living "with that demon", about whom, I'm ready to wager, she doesn't know the first thing.

"What a horrid place, ma'am," she kept repeating. "If I were the captain I'd ask for a transfer at once."

"Men have their reasons, Angelica, which we cannot always understand."

"Of course, ma'am, but by your leave, we women have ours too. A person like you, so young, so refined, forced to live in this desert, miles from everything . . ."

"You're not to distress yourself on my account. I'm content, believe me, and you'll get used to it soon enough. Come, I'll show you our quarters."

I stopped to watch the gracious figure of Adele climbing the stairs followed by the maid. I ask myself if I've really done the right thing, bringing her to this place, wrenching her from her women-friends, from the concerts, from the thousand familiar habits, great and small, which determine a woman's life. "I'm content," she says, but she does miss it all – else she wouldn't be looking forward so impatiently to Teresa's visit. Besides, looked at from down here, in this solitude, men's reasons, mine, those of my superiors, seem to me remote, incomprehensible, like the tunes Adele sketches out on the piano in the evening, in the big drawing room. Suddenly I can no longer imagine why I've come, whatever induced me to accept the posting. I've no idea where I am, nor who is the invisible prisoner in my charge. I sent him further notes, but obtained no reply; without that brief sentence that reached me the first evening I might perhaps be

asking myself whether there really was anyone behind the barred
windows, whether there was a man, or only some incubus forgotten
from my childhood nights.

It's impossible to discover anything about him. In vain did I question the soldiers, in vain did I rummage through the prison archives
in search of the name, or a portrait: nothing refers back to what
happened then, in that stormy era preceding his capture, and the
documents and reports list him simply as "the prisoner" – a vague,
abstract form of words which has nonetheless assumed in my eyes a
strange precision, a concreteness I'd be hard put to define.

"The prisoner", or "He", or "the man", is the hidden centre around
which this enormous edifice has been raised. For him it was constructed and it's due to be pulled down the day he dies. On that day
the seals will finally be removed, the door opened and those present
will be able to behold the corpse.

Some evenings, for no particular reason, I walk through the series
of rooms, drawing the twelve bolts one after the other, until I reach
the prisoner's door. Then, for no reason, I turn back.

30 MAY

A serene day, today, a consecration of our new home, as it were. An
aura of solemnity now vests our newly rediscovered rhythm of life,
which has lost none of its old charm. Adele's quiet activity, Ottaviano
at play, the old maidservant's constant bustle, every action a taking
possession, extending our ownership to those alien surroundings.

Papers, tableware, items of furniture, so many things still boxed
up in the wooden crates, but here and there we have the odd corner,
the odd detail that reminds us of our accustomed life, and the home
we left comes slowly back to life under our eyes.

The women are busy setting the place to rights and turn their eyes
less and less across to the frosted windows of the opposite block; I,
too, momentarily forget my anxiety, in their company.

A letter this morning from cousin Teresa, to confirm her impending
visit: she's coming in July, with her husband and her mother-in-law.
Adele highly pleased.

Angelica asks me to detail a soldier to escort her to the neighbouring village to shop. It seems no one has a strong wish to go "out
yonder". Entrusted the duty to Gaspare, the rustic-faced lad, and off
the two went in the trap.

On her return, Angelica took me aside. "An odd type, that Gaspare, sir. A young lad like him, in good health, I'd have thought he'd have a girl in the village, as soldiers usually do. But instead of going off after her, he stayed with me the whole time, tied to my apron-strings. He looked like a frightened child."

I shrugged. I take no particular interest in Gaspare, and his love-life leaves me even more indifferent.

So all in all, a quiet day, pretty uneventful.

Forgot to mention a strange fancy of Ottaviano. He's come in at night to inform us that he's seen a giant at one of the windows opposite – a great black giant with a beast perched on one shoulder. Must be a monkey, says he, or perhaps a parrot, and to show what he means he pats his little hand on his left shoulder.

2 JUNE

There still is a world out there, peopled with plants and animals, pervaded with the odours of spring, as I've had the means to establish this morning, on finally being able to take Adele and Ottaviano out on to the moors.

The child would occasionally slip his hand from his mother's grasp and set off running and skipping. Then Adele would give her skirt a slight hitch and hasten after him; she'd clasp him to herself and lift him right up in her arms. There's not a prettier sight in the world than this sort of dance they performed as they pursued each other along the paths, losing and finding each other; they made burgeoning Nature the chosen companion and accomplice in their games.

Never had Adele looked to me so youthful – a tranquil, recollected youthfulness whose vital forces didn't run riot but settled into a fragile harmony. Her gracefulness, the childlike abandon evident in her every gesture, created an impression of evanescence which, far from tarnishing its splendour, enhanced it, and if my joy in contemplating her was blended with a fleeting sadness, this made it only the sweeter.

This spell of youth, I could see it passing within her like the enchantment of spring, only to evaporate with the passage of the seasons. I imagined grey hair rather than brown framing her features, but however hard I tried, I could not imagine the lineaments other than they are, so I came to picture her quite bizarrely as a young girl with grey hair, and the old age which I felt encroaching on her seemed to me unreal, spurious, like an actress's make-up.

Adele eventually tired of running, and Ottaviano panted, his cheeks flushed. So we sat down on a mossy boulder to rest, in a patch clear of scrub. The child stretched out on the grass at our feet and asked his mother to tell him a story.

"Once upon a time there was a most beautiful maiden," she began, "who sat on the top of a rock, by a river's edge. She combed her golden tresses with a golden comb, and all the while she sang a song."

But Ottaviano interrupted her. "No, I don't like that story. I want the one about the giant, the black giant with the monkey on his shoulder."

"My son," said I with a chuckle, "there is no story about the black giant."

"What? No story about him?"

"Not that I know of."

Ottaviano seemed upset. "And we?" he asked, a slight quaver in his voice. "Do we have a story?"

As I hesitated to answer, he burst into floods of tears. "We don't have a story," he repeated between sobs, as if he had learnt on a sudden that he belonged to an inferior rank in the scale of beings.

Adele stooped down to caress him. "Don't cry," she murmured, "we all have a story. However, we cannot know ours, only those of other people."

Ottaviano's sobs became ever more plaintive, while his mother continued to cuddle him. "The maiden combed her golden tresses, and all the while she sang a song. Her song had a strange melody, mysterious and powerful . . ."

Little by little, lulled by Adele's words, the child drowsed off. We looked each other in the eye and burst out laughing, but softly, so as not to waken him.

7 JUNE

A grey sky. It's been a thin, continuous drizzle for the last three days with no sign of stopping. The walk on the moors seems ages ago now and so does the sense of freedom we'd been breathing.

The bad weather keeps Adele confined to our quarters. She sometimes plays the piano, but not even music seems to afford her much joy any more. Perhaps because she has no one to share it with, this passion of hers becomes wearisome, like those longstanding friendships which only habit prevents one from breaking off. She plays out of boredom, not out of passion. Beneath her fingers the notes run out listlessly, and seem to obey the laws of some blind mechanism devoid of any goal, just like the rain beating on the window-panes.

Nothing would change in a person's physiognomy, in the features of a face, if the sustaining spirit suddenly took its leave, and in the same way nothing has changed in Adele's performance. But the spirit's gone out of it: the absence is evident even to my untutored ears, and the child, who used to stop playing when his mother was at the piano, to listen to her spellbound, now carries on with his game regardless; he seems not even to hear the piano.

Crossing the courtyard this morning, I looked at the windows of both apartments, the one on the right and the one on the left, and I couldn't help thinking of my wife as the second prisoner in this jail.

It cannot go on like this. I went upstairs and suggested to her that she take Ottaviano and go to spend a week at her mother's. Being back in town is sure to do her good. She'll have a lovely time and when she's back, before she can start drooping again, Teresa's visit will come to raise her spirits. But then what, once Teresa has gone?

9 JUNE

The mystery of the giant with the monkey on his shoulder has finally been revealed. Yesterday evening, as I was sitting at the desk sorting through my papers, I chanced to raise my eyes towards the window, and I saw across the way, projected on to the window-panes, the shadow of the prisoner.

It is gigantic, as Ottaviano affirms, and there is indeed something on his left shoulder. Realized at once it was not a question of some exotic beast, but more simply of a violin. The prisoner was standing at the window, playing the violin.

Called Adele, and we spent a long time watching the rapid movements of his right arm. Then we saw the black line of the bow detach itself from the instrument and lift up to hover for a second; I tried to imagine the sudden silence that must have descended on the room, a shadow or maybe penumbra illuminated still by the echo of the last note.

The bow dropped once and the movement of the arm resumed, but slowly. The elbow moved continually to and fro in a motion reminiscent of regular breathing, or of a sea barely ruffled.

Adele looked on, fascinated. "It's the Adagio," she murmured in a

hushed voice, as if she feared that in talking she would disturb that
music as it evolved beyond our hearing. Her attitude remained one
of respectful attention, and from time to time she laid her hands on
her forehead, as she often does when listening to a concert. I found
her gesture profoundly moving for all its absurdity, or perhaps because
it *was* absurd. Thus it is that people will often feel a sense of ambiva-
lence, if they're used to shaping their lives on the basis of the dictates
of reason, when they observe the meaningless actions of a child or an
animal: they'll feel pity and respect in equal measure, as at the
expression of a higher nobility, an innocence which has been lost in
us.

Meanwhile little Ottaviano came into the room, unnoticed by
Adele, who gave a start on finding him suddenly beside her.

I took him in my arms so that he could look out, and I explained
to him that the black giant was really the shadow of a man, and that
what he had on his shoulder was not a monkey but a violin.

He observed the black figure in perplexity.

"If it's a violin," he finally said, "it must be a magic violin." And
he returned to bed, satisfied with this conclusion.

13 JUNE

My mother-in-law's answer has arrived, saying that she is ready to
accommodate her daughter next week. Adele barely glanced at the
letter. She is distrait, absorbed in her own thoughts, and leaves it to
Angelica to take care of the preparations.

She spends hours seated at the piano, but instead of the usual
pieces, she plays short passages left incomplete, or enjoys herself
inventing chords which she holds sustained with the pedal, and then
leaves them to die gradually away. She seems all of a sudden to have
quite lost her confidence with this instrument, her companion ever
since her childhood, the vehicle of innocent habits and carefree
recreation. She approaches it with a strange disquiet, and, more than
playing, she seems to be auscultating it, to be expecting some revelation from it; every time she rests her fingers on the keyboard it's as
if she were formulating a question, a timid, hesitant question that
obtains no reply.

I wish she would gird herself up to play a piece, any piece, from
start to finish, or give up the piano altogether.

Outside it continues to rain. Each evening, at the window opposite,

the shadow of the prisoner appears with his violin, and each evening
it seems to me bigger than I remembered it.

16 JUNE

Only a few days to go until Adele's departure, fixed for the
twenty-third.

The weather has improved, and this morning I suggested to her
that we go out for a walk. "I've got too much to do," she answered.
But the trunks are still in the cellar, the clothes in the wardrobes, and
when Angelica comes to ask her for instructions she replies with a
touch of impatience.

Eventually, in the late afternoon, I contrived to persuade her.
Ottaviano stayed back with the maid, and the pair of us walked alone,
side by side. Adele was plunged in her thoughts, heedless of her
surroundings. We reached the edge of the esplanade, where the moorland begins. Adele turned to look at the prison, a great dark mass
which stood out against the light of the evening sky. "It's cold, we'd
better go back in."

"It's a splendid evening," I protested, and offered her my uniform
jacket to cover her shoulders. But she refused, and I had to take her
back.

We found the child busy telling Angelica a very complicated story
he'd invented: the protagonists were an all-black giant and a magic
violin.

When he saw us, he broke off to ask what a violin was. Our ex-
planations disappointed him. "So it isn't an animal? It's a dead thing?"

"It's a wooden thing, Ottaviano. Like this table, like your rocking
horse."

"But perhaps my giant's one is different."

"Please yourself," said I, laughing.

He turned back to Angelica. "Once upon a time there was a giant
who pretended to be the shadow of a man, and on his shoulder he
had a monkey which pretended to be a violin . . ."

20 JUNE

Spring has now given place to the first heat of summer, and in the
clear light things stand out in sharper relief. The sun sets late, slowly:
a chain of colours that merge, the one into the other, with the most

delicate nuances linking day to night, as in those word-games in which you change one letter at a time to arrive at another word that means the opposite.

Yesterday evening the drawing room was still illuminated after supper with a purple light. Adele, seated across from me, attended with no great application to a piece of embroidery begun some time back. She was wearing a light cotton dress which left her arms bare from the elbows, but the heat was so stifling that we could not shut the windows.

In the building opposite the transoms were open too, and with the twilight, when the shadow appeared on the window-panes, we heard for the first time the sound of the violin. It came to us distinctly across the silence of the courtyard.

Adele laid down the embroidery and closed her eyes the better to listen to that distant melody. It was a playful *cantabile* that suggested a dance. "How can someone of his sort play so well?" she murmured.

"It is indeed strange. This music expresses such a simplicity, such a childlike purity . . ."

"Or perhaps a longing for these. Listen closer: can't you hear something murky, aching?"

That playful motif did in fact keep disappearing into a series of dark notes, whence it would re-emerge, each time that much less intimate, more charged with yearning, a frail skiff, laden with memories, sailing the black waters of the Styx.

"Who's that piece by? Do you recognize it?" I asked.

She didn't answer. She seemed to be gradually sinking into the extreme languor that emanated from the music. Her face was expressionless, her body inert. Only her hands, resting on the armrests, traced the path of the music with a barely perceptible movement.

26 JUNE

Adele wouldn't go – not that there was any further need to: she's found her feet now, and recovered her serenity. In fact I have the impression that in the solitude of this place our union has become deeper and stronger: an unhoped-for stroke of fortune, which I owe to the prisoner and the sound of his violin, which every evening Adele and I listen to together, sitting side by side in the semi-darkness of the drawing room.

That music becomes daily more precious to me. It's as if at the very moment of experiencing it the music gave us a reflection of our happiness which had receded to a distant memory; and as I listen to it I'm seized by a strange paradoxical sensation, almost a nostalgia for the present.

Adele too has gone back to playing some pieces, but only when I'm not around. I hear her from the courtyard or from the open windows of my office. That way she is present through those sounds even when I have to leave her: she accompanies the various duties to which I am constrained each day, and which sometimes seem to me to have the single purpose of banishing me from her presence, thus affording me the pleasure of finding her again.

And perhaps the prison, the guard towers, the thick windowless walls, perhaps all of this exists only to remove us from the world and permit our lives to flow undisturbed, protected by the squads of soldiers that patrol the building.

1 JULY

In a week Teresa and her family will be arriving. A letter came this morning with the announcement; among other things it informed Adele that "those purchases" had been made for her.

"I didn't know you'd written to your cousin. What purchases, anyway? What's it all about?"

"Nothing of consequence."

"Tell me, darling, I promise not to scold. You have every right to buy yourself something chic every now and then, and you know I like to see you looking smart."

Adele smiled. "You'll have to get used to seeing me the way I am, at least for a while."

"I ask for nothing better. And yet I am not convinced: you're hiding something from me, you're preparing me some surprise . . ."

"It's almost lunchtime. I'm going to have the table set."

So our idyll will soon be at an end. This isolated existence of ours, which at the start aroused in me a sense of anguish, seems to me now perfectly normal, and I cannot but feel a little put out at the prospect of a visit. Adele seems cross too, but consoles herself with the thought that Ottaviano and I will be able to take our guests out on to the moors and spend long afternoons with them in the open air.

"At least you'll enjoy yourselves. The weather is so fine . . ."

"Won't you be coming?"

"Oh, I'll have things to do."

"But leaving you here all on your own . . ."

"I like being on my own."

"Without me?"

"I'll be able to get on with my things, play the piano . . ."

"I thought you played for me."

Adele went over to the window. "And him? D'you think he plays for someone? D'you think he knows we're listening?"

6 JULY

My wife seems to be a bundle of nerves. She's normally so sweet-tempered and kind with even the humblest of people, but she was so sharp with Angelica, she reduced her to tears; her reaction was abnormal and quite inexplicable.

Of course the maid shouldn't have interrupted while she was at the piano but, after all, there's more in this world than just music, and Adele has lately been all too negligent of her duties.

So she was sitting at the piano when Angelica, as she herself told me, came into the room. "I need instructions, ma'am, to get the guest-rooms ready."

She had to repeat this a second time because Adele did not so much as answer the first, so totally absorbed was she in the passage she was playing. Eventually she raised her eyes and, according to Angelica, she looked like a sleepwalker who'd just woken up, or "one of those people who speak with ghosts", as she imagined they must look if they're abruptly interrupted during their supernatural dialogues.

"What d'you want?" she said in a flat voice.

Angelica put her request for the third time.

"I'm busy now. You'll have to see to it yourself."

But the maid persisted. "I was thinking of putting flowers in the guest-rooms, ma'am. There are some very pretty ones on the moors."

"Good idea. Go and pick some."

"But ma'am, I'm too ignorant, I've no feeling for these things. You'd have to come with me."

"I'm busy, I tell you."

"Tomorrow perhaps, before they arrive . . ."

"Can't you see you're interrupting me?" Adele burst out in a temper. "Now be off with you, leave me in peace. I'm not interested in you or your flowers."

At this point in her story Angelica could not hold back her tears. "She never used to be like that, sir, never before. It's this confounded place, it's ruining her character."

"What rubbish! Anyway, you know perfectly well that when she's playing she's not to be disturbed."

This evening, though, I did feel it was my duty to scold my wife. She listened meekly.

"You're right," she finally conceded, "I treated the poor thing very badly. I'll try to be kinder in future."

"So will you go with her to pick the flowers?"

"No, I don't want to go out. She can do it perfectly well on her own."

8 JULY

Yesterday afternoon the guests arrived. Teresa made a point at once of informing us, in an excited tone, that the prison aroused in her "a sinister impression". She grasped Adele's hands sympathetically. "Well, my dear, how are you managing in this cloistered place? I could never put up with such a life. But you've always been so courageous."

Adele looked at her with a smile, part affectionate, part ironical.

"Anyway, I've brought you what you asked me for, and I hope it will serve to alleviate your boredom a little. To tell you the truth, though, I can't understand the object of these . . ."

"I'll explain later."

I've never been able to endure Teresa, with that woman-of-the-world façade of hers, but my wife is very fond of her, in view, I think, of their shared childhood. Who knows? Maybe the Teresa she knew in those days was different, one I cannot imagine, and it's with that recollected one she's keeping faith. Perhaps beneath those airs and graces, the girl of former times still subsists, just as in each one of us there is the kernel, the original nucleus, that the years obscure without being able to efface. And I've always noticed, seeing Adele with her cousin, that behind their apparent dialogue, made up of conventional set pieces, there's another one, a continuous, silent one, from which I'm excluded.

But yesterday, the moment the guests arrived and again during dinner, I had the clearest sense that this usual rapport was not being established. As a rule, in Teresa's company, Adele tended rather to grow into Teresa, unwittingly adopting something of her mannerisms, her inflexions. This time, though, she stood out from her in the fullest, most irreconcilable contrast of her own character. She spoke in a different key and paid scant attention to the news the other brought from town. Even her discreet, delicate beauty was totally at odds with her cousin's flamboyant good looks, to which her beauty was normally a simple complement.

Scarcely was she upstairs than Teresa produced a package from a travel bag, and handed it to my wife, who hastened to take it to her own room.

I chatted idly with Oreste, a quiet, down-to-earth fellow whose personality, if he possesses such a thing, is not one of those that are readily identified. At first glance, everything points to the notion that he's merely a grey background to set off his wife's strident colours. It's easy to forget he's even there, and he in turn seems bent on hiding behind Teresa's endless chatter, to which he listens with a smile of timid complacency.

As for Oreste's mother, she's a little old woman with no longer a trace of individuality — it's been overlaid by the characteristics of her age, which are ruthlessly generic. Her mind is enfeebled, and her bluish eyelids, drooping beneath a continual somnolence, are never raised except to dart cautious and vaguely hostile glances about her. Oreste explained to me that they've brought her along because she can't be left on her own, as she can no longer look after herself.

In the evening, Adele sat by the drawing-room window and when she thought no one was watching she turned a furtive glance towards the building opposite. The prisoner's shadow stood out as usual on the frosted panes, but the sound of the violin was completely drowned by the voice of Teresa, who perhaps thought she was making conversation but was in fact indulging in a long monologue, interrupted at intervals by her husband's peaceable interjections or some bland one of my own.

13 JULY

Teresa has finally exhausted her baggage of news, and the urge to talk has given place to a wish for information. At lunch today she kept on questioning us about the prisoner.

"What? Can you really not see him? Get along with you, Eugenio, try another one! You must have been into his rooms at least once. You're in charge so they will have entrusted the key to you."

"The key's in my office, in a safe. But I couldn't have made use of it even if I'd wanted to; the prison entrance is sealed off."

The old woman roused herself from her torpor. "All to the good," she muttered. "Better no one should see him."

"Well, Mama, you remember? What can you tell us about that monster of a man?"

"I don't remember anything. Remembering is not a good thing."

Strident, nervous laughter from Teresa. "She keeps stirring up our curiosity this way. I'll confess, though, I've always had a weakness for grisly tales."

At this point Adele, who had found the conversation irritating, got up from the table. "Excuse me, I have some instructions to give in the kitchen."

But before she could leave the room, the old woman took up again: "It was like a chasm. An enormous chasm that had suddenly opened up."

Teresa clapped her hands enthusiastically. "Well done, Mama, that's a really fine start, it's worthy of a novel. But if you don't mind my saying, you're being a bit vague. Come on, tell us something more . . ."

But the old woman's eyelids had drooped again and her breathing was becoming heavier.

Teresa turned back to me. "You must have an archive in this prison; there'll be documents."

"What makes you so interested?" asked Adele, and I hoped that her cousin would not notice the shortness, almost the rudeness, with which she said this.

I have to say that I too found Teresa's curiosity irritating. I saw her questions as a violation of our intimacy, an essential ingredient of which was the secret kept close behind the barred windows. We've been living in contact with it for some time, and though this proximity's been no help towards its exposure, it does make us in a way accessories. I feel bound to protect it from the encroachments of outsiders, people from "out yonder", even though I'm as ignorant as they are of what it is in effect I'm protecting. If I scrutinize this feeling with Teresa's eyes, or with Oreste's, it seems to me absurd, but their eyes are no longer ours: something's happened these past weeks, a

change whose implications I'm only beginning to weigh. The threads
that bound us to our previous life have snapped without our even
noticing and some obscure bond has replaced them.

16 JULY

Took the guests out for a walk this morning. Oreste went ahead with
the child, while I gave my arm to Teresa. We walked more slowly
and soon lost sight of our companions.

Thought back to that spring day, shortly after our arrival, when I
took Adele and Ottaviano on to the moors for the first time; compar-
ing that memory with all that now surrounded me, the contrast was
a disappointment at every turn. Nature in its high-summer bloom
seemed to flaunt itself in comparison with the subdued, suggestive
enchantment of its first flowering; such too was Teresa's brazen, pre-
tentious glamour next to Adele's unaffected charm. My mind would
conjure up the hasty errands Adele used to run, the occasional loss
of energy to which she would tenderly succumb, and contrast these
with her cousin's measured advance; and Adele's soothing voice, like
the echo of a purer world, blended distantly into our conversation –
a voice which told the child stories of artless spells.

I was sorry that she had refused to come with us on our walk: after
all, Oreste's mother could have stayed on her own for an hour or
two, with the maid to look after her. But Adele would not hear of
it; she'd insisted on staying behind, alleging her duties as hostess.

"Tell me, dear cousin," said Teresa suddenly, jolting me out of my
thoughts, "tell me what's the matter."

"Nothing. Why d'you ask?"

"Oh, no particular reason. There's something odd about Adele,
that's all. Something's changed. I've not managed to have a proper
tête-à-tête with her since I arrived – almost as if she's avoiding me."

"Nonsense. On the contrary, she's thrilled with your visit."

"D'you think so?"

"Of course. She's simply a bit tired. With us, too, she sometimes
behaves oddly."

Teresa's face lit up with a malicious smile. "I've got it. And you,
you never told us a thing, you naughty man!"

"What was I supposed to tell you?"

"Get on with you! I'm a married woman, too."

"Honestly, Teresa, I don't follow you."

She threw a questioning glance at me. "Either you're a seasoned liar, or Adele hasn't yet told you."

"Be good enough to explain yourself, dear cousin."

She put her lips to my ear. "Believe you me, I'm an expert in these matters: Ottaviano will shortly have a little brother."

I don't know why, but the conjecture struck me at once as absurd. Not that there was in fact anything to prevent it, and indeed many things would thus receive their most logical explanation; and yet I'm unable to believe that a new life can be brought to birth down here, inside the prison walls. I think back over the days we have spent here, and to the elegiac sweetness indissolubly woven into the melodies of the violin, and I detect an element of insanity, of unreality, which denies any hope of fecundity.

I did not of course share my scepticism with Teresa. "Should I have news in that direction," I limited myself to replying, "you will be the first to be informed."

"Bear in mind, this time I want to be the godmother, otherwise I'll be mortally offended."

Why is it that this all seems to me so unspeakably vulgar?

21 JULY

The custody of the prison is regulated by an iron mechanism. The soldiers are divided into two groups of ten, each group serving for about one year, after which it is posted elsewhere. The dates of arrival and departure of the two groups do not coincide, so that at every moment new elements blend with others already familiar with the place. Thus is continuity assured, at the same time relieving the men, which should avoid the pernicious effects of too prolonged an isolation.

Yesterday I received the order for the transfer of the first group, and signed it at once. Departure fixed for today. Called those involved into my office; they received the news with something like dismay. The most stunned was Gaspare, who seemed at first quite simply not to grasp my drift, and had his fellows repeat it all to him several times. "Tomorrow?" he asked wide-eyed. "For good?"

This morning, as he climbed into the wagon, a few tears bathed his pink cheeks, which Teresa found amusing – she'd come to watch the departure.

"Come along, boy," she told him with a chuckle, "there's no reason to take on so. Indeed, in your place I'd be only too happy to leave this prison."

"Yes, ma'am, but you see . . . I've grown used to it."

"You won't take long to grow unused to it: the world offers many consolations, especially when one is young."

Gaspare looked obtuse as he listened. "I'd got used to being here," he repeated.

Teresa shrugged and moved away from the wagon. "That young man does have a thick head," she said to me. "Peasants – they're all like that: they put down roots, never mind where. I hope that at any rate you won't weep when you can finally return to town."

I smiled, but deep down was sorry I'd been unable to protect that young peasant's wretchedness from Teresa's glint of sarcasm. She can have no idea how far the city is for us, how hard for us to believe in the idea of returning to it. It's as if we had been here forever and were destined to remain here forever, and this is certainly how it would have appeared to Gaspare.

I feel a sudden urge to leave too, to take Adele away, and the child. Only now, seeing her next to Teresa, do I notice my wife's pallor and remember that it's almost three weeks since she last set foot outside the prison. But there's no persuading her to go out: any proposal to that effect makes her strangely apprehensive, a bit as it does with Gaspare, and I too am happy enough to stay within these walls. Sometimes I feel I'm under the influence of one of those mild but insidious poisons that invade our organism and little by little take it over, replacing sound health with a deceptive sense of wellbeing, a pleasure mixed with revulsion, which one can no longer do without.

I ought to react, put in for leave, conquer the inertia that holds me confined here. Or at least I should find the strength to send Adele away: she ought to leave, go back to town, to her mother's or to Teresa's. We often speak of it, and the guests too invite her to come and stay, but she puts into her refusal an unexpected vehemence which contrasts with the indolence, with the now chronic apathy that seems to possess her.

None of this worries Teresa, who sees in it a blindingly obvious confirmation of her theory. "Women in that condition often become obstinate," she tells me with the supercilious air of one explaining to a novice the first rudiments of her own science. She scrupulously observes all her cousin's oddities and reports them to me in a tone of amused compassion.

28 JULY

The guests have decided to suspend their visit, which was supposed to continue until the first days of autumn. Find it difficult to pretend regret; Adele does not even try. The company of strangers depresses her, as solitude used to do, whereas now this seems to attract her irresistibly. She awaits it anxiously, tensely. She does all she can to help Teresa pack her bags, and Teresa thanks her, surprised at her cousin's solicitude. I read in it, however, the measure of her impatience.

There has always been in Adele a propensity to isolate herself, a contemplative disposition, but only down here have these vague tendencies fully revealed themselves. She is little by little freeing herself from the external, the incidental, to disclose the authentic nucleus of her personality.

As though obeying a command of nature she rejects out of hand everything that might obstruct such a process, and to this category Teresa's visit is certainly to be ascribed. Her cousin's departure seems to me a victory of Adele's, or of the tenacious will that possesses and guides her towards an outcome I cannot yet imagine.

31 JULY

This evening after the guests had gone, I was in my office attending to my correspondence, and heard once again, after so long, the prisoner's violin.

He was playing a slow melody. It possessed the same ambiguous simplicity, the same melancholy grace that had enthralled us night after night before Teresa's arrival. To the natural enchantment of those sounds was now added the pleasure of rediscovering an old habit.

But the violin was all of a sudden answered by a piano, which took up the theme with its pure, liquid voice.

Left my papers and went into the drawing room. Adele was seated at the instrument, so absorbed as not to be aware of my presence. She kept her eyes fixed on the music and her playing had that tentative, slightly mechanical approach that's perhaps inevitable when one addresses an unfamiliar piece. But the violin was guiding her along that arduous path, with which she was unacquainted, and she followed meekly in its footsteps.

She repeated the theme with a light touch, while from afar, from

the open windows, there came deep, mournful sounds, like the breathing of a titan shut up in the bowels of the earth. Then Adele's hands
moved to the left-hand side of the keyboard, and it was her turn to
spread a carpet of shadow beneath the violin's limpid tune, which
imparted to the theme a faster, whirling pace, charging its sweetness
with a note of desperation.

The melody lost itself in a series of complicated variations, and
only recovered its outline for a second at the end, an outline remote
and fleeting, like images in the memory. Then it faded out in the long
final chord sustained by the two instruments.

When the music was ended, Adele sat motionless at the piano. In
the room silence reigned.

I approached and flipped through the score in search of the title
page. It was a sonata for violin and piano, the work of a composer
whom till now I knew only by reputation. I asked myself how she
obtained it, and suddenly remembered the mysterious package
brought by Teresa.

And yet, I still fail to understand. I don't understand what secret
correspondence, or what trick of fate, could have brought Adele and
the prisoner to play the same piece, and how they could play together
without ever having exchanged a word.

Adele replies evasively to my questions. "It just happened that
way," she'll say, and the matter doesn't seem to surprise her in the
least. As I write she has not yet gone to bed: she continues to study
the score by candlelight.

3 AUGUST

Adele and the prisoner have moved on from the Adagio to the first
movement of the sonata, which is far more extended and complex,
composed as it is of two themes which seem for a long time to elude
each other, only to find in each other their eventual fulfilment. I
have christened the themes Apollo and Daphne, but Daphne, after
wandering restlessly from the piano to the violin, undergoing the
most varied metamorphoses, eventually concedes to Apollo the soft
embrace of her foliage, tempering the god's ardent passion in tender
wistfulness.

Thus do I strive in my own way to interpret a language I cannot
understand, aware though I am that it doesn't need the support of
such images – only I do. Apollo is not Apollo, Daphne is not Daphne,

those musical figures have nothing to do with the love of the god for the nymph, and in the embrace that unites them at the end are no bodies, no members, no laurel branches. Each time, at the end of my poetic musings, my allegorical play, I realize that I've not moved a single step closer to that inaccessible force which reposes in self-fulfilment, as though it possessed nothing outside of itself.

My little musical fable has not tickled even Ottaviano. "Why don't you teach me the violin instead?" said he. "That way I can play with Mama."

But I have nothing to teach him, and Mama seems to be totally oblivious of him. She lives in the world of sounds, where she blends her solitude with that of the prisoner.

7 AUGUST

Impossible to speak with Adele: by day she studies, in the evening she and the prisoner play, always those two movements, which she now executes with perfect confidence.

Ottaviano listens from his bed. "Mama's never played so well. Is it the giant who's taught her?"

I don't know whether it's been the giant, but Adele's style has certainly changed. It cannot be said, as once upon a time, that she plays nicely. There is indeed something painful in listening to her, something almost disturbing: I feel as if every cord of my being has been set vibrating one at a time, from the happiest ones to those that are tender, shadowed. Once, hearing the opaque dialogue of the piano and violin, I thought that those were the conversations the Fates must hold as they spin the threads of human destiny, and I asked myself what on earth "the giant" could be slowly imparting to my wife – was it a sonata or the secrets of the universe? For if the essence of the world possesses a tongue, it is comprised not of words but of silences and of notes of music. Therefore as I watch Adele playing, I feel a sense of veneration, as a profane man before a priestess.

10 AUGUST

Yesterday a letter from Teresa, addressed to both of us: thanks us for our "exquisite hospitality", and expresses her regret at having had to leave before the appointed time. The letter ends with these words: "I am expecting from you, very soon, glad tidings."

"What does she mean?" asked Adele with a frown.

"I don't really know," I lied. There's no point speaking to her about her cousin's fancies, least of all now while her mind is occupied with quite different thoughts.

"Eugenio, please write a reply."

"What am I to write?"

"Anything you like."

"I'll tell her that you're thrilled with her scores, that you do nothing but play them over."

"Why?" she retorted drily. "What's Teresa got to do with it?"

I was surprised. "Just as you think, darling. If you don't want her to know . . ."

"Whether she knows or not is a matter of utter indifference to me."

"In that case, why lose your temper?"

"Lose my temper?" She came up and gave me a peck on the cheek: an absent, hasty gesture, not so much an expression of affection as an attempt to reassure me that this still existed.

Dreamed last night that I was sitting for hours in a little bare room, waiting before a closed door. Eventually the doors opened, allowing a glimpse of Teresa. She was dressed in white and was pressing her forefinger to her smiling lips. She signed to me to follow her, and on tiptoe guided me across the threshold.

I found myself in Adele's bedroom. The curtains were drawn, and in the half-darkness I barely descried the big bed in which she was lying, her face as pale as could be, her brown hair loose on the pillow. Beneath the covers one could divine, next to her body, a smaller frame, as of a baby she was clasping to her breast.

I spoke to her, but she looked at me without answering. It was Teresa who told me to draw near.

I approached the bed and delicately drew back the covers. In her arms, lying tenderly against her breast, Adele was holding a violin.

13 AUGUST

The sonata is finally completed: this evening they've played through the whole of it for the first time, and I as usual have stayed to listen, a fascinated outcast.

After the boisterous sport of the first movement the music goes on to weep for itself in the self-absorption of the Adagio; it laments over a wound of which I know nothing, and yet I seem to feel it in my own heart as I listen. Never would I have believed that there could be so intimate a connection between suffering and solace, that they could belong to each other, making as it were the two sides of the same coin. Their bond is so subtle, their confines so finely discriminated, so imperceptible, it is impossible to grasp where the one finishes and the other begins.

Then the Scherzo explodes like a carefree dance seen through a veil of sadness, and it reminds one of youth perceived through an old man's eyes. With a lively, clear-cut rhythm, piano and violin take it in turns to pursue this phantom of a lost joy which, in the central, more rarefied section, seems to let itself finally be captured, only to reveal its own unreality. Then it again takes flight and the illusion begins all over.

In the final movement a serene, majestic motif returns, entrusted now to one instrument now to the other, after various meanders which each time overrun the fragile equilibrium, dissolving its limpid and precise shape into a thousand restless streams through which there steals a suppressed anguish. At the conclusion the principal theme restores the note of triumph, but it is as if the laurel leaves already looked withered on the victor's brow.

I continue to experience each proposition of that enigmatic discourse, which has no object and yet describes one with a precision not available to any other language; and feel as if I've approached the sacred book of some paradoxical religion, in which the unknown name of an absent deity is set down in every conceivable way.

18 AUGUST

Captain B., commandant of the *** Barracks, has written to enquire about the conduct of Gaspare during his tour at this prison. It seems he has deserted. One morning at reveille his room-mates found his bed still made, and his uniform gone, together with the few objects he kept on his bedside cupboard: a wooden pipe, his little baptismal chain and a portrait of his mother painted on an oval panel by some rustic artist. He had left behind only his weapons, piled at the foot of the bed.

They're looking for him all over the place and they'll find him soon enough. I think with pity of that poor young man. His actions, his reactions, were guided by a naive, almost brute instinct, and this very immediacy made him quite difficult for us to understand; we are so much more evolved and complicated, accustomed as we are to perceiving the essentials in others – and in ourselves – through the norms to which we have been educated, and blind, perhaps irredeemably, to whatever does not correspond to these. All the time we spent together, the only thing I understood in him was that look of bewilderment and dismay he cast about him as he took in the prison walls before he climbed into the wagon; and this, probably, is the one and only impression of him that will stay with me forever.

As I write, the notes of the piano and violin reach me. Every evening they rehearse their sonata, which has no message and formulates it so precisely. I get lost in speculations, hoping they will offer me an access to that remote world, but perhaps all they do is distance me from it. When Adele sits at the piano she certainly does not ask herself about the essence of the music: she herself embodies that essence at the very moment of placing her fingers on the keyboard, and I believe that her mind is emptied then of every thought, that everything that surrounds her drops away into oblivion and indifference. All that remain are the white and black keys, which glint in the penumbra of the drawing room, and the music open on the stand, and the notes of the violin which respond from the barred window.

23 AUGUST

Yesterday evening, while the two were playing, I went into Ottaviano's room. Expected to find him sitting up in bed, intent as usual on listening to the music: instead he lay on his back, his head buried under the pillow. Thought he must be asleep, and left the bedroom on tiptoe, slowly shutting the door behind me.

"Papa," called the boy. He must have heard the snap of the handle.

I went back in. "Forgive me, Ottaviano, I didn't mean to wake you."

"I wasn't asleep," he replied, turning his big dark eyes towards me.

"Then what were you doing lying with your head under the pillow?"

"So as not to hear the music."

"I thought you liked it."

"No. Not any more."

On his face there was a solemn, resolute expression which contrasted with the childlike softness of his features.

I sat down beside him. "What's the matter, Ottaviano? Why don't you like the music any more?"

"Because it is a spell."

"A what?"

"It's a spell of the giant to carry Mama away."

I smiled. "No one can carry Mama away, you ought to know that: she loves you too much."

"But she never keeps me company."

"That's because she has things to do, and you know that you're a big boy now and can be on your own."

"I'm not big. I don't want to be on my own. It's all the fault of the giant and his spell."

Stayed in the room until he had fallen asleep. Even in his sleep he seemed to be prey to a lively agitation. Of course he senses Adele's abstraction – absorbed as she is in her music, she takes barely any notice of her son.

This morning, finally decided to rebuke her. "It would be as well if you spent more time with him, especially during the day."

"You're right. Poor child, I really am neglecting him too much."

Spent the whole morning in my office, looking over Gaspare's service record, and drew up a brief résumé, which tomorrow I'll send to Captain B.

Going back into our living quarters, I found Adele at the piano, intent on practising.

"Where's Ottaviano?"

"Out for a walk with Angelica."

"I asked you to stay with him."

She lifted her eyes from the music. "I did ask him to keep me company as I played. He didn't want to."

30 AUGUST

Adele and the prisoner have embarked on another sonata by the same composer. It's from the same stack of music brought by Teresa. This time the piano was first to start, but the violin leapt straight in with amazing alacrity, as if the man knew in advance that Adele was going to play that very piece.

Her progress is remarkable: she's learning even the most difficult passages with an extreme rapidity. Her style is achieving an ever more perfect rapport with that of the prisoner, and sometimes I have the feeling that the two instruments are played by the same hand, governed by the same will.

For Adele music is no longer a pleasure, it has become an obsession. When she is far from the piano she seems to be suffering, and her entire day is now reduced to a feverish expectation of those few hours after sundown when the soldiers withdraw and the prisoner begins to play.

She herself is aware of the morbid character of her passion; it fills her with remorse on my account and Ottaviano's, but if I suggest to her that she give up music she shakes her head firmly and says, "I can't." Her anguished tone is unanswerable.

I wonder whether I really would want her to give it up: when I hear her play, it sometimes seems to me as if one of the Graces has torn her from the serene drabness of her previous existence to place her in charge of a supreme revelation.

The cloistered state in which she lives has banished the bloom of youth from her cheeks. Her face has become more hollowed, her cheekbones more prominent and her eyes deeply inset, achieving an opalescent splendour in the feeble light of the candles.

Her eyes, which were always most beautiful, have now acquired a fleetingly intense expression, as if the music had night after night formed a sediment in those dark irises.

8 SEPTEMBER

Today the sky has been overcast all day, with a leaden oppressive greyness. At twilight one of those violent thunderstorms that signal the end of summer broke out. The air turned suddenly chilly, but Adele insisted that the windows remain open so that she could accompany the prisoner.

The sound of the instruments was now and then overwhelmed by the powerful voice of the thunder, only to re-emerge with each time a more noticeable sense of fragility. Thought about these human things, how ephemeral they are, tied to life as they are by the slenderest of threads, and how immutable are the things of Nature. We'll be gone, and the room, and the piano, and the music itself will be destroyed, or there'll no longer be eyes capable of reading it, but the same sky, streaked occasionally, as now, by veins of lightning, will continue to stretch over this countryside.

Or maybe that music, which seems ever on the point of expiring, is destined to a paradoxical immortality which will render it the perpetual witness to its very dissolution. Perhaps the prison somehow participates in this eternity, and the prisoner's life, to which it is tied, will have no end. His shadow will continue to be projected on the window, the violin will continue to play when, all about, the world of men will have vanished, a world which for him has anyway long ceased to exist.

9 SEPTEMBER

This morning we waited in vain for Adele in the dining room. When lunch was over I went to look for her in her bedroom and found her still in bed. She was shivering under the covers, even though the weather is at present very mild and the room's in a sheltered position. Her forehead was burning and her eyes glinted unnaturally.

I sent at once for a doctor, but we had to wait until evening before he arrived from a town not far distant.

From the window I saw the trap arrive. A man got out and took down a bag. The soldiers directed him to our entrance.

I woke Adele from the vague slumber into which she had sunk. "Don't worry, the doctor's come."

She raised herself on the pillows. "It wasn't necessary for so little."

"Whether it's little or not let's leave him to judge."

But the doctor, after examining her, confirmed that it was nothing serious and ought to clear up soon. "It's probably a chill. It happens, at the end of the summer, if one fails to notice in time that the weather has changed."

"True, yesterday evening we left the windows open, in spite of the storm."

"Well, that explains it. The lady must rest for a few days, and above all she's to stay in the warmth. Then, should the fever not abate, send for me again."

Outside, the heavens had started to rumble again. It happens at this season that the rain comes punctually, always at the same hour, as though keeping an appointment.

The prisoner's shadow, punctual too, appeared at the window. When I saw it I closed the curtains.

"Well done, sir, that's an excellent precaution. The material will also serve to screen off the dampness. You cannot imagine what damage the damp can do, when it gets into one's bones."

The doctor settled into an armchair and embarked on a minute and joyless depiction of the evils caused by humidity: pains in the joints, persistent fevers deteriorating until they brought on cardiac palpitations, and various other calamities which he presented to us in closely ordered detail, from the mildest to the most severe.

"To tell you the truth, there is no proof that it is the damp that causes these illnesses, but it's as well not to overlook this hypothesis."

The cloudburst had now exploded in all its violence and he had to wait for the weather to improve.

"In the meantime I shall prepare your good lady a poultice."

"Will that do her any good?"

"In all honesty, we cannot yet say with certainty that a poultice helps in these cases, nor on the other hand are we to discount the possibility. At all events, it'll certainly do no harm."

He had himself taken to the kitchen, and told Angelica to put water on to boil. Meanwhile I looked on curiously as he mixed together certain herbs he had taken from his bag. When the water was hot he threw in the mixture.

The maid went out to look for some gauze for the poultice and we waited on alone.

"Doctor, tell me the truth . . ."

"About what? Ah, you want to know about your wife. Believe me, there is no cause for alarm. Besides, she is so young . . . She'll get better in no time."

"What is the exact name of her illness?"

"It's hard to say. You see, strictly speaking there is no illness: merely a very slight indisposition."

Angelica returned with the gauze, and he spread it out in a basin and poured the herbal mixture on to it.

Back in the patient's room, I saw that the curtains had been opened again. Adele was staring at the window and kept her eyes on it while the doctor applied the poultice.

12 SEPTEMBER

My wife's temperature is now completely back to normal and she has got up. She's spent the entire day wandering from room to room with the restless joy often experienced by convalescents on recovering their freedom of movement.

Towards evening I heard the notes of the piano coming from the drawing room, and hastened to join Adele. Found her intent on her playing in front of the open window. Beneath what was still a summer dress, her shoulders trembled slightly.

"D'you want to fall ill again?" I said to her severely, and made to close the windows.

She stopped playing and shot an imploring look at me. "Please, do leave it open. I'm well again, and it's not a cold evening."

"The doctor insisted . . ."

She smiled. "The doctor's unable to rule anything out or prove anything."

"Even so . . ."

"If you love me you'll not refuse me this pleasure."

She read surrender at once in my face and went straight back to her playing, without a further glance at me. The violin, too, which had broken off at the same time as she did, resumed its melody from afar.

I left the room in search of a shawl, then returned and gently wrapped it round Adele's shoulders. My activity seemed to unsettle her, so that she played a wrong note, but she said nothing and carried on.

The shawl slipped down her back and fell to the floor.

20 SEPTEMBER

There's a rumour that a man is hiding out on the moors, concealed amid the bushes. The slightest noise is enough to scare him off like a wild animal, and no one has ever been able to obtain a close view of him. For some time the soldiers have been telling each other this strange story, at table or in their rooms, but as soon as they're aware of my presence they quickly change the subject, exchanging glances of timid complicity.

I don't wish to know the secret they're guarding with such care, nor to know the identity of the mysterious figure who lives in the scrub; they say he's dressed in a soldier's uniform. Sometimes I imagine him roaming about amid the grey of the vegetation, beneath the grey sky, and stealing furtively as far as the edge of the esplanade to espy the mass of the prison from a distance.

It's turning progressively colder, and I've firmly told my wife she's not to play the piano with the windows open. She obeys, but she's grown sullen and dispirited. In the evenings, when we sit together in the drawing room, she keeps gazing at the prisoner's shadow and then flashes a resentful look at me.

Her lips are now a tenuous, dusty pink that can barely be distinguished from her complexion. Her hair falls inertly, like an opaque curtain, to frame her oval face, and her eyes seem to grow larger every day, as if their sad flame is gradually consuming the rest of her face.

Her nights have become a long tormenting vigil. Often, when I see her lamp lit, I go to her in her room and find her sitting up in bed, her back propped against the pillows. I should like to stay and keep her company, but Adele welcomes my presence with ill-concealed vexation and when finally I decide to bid her goodnight, she looks relieved.

Her condition worries me and often I suggest sending for the doctor, but every time she refuses. "I'm perfectly well, I promise," she obstinately repeats. And yet while she's talking she keeps her hands gathered in her lap, to hide their trembling.

23 SEPTEMBER

This morning Adele was unable to get up. She has a high temperature and is verging on a semi-comatose state. I stayed to observe her in silence while the doctor felt her pulse. He too remained silent, and only when we were outside the room did he decide to answer my look of alarm with a word or two. "A relapse, sir, it could be a pretty serious affair."

"Is she in danger, then?"

"I'm not in a position to rule it out."

He'll be back tomorrow, to apply remedies in whose effectiveness he himself does not believe. "What counts above all is the patient's general condition, her ability to rally. And I have, alas, found the lady somewhat debilitated since the last time. If my precautions had been better observed . . ."

"Doctor, what can I say? She's always stayed in the warmth lately, and I've forbidden her any effort."

"Even so . . ."

"If this indisposition . . ."

"I'm afraid that it's no longer a question of indisposition, my dear sir; it's a real and proper illness."

"What illness?"

"It's early to say. Let us wait for further symptoms to show."

Spent the entire day at her bedside, and in her room I'm now writing these lines. She is asleep, a deep sleep to which she seems to abandon herself without reserve. The few sounds, the movements that we have to make around her, do not reach her. She didn't even wake when Angelica delicately applied the poultice at dusk.

"Sleep heals, sir."

I nodded at those words, and continue to repeat them to myself as the shade of evening falls slowly on Adele's sleeping face.

26 SEPTEMBER

The doctor comes daily and continues to await the appearance of further symptoms. But Adele's illness manifests itself exclusively in fever which, despite the compresses, shows no sign of abating. It leaves her in a daze, and she passes continuously from sleep to a state which is barely distinguishable from it. Her breathing is heavy, laboured, yet there is no catarrh in the chest.

"Your wife," the doctor told me yesterday, "is not suffering from any definable illness. One ought to conclude from this that she is in good health."

"And the fever? How is that explained?"

"I cannot yet say for a certainty, but I am weighing up the theory that it has to do with her nerves."

Thus does he weigh up his theory, and Adele's condition deteriorates.

I cannot even remember when it was that I heard her voice for the last time. Now she does not answer me, she is not aware of anything. Angelica prepares cups of broth and feeds it to her patiently, a spoonful at a time, while I hold her up in a sitting position. She swallows without opening her eyes.

1 OCTOBER

The sky is clear, but the days have noticeably drawn in. Outside there is an autumnal nip in the air; in the morning, I throw open my bedroom window the moment I get up, and inhale a little of it – a rare pleasure, without which I'd perhaps be unable to endure the oppressive atmosphere that reigns in Adele's room. There it's like being in a greenhouse: the fire is kept burning without interruption, and I gaze at the logs releasing a fine dust as they are consumed, one after the other.

The silence, too, is oppressive, and the penumbra, barely lit by the flames in the hearth.

Often I lose all notion of time, and to tell whether it is day or night I have to look at the thin strip of light that filters through the curtained windows. When the strip disappears I approach the curtains, open them a chink to see the shadow of the prisoner, and think back to the summer evenings when the sound of the violin reached me, blending with that of the piano.

It's days since I've gone down to my office, as I have to look after the patient. I've entrusted the child to Angelica, who certainly knows better than I how to take care of him. Every afternoon she takes him out for a little diversion: they go for long walks on the moors and come back only at sundown. Ottaviano always carries a posy of flowers which he wants to give his mother. He hands them to me and waits for me outside Adele's room, as I find some pretext to stop him going in. The moment he sees me he asks me if she liked them. I answer yes.

Angelica brings him supper in his bedroom and stays with him till late. Sometimes they play for a while, without making a noise, sometimes Ottaviano goes straight to bed and the maid tells him a story, always the same story; he listens to it with his eyes shut, drifting off to sleep.

6 OCTOBER

Adele died at four in the afternoon. The doctor and I attended her brief agony helplessly while Angelica kept the child in another room so that he would remain unaware.

She expired quietly, without uttering a word. After the doctor had taken his leave I myself closed her eyes. Gently I unclasped her hands, which in a final spasm had clutched the hem of the sheet, and crossed them on her breast.

I stayed beside her a long time. My throat was constricted by a knot of anguish; it prevented me from weeping. Watched the immobile face, the slight figure outlined beneath the covers, the slender, lightly contracted fingers, whose pallor set off the gold circle of her wedding ring, and I asked myself who that woman could be who for seven years had lived at my side. She seemed a stranger all of a sudden, as if death had shed a cruel light on the solitude in which we are all confined.

So many things that we take to be an essential part of us die before we do, so many things are taken from us, and life is seen to be a continual expenditure, a cruel squandering of sounds, images, feelings, which our memory labours to keep after, as one might administer the fortune of a spendthrift master and, in anticipation of bankruptcy, strive to salvage the small change.

So do I wrap Adele's body in the veil of memories, to conquer her indifference, her almost hostile reserve.

Tonight, too, the soldiers go along the sides of the courtyard to put out the lights, and the prisoner's shadow has appeared at the window. Only the piano remains silent, sealed, like a casket the key to which has been mislaid.

20 OCTOBER

It was the evening after the funeral that I saw the prisoner's shadow for the last time. Already for some while the dishes the soldiers passed to him through the turntable had been coming back almost untouched, but only on that day was I informed of it.

The news left me somewhat apprehensive, and I felt better on seeing the giant's silhouette projected on the window-panes. He was not, in truth, holding the violin to his shoulder, nor did he remain long at the window, and yet that fleeting apparition was enough to reassure me that he was up and about, and that I was not to worry about his health.

Since Adele's death I've never been able to recover my self-possession. Back in those first, terrible days as I tried to re-adapt to normal life, its rhythm bewildered me, not because it was in a ferment, but on the contrary because its quiet, regular pace conflicted with the utter devastation of my spirit: they were like incompatible sizes, and the contrast was painful when not grotesque.

I lived in an amphibious condition, in a continual state of stupor, and it took me some time to realize that the shadow had stopped appearing at the windows opposite. I did notice eventually and, as duty dictated, I wrote to the prisoner to enquire about his health and offer him, in case of need, every possible attention.

The note came back still sealed, along with the dinner. Nothing had been touched: the plates, the glasses, the cutlery, everything had been left in the identical position in which the soldiers had assembled them an hour or two earlier.

Gave orders to try calling him, from the courtyard or through the prison door, but no reply was obtained. Someone put his ear to the keyhole: from within not the smallest sound was to be heard.

Finally I took the keys from my office safe and, escorted by two soldiers, I passed through the twelve rooms. When we reached the last door I told the men to remove the seals, then I put the key in the lock and turned it.

We went in. I tried calling once more, but in vain. Very soon I noticed that the prisoner's rooms had the same lay-out as our own, but they were quite bare and unadorned. I remembered our quarters as I had seen them our first evening, but when I recalled Adele's face and the expression of dismay with which she had looked about her, I no longer wanted to remember, and set off with rapid steps to complete the inspection.

We found him in the last room. He was lying on a camp-bed, already rigid; he was a little man, tiny in fact, and the years had bent and shrivelled him still further.

I cannot recollect his features any differently from the way I saw them then, fixed in the immobility of death. They seemed to be sculpted in a rough stone, scored with deep crevices. As time continued to excavate, it had abstracted from those features anything that might have softened the sharper angles, transforming that face into a ruthless caricature of itself.

"Is that him? Is that the giant?" asked a child's voice at my shoulder. Only then, turning round, did I notice Ottaviano: he must have followed me and managed somehow to slip into the room.

"What are you doing here?"

"I've come to see the giant."

"Now you've seen him: go home."

He didn't obey me, but I didn't have the heart to show severity. It was the first time since his mother's departure that he had shown an interest in anything. He went to explore every corner, walking on tiptoe, I don't know whether out of respect for the deceased or for fear that the deceased might hear him.

"Look," he suddenly exclaimed, "I've found the monkey!"

I saw that he was grasping the violin in his little arms.

"Put it down, Ottaviano. Put it back where you found it."

"No. I want to learn to play it."

"If you want to become a violinist I'll buy you another instrument: this one does not belong to us." But the child could not bring himself to put it down; indeed, when I approached to take it from him he clasped it to his chest with all his might and stared at me in silence, with a look that threatened tears.

The violin is now in our quarters, and tomorrow we shall take it away with us. We couldn't put it in a trunk because Ottaviano absolutely refuses to be separated from it, not even during the journey.

As I write, he is in his room, stroking the bow on to the strings and extracting from the instrument bizarre sounds that have little to do with music.

The wagon has already left with the furniture; the rooms are cold and practically empty. Angelica has left us our supper and a bit of dessert to eat for lunch.

All day, beneath a lowering sky, the soldiers have been preparing the charges. I supervised the work and occasionally from the courtyard I would raise my eyes to our windows. Ottaviano kept observing us attentively, his face pressed to the window-pane, and he clasped the prisoner's violin tightly to himself.

Tomorrow I shall accompany the coffin to the village cemetery, where a grave has already been dug, not far from Adele's, to receive the little man with the giant's shadow. Then I shall return to fetch my son and together, for the last time, we shall pass through the prison gateway.

I ask myself whether for us there can still be a life, whether there is a world out there.

Translated from the Italian by Guido Waldman

PAOLA CAPRIOLO

Letters to Luisa

Dear Luisa,

My little prison is finished at last. I can't tell you what patience, or what labour of ingenuity it's taken me to construct the dozen cells with their paper walls, and to cut out of each one an opening large enough to allow our guest to pass through. I've covered the prison with a transparent sheet: that way he'll not be able to escape and I'll be able to observe his every movement. And there is a little door, also made out of paper, which gives on to the outside, and which only I can open or shut. As you'll already have gathered, I'll use it to pass through to the prisoner as much as is needed for his sustenance.

But I'm still faced with the hardest part of the project, that is, the capture, and this, I'll make no secret of it, leaves me somewhat apprehensive. The thing is, as you'll agree, it's absolutely vital to take him alive. I've been watching his behaviour for some while, and I know he's capable of a thousand tricks. He can climb with an extraordinary speed, and this place, moreover, is not short of hiding-holes.

Still, I don't despair of bringing it off: in my life I've defeated considerably harder problems, as you know. Or perhaps you don't know. One day I'll have to make up my mind to tell you everything precisely as it happened, in accordance with the truth, so as to dissipate certain misunderstandings that might come between you and me.

I desire nothing else but your understanding and your affection.

Dear Luisa,

I'm glad to inform you that my adversary has shown himself far less astute than I expected. With a childlike trust he

abandoned the ceiling to cling with all eight legs to the end of
the stick I stretched up to him. What d'you say to that? Would
you have imagined he could be so naive?

I have to confess I was deeply disappointed that his capture
proved so easy; you'll remember the pleasure I derive from running risks, taking chances, pitting myself against men or Fate.
For all the tenderness you often showed me, you always were a
challenge to me, and you still are. Which is why I continue
to seek your understanding, and yours alone. What does the
judgment of the world matter to me now? And why should I
lie? Even the spider, shut in the paper prison, has stopped spinning his webs of lies: he is motionless, resigned, awaiting the
end. If he could speak, he would say nothing but the truth.

But the truth, dear friend, is nearly always tiresome, and I've
therefore left our guest to his glum reflections so as to dedicate
myself to the violin.

I hope that you have not given up music: I should consider
it the worst of betrayals. I play every evening, after dinner, when
there's an end to the noises from the courtyard. My notes need
silence the way fish need water, the way I need you. For you,
dear Luisa, I should perhaps still be able to lie.

Dear friend,

Today I heard a great rumpus in the courtyard, and in the
evening, as I was playing, I was interrupted by someone knocking at the door. A note was passed to me on the turntable; I
read with difficulty, for my eyesight is getting worse by the day.
I could make a request for an optician to examine me and pre-
scribe suitable lenses, but I don't want anyone coming in here.
In the early days, years ago, I wanted nothing better, and would
have welcomed any visit with delight. But not any more.
Besides, there'd be no point putting on a pair of glasses to
decipher the futile messages that get passed to me: "Be it known
to the prisoner . . . From today . . . The new commandant of
the fortress . . . " With this idiotic rotating of the troops they
delude themselves into imagining that they're marking the passage of time for me too, but I'd no longer be able to look up my
days on their calendar.

I've learnt to capture flies with the aid of an old wicker sieve. I open the transoms in the morning to air the place, and there are always some that find their way into the rooms: from this abundance of fauna, and from a certain mildness of the weather, I infer that it must be spring – April, or perhaps even May.

I watch the insect as it circles about, and wait, motionless, for it to settle. Then I dive on it like a predator and cover it with the sieve. I doubt even our guest could do better.

Once I've effected the capture I open the paper door and introduce the little victim into the prisoner's rooms. Through the transparent sheet I watch him at his savage meal, and each time I think of you, Luisa, and that pure, childlike faith of yours with which you always countered my scepticism. Forgive me for wondering: have you never considered what a monstrous notion it is – the notion of a heavenly spectator looking down through the clouds, impassive or perhaps vaguely curious, at the mutual lacerations of his creatures? If he's satisfied with the paltry pleasure offered by such spectacles, he must assuredly be getting bored to death up there. Thus do I, bored as I am by endless imprisonment, watch the little fly disappear amid the spider's legs, and you would certainly be horrified at the pleasure I derive from the sight – or at least the soft-hearted girl I used to know would be.

But why, Luisa, do you refuse me your pardon if you can forgive that God of yours?

My dear,

I continue to receive messages from that new commandant, though I made it clear enough to him, in my very laconic reply to his first note, that I have absolutely no intention of engaging in correspondence with him. I'm so fed up I've decided to leave the letters unopened in future. I would open only yours, if eventually you deigned to write to me.

I wonder whether I'd still be able to recognize your hand-writing, that neat, graceful hand that used to be so familiar to me. The years could have altered it, as they have altered mine; so many things have happened in the meantime, so many pictures, perhaps too many, have passed before my eyes. First the triumph, then the ruin, have dug a deep chasm which severs me from my past, and only the memory of you still succeeds in bridging it, like one of those long bridges made out of creepers which the American Indians used to stretch across precipices: they looked fragile but were perfectly strong and safe for whoever dared set foot on them.

You too, Luisa, should take the risk, you should try to understand. Yesterday I heard a woman's voice in the courtyard; it was shrill, and the accent was plebeian. She was shouting about some "demon" or other and I understood she was referring to me.

You're not to believe that such a thing bothers me: on the contrary. I imagine that the spider, too, would feel relieved if, from his paper prison, he could hear the voices of the little insects that are still in dread of him. But he devours his flies wearily, listlessly, wounded as he is in his pride as a predator.

The creature's prostration moves me to the point where I've decided to capture another spider for him. Their encounter is bound to lead to a fight to the death, and I'll not disguise from you that I'm thrilled at the prospect of watching it. I should feel I was a Caesar, with absolute power of life and death, contemplating the gory dance of a pair of gladiators.

The trouble would be if the two spiders were of opposite sex and, instead of fighting, chose to proliferate. In that case I think I'd free them so that they could go somewhere else to enjoy their obnoxious domestic bliss.

I hope, sweet Luisa, that my proclivities do not scandalize you too much. At bottom even music is combat, and time was when you liked to engage in duels with my violin. I still remember you as one of the worthiest opponents I was ever given to meet.

My dearest,

For days now I've been hearing the rain beat against the frosted window-panes, and I can't open the transoms for fear of flooding the rooms. My advanced years do not permit me to expose myself to the damp.

I have scanned every wall of the prison but it's been impossible to find a single spider. The supply of flies is also proving difficult, though the situation is not yet desperate because I've had the wit to store a dozen, alive, in a glass jar.

I've replaced the lid with a cambric handkerchief to let them breathe, and I've made little holes through which I drop bread-crumbs every now and then. Thanks to this precaution we are in a position to face this period of famine, buoyed by the hope that the fine weather will return before our resources are totally exhausted.

I believe our guest finds the taste of those flies insipid, arriv-ing in his lair as they do already more dead than alive – and so do I find the more elaborate fare the soldiers pass to me punctu-ally twice a day by the turntable.

They treat me with respect and, what counts more, with utter discretion. No one is authorized to enter the rooms in which I am confined and even my windows are screened, so that I can't see anything going on outside. Total isolation for the rest of my days is the punishment with which I am to make amends for my misdeeds and, believe me, Luisa, as a punishment it is far less harsh than it might seem. One gets used to it, one finds companionship among the insects, or among the ghosts.

True enough, it is impossible to imagine anything at greater variance with the dreams of our youth. What I dreamed came true in part, and others, looking into my dream as into a mirror, have seen in it the distorted features of a nightmare. You dreamed of a world in your own image, a sort of paradise, and already in those days I smiled at such illusions because I knew that paradise simply cannot be achieved on this earth. Hell, on the other hand, has given rise, you must allow, to some excellent approximations.

I realize, poor angel, how much this cynicism of mine offends you, and how distressing you find it that a demon of my type dare address you in such a confidential tone. But who knows whether the years have not wrested the odd feather from your pretty wings, or sullied their whiteness. Perhaps those blemishes, those tiny wounds which have opened in your flesh where once those feathers sprouted speak to you of me as well, of the ever-rebellious, the ever-fallen angel. Gradually they'll teach you to understand him and to forgive his fatal dreams.

My Luisa,

Forgive me if I've neglected you for a few days, but I've had an extraordinary adventure which has completely absorbed my attention.

I define as "adventure", and also qualify as "extraordinary", an event which formerly I'd not even have heeded. You must sympathize with me: I already explained to you earlier that for decades I've been living in the company of insects and ghosts; no sounds have reached me beyond the raucous shouts of the soldiers, the din of horses' hooves and carriage wheels, and the melodies I myself produce on the violin. So imagine my amazement when I suddenly heard from across the prison courtyard the alien voice of a piano. Someone somewhere was playing a jolly if undemanding piece of music. He was playing it neither badly nor well — or perhaps more badly than well — and the performance certainly had nothing in common with your own incomparable mastery; and yet I was quite bowled over by that music, and I've been waiting impatiently each day ever since for its return through my prison transoms, which I always keep open, taking advantage of the summer warmth.

I wonder whence those notes arose, from what hands. I think the player must be someone in the new commandant's household: he himself, perhaps, or more likely his wife or daughter. There's something mawkish in the style and a lack of fibre which point to a woman. Don't mistake me, please: I mean women in general, without any personal reference to you. You too were mawkish in many respects, but not when you were sitting at the piano.

As I listen to that music, I'm reminded of certain well brought-up young ladies at parties who'd consent to "play something" for the delight or torment of the guests. I still remember how it amused me to watch the embarrassment that possessed them when I entered the room: straightaway their fingers faltered and hesitated. Sometimes the poor creatures broke off altogether and peered foolishly at the music, as if they had suddenly lost the art of reading the notes. Then if I approached the piano, a violent blush would spread across their cheeks.

Perhaps the mysterious pianist would blush too if I appeared before her, and would be unable to pursue her mediocre exercises. The mirror, at which I look as little as possible, delivers back to me the depressing sight of a head of grey hair, a face ravaged by time; but the glance remains steady, and I still recognize in it the terrible me of former days. You too, dear friend, would recognize it, and perhaps in its presence your face would revert to the expression you were wearing when I saw you for the last time. You didn't blush, but there was a gleam in your eyes – it betokened at once pity and revulsion. That was at the trial, you remember, and you were dressed in black.

Dear Luisa,

You should hear the way she thumps on the keys, that amateur musician – the whole time, even when there's simply no need to. Her little twopenny tunes, those vapid little waltzes of hers would perhaps be more endurable if they were played with a light touch, with a measure of detachment. Instead of which she does seem to go out of her way to imbue them with accents of frantic passion, and the result, in party pieces of this kind, is utterly grotesque.

I'm writing you all this to show that imprisonment has not been sufficient to make me lose my mental lucidity or my ability to form judgments. But where my judgment pulls back in disgust, I'm assailed by an odd disquiet, an agitation I can't explain, in a different part of my being – the shadow part, beyond the reach of reason, the part that you, with those nebulous formulae you're accustomed to, would perhaps call my heart or, worse still, my soul. Exasperating though I find it, I can't prevent myself feeling a sense of pleasure as I listen to the notes from that instrument.

I've asked myself what makes her play so loudly, and I've come to the conclusion that she wants somebody to overhear her. Now who on earth could that somebody be? Certainly not one of their household, because in such a case a din like that would be wholly superfluous; it must be someone at a distance, who does not live in her quarters. You will already have guessed where this argument is leading: the somebody, the distant person, can only be me, it is for me that the girl pounds the keys of her piano so brutally.

She will have heard people talk about me, it is natural; they'll

have given her an account of my deeds many and many a time,
I'll wager, since childhood, omitting no doubt the odd detail
unsuitable for the genteel ears of a young lady. She knows that
I'm living in here, a few steps from her, still glowing from the
last rays of my glory: how could she resist such a temptation?
Of course she's heard me play, and she deludes herself, poor
child, that she's in correspondence with me as she lays about
the keyboard that way.

She deludes herself and she does not delude herself, because
I've already confessed to you that her music affords me a certain
pleasure. And yet, my Luisa, what on earth is such a pleasure if
it's not a shadow of the sublime pleasure that you and I were
able to derive from each other as we played together?

Dear child,
I fear I've painful tidings to communicate. Yesterday about
midnight our guest expired, from natural causes I believe. I
found him lying on his back, his eight legs clasped about his
last prey, which he did not have the time to ingest.

The obsequies will be held this evening, in solemn pomp,
and though you are unable to participate, I would ask you at
least to wear in his memory the black attire lately alluded to, in
which I saw you at the trial. Tell me, did you wear mourning
for me? I know you did, I am certain of it, but I should like
you to confirm this for me. And I should like you to confirm
that it was indeed black, rather than dark green as it used to
appear to me.

The defunct companion of my solitude now lies in a small
wooden box. I observed him for a while during which the piano,
instead of playing the funeral march, was engaged in the usual
drivel.

You know, dear, that in the course of my existence I've
acquired a certain familiarity with death, not least with that of
others, but also with the thought of the end that inevitably
awaits me. Did you see me wince, perhaps, you who were watching from one of the back rows, when I was under threat of the
capital penalty? No, I did not bat an eyelid, neither on that
occasion nor on any other: amid the perils of victory and those

of defeat, I always dared to proclaim myself, before the dismal spectre, the proud master of my fate.

Nobody will attend my funeral, apart from one or two distrait soldiers, and everything will take place in haste, and in silence. But this evening my violin will intone for that dead spider the sweetest of laments.

Dear friend,

I could not resist. The other day, before the hour fixed for the ceremony, I shut the little wooden box and tied it with string. Then I pulled a chair up to one of the windows, stood on it, reached up on tiptoe as high as I could and threw the coffin out through the transom.

I'm consoling myself with a new companion. This one belongs to a different breed, it's not black but of a yellowish hue and spotted; its body is smaller and its legs longer and thinner. Unlike the other, which barely moved, this one runs with feverish anxiety from one corner of the prison to the other, seeking the way out for an impossible escape. See what enormous differences of character are to be met with even amid the representatives of the inferior species!

Even his way of devouring flies betrays a singular disquiet. He is greedy, frantic – I've scarcely passed him the insect than it's already disappeared, wrapped in the arms of his executioner.

All this makes for novelty and helps to pass the time most agreeably. The spectacle of violent death has about it something deeply reassuring; it allows one to banish from one's mind for a moment the thought of that other, that anonymous, faceless one.

At all events, these are my little pastimes, indeed the only ones, because for some while the piano has remained silent. Certain sounds I hear lead me to suppose that the commandant has house-guests. It is odd, though, that no one ever invites the girl to "play something".

I detest them all, from the first to the last. The echo of their conversation reaches me from a distance, and I'm sure they're talking about me. What else could they be talking about?

I play the violin for long stretches, to cover the unbearable sound of their voices, perhaps also to annoy them. I'd like to be able to go in there, confound the fathers and the mothers with my presence, terrorize the girls.

You, I remember, always sustained my stare, and I never succeeded in making you break off while you were playing. And to think that you're so young, so timid . . .

Dearest Luisa,
My days drag by with infinite tedium. Time, as you know, lengthens and shrinks, and invariably does the opposite to what we wish, so that there is not an instant but seems to us to be passing too slowly, or else too fast. If I were you I'd lodge a complaint about this with that Lord of yours up there, assuming that the two of you are still on good terms.

My time is stretching out, Luisa, it is stretching out immeasurably. The seconds go by with the listless tread of a tortoise, and my nostalgia for the piano increases daily.

It sometimes happens that after lunch there is a total silence in the prison, as if everyone were sleeping. Then I take the violin, approach one of the screened windows and begin to play, in the hope of being heard by the unknown pianist. At night too I play for her sometimes when the veiled glow of the lamps that light the courtyard no longer reaches me through the windows.

It is a sort of summons that I send her through the narrow aperture of the transom, or better, a web that I'm spinning to capture her. Who knows if I shan't succeed in persuading her to return to her instrument a little, and perhaps in making her understand that there's better music in the world than that to which she is accustomed?

I devote myself to this project with the boundless patience of one who has nothing else to do.

My dear,
The mawkish little fly has finally fallen into the net: yesterday evening, after the long silence, she started playing again, and

the notes that came out of the piano were no longer her music, but mine.

To lure her I was playing a slow and persuasive melody, the slowest and most persuasive one I know. Yes, Luisa, it was the Adagio, that very Adagio from the sonata we both loved above all others. I played it, I'll admit, in a rather pedantic manner, not because I've mislaid my ability as a virtuoso, but to ensure that the girl understood all the more clearly.

And indeed after a while she began to respond to me.

Her fingers moved timidly, hesitantly, and she often seemed to find difficulty in following the music, but, as I have told you, I have patience, boundless patience, and I shall continue repeating the piece every evening until my companion has learnt to play it properly.

I say "my companion", and I'm almost ashamed of these words, for I know that such an expression must refer to you and to you alone. This one will never be in a position to equal your exquisite renderings, nor will it ever be possible to establish between her and me that deep sympathy which turned our instruments into the double echo of a single voice.

But pity me, for I must be content with what I find, and it is already a great deal for me to have found at last someone with whom to play. Would you by chance be jealous? Ah Luisa, I hope so with all my heart!

Sweet friend,

My pupil is beginning to make some progress, while lagging a thousand miles behind perfection. There is now a certain finesse in the way she executes the Adagio, and you yourself might perhaps be able to listen to her without undue irritation.

You'll see: little by little I shall succeed in teaching her my language, our language. Slowly I'm drawing her towards unknown regions: gone now forever is the era of naive pleasures, of syrupy melodies. I don't believe that she could go back to them any more even if she wanted to.

Suddenly, as I play with my new victim, I find myself in clothes which I'm not accustomed to wear: those of the philanthropist. Because, you'll have to concede, it has been really

and truly an act of mercy to have snatched that unknown creature from her polished barbarity to raise her up with me to the
spheres of art.

In fact, dear Luisa, you must henceforth accord me all the
honours that go as of right to a spider in the odour of sanctity.

My dearest,

The girl is beginning to repay my efforts with a few happy
surprises. She certainly no longer seems the same person: she is
rapidly losing the traces of that insufferable amateurishness
which bedevilled her playing at the start, and little by little,
from the touch of her fingers, a new, more delicate sensitivity
is surfacing, which occasionally reminds me of yours.

That's it so far as the Adagio is concerned. With the first
movement, on the other hand, we are barely at the beginning,
and I have to try to forget you if I want to be indulgent. Nevertheless her interpretation is already quite tolerable, and I'm
pleased to note how remarkably well and quickly she's picking
it all up. If you hadn't spoiled me, I'd perhaps be more than
satisfied.

My friend,

I realize that lately I've not given you news of the spider, but
you're not to do me the injustice of imagining that my new
pedagogical mission is inducing me to neglect my duties as host.
I spend long hours hunting for insects, especially in the morning,
both because it seems to me that the prey is then available in
greater abundance, and because music, you will agree, is certainly not something to be tackled before lunch.

The weather is warm, the sky serene, but I have the impression that this has all lasted now for a long time, perhaps for
months; the slanting rays of the sun that warm my rooms as
they filter through the transoms retire ever earlier, leaving me
at the mercy of a vague shadow. I'm afraid that summer will
soon come to end, and with it the season of flies.

Our friend does not seem to be worried in the slightest; he

continues to consume his meals with his accustomed voracity, as if he had committed his own fate to the benevolent hands of a special providence which guarantees him an abundance of food until the end of his days. And who's to say that this is not precisely the case?

As you will perhaps remember, I never had a great inclination for study, and the troublesome vicissitudes have divorced me from it totally. Now, though, I should like to be an entomologist and to know whether spiders survive the first intimations of winter.

Dear Luisa,

After happily surmounting the obstacles in the first movement, the girl has mastered the Scherzo and the Rondo with quite breathtaking speed. Now we are in a position to play the sonata through from start to finish in all tranquillity. There is, of course, still the odd roughness here and there, but you'll remember what an intricate score it is. By and large I can pronounce myself proud of my pupil. She is highly receptive and succeeds in compensating for the deficiencies in her training with a musical instinct I'd never have credited her with possessing. This instinct is gradually awakening, thanks to those maieutic gifts of mine, and I imagine she's no less surprised about it than I am.

Spiders' webs, dear friend, are spun from the most impalpable of elements, and yet they know how to enwrap the prey, and how to retain a hold on it. Thus have I used an invisible thread to tie her hands to my hands, her will to my will. I lead her, she follows me. Slowly, with no need for words, I teach her to respond precisely to my every request, to pose the exact question to which I want to reply, and sometimes it seems to me that I've returned to those happy days when you and I used to hold such dialogues.

My God, Luisa, how she resembles you! When we play our sonata I'm unable to imagine her other than as a blonde and dressed in black. And she's forever watching me with that equivocal, woeful expression as she sits way off, at the back of the hall. I've never doubted that it was you back there, watching me

like that while I was in the dock. I've never doubted it for all
that my eyesight, even then, was slightly weak. She looked too
much like you to be another. Who other than you would have
dared fix your eye on me and hold my gaze for so long?

But if the guards had not at that very moment escorted me
from the room, I'm certain that even you would have dropped
your eyes, just as the unknown pianist has made herself meek
and docile to my will. She follows in my steps and penetrates
into the most insidious labyrinths of the music, into that obscure
paradise that was our kingdom once upon a time.

I sometimes wonder how you succeeded negotiating it while
maintaining your candour intact. No shadow, not even then,
obscured the splendour of your wings. I opened chasms beneath
your feet, and you'd hover over them, all confident and unwary.

I found you an exasperating companion, especially then,
when we played together and were like brother and sister, like
bride and groom.

This other one, too, might perhaps exasperate me were I not
mellowed in thinking of you. Tenderness is a luxury which I
may now permit myself, but in moderation: too high a dose
would poison me. There are times, therefore, when I'd like to
banish your memory, when I could wish you'd leave me a little
to my solitude.

Dear Luisa,
That girl frightens me. There is something in her way of
playing that frightens me. The overwhelming sweetness, the
extraordinary similarity . . . I believe that this kind of dismay
imbues the spirit with joy on its approach – and I don't know
whether I ought to resist it or give in.

I beg you, Luisa, have pity.

My angel,
This evening, when you were the first to start playing, and
with so light a touch, I felt as if you'd opened before me the
gates of my happier past.

Little angel, your white wings make a pair with my dark ones; your innocence belongs to me, and my cruelty belongs to you.

I've never doubted that we were the two halves of the same thing, that the hand that strikes and the flesh that receives the blow are one and the same thing. My Luisa, raise your eyes from the piano and see how gently the spider grips in its legs the body of the fly. Do you not feel it too, that all this is right?

All is right, my girl, all is redeemed, and everything discovers itself in its own opposite. I've never doubted it, I've never doubted that it was you sitting there at the back in the court-room. You were dressed in black, with your white wings. What else do the piano and violin talk about if it is not of this mystery and its double face?

Of what else did we then speak, when we still did not understand, when we thought we were remote from each other? When the brother did not recognize the sister, and the bride denied herself to the groom?

Look: the little fly has disappeared in the spider's embrace.

My beloved child,

I no longer know which one of us is leading and which being led. Our notes melt into each other and blend, and yesterday evening the sky lit all its lights to solemnize our union.

Did the lightning flashes upset you, I wonder? Were you perhaps frightened by the dull rumble of the thunder? Ah no, you went confidently through our garden of notes, you flitted about there, you little winged insect, over the abyss which is yours and mine, which is my cruelty and your innocence.

Look, my twin, how everything melts into everything else, how everything leads and everything allows itself to be led.

My pretty angel,

After these long days of silence I despaired of ever hearing your voice again. Thanks be to you, and to the cool evening air, which has brought it back to me.

And yet there is something different in that sound, something oddly remote. Your eyes, beneath the light veil, were fixed on me, and yet seemed to elude me.

Angel, why do you no longer answer me? I beg you, say something to me with that liquid voice of yours, some words of love on your white and black keys. I want to go on reflecting myself in you.

Sweet Luisa,

The violin is tired of playing on its own, and the spider devours its flies with little appetite. Why this silence? Why do you abandon me now, after being my guide on the edge of the final abyss?

Dear Madam,

I am writing to you again after this long interval to advise you of my state of health.

I am too weak to play, and ever since you deserted me I find no pleasure in the violin. The soldiers continue their importunities, passing me enormous trays of flies twice a day through the turntable. I still eat a fly every now and then, but with little appetite. I no longer even have the energy to run from one corner of the paper prison to the other in search of the way out.

I lie on my back most of the time with my legs in the air and, stretched out on this camp bed of mine, I'm now writing you this last letter.

I shall make the effort to get up to go to put it in the drawer with all the rest. Who knows, perhaps after my death someone will have them delivered to you, assuming that they succeed in finding you and that you've not yet left this world to reach the heavenly dwelling to which once upon a time you aspired. There you will certainly never have the opportunity to meet me, and so I bid you farewell, my cruel and innocent other half, eternally sundered.

Translated from the Italian by Guido Waldman

PETER HØEG

Compassion for the Children of Vaden Town

Throughout the nineteenth century the particular form of love known as compassion was growing in Denmark. It first appeared among the upper classes but later spread to the rest of the populace, and for more than any other cause its heart beat for defenceless children. At the turn of the century the citizens of Denmark saw their children in a deeply melancholy light like a sunset stretching into infinity, and in an attempt to grasp this painful compassion they turned to history and religion as if to say: See how the genesis of our nation is the history of unique parental love.

They were agreed that the original discovery of childhood frailty was made only a hundred years before, and that it was in Denmark more than any other place that the early nineteenth century with a constantly fearful and never resting solicitude had begun to protect the young and fragile, and for the first time in science and art had tried to give expression to the discovery that every child carries within it a portion of Paradise. It was in the light of the heaven of Romanticism that the Saviour had revealed himself in earnest as a heavenly mother, from whose wounds flow not blood but milk, and to whose call: "Suffer the little children to come unto me", the Danish congregation had risen and wept: "That is us!" It was the painters of the Danish Golden Age who captured the divine nature of childishness for the first time, who depicted mothers who regarded their newborn both happily moved and as if looking for something they themselves had definitively lost.

Compassion engenders the urge to protect, and the nineteenth century became the age of munificent private initiative. Collections were instituted in aid of children and widows after the Napoleonic Wars and the war of 1864 against Germany, schools and orphanages were built, and in the hour of darkness the women of the bourgeoisie gathered in the bay windows of great houses to sew and embroider to help the Sudan Mission for the conversion of children. These women had a vague and uneasy concept of Africa but they felt that with every careful stitch in the tapestry canvas they drew the remote, dark children closer to the light of civilization and their own beating hearts. And they laid down their sewing and thought of the Danish children's poet Hans Christian Andersen, and those lines in which he had lifted himself above his own tragic childhood and written:

> *Thou Danish tongue, thou art my Mother's voice,*
> *Thou comest to my heart so sweetly blessed.*

With the beginnings of material development in the early twentieth century self-sacrifice spread to all classes of society, and a comprehensive, always audible note sounded in the consciousness of the country which was concentrated in monuments, orphanages and children's hospitals, in legislation against neglect and epitaphs to benefactors of children in art and science, and never was it called into question that this was an element in an all-embracing material and emotional enrichment of the nation.

There was one place in Denmark from where, more than anywhere else, a number of those impulses for the improvement of children's conditions emanated and made a lasting impression, and that was Vaden Town, beside Vaden Fjord on the east coast of Jutland. For a hundred years this prosperous provincial town had provided the ideals of parental love for the rest of Denmark. Citizens from Vaden Town had sponsored the great bill laid before both houses of parliament, which from the middle of the previous century onward curtailed cruelty to children and child-labour. And it was these same citizens who later, in ministries and committees, had seen to it with dogged perseverance that the legislation was enacted. It was the cathedral school of Vaden Town which had produced some of the pioneers of medicine in their time, great doctors who had risked their lives – in the battle against wrong and malnutrition and the chief infectious diseases – to secure the future for those who survived to maturity. Many of them returned to their childhood town, and at the beginning of this century when the sanatorium for tuberculosis was built in Vaden – the first child sanatorium of its kind – the town had a hospital and medical service admired throughout Europe.

The hymnist and educationalist Nikolaj Severin Grundtvig was a priest in Vaden Town for a short period in his youth, and although he was not actually a son of Vaden, those few years of ministry marked him for life. It was here that he managed for the first time to conquer the depression that had pulled him down, and evolve for himself the truth on which he would later build his life's work, that there is no way for the adult to find himself except through the child. And even if this wise aphorism, like most words spoken by the great writer from his pulpit, was somewhat obscure – like the light of truth glimpsed through a thick fog of words – yet the citizens of the town noticed that they like the priest were glowing with heartfelt inner warmth, and they took him to their hearts. When a tablet was placed at the entrance of the sanatorium in memory of those doctors among the town's sons who had given their lives in the service of medicine during the great cholera epidemics in the middle of the last century, three lines of verse by Grundtvig were chosen to be engraved on the stone tablet, in which he had given expression to the truth he had experienced that compassion was the truly distinctive characteristic of the Danish nation:

> *For the living and the dead*
> *can the hearts of all Danes bleed,*
> *but never can they freeze!*

And yet it was not for official, monumental philanthropy that Vaden Town was known to the rest of Denmark. The town owed its fame to the fact that it was generally acknowledged that its inhabitants nourished a feeling of mythological depth: in Vaden Town the citizens loved their children with a fierce, fanatical love that would never tolerate that anything bad should happen to them.

People speculated over why the universe should have picked on Vaden as the target for such intense feelings, and some did point to its wellbeing and said that in Vaden Town they loved because they could afford to. The town was never heard to respond to this objection, but that was because the response was the obvious one, that the opposite was the truth: out of feeling for little ones follows – according to an inexplicable but incontrovertible regularity – material increase.

In the early spring of 1929 a gentle wind blew across the southern Funen archipelago and in over Jutland, as if it wanted to push the country softly and kindly into a long early summer. With the wind came, its course set towards Vaden, a large, black, schooner-rigged ketch. The curve of the hull and two big retractable keels showed that the ship had been built to go close in to modest harbours in Denmark and along the German and Dutch North Sea coasts. But its rigging was high and its polished swung hull shiny and well-kept like that of a royal yacht, and it flew the swallow-tailed *Dannebrog* with the national coat of arms, the flag reserved for the Danish monarch.

The ship sailed along swiftly, and from its deck Vaden Town, in the white light of the low-lying sun, resembled a toytown expecting someone to assent to its right to be given to a child as a gift. The shores of the fjord stretched out into the sea like welcoming arms, and at the head of the fjord the town rose over its harbour with clear, almost laughing colours. Nearest the water were fishermen's and sea captains' houses, higher up the larger citizens' and merchants' dwellings, and uppermost the church and the sanatorium, but everywhere the old cobblestones and the old street lamps had been preserved, and around the harbour among the modern shops they had kept the old warehouses. Thus the past was immediately visible in Vaden Town, thus the new grew harmoniously out of the old, like the child from its parents.

The town was still encircled by the old city wall. By means of comprehensive restoration work and a well-planned system of gates and bridges to the outside world, the town had remained in this embrace of dark brown stone as a symbol of the conditions it offered its children: the open heart inwards, and the protecting back towards the world outside.

The ship quickly drew near to the town, with a trustfulness as if no one on board knew that the harbour in front of it was as closed up as a grave, that the previous week first the town council and then the whole town, at a meeting in the market place, had unanimously decided to close the town gates and harbour, and man them with the 200 soldiers selected from the 6th North Schleswig battalion recruited from and stationed in the town.

At this time, at the epidemiological department of the National Hospital in Copenhagen, there was a chief physician by the name of Christian Windslov, whose origins, grandchildren and heart were in Vaden Town. He was a descendant of Professor Frederik Christian Windslov, who from 1810 onwards had brought in compulsory vaccination against smallpox, and thus by and large stamped out the disease in Denmark. His successors had retained a thorough knowledge and fear of the disease, and for a hundred years the few and rare cases of smallpox that occurred had been sent to them. In the middle of February, when two children from two different places in Zealand were sent to Christian Windslov, he looked into their feverishly shining eyes then pushed the hair back from their foreheads to look for the typical red blotches, but found none. An instinct made him spread out the children's fingers, and between two of them he saw two burning red patches, and beneath them the bones shone with a yellowish gleam through the skin, as if the skeleton was already demanding its rights.

Swabs from the children's throats and nasal mucus proved to contain the smallpox virus. And yet their upper arms bore evidence of smallpox vaccination, which, said the doctor to himself, showed that everything possible had been done to protect these children. What he was witness to here should not and must not be possible.

He had had the children isolated on admission to hospital. On the third day he saw the disease had spread to the rest of their bodies, which in another forty-eight hours bore large, connected areas of inflammation that broke out in white pus on the fifth day. On the seventh day Christian Windslov watched the children die, a more horrible death than he had ever before experienced. The normal weakness was absent; in this instance nature offered no narcosis, the disease produced a remarkably clear fever, in which the children, despite doses of morphine and the periodical cramps, watched how death came and sat on their chests, and little by little crushed the life out of them.

The following week eight afflicted children arrived at the hospital. The week after that twenty more. On 1 March Christian Windslov locked himself into his office. At that point he had not slept for a week, but his mind was piercingly clear. Now, slowly and clearly, he wrote a letter to his childhood friend, the mayor of Vaden Town, merchant Nikolaj Holmer.

"I must first tell you," he wrote, "that with this letter I hereby break my oath of silence. At this present moment I am the only person in this country who knows that a new, unknown type of smallpox has broken out in Denmark. The form of the disease bears a certain similarity to the known types, but it develops faster, is far more painful, and apparently irreversibly fatal.

"I have tried everything to inoculate the new disease. But I have apparently not been successful. And we have no other means. I am afraid the disease is incurable, that, in spite of all our efforts, we are confronted with a curse which is beyond our powers to remedy.

"To date we have had fifty cases at the hospital. Today I have received reports that indicate another two hundred. And Nikolaj, listen to me: by far the majority are children. The infection must have taken root in Zealand, and as far as I can see it has spread from there to Funen and then to Jutland. But it has not yet reached as far south as Vaden, there is still time. I do not know for what, I am a scientist and not an organizer and consul like you. But I feel, indeed I beg you: make use of this time, Nikolaj, use it for the sake of our children."

Well aware that this was the strangest and most important letter he had written in his whole life the doctor signed his name, and when his pen left the paper he felt between his middle and index fingers a light pressure, and when he spread his fingers out on the paper in front of him he saw the two red spots. Then he was filled with a great rage. Not on his own account, for during the past fifty years Christian Windslov had conversed with death formally but politely, as with an equally placed opponent, no, his rage was for the young, the living, those he had watched being born, whom he had carried on his shoulders when they had overeaten, and had read aloud to, and who were already now threatened by this strange, mortal inexplicability that could cross the barrier of safety which he had lived to establish and was now to die for. It was a savage maternal instinct which now welled up in the doctor's exhausted body and which caused him to recall a motto he had shared with Nikolaj Holmer in their youth, and with tears in his eyes he leaned forward and wrote under his name:

"*Nunc aut numquam*" – now or never.

Then he calmly disinfected the letter and envelope with carbolic powder, and when he went out to post it he kept a rubber glove between the paper and his infected hand.

Nikolaj Holmer received the letter in the afternoon. He had always been a man who never hesitated to do what he thought necessary, and when he read what his friend had written he felt that the words came to him from the grave, and by the time he called the town council to a meeting that same afternoon he had decided what must be done.

He read out the letter to the assembly and then allowed the horror to spread. It was the minister who expressed the thoughts of everyone by saying that he felt that this was a kind of punishment for the rest of Denmark's home of death, a punishment which the living land of Vaden Town was now to suffer the injustice of paying.

Then Nikolaj Holmer stood up. "Reverend sir," he said, "I shall give your words and this infection a secular interpretation. There can be no possible doubt that this disease is a question of hygiene and care. It has struck the rest of the country first because in the rest of Denmark people do not have our drainage system, our cleanliness in the home, our care for minors. It will be madness for us to pay for others' neglect. It is probable that Denmark is confronted with an epidemic which may prove to be the greatest and most terrible in the history of our country. Our children must not perish in this Ragnarok. I suggest then that we close the town gates, that we place a guard of soldiers from the 6th Schleswig battalion, who are all children of our town, and that we then keep them closed until a vaccine has been found or until the epidemic has died out. Do you understand what I am saying, gentlemen? I suggest that we show we are possessed of enough courage to put the rest of Denmark in quarantine."

Even before Nikolaj Holmer had finished speaking his fellow citizens had realized that this was the only way forward. All shared the conviction that not only was Vaden Town a reservoir of emotions for the rest of the country but that their town was Denmark's heart, and it seemed to them sensible and right to close off the blood supply to the body that had neglected itself. "If thine arm offend thee, cut it off," thought the priest enthusiastically, but then it occurred to him that man does not live on great emotions alone. But Nikolaj Holmer forestalled him. He walked slowly over to the great windows from which you could look down on the town, and with a sweeping movement included the grain silos, the warehouses and the cargo ships. "Holmer & Son," he said, "can feed the town. And not with one meal only. And not only with bread and fish." He paused. Then added quietly: "Now or never."

On the evening of the next day the rest of the town affirmed the council's decision at a meeting in the market place, where Nikolaj Holmer drew attention to the fact that there was no constitutional authority for this popular assembly and its decisions. "But," he added, "it is only for the sake of order that I say this. I regard this meeting as an Athenian assembly; we in this place are now the highest decision-making authority. From this time on I consider that in this town no other law is valid apart from that right a man has to guard his family against a deadly threat from without," and so strong was the feeling of solidarity in those present that all remained silent. Instead of rounds of applause a quiet wave of purposeful agreement flowed towards the mayor.

This wave also reached up to Nikolaj Holmer's son Kristoffer, who sat looking out over the town from a trap-door at the top of the warehouse in his father's quadrangular merchant's house. Kristoffer was the only one apart from the members of the town council who had prior knowledge of what the meeting was about. On the afternoon when Nikolaj Holmer had received the letter from his childhood friend he had sent a telegram calling Kristoffer home from the boarding school he had attended for the past three years. Kristoffer was the merchant's only son, and hopes for the boy's future were the mainstay for the merchant and his business. What Nikolaj Holmer said to the citizens in the market place he said from the depths of his heart for the sake of his son. And yet at this moment Kristoffer stared down over the town unseeing, in dull inner desperation.

For two hundred years Nikolaj Holmer's forefathers had been wealthy merchants, who had built up, maintained and gradually increased the family fortunes through small, carefully calculated business ventures. Behind this moderation lay a deep fear of poverty, which the Holmer family could observe every day from their rooms looking down over the low-lying districts of Vaden. In no member of the family was this fear stronger than in Nikolaj, but in him it was demonstrated very early as a distrust of frugality. Hardly had he learned to speak before he raised his head from the thin gruel of the evening meal and said to his sister: "When I grow up I shall have dumplings in my soup." He was not beaten for this presumption, for children were not beaten in Vaden, not even for such arrogance. But he was sent to bed, and his mother came and sat with him, and sang in a broken voice:

> *Seek for the humble places*
> *In the dust where the Saviour weeps*
> *There you may speak to Child Jesus*
> *For the roses grow in the vale.*

Nikolaj hardened his thistly temperament against this humility and turned to face the wall. He realized that the Saviour, like his own parents, had been an unsuccessful woolseller, trudging dusty roads to sell goods that would earn him nothing and only brought him fame that came too late. And from an early age little Nikolaj knew why: it was because the Saviour had encouraged laziness. Wherever he went people had laid down their fishing nets and tools to follow him and hear him preach the gospel of idleness, about how it does not help to store up in barns and win the world, for as the birds of the field eat without sowing and harvesting, so shall ye also eat.

From this sermon, which could not possibly lead anywhere but certain bankruptcy, Nikolaj Holmer turned away to find a road which led outwards and upwards, and he created his own idea of ascension. He pictured to himself that an angel would come and give him a sign, and then they would ascend together.

One day when he was seventeen years old he saw the angel. She was playing ball on a lawn behind the private girls' school. Several other lofty heavenly beings hovered about the lawn, all clad in long blue skirts and white blouses, but there was only one angel, and when she left Nikolaj followed her at a discreet distance, not because he was afraid, but because one who has seen God is filled with a huge respect.

The girl's parents had a property that was bigger and situated higher up than the Holmer family's, and where his people were careful, hers were known to have achieved their position through a large-scale meanness which had let nothing run through their fingers, and least of all a daughter. These people had been able to accomplish everything, they had lifted up other families or thrown them into the abyss, they had influenced governments and given the history of Denmark a direct push, but it was soon clear that the love between their daughter and Nikolaj Holmer was such that, hand in hand, the two young people directly confronted every obstacle and would either break on it or annihilate it. They moved in together into two small rooms down by the harbour, and one day, seven months after they had met, the girl donned a loose white dress, stuck a big yellow dahlia in her hair, took Nikolaj's arm and promenaded her pregnancy up and down Vaden Town.

Up to that time Nikolaj had not given a thought to money. Dazed with love as he was, for seven months the world had appeared to him as if the only question of significance was love and a roof over their heads, and he could not work out if this was because his emotions had thrown him into deep unconsciousness or because they had raised him up to a higher and clearer viewpoint. But on that day when his and her parents realized she was pregnant both families declared they would break off all connections with the pair. In a flash Nikolaj saw his wife and child as something he might lose; the angel image dissolved before his eyes and he saw living beings who could be struck down by sickness and hunger. This nightmare lasted only a short time before the families relented, for in Vaden Town it was believed that that which children and young people had joined together, adults should not put asunder, particularly not when each was a suitable match for the other, as in this case.

But by then it was too late – Nikolaj Holmer had been hurled back into the panic fear his family and childhood had nurtured for poverty. He had looked at the woman in his life and said to himself: "I must safeguard her."

It was to be one of the most rapid rises Denmark had ever seen. From his family's fund of experience Nikolaj knew everything about trade, and now he combined this knowledge with a new fearlessness bordering on a contempt for death, and in this state he invested the family savings in what amounted to financial suicide: a shareholding company building a huge sailing ship in Rostock, a full-rigger with a steel hull which was to engage in the already lost battle of sail against steam, and join the annual race from Europe to Australia for the first precious grain harvest. The first year the *Vincent* made the voyage around the Cape of Good Hope in two hundred days, and the sale of corn in London gave the investors 7000 per cent, the biggest profit ever seen in this market. The following year was even better. The third year the ship vanished off Madagascar, but by then Nikolaj Holmer had withdrawn his money and had bought a freighter of his own, his first. Two years later he and his wife and their son Kristoffer moved in to the white quadrangular merchant's house and that year in Helsinki Nikolaj built the full-rigger *Kronos*, the world's largest sailing ship, which the following year, on the same grain route to Australia on which he had embarked on his financial heavenly flight, beat the renowned tea clipper *Cutty Sark*'s old speed record. Two years later he had extended the foundations on which his family's security rested far outside the boundaries of Denmark, to branches in Bergen, Stockholm and Riga. And from extensive storehouses in Cuxhaven at the mouth of the Elbe the firm looked meditatively out over the North Sea.

Although Nikolaj Holmer saw his wife daily during these years, he lived in a different world from hers, a world of stocktaking, shipping lists and calculations. Out of the loneliness in which her husband had left her she began to hear voices. A faint echo of these voices reached the merchant, then he began to see a new, hunted expression on her face. He realized that in some way or other she needed him, and with his trained eye for future prospects he calculated that in at most five years he would have safeguarded his family, in five years he would be able to put himself at the disposal of love. But the voices could not wait so long, and one spring day they persuaded her to slash her wrists. Nikolaj Holmer himself was the one who found her in her bedroom. In a last attempt to show consideration to those she had left she had managed to let her blood run into one of the large porcelain vases he had had one of his ships bring her from the Far East, and not a drop had been spilt.

There before his wife's corpse Nikolaj Holmer saw that she really was an angel, for she had succeeded in taking her beauty with her to the other side of the divide between life and death. The next thing he thought was that he must have made a mistake, since he had been deprived of all reason for living. He could not perceive what this mistake had been, but he met sorrow with the only reply he knew: work. Although Kristoffer was only seven years old he changed the name of the firm to "Holmer & Son", and when Vaden Town closed its gates ten years later it was one of the largest trading businesses in Denmark, and he himself the owner of one of Denmark's largest private fortunes.

Probably no other town in Denmark could have done what Vaden Town did. Of no other place would it have been accepted that it cut itself off from the body of society. But week after week went by and the town remained hermetically sealed.

This was due partly to the powerfulness of the town, to the respect produced by wealth and position, partly to the fact that thirty members of the upper and lower houses of parliament and four government ministers had been born in the town. But mostly it was connected with the reaction of the rest of Denmark to the news of an unknown, deadly disease.

When the National Hospital published the announcement the country was stunned, and it remained for week after week in a state of rigid despair. It was as if the mere thought of the disease, the fearful intimation of what these two hundred cases could develop into, was in itself an infection. It was if the doctors, hospitals, maternity homes and disinfection plants, the whole mighty apparatus of physical health, had become a weakness. As if it was no longer possible for the nation to live in the consciousness of its failure to conquer death.

In this state it was impossible to react against Vaden Town. Not one member of the government, hardly a single person in Denmark, could deny the thought that Vaden's lofty isolation was the only possible sensible act against the threatening disease's anarchy.

During the period the town was closed it received visitors only once. On the fourteenth day of the closure, Kristoffer, from his lookout, saw the big ketch anchor outside the town and signal for a pilot. None set off. Instead, the blue-and-white signal flag which means "no" was hoisted on the harbour flagstaff and thereby Vaden Town slowly and unmistakably spelled out its refusal. A small boat was launched from the ketch, a shining little boat of polished mahogany with a canopied cabin at the bow, and a steam engine of brightly polished copper and brass at the stern. This craft was met at the furthermost quay by the harbour master, Nikolaj Holmer and four armed soldiers, and even Kristoffer was surprised when the little boat was not immediately turned away but turned round only after a lengthy parley, after which one of the Vaden pilot boats put out from the harbour and towed the ketch up to the quay, thus making an inexplicable break in the isolation of the town.

Despite its swallow-tailed pennant the ship did not belong to the royal family. Its name was *Alanda Gleim* and it had on board animals, artists, craftsmen and the management of the Circus Gleim, Europe's finest circus of all time. At the end of the last century at a special performance at Fredensborg Castle for Christian the Ninth and the whole of the European family of the royal house, the King had given permission for this circus, which travelled around Europe by sea, to fly the flag of the royal family, as it was considered that the circus in itself was a kind of voyaging kingdom, a Noah's ark for the only art form beloved of every class of society.

The director of the circus, Herr Gleim himself, had been one of the two passengers on the launch. The other was an old man with a grey moustache and a sensitive face. He was a dwarf, only one metre twenty high, but his fame spread, the placards said – and Circus Gleim's placards did not exaggerate – from the Cape of Good Hope to the northernmost Gulf of Bothnia. This was Monsieur Andress, a clown adored by a whole world.

Monsieur Andress had combined the popularity of the circus clown with the highest European culture. Born of wealthy exiled Hungarian parents and brought up in southern Europe, he had grown up as a cosmopolitan. He had received a classical education, had early determined to become a priest, and had apparently almost completed his studies at the Jesuit college when an irresistible attraction to music had led him to some of the most famous conservatories in Italy. Despite his small size he turned out to have a formidable voice. Several composers had written pieces specially for this dwarf's counter-tenor, until he deserted the opera for conducting, and it was realized that from this small but perfect body issued a musical magnetism which led the Vienna Opera House to offer him the post of musical director that fell vacant after Gustav Mahler. But Monsieur Andress said no. From some place in the universe – incomprehensible to the rest of the world and to his family in particular – the conviction had come to him that he must be a circus clown. And when he stood in the ring for the first time everyone saw that the idea must have come at the same time from Our Lord and his own generous heart. No one before had thought that this musical dwarf was funny, but that he had been created to receive, in a diminutive suit of evening dress and a child's patent-leather shoes, the homage of a concert audience. From his first entrance into the ring people understood that in this very guise, in shoes too big for him and enveloped in the smells of the stable, while the whole world wept and laughed by turns, the universe was fulfilling its intentions for Monsieur Andress. Without losing the touching simplicity of the clown he took up its mask, refined it, magnified its childishness and dissolved its traditional malice, until he entered and left the ring like a study in irresistible childish awkwardness.

It was with this past and renown behind him that Monsieur Andress, from the small boat, faced with the barrels of the soldiers' rifles, now directed a plea to Nikolaj Holmer.

For three months, the clown explained, their circus had toured the

Baltic coasts. On the way down through the Baltic they had run into a severe winter gale, the flat-bottomed, violently rolling ship had been forced to heave to, and then try to ride out the storm. The constantly changing wind direction had driven them now southwards, now back in the direction they came from; with the horses screaming with terror they had sailed twelve knots on bare poles. In the poor visibility they had lost their bearings, and when the first sunlight appeared, and they caught sight of land astern, it turned out to be Aero in the perilous archipelago in which only skippers with a knowledge of the area can navigate. The ship had in fact been on its way to Kiel, but for the sake of the animals and especially for the children, the children who were terrified and weak from not being able to take nourishment for so long, they had decided to sail before the wind towards Vaden Town.

Faced with the prospect of having to reject sick children, and with this ancient, who was the soul of the European circus tradition, and who would be received with gratitude by every head of state, Nikolaj Holmer decided to relent, relax the rule and offer welcome. "For they like us," he thought, "have been isolated, they too seek protection for their feeblest, for the women and children."

With the coming of Circus Gleim the feelings released in Vaden Town were given the focus they had lacked.

Among the members of the town council there were some who had feared that the unusual situation, its having taken the law into its own hands and set itself apart from the rest of Denmark, would lead to personal lawlessness. They had recalled stories of towns that had closed their gates in the Middle Ages, and whose inhabitants had started to burn their candles first at both ends and then on a bonfire of debauchery in an attempt to compress a whole life into the brief time remaining to them.

Things took a different course in Vaden.

Everything seemed to go on as if nothing had happened. Every morning people got up and went to work, and children to school, and yet nothing was as it had been. For in contrast to the frenzy that the plague had induced in medieval citizens and made them dance until they dropped, the adults and children in Vaden had been filled with a great, new patience which resulted from a feeling that they would live forever. They were able to go on taking part every day in a life whose conditions were completely changed because this life had suddenly been illuminated by a fresh clarity. From several places in the town they had had a view over the fertile Danish countryside. When the gates were closed this view seemed to vanish. The townsfolk quite simply gave up looking along a street or over the town wall towards the small farms to the south. As soon as the newspapers were no longer delivered thoughts stopped of their own accord on their way to the larger towns or out over the sea. One day, without anyone being aware of who took the decision, the telegraph service at the post office closed, and from then on the rest of Denmark seemed to cease to exist. To children, only what is close to them has any existence, things at a distance fade into darkness. Now the adults of Vaden Town began to regard the world like this. They did not mention it to each other. But they wondered why they had not isolated themselves much earlier, why it should take an epidemic to make them understand that the essence of security is to mount barricades.

This new immortality was a powerful emotion that drew people to meet every afternoon in the market square, in that place where they had, so to speak, voted themselves democratically into eternity, and here, in front of the town hall, Nikolaj Holmer and the other merchants distributed the daily allocation of food. At these gatherings Circus Gleim and above all Monsieur Andress became the leading lights.

Proceedings began with a performance in the great salon of the town hall, but because of the overwhelming attendance, since the whole of Vaden Town wanted to be there, and also on account of the surprisingly early spring rise in temperature, the event was transferred outside to the square, under the open, bright afternoon sky, which, as the performance took its course, faded, turned blue and then grew dark.

It was not a complete programme, for the people's intense air of attending a religious ceremony was not suited to Circus Gleim's great international gala performance. The inhabitants of Vaden were shown three items, were moved by them and afterwards demanded to see them every evening. A tall Mongol in white who demonstrated six Lippizaner horses in free dressage without a whip, a strong lithe girl who hung from a rope and carried out quiet, contemplative acrobatics, and finally Monsieur Andress, the great little clown.

They all felt that with him a king had come to town, with him the universe had sent them a sign confirming that what they had done

was right, for what this dwarf had done was to find the child in the
adult, and then turn it into God. He invariably made the same
entrance, without make-up, in a velvet costume slightly too big for
him. To start with he brought with him a twelve-year-old boy, with
whom he began to play, and during this game the ancient vanished,
age fell away and out of the old man's body grew the boy in them
all, *puer æternus*, like a shining symbol of that for which each one of
the spectators had been willing to offer his life: the love of childhood.

In the course of his first two weeks in the town Monsieur Andress
simplified his performance each day until finally he dispensed with his
assistant and took the stage alone. He was always presented by the
circus manager, who had been the first to recognize the professional
potential in this audience's blend of warmth and self-sacrifice, and
who soon firmly decided to present the great clown in a manner which
no one coming from outside would have understood. Every evening
Director Gleim threw out his hands and said: "Ladies and gentlemen.
The musical clown Monsieur Andress in Vaden Town. A heart in a
heart in a heart!"

Each of these performances was a divine service from which people
went home moved, dazed, with shining eyes and the clown's voice in
their ears, a voice which seemed able to speak in every language,
including mellifluous soft Danish.

Kristoffer Holmer too emerged deeply moved one day when, half
unwillingly and after passing the square by chance, he had attended
a performance.

The concepts on which Vaden Town based its existence were those
of trade, craftsmanship and navigation. Even the religion preached in
the churches was adapted to an industrious daily life. No one in Vaden
Town doubted that what the Saviour had proclaimed was that those
who seek shall find, providing that they rise at 5.30 six days a week
and go to work. Anything over and above that, anything that smacked
of philosophy or pleasure was regarded on the whole as superfluous.
When the inhabitants of Vaden wished to look beyond daily life to
the golden realms behind it, they looked at their children. Still, most
of them would have been ready with an answer if someone had asked
them what a prince looked like. They would have replied that a prince
looked like Nikolaj Holmer's son.

Kristoffer Holmer had always been a strong boy, the fastest runner and most skilled at ball games among his contemporaries, and he also had a solemn dignity about him that made adults listen to him even before he reached the age of seven. He could play the piano as soon as he was placed before the instrument, he could draw when a pencil was put into his hand, and yet he was reticent about his accomplishments as if wanting to make light of them, as if he wished to ask pardon from life for letting everything come so easily. He had deep-set dark grey eyes which gave his whole face a withdrawn character. The women of Vaden thought Kristoffer resembled a saint, and they surrounded him with a halo of compassion as they remembered how he had lost his mother when he was quite small.

People had always agreed that a more worthy crown prince for the firm of Holmer & Son could not be imagined, and his formative years passed like a complete redemption of the trust the world had placed in him. Even the grief at his mother's death seemed to have been transformed in this little boy and lent him unnatural maturity. Without doubting his son for a second, Nikolaj Holmer had sent him to the finest boarding school in the country at the age of fourteen. During Kristoffer's years there father and son saw each other only in the holidays, and every time it seemed to Nikolaj Holmer that his son had steadily grown more like his own and everyone else's dream of a son and successor.

When his father's telegram recalled Kristoffer and the two met each other for the first time in six months, his father saw that something was wrong, for Kristoffer seemed more absent, his character more withdrawn, with a deeper, more searching gaze than his father had ever seen in him.

Nikolaj Holmer was a poor student of human nature. It is true that no one understood better than he did how to expose a rake-off or faked accounts, and how to break embargoes. But that portion of the human heart not concerned with buying and selling remained a closed book to the great merchant. His authority and power at the counter and the negotiation table were unassailable. Now, night after night, he sat at table opposite the only person in the world that he loved and with whom it had suddenly become impossible to exchange even the simplest generality, and he felt confused, humbled and angry. They ate in total silence, and afterwards Kristoffer rose and went away, and usually the merchant did not see anything more of him until breakfast-time next day.

What had happened was that immediately before he was recalled to his childhood home Kristoffer had made the discovery that he himself most likely did not exist. This probability had confronted him in the school gymnasium during a fencing lesson, and it had come without warning.

Since the establishment of the school in the eighteenth century fencing had been an approved sport, and the best foreign instructors had been brought in to teach it. When the French fencing master saw Kristoffer evaluating a foil by weighing it in his hand, and later gave him his first ever lesson, he recognized in his new pupil that combination of psycho-physical balance and sudden flick of danger that is the essential character of fencing. And Kristoffer seemed to form a lasting interest in the sport. After three years of training the school gave him a week's leave in April and after devoting that week to intensive preparation under the supervision of his French teacher, he won the Danish championship, beating captains who were fifteen years older than he was and wore curled moustaches and had ten years' experience of contests behind them.

At this time the twentieth-century upsurge of interest in the sport was building up in Denmark, and in the boy from Vaden Town the Danes saw a new candidate for the next great Olympiad. With the prospect of this challenge Kristoffer's training was now directed towards it, and it was during this training, when his championship was only a few weeks old, that he was seized with despair. During a contest with the only other pupil at the school who could offer him opposition, Kristoffer looked inwards for the first time in his life.

Hitherto he had seen himself through others' eyes. In the upturned, trustful and admiring faces of people around him he had seen his own reflection, and had understood that he really was Kristoffer, who was to set out on a journey to discover a new part of the world for himself and others. His teachers and his schoolmates had assured him of this, and he had seen it in his father's eyes. But in the fencing hall, behind the mask, the opponent's face is invisible, and suddenly it seemed to Kristoffer that he was fighting with himself. Then he glanced back and into himself. He knew what he ought to have seen. There should have been a boy filled with purposeful self-confidence, a great sportsman, a wealthy young man engaged in a superlative process of education, a slightly awkward and therefore irresistible worshipper and lover of women, and a powerful business man in embryo. None of this was to be seen. There was a black echoing emptiness surrounded by the frail shell which people wrongly imagined to be the exterior casing of Kristoffer Holmer's supereminent personality. Then he low-ered his foil and turned his back, thereby exposing the white plastron that indicates the hit area; he did not feel his opponent striking and making a hit but walked away through the judges' upraised arms without noticing the shocked faces, for all these feelings were merely, he knew, a mask. The world had never set eyes on the real Kristoffer Holmer, if he really existed somewhere in the emptiness.

It is a terrible thing for a human being to see his own life or that of others threatened with annihilation. But far worse is it to know that he himself is apparently dead and perhaps has never in fact been alive, while his fellow beings behave as if he is still amongst them. This was Kristoffer's situation when he returned to Vaden Town in March 1929 and heard the gates clang shut behind him so that he might be protected from a threat from without, which must have seemed to him to be far less harmful than the death he carried within himself.

He had received his father's telegram at a time when he was still paralysed. In Vaden Town, during the first weeks of quarantine, he had the opportunity to mull over his situation, and his first thoughts alighted on suicide, cruised around this tempting possibility, but then gave it up. Suicide presupposes an unbearable tension which one hopes death will release. Kristoffer had been struck down by some-thing different. He had been, he felt, struck by a despair so deep that it extended beyond the far side of death. He was not religious but he was convinced that if he did away with himself he would leave behind him only the worthless mask, and the inner emptiness would go with him and smile at him and envelop him in its horror on the other side of the grave.

He tried once to explain himself to his father. Nikolaj Holmer had listened attentively and then nodded. "I understand you," he said, "perfectly. I too have experienced, faced with a sure business deal, the wish to get up and leave, because I felt the trick was not mature enough to take. What is most important, Kristoffer, is not to win every time. The most important thing is to be sure in oneself that one could have won every time."

After this conversation Kristoffer had drifted around the streets in a state of utter hopelessness, and it was then that he had found himself in the square and had seen Monsieur Andress perform, and the experi-ence had moved him deeply. It did not make him happy, it promised him nothing, but it spoke to his inner self and told him he was not alone, that here on earth, in this very town, there was a human being who felt the same pain as he did and could give expression to it.

Kristoffer's first impulse after the performance was to make his way through the crowd and grasp the little hand, perhaps to kiss it, and anyway to assure the clown that he, Kristoffer, completely and perfectly and the only person in the town, had understood that childish confusion in an incalculable world to which the old man had given expression. But he stayed where he was, held back by the respect that surrounded the artist. Apart from the mayor and some few council members no one went closer to the old man than the distance separating the edge of the ring from the first rows of seats, for they all felt that the warmth they had sensed between themselves and the dwarf must not be grabbed at, that it was a materialization of a higher truth of which the dwarf was a kind of medium. When the performance came to an end they watched him leave without daring to follow him, and if they happened to meet the small meticulously dressed figure in the street they turned aside, and the women involuntarily bobbed with the respect people intuitively show to a high priest. Yet Kristoffer knew in his heart that he could have broken through this ring – all his life he had been allowed to do what no other could do. The reason for his turning his back on the square and going home was because he had realized that he had nothing to offer. How could he think of going up to a person possessed of such inward wealth when he himself in fact did not exist?

From the place within the four wings of the merchant's house he made his way upwards, to the top floor of the tall warehouse and there opened the hatch on to the yard, sat on a sack and looked down over his childhood home and across the town. During the past weeks he had taken to sitting here, in part because in this place he could be alone with his emptiness, but also because he had played here as a child. Now the view and the particular atmosphere of the loft assured him like a very faint whisper from the past that there had in fact been some meaningful moments in his life.

In the previous century this loft had been a storeroom, but now the development of modern cranes and trade in perishable goods had rendered it superfluous. The antennae of the great trading house, which sensitively registered the least variation on the stock exchanges of Great Britain and the United States, had by extending themselves such distances lost contact with what was close at hand. Quite simply, the firm had forgotten this loft. As a small boy Kristoffer had discovered it, and with an instinctive feeling that, in contrast to other secrets which would grow and shine by being shared with others, this one would vanish if he mentioned it, and with a deep discretion of the kind adults never ascribe to children, he had succeeded in keeping this place to himself. Earlier he had kept the hatch closed for fear of being discovered, but now after opening it daily he had realized that no one in Vaden Town, not even his own father, ever looked up, that their thoughts were horizontal, and in his father's case stretched out over all seven seas but were never directed upwards towards a point just over his head.

The loft still contained the carefully stacked remains of a forgotten past, from the time when Vaden was establishing its fame as a maritime town. Sacks of strong-scented spice from Sumatra for which no name had existed either in English or Danish, which had turned out to cause hallucinations and thus been impossible to sell, had been stowed here out of harm's way. Finely crafted wooden boxes holding compasses from a time when compass cards were lavishly embellished but did not give more exact degree measurements than the four corners of the world. Metal crates with piles of charts covering areas whose coasts offered but few harbours, on which the cartographers had drawn fabulous creatures on the hinterland. Now from this room Kristoffer watched the sun go down and a great storm gather.

It started inland, like a dull pulsing glow that did not seem to belong to the evening sky. Then all colour was drained from the sunset, the sky grew quite dark, and slowly a coal-black haze moved towards Vaden, like the shadow of a not yet visible, inconceivably huge body that was approaching the town from outer space. At first this shadow seemed far away, then it put on speed and reached the town in a single movement. One moment houses and sea lay illuminated in the last narrow field of daylight, the next Vaden was enveloped in darkness, as if a black cloth had been thrown over it. Then the cloth was split by the first flash of lightning. For an instant a long vertical snake of white light was chiselled out of the blackness, then it was gone, taking with it the electric light and leaving the town in total darkness as if the rest of the world had wanted to take revenge and pay Vaden back for its defiance.

When the light disappeared the courtyard beneath Kristoffer was plunged into pitch darkness. Then the darkness was rent by a new flash, lightning of a kind Kristoffer had never seen before, a lengthy painful discharge of white energy. The rain followed, as yet only as a warning, a swift triumphant drum roll of water that ebbed out in a distant rumble of thunder.

Kristoffer felt an irresistible impulse to pray to the black sky for help.

As a child he had made himself slings, and with other boys on the beach competed as to who could hurl highest. He had always regarded other people's prayers as similar shots at heaven. If there was anything certain in this world it was that the stone and the words would return to the thrower – his own stone later than the others – without having caused any other effect in the universe than once more to confirm what everyone knew: that Kristoffer Holmer had hurled highest. Now he felt, even though he did not move, that he placed a shiny round stone in his sling and, well aware that there was no small element of madness in the action, threw the words out into the emptiness in an entreaty that for him too there might be a meaning, that there might be a human core within the shell of Kristoffer Holmer. Then he tensed every fibre listening for an answer or the echo that would show the stone had merely fallen back to earth.

His suspense was broken by a crack of thunder. When the next lightning flash lit up the courtyard beneath him a figure stood in the gateway. In the lightning which followed like a long, connected series of flashes, Kristoffer recognized the figure. It was the dwarf, the great Monsieur Andress. He stood sheltered from the rain but visible in the flashes of lightning, and he looked around him like an actor who has made his entrance, and the darkness between the flashes made it look as if he made quick jerking movements with his head. It seemed impossible to Kristoffer that the little man could see anything at all against the alternately inky black and dazzling sky, and yet for a moment it appeared that the dwarf gazed intently into his eyes. Then everything grew dark and an earsplitting crash caused the air around him to tremble.

In the silence that followed he heard footsteps. The measured steps of a small person. Someone must have lit a paraffin lamp which the dwarf carried with him on his way up, for its glow flickered up the staircase and shone into the loft.

Then Monsieur Andress stood in the room.

Kristoffer had been brought up to be polite and to anticipate and prepare himself for all eventualities, and while the clown's steps approached he had planned a worthy reception. He had intended to take a step or two forwards, go down on his knees, which would bring his head to the height of that of the new arrival, utter his name and then improvise a welcoming speech.

But what actually happened was that he stayed sitting down, unmoving. In one hand the clown held a violin case, in the other a lamp, but the light which now flickeringly lit the loft came, thought Kristoffer, from his face. It seemed to be lit up from within; through the fine net of wrinkles and the bushy moustache shone a light that seemed to issue from a brightly burning source of warmth and humanity which dispersed Kristoffer's plans and brought them to nothing. With slow dignified movements the clown put down the lamp and took off his cloak; beneath it he still wore his costume of flowing white material. Then he went over to the hatch and looked out.

A fresh onslaught of lightning burst out and for a moment, over the black streets, the flashes showed the shining rainwet roofs like rows of tombstones on black earth, and Kristoffer recalled that the town was entrenched against death.

When the dwarf spoke his voice was like worn velvet, with a delicate gloss of the various linguistic territories his long life had taken him through.

"From my height," he said, "it can be quite pleasing to see the world *von oben*, like this."

The thought struck Kristoffer that the clown's stature had not only since his birth placed him beneath other people's eye-level but might also have transferred him into another world, that the pain he had recognized in his performance perhaps stemmed from an experience similar to his own in that both of them, by a definitive abnormality of growth, had been set outside the world that surrounded them.

"From up here," the clown went on gently, "one can easily imagine that the land and the town down there are *morte*, that we are the last living people in the world."

This observation made its way effortlessly into Kristoffer's innermost dreams, from where he made reply.

"Yes," he said, "that would be awful. But there is something that is even worse than being alone in the world, and that is never to have existed at all."

The dwarf made no answer to this, but for Kristoffer an answer was unnecessary, because at this moment he felt he had been understood. With equal amounts of deep gratitude and disquiet over the inexplicable, he felt that the universe had heard his prayer, that he was in the presence of a higher being who could see through what the world hitherto had confused with Kristoffer Holmer. "Monsieur Andress, too," he thought, "surely feels that he does not really exist among other people," and he recollected the end of the performance, when the clown collected the jewels of the audience and put them on, and afterwards strutted around the square like a child begging to be loved because it sparkles, and then the next day gave the precious things back with unerring certainty to their owners, this time as if begging for their attention because he had returned something that had been missing. Kristoffer felt his eyes fill with tears.

"I don't know if you saw me," he said. "But I was down there on the square during your performance. It was . . ." – his voice failed him for a moment – "it was magnificent."

Almost unwillingly the old man tore his gaze from the darkness over the town and looked at Kristoffer vaguely.

"When I am performing," he said, "I am never anything but marvellous."

Trained as he was to seek the highest thing but to keep silent about his own merits, this candid self-evaluation made Kristoffer lose his breath. "You can only speak like that," he thought, "when you are a saint, when you have risen above all other human beings, up above the endless work of making yourself deserving of a place in the world."

"I have," the dwarf said, "seen you sitting up here several times."

It was a long leap between Kristoffer's feeling of unworthiness and the fact that the person addressing him had seen him before; he was, so to speak, mentally reeling in the stream of merciful light that had made him visible. But again he answered from within himself, that part which the clown seemed to address directly.

"I have," he said, "discovered that I somehow do not exist."

"And where," asked the clown, "did you discover that?"

"At school," replied Kristoffer.

A painful spasm crossed Monsieur Andress's face. "Everything one receives at school," he said, "is bad . . ." then, after a pause, ". . . is a dreadful headache," he finished the sentence.

This plain statement again brought tears to Kristoffer's eyes. Again he felt the little man coming to meet him across the human ages in time and experience that separated them.

The world knew that Monsieur Andress had spent twenty years in conventual school, at Jesuit colleges and the world's strictest conservatories. From his learning and his experience of educational institutions, experience that extended infinitely far beyond Kristoffer's own, he had gleaned this gem, which shone in Kristoffer's eyes like a crystallization of his own chaotic feelings.

"That," he said in deep gratitude, "was precisely how it began. With a headache."

The golden light of the lamp threw, above the hatch, a huge enlargement of the clown's figure, like a big dark wall. Kristoffer leaned against this weeping wall and opened his heart, and to his immense astonishment discovered it was not empty.

"One day in the gymnasium when I was having a fencing lesson I turned my back on Castenskiold," he said.

"When one is fighting," said the dwarf, "one must never turn one's back."

"It was not like that," said Kristoffer. "I suddenly discovered that it was not him I was fighting with. In some way it was myself. I wonder if you understand that?"

The clown took a step closer. "Yes," he said, "it happens to some people. And precisely at school. There was" – he looked intently at Kristoffer – "a voice that spoke to you, was there not?"

Kristoffer had never felt before that there had been a voice. But now the clown's eyes, which had gleamed before him in the darkness, seemed to throw new light over his overshadowed memory, and when he recalled the echoes of the gymnasium, the sound of canvas shoes on the copper covering of the piste, the sound of the blades striking each other, he heard the still more distant but unmistakable sound of a voice speaking to him.

"Yes," he said quietly, "there was a voice. But" – he looked pleadingly at Monsieur Andress – "it is so faint that I can hardly hear it."

The clown leaned forward and at that moment the ceiling of the loft changed and Kristoffer saw the timbers of the gymnasium roof, and through the shouts of command he heard a voice barely distinguishable from that of Monsieur Andress ask: "Why do you fight?"

With a start Kristoffer jumped to his feet as if in an attempt to shake off a nightmare, but the question nailed him to the spot. In self-defence he grasped at the first words that occurred to him.

"Because," he said, "it is important to take part."

Close to his face he saw the old man's grey hair and he realized he was on his knees. He wanted to say something, he wanted to change the course of the conversation, but something relentless had come over the dwarf.

"You know all the same," said the voice, "that if you lose today you will make the people looking on still more unhappy than if you had not fallen into line."

"Yes," said Kristoffer.

"So why do you fight?" the voice pressed him.

"To win," replied Kristoffer.

"And if you win," the voice went on, "how long will you and the spectators rejoice in your victory?"

Kristoffer made no answer.

"Perhaps for one night," said the voice. "Perhaps for an hour. Perhaps for a minute. Isn't that how it is?"

"Yes," said Kristoffer.

"That is," said the voice, "*porca madonna*, a brief moment to wear away your youth for."

Like a priest who has blessed the congregation and then turns towards the altar, the dwarf turned away. But now Kristoffer would not let him go. With an effort he pushed himself up from the homespun sack beside him and followed the clown, divided between his terror at apparently being transparent before the clear eyes in the darkness and his need to hear the voice giving its answers.

"What about school?" he asked. "What about going to school?"

Monsieur Andress made a gesture to him to stand still.

"Do they still say that you are learning for life?" he asked.

"Yes," said Kristoffer.

"And when life begins," said the clown, "then they will say that you live to work, and that you must work for the fatherland and for your children. Those children who are already getting to know in school they are learning for life, and that is the way it continues, in that way they all – *i coglioni* – push life before them, while they scream that they cannot manage it." And he quoted slowly: "*Più le cose cambiano, più sono le stesse cose.*"

With the assurance that comes of knowing the effect of one's remarks in advance, Monsieur Andress turned his back on Kristoffer, took up his stance in the hatchway and looked down into the courtyard, and as if he had called up an effective underlining of his own words, a series of lightning flashes caused him to stand out like a black silhouette against a sky boiling with electricity.

Although Kristoffer felt a slight trickle of cold fear in his blood of what he was taking part in, he was carried forward by the thought that a chance like this would probably never be offered him again.

"How," he asked, "could you know there was a voice?"

Monsieur Andress turned round slowly and now when he stepped down towards Kristoffer there was something cunning in his attitude. "There is always a voice," he said. "All you have to do is listen. That is how I work in the ring."

His eyes grew distant, and Kristoffer pictured him in the market square, head inclined, listening into the night for something only he could hear.

"I have the audience with me," he said, and his voice was slow and ecstatic. "I have collected the jewels, I have been out among people. And then I hear the voice, far-off, a little faint, but still absolutely clear. And it tells me I must take a boy on to the stage."

He took Kristoffer's hand, and unresisting he followed the dwarf on to the floor. For a brief moment he thought of the assistant the clown had used for a time in his performance, and who had been the envy of all. "Now," he thought, "I am in that boy's place."

"We stand on the stage," said Monsieur Andress, "the audience is tense, and I feel it spread out into the night, I hear the voice whisper the show is going well. It whispers: 'Now you have a boy. Now you must get a girl as well. Then you will create something great tonight. Something that will make the bells ring.' And they are already ringing." He turned towards Kristoffer. "When the bells ring," he said, "something big is on the way."

"The church bells?" asked Kristoffer, and thought of Monsieur Andress's clerical past.

"No," whispered the clown and his eyes were distant. "No, not the church bells. It's the cash-till bells that are ringing. If only we get hold of a girl."

Kristoffer became aware that someone was on the way up the stairs. In other circumstances this event would have filled him with surprise and sorrow because someone had discovered his hiding place. But on this night under the spell of the clown's magnetism he chose, without quite realizing why, not to wonder over it.

Then the girl stood before them. At another time Kristoffer would have stared at her, but he was not sure of her existence. Like the voice that had spoken to him and which was still ringing in his ears, she seemed to be a partially unreal stage requisite in a supernatural performance. All that he saw was that she was soaking wet, so wet that her long hair, which, under other conditions, – if she existed under other conditions – must be curly, now hung down over her shoulder and sent a long succession of big water-drops running down over her body and on to the floor. A further contribution to the absolute improbability of her figure was the fact that she was barefoot and apparently naked. Then Monsieur Andress recovered his attention, seized the girl's hand and drew them both out on to the floor, and as he bowed to an imaginary audience, Kristoffer recognized his characteristic form of greeting from the performance on the square, a greeting which kept a firm hold on the spectators' hearts and attention beneath its outward humility.

"Ladies and gentlemen," said the clown, "a young lady and a young man."

He turned towards them. "There is," he said slowly, "something big in store this evening. Something that will make us all richer, in experience and wisdom. It is my art to obtain this feeling, and to allow the audience to feel it. We expect the incredible, the audience and I. It is true that I don't know what form it will take, I have no ideas. But I am listening," and he inclined his head as if listening to the night sky.

Then the girl took two steps forwards and uttered a deep, wailing sound, a cross between a snarl and the onset of a vomiting attack.

Now for the first time Kristoffer looked directly at her and he saw she was not naked but so drenched that her dress stuck to her body. He had been brought up to the world of sound realities which uses language that is plain, cheerful and effective. The events of the past week and in particular the past hour had transported him to a different and more dangerous landscape, in which unexpected and fabulous turns of phrase came to him. He could not recall ever having seen this girl before and yet he knew she was a princess. At this moment he had no access to his school learning and could not place her in any familiar mythology, but she resembled, he thought, one of the tragic heroines from great drama. She was pale. Not dull and colourless, but her neck and face appeared chalk-white, a cold wind suffused her clothes and he had no doubt that she had brought some terrible experience with her. Monsieur Andress had come to the loft with the light of transfiguration; the girl radiated a kind of uplifted insanity.

She took two uncertain steps across the floor and seemed for the first time now to have seen the young man and the elderly one. She gave no indication of what chaotic thoughts passed through her head and yet she seemed to have gathered the solemnity of the situation, for she slowly straightened herself as if preparing the significant opening comment expected of her. Then she raised one arm and looked straight at Monsieur Andress.

"I know," she said slowly, "everything about codfish."

Then she fell forwards without trying to prevent herself and would have struck the floor with her face if Kristoffer had not caught her.

That moment when he felt her weight the cold air around her reached him too. It was the air from the sea and for a moment he wondered if she might have been close to drowning.

Then he recognized her.

There had been one person in Kristoffer's life with whom he had shared the secret of his loft, and it had been to this person – whom he had never mentioned to anyone else – his thoughts had returned during the past weeks as to a warm rock in the midst of the flood of meaninglessness he felt his life had become. That person was Sonja Vaden. She was the same age as Kristoffer, the daughter of a fisherman whose family, in spite of bearing the name of the town, had long since been forced outside the town walls to take up existence in a windswept district beside the fjord. In other parts of Denmark the two children would have been separated for their own good and told that the social realities that divided them were such as it was not in human power to alter. But in Vaden Town people did not harden their hearts so much, and so the two children continued to play beside the water and in the hills above the town. Sonja had lost her mother when she was five, and she had met grief head on without breaking down. When Kristoffer's mother turned away from her husband and child to follow her voices, Sonja offered Kristoffer, wordlessly but immediately and without reservation, her companionship and her slight but remarkably strong shoulders as an aid to get over the horror. For weeks and months Kristoffer wept every day in Sonja's company, an inconsolable weeping that no other person but she was witness to. Later on came a spring in which he remembered pulling the truck up to the highest point overlooking the town and then he had driven Sonja down the winding road with the sun and the wind from the sea in their faces and a cloud of dust behind them.

After that she disappeared. Throughout his childhood her father had regularly taken her out fishing with him. One day in October they had gone out quite early in the morning. About midday it had started to blow and when at last from the hatchway Kristoffer caught sight of the little boat the wind had strengthened to a gale which rushed over the sea like a great cold scythe, flayed off the tops of the waves and pulled them over the water in white ribbons of foam. At some point in the howling gale a wave crashed sideways over the stern into the boat and took Sonja's father with it. The girl had tied herself to the tiller with rope and steered the boat through the storm towards land. The entrance to Vaden harbour was narrow, and the townsfolk stood by helplessly at a loss watching the girl in the little boat approaching the cruelly smiling stone fangs of the quays, hidden in the frothing waves by white foam. There was not a soul among them who would not have risked his life for a child in distress if it could have helped, but the gale had now become so violent that help was impossible, and they clenched their jaws around their grief and thought with bitter hatred of the sea that they would remember this, there would come a day when even nature would not be able to take a child from them.

Kristoffer had gone down to the harbour. But in contrast to most of the people standing there he did not weep. He went further out than anyone else and no one had the strength to keep him back. Clinging to the tall green pole of the leading light he gazed out at the boat and the only liquid that came into his eyes was spray. He had learned from Sonja that there is a time for everything. There had been a time to weep, but not now, now it was a time to be strong, and Kristoffer concentrated all his attention on reaching the girl at the tiller. Immediately in front of the harbour entrance Sonja put the engine into reverse and, strangely coldbloodedly, as if something of the sea had entered her veins, she held the boat against the wind and the sea. Kristoffer alone knew why she did this. Once, when he seemed about to be overcome by despair, she had told him that all misfortunes in life come in waves. "And Kristoffer," she had said, "you must count, for every seventh wave is smaller than the other. That is the one you must try to sail along on."

Now Kristoffer saw that Sonja was counting the waves; just before the seventh she straightened the boat, increased the engine to full throttle, and on the high, completely straight and sharp crest of the wave she sailed into harbour only a few inches from the starboard outer sea wall.

In the inner harbour she had collapsed. When they had brought the boat to the quay Kristoffer had stood and watched them lifting her up, and she had been just as white-faced then as she was now. Just as she came up to him she had opened her eyes and he was the first person she saw. "Kristoffer," she had said, and Kristoffer had bent down to her and she had whispered, so only he could hear her: "Will you take the tiller for a while?"

As far as he could remember, that was the last time he had really seen her.

It is true that she stayed on in the town, in the home of a taciturn uncle and a careworn aunt, people who had expected the worst from life and had got it. Their only child had been stillborn, the fishery had been meagre and dangerous, only in religion had they found fruitfulness and calm. They looked upon life in Vaden Town as they had looked upon the sea, unwillingly, trembling and with the feeling that it was an unavoidable evil that awaited them every morning at their street door, accompanied them through the day and let them go only when they returned and could lock the door of their home behind them.

The awareness of the sorrows Sonja brought with her weighed them even more heavily towards the earth and made them turn still further from the world and draw ever closer to the girl. They consulted a doctor and after this visit Sonja was taken out of the mixed school and sent to Countess Moltke's school for girls, where her new mother took her each day. Her foster parents were not members of the dramatic or music societies, they did not go for walks or to balls, so from then on Kristoffer only had glimpses of Sonja, and she was always accompanied by an adult. At one time he made efforts to find a way of contacting her, but the situation was new and confusing for him. He started to go to church every Sunday because he was sure he would see her there. Then her aunt and uncle changed their place of worship to one of the small thin-lipped denominations whose temple was near the harbour, and no one was admitted to this little white house before his heart had been scrutinized and carefully weighed, and as Kristoffer felt that his interior self could not stand such an inspection, he stayed away. Furthermore, all the adults in Vaden said that what Sonja needed was to be sheltered, and that was best done by leaving her in peace. So unwillingly, with the longing for her always alive in him, Kristoffer gave up searching for his lost friend.

Now that he had her in his arms and discovered he was big enough to carry her, and that she had changed and seemed a stranger, he thought that, like the rest of his life, it was too late now anyway.

Monsieur Andress removed the cork from a flat slightly curved silver flask and leaned over the unconscious girl. Kristoffer had seen him on the stage making a show of drinking from this flask and afterwards tottering apparently intoxicated among the spectators, but he had been sure the flask was empty. Now the scent of well-matured rum filtered through his nostrils. He said nothing, but Monsieur Andress read his thoughts.

"To drink from a bottle that everyone knows is empty," said the clown, "and then walk around as if drunk, that is art. But to drink from a bottle that everyone knows is empty, and yet have a drop of rum in it, do you know what that is?"

"No," said Kristoffer.

"That is divine," said Monsieur Andress.

He poured a few drops of the liquid between the girl's lips. She swallowed without coughing, then opened her eyes and looked straight at Kristoffer with a glance of immediate recognition. Something that might have been a cold draught swept between them and with a leap she freed herself from him and stood up, and moved away from the staircase in terror.

"They are coming," she whispered.

The dwarf seized her by the arm, and Kristoffer saw again the surprising strength that dwelt in Monsieur Andress's small body, and when he spoke his voice was authoritative and sure.

"If they come," he said, "I shall stand on the stairs, and I shall give them . . ." – he hesitated a moment with the dramatic artist's fastidiousness for the right words of welcome – "a courteous but definite repulse," he said.

Kristoffer saw that the clown's power had penetrated Sonja's clouded consciousness, for she lowered her shoulders. Then she looked at the clown.

"I found it," she said to him. "I found the way here. I have been here before."

Monsieur Andress made no reply, he merely looked into the girl's eyes, and Kristoffer realized they must have met each other before, that they knew each other, and that what was happening now, to a greater or lesser extent – in a way that far surpassed his understanding – must have been planned.

Without a word Monsieur Andress handed his silver flask to Sonja. Kristoffer could not imagine she had drunk neat spirit before, and in no circumstances straight from the bottle. Now she took a long deep slurp and afterwards wiped her mouth slowly with the back of her hand.

Earlier her face had been distant and expressionless, as if she had come to the loft with the intention of saying as little as possible and preferably nothing. Now the alcohol rose through her like a deep blush, sparkling in her eyes like tears, and made her talk.

"The warmth," she said, "that comes from spirits is false. He often said that. But it feels genuine enough now." She made a long pause.

Then: "Surely," she said, "it can never be taught from the Bible to murder another human being. That's what I said to him. But he did not hear me. I could have got those codfish. I know everything about codfish." She looked past Kristoffer out into the night. "When you have need of them," she said, "there is never anyone who listens."

"There is," said the dwarf without taking his eyes from hers, "always someone who listens."

"Even now?" the girl asked.

"Precisely now," replied Monsieur Andress, "precisely now someone is listening."

The girl closed her eyes and then quoted slowly:

Hold fast to what you have
so none shall take thy crown.

She opened her eyes. "That is what he wrote," she said, "in my hymn-book. It was the text for confirmation. For he is a lay preacher. He prepared me himself. And then he gave me a gold ten-kroner piece."

She stopped, as if talking was a useless effort, and when she did continue Kristoffer knew that it was the dwarf's questioning face before her which assured her the world was listening.

"It was a little hymn-book," she said, "so small you had to turn the pages with a pin. And yet it is like that they picture Paradise. Very small, very flimsy pages." She looked despairingly at her two listeners, as if she realized how disjointedly she spoke.

"They say you must be still. Only by sitting still can you enter Paradise. It must be a very small Paradise they are preparing themselves for." She paused. "Countess Moltke too," she said, "is preparing herself for a very narrow Paradise. So narrow that there certainly won't be room for anyone except herself, and" – she made a face – "her French bulldog."

A deep rattling roar shook the room and in the noise Sonja took another long gulp from the flask. When quiet returned her thoughts had run on. Now she looked straight at Kristoffer.

"Kristoffer," she said, "do you remember *The Bayadère* at the dramatic society?"

Kristoffer nodded.

"Father took me there. When they began to dance" – her eyes shone at the memory – "when they began to dance I wet my knickers. But Father put his coat under me. And then he whispered: 'Sit on it. To hell with it, you'll soon be dry.' And I was. And afterwards I danced at the ball. And nothing showed." She laughed triumphantly. "And you were the only one I danced with."

Kristoffer nodded again.

"But you didn't know I had wet my knickers."

Kristoffer shook his head.

She looked straight at Monsieur Andress. "But he disappeared, sad to say," she said.

The clown watched her intently.

"Yes, well, he died," she went on matter-of-factly. "The sea took him. The motor was no good. He's told me that many times since. 'It happened because we couldn't beat the waves,' he says."

"How could he tell you that when he was dead?" asked Monsieur Andress.

The girl looked at him distantly. "Oh," she said. "But he came back, didn't he? You see, I went down to the water every day, and one day he came back, and he lifted himself up on his tail and smiled at me with all his teeth. He always boasted, you know, that he'd kept all his teeth."

"Did he have a tail?" asked Monsieur Andress.

The girl nodded at him. "It might be as long as a week before he came back," she said. "That's a long time to wait when you're alone. But he always came. Because we had to talk, didn't we?"

"What did you talk about?" asked Kristoffer.

"About everything you can think of," said the girl. "About Uncle and Aunt. And the accident. And about you, too. At the beginning . . ." she paused, "at the beginning we agreed you would come and fetch me. Father said you would be sure to. One day you would come with the truck and we would drive away. But you didn't come, did you? You can go on believing in something like that for quite a time. And I did see you now and then in the street. But you can't go on believing it."

Kristoffer felt something on his hands and when he looked down he discovered it to be his own tears, and in wonderment he found

that from inside himself, from where he had believed was only emptiness, there now flowed tears he was unable to stop.

"Hold fast to what you hold," the girl said. "That's what they think
about."

"Yes," said Monsieur Andress. "That is more or less what they
think about, *i coglioni*."

"You see," said Sonja, "Father used to take cod from the storage
tanks. I took the lid off for him and he used to take a couple. Never
many. Just enough to take the edge off the hunger. Just two or three.
We have to live, don't we? And it went well for a long time. He
leaned over the edge and put his nose into the water and caught them
easy as anything. By casting with his head."

"Was your father a kind of fish?" asked the clown.

"A porpoise," said the girl.

A puzzled expression crossed Monsieur Andress's face, as if his
understanding was eluding him, and it occurred to Kristoffer that the
old man's extensive knowledge, despite his many years at sea with
Circus Gleim, might not after all extend to the creatures in Danish
waters.

"Aunt," the girl went on, "often said that it may be true that not
much good comes from the sea, but you know all about the evil it
sends. It's different with people. So they let me go down there alone.
But that day he must have noticed something or other, because he
followed me. It was Father who saw him. I had pushed the lid off
the tank and he had eaten. He hadn't said a word. But I felt he was
looking at something. And he says, 'Hey, brother!' And then I see
Uncle. He's standing just behind me and he's holding his gun to his
side, so I don't see it at first, but then he raises it, sort of slowly. I
say to Father: 'Cripes, Dad,' I say, 'you'd better swim off or Uncle
will shoot you.' But he doesn't seem to hear what I say. He just looks
Uncle in the face and then he beats the water and then he lifts himself
up on his tail and stands there while the water gets white with foam
around him, and then he shows Uncle all his teeth. So then I understand why he doesn't swim away. He'll allow himself to be shot. He
thinks that if he gets away I shall suffer for it. He thinks Uncle will
ill-treat me." She shook her head slowly. "So stupid of Father, wasn't
it, to think they could lay hands on me. He should have just tried. I
would have strangled him. I would have got up in the night and
fetched a string from the piano." She thought for a moment. "A
C-string," she went on, "because 'Our God he is a fortress strong' is

in C-major. And then I would have strangled him. I know he's bigger
and stronger than me. But I would have the night on my side. And
it's hard to defend yourself, when you've been asleep and have a
C-string round your neck."

Kristoffer felt himself swallow and caught himself feeling his neck
with a couple of fingers.

"But then," said Sonja, "then Uncle took aim. It was a double-
barrelled shotgun. Father never used buckshot. He said that was for
people who couldn't shoot. I try to stop him. 'Uncle,' I say, 'that
couple of fish, I can get them for you any time, just take me out with
you, I know everything about cod.' But he just cocks the gun. Then
I say: 'Surely the Bible doesn't say you should murder your own
brother, does it?' but he doesn't hear me, he's beside himself. And I
seem to be paralysed. That's because they want you to be quiet all
the time. You get out of the habit of doing anything, don't you? But
then I see him start to pull the trigger, then I wake up, and then I
hit at the gun and both barrels go off. I must have closed my eyes
for when I open them again Father has gone and for a moment I
think he's been hit, but then I see Uncle lying on the ground with
blood all over the place, and he must have shot himself in the legs.
But he moves all the same, he tries to get hold of me, but I don't
stay, I just go away."

Monsieur Andress looked at the girl with narrowed eyes.

"When was this?" he asked.

She hesitated a moment as if she had lost the sense of time. "Well,"
she said, "it was today."

"So you have come," the clown reasoned slowly, "straight from
there."

The girl nodded slowly. "Straight from there," she said.

Monsieur Andress drew a deep breath. "That is," he said, half to
himself, half to the two young people, "what age and experience gives.
The knowledge that a stunning turn is on the way. First you feel the
power, and then there is nothing for a moment. You are confused,
un sentimento di essere abbandonato, and it is then you listen, and then
it comes, and then it is . . ." – he looked at the girl – "that you hear
the most amazing things."

Slowly and laboriously Kristoffer rose to his feet and with stiff
steps went over to Sonja. He knew that now the world had encapsu-
lated him, and was on the point of casting him out. Still he felt he
would be permitted a final word.

He placed himself before the girl and stretched out his arms in a searching gesture, but no word came from his lips.

"Why," she asked, "didn't you come?"

"They said you had to be shielded," Kristoffer replied uncertainly.

The girl looked at him intently, without reproach and without judgment.

"Yes," she said then. "And when they come to fetch me they will shield me in earnest."

At that moment, Kristoffer was struck from outer space by the full extent of his own treachery and he grasped the fact that behind the shell was not merely emptiness, behind his name was one who had failed the human being without whom he could not conceive the world at all, and from whom he was now to be parted for ever. Staggering like a drunkard he spun round on his heel and reached out as if he wanted to recall his previous emptiness, which was far preferable to this knowledge that every possibility had been thrown away. In that moment, above the lamentation of the rain, he became aware of voices around him, a mumbling chorus of insistent speech, and one of the voices separated itself, more audible and imperative than the others. In front of Kristoffer, two eyes caught the golden light of the lamp, and he realized that it was Monsieur Andress's voice he heard.

"One can, you know," said the clown, almost kindly, "one can always jump, Kristoffer."

A great warm wave of gratitude washed over Kristoffer because the little sage had again looked into his soul, seen his despair and shown him a way out. And like all final deliverances this one too had the effect, at the moment it was suggested, of being completely beautiful and right.

In a single movement Kristoffer put all his sorrows aside and stepped up into the hatchway. Beneath him the darkness was bottomless and yet at the same time welcoming. Then Monsieur Andress's voice came to him again, low and insistent.

"On the other hand, jumping down into Daddy's courtyard would be to choose a very quick and easy way," he whispered.

In a nightmarish change of scene Kristoffer was back in the fencing hall, and there he slowly turned round so he stood with his back to the darkness. From behind, from the depths beneath him, a gentle pulling drew him backwards. In the room in front of him the girl and the dwarf were watching him closely.

"That time," said Kristoffer as if what he was talking about was obvious, "I turned round and went away. That's what I want to do now."

The dwarf laughed quietly. "That time you were wiser," he said. "Now you'll just disappear. That leap, my boy, will be the last and longest step backwards you'll ever take."

It was no longer possible for Kristoffer to decide whether the figure of the little man pulled him in to life or pushed him back towards annihilation, all he knew was that the dwarf must have been sent from elsewhere, that he was a great, a universal disintegrator and tempter. With difficulty he took his eyes away from him and directed them at the girl. She looked at him as she had done before, many times, infinitely long ago, when he wept: without fear, without reproach, but attentively, almost insistently, as if he were a human being like all the others.

This look made Kristoffer step back into the loft and sink down. The girl came up to his side and silently took him by the hand.

"That," said Monsieur Andress, "looks like a finale." He turned to the hatchway as if to an audience. "It is now time," he said, stopped, listened into the night for a moment, and then continued, "to declare these two young people, who have been separated, but whom I, Monsieur Andress, have brought together as if I were Our Lord himself, to be betrothed, at least on this stage and for this evening. And allow me to sing a pious hope for their future and mine, with the voice that called forth a deluge of tears over the whole of Europe."

He loudly cleared his throat and then he sang:

> *Lieber Gott*
> *gibt doch zu*
> *daß ich klüger bin als du.*

Kristoffer and Sonja had been looking at each other, but the moment the first note sounded they looked up, for at that moment the great clown's world-renowned tenor cracked and grew thin and quavering, like falsetto laughter. Then he fell silent and stood completely still for a moment.

"Yes," he said quietly, "the voice has gone. But I am still here."

He lifted his right hand as if to wave goodbye and with a movement like a greeting he pushed his thick grey hair from his head. Under the wig was straw-coloured stubble through which the scalp shone pinkly.

"Allow me," he said, "to introduce you to a young person washed up on the immortal rocky shores of dramatic art by cruel destiny."

Carefully, as if not to tear his skin, he took off his grey moustache. He passed his sleeve over his face, and on the white velvet rested the remains of what had been the face of the great Monsieur Andress. Before them Kristoffer and Sonja now saw a boy of at most twelve years of age.

"Cor," said the boy triumphantly, "I must do this in the ring one day."

"Who are you?" asked Kristoffer.

"I am assistant to the great Monsieur Andress," said the boy.

"Where," asked Kristoffer, "where is Monsieur Andress?"

"Monsieur Andress," the boy replied, "died a week ago. You see," he said slowly, "he brought this new smallpox into town with him." He reflected for a moment. Then: "We had been on tour," he said, "and on the way back we decide to go in to Rödby. But they don't want a show there. Which, my children, was right shitty, for we were hungry." He smiled at the two facing him. "Circus Gleim looks grand enough," he said, "but it costs to look grand. So we were starving." He laughed at the thought. "That's the world for you," he said. "Even the great Monsieur Andress was starving. That's when we tried to get into Vaden. And hunger got the imagination going. And Andress told that story about the storm, and that did it, we are in harbour, there's food for all. And Andress brings luck and boasts it's all due to him. But one day he's covered in red spots and he falls ill. There's just him and me in the cabin, he gets cramps that throw him fathoms up in the air and on to the floor, so in the end I have to tie him down, and towards the end he's so bad I think: *Scheisse*, now it's better for him to die than live, and then he dies. And what shall we do? *Mann weis'nicht, und* one is too polite to ask. And then I get the idea of putting on his wig – he was bald, wasn't he? – and I make a moustache, because I wasn't born yesterday, and then I take the stage. All the others notice at once something's wrong, but of course they're frightened, so they let me do it, and the audience don't notice anything, no, *nichts*." He looked in front of him dreamily. "Actually the audiences love me," he said. "In fact I must say that I was no worse than the old idiot ever."

The two young people stared at the boy in a vain attempt to bridge the transformation they had witnessed.

"Have you," asked Sonja after a while, "been infected with smallpox now?"

"Who knows," said the boy, "and I'm too polite to ask."

At that moment the rain increased in force, it rose from an unbroken mumble to a triumphant cascade, and irresistibly attracted by the wildness outside the three went over to the hatchway. Above them the sky gaped bluish-white in a long, linked series of lightning flashes, and from this whiteness the rain fell in great heavy drops that struck the roof of the merchant's house, then bounced up and were splintered by the following drops into white foam until the town beneath them was enveloped in a white vaporous fog.

Kristoffer and Sonja still clasped each other's hands, and now in a mutual vision they saw through the storm. For a brief moment the shining watery mists gathered together, and above the town rose a figure that stretched from the earth into the heavens, and they recognized Death, a huge, upright, shining skeleton, and at its summit the skull smiled rapturously at them, and on the roofs of the town the wet bone fingers played a savage tympani of water. The vision stood out against the sky for only a moment, then it was gone, and in horror they stared at the boy at their side as if to seek an explanation or at least confirmation, but the white tense face revealed nothing.

"Tonight I shall leave," said the boy. "I have found a gate in the wall that opens. I have decided to allow you to come with me."

"Then shall we die out there, all of us?" asked Sonja, and she asked without any suggestion of fear, as if it were a question of nothing more serious than tomorrow's weather.

"Who knows," said the boy. "And one is too polite to ask."

"– But death," he added after a moment's pause, "can't be shut out, after all." And he went on, thoughtfully: "Where I have lived most of my life people don't live to more than . . . than . . ." he hesitated confronted with difficult figures, "perhaps half the age of folk here," he finished his sentence. "But what's the use of living to a hundred and fifty with the artificial this and that they talk about, if you don't live properly?"

"What are we going to live on?" asked Kristoffer, and this was his first objection.

In the light of the lamp the boy opened his violin case, and the contents sparkled and dazzled the eyes against the blue velvet. "On the crumbs from the rich man's table," he said. "Today the women of Vaden Town came along in their most magnificent finery to see Monsieur Andress wear their *bijoux* and jewels."

Kristoffer looked out of the hatch and down on the main building. The great chandeliers had been extinguished, but a solitary light went flickering through the darkened rooms. It was, he knew, his father, Nikolaj Holmer, keeping watch over his valuables against fire and over the only person in the world he cared for, his son, Kristoffer, whom he believed to be safe in bed.

"How," asked Kristoffer, and this was his second objection, "will it be possible to forget what one has left behind?"

"No one who lives life aright," said the boy coldly, "*can ever forget.* I personally," he added proudly, "remember every single arseful I've had in my life. What you can do is live so you don't need to blub over what you remember."

"Do we," asked Kristoffer, "do we really *have* to go away?" and this was his final objection.

"That," said the boy, "is something I can't tell you. And one is too polite to ask."

Then from the violin case he took out a wooden flute, the famous flute that had belonged to Monsieur Andress, the great clown.

"I've promised," he said, "to play outside one or two windows where a few other young folk who want to come with us live."

He looked at Sonja and Kristoffer. "Ladies and gentlemen," he said dreamily, "think of the performance we have given you tonight, my children and I. They have told you two stories that – don't deny it – have touched our hearts. And now see how he stands, as straight as a soldier, and how lovely she is, like a doll. And when they were small, it was soldiers he played with, and she had painted dolls. Now, ladies and gentlemen, the tables are turned! Thank you very much indeed."

Then he closed the case, picked it up, threw his cloak over his shoulders and made his way down the stairs. Kristoffer and Sonja followed him silently and Kristoffer remembered they had each gone up those stairs alone. He himself as if he were going to the scaffold, Monsieur Andress as if he were stepping up on to his throne. He could find no words to describe the girl's ascent, but into his mind came the sight of her bare legs when they had played on the beach.

When they went out of the gateway the rain had eased off and the town lay shining brilliantly under the moon. It occurred to Kristoffer that they had not had an answer to the real question. He caught up with the boy in two long, purposeful strides. "What," he asked of the back lit by the moon, "what do you want of us?" And the back answered him: "It is not good for us to travel alone," and it was impossible to tell whether that "us" was *pluralis majestatis*, the self-confident plural of a ruler of the world, or the astute businessman's attempt to make his affairs seem more impressive than they are.

That night a snatch of flute music was played outside several windows in Vaden Town and later on a gate in the wall was opened. Through it a carriage passed and drove away. It bore no light and so almost at once vanished into the night. That is how the great clown Monsieur Andress took the children away from Vaden Town.

Translated from the Danish by Anne Born

MA YUAN

Three Ways to Fold a Paper Kite

1

The Tibetan New Year fell on the third day of the third lunar month (according to the Tibetan calendar). That morning I had been poured several glasses of *chang* beer by colleagues who had dropped in to celebrate. Feeling rather heavy-headed, I went back to bed at midday and didn't wake again until after nightfall. When I got up, I washed my face with cold water, only to discover a boil on the right side of my mouth. An item of little consequence.

Over the next few days, the boil continued to grow until it oozed a disgusting mix of pus and blood. This bloody mixture flowed unchecked and a crust the size of a walnut formed in the corner of my mouth. One side of my face had begun to change shape and swelled up into a frightful mess. This state of affairs is commonly known as the "dangerous triangle", the danger being that toxic bacteria from the boil can enter the blood vessels in the mouth and go directly to the brain. I hadn't realized this. However, even if some of you find it funny, the pain was so intense it made me weep on more than one occasion. This was no longer an item of little consequence.

I began making frequent trips to the hospital.

The first day of the Tibetan New Year is a great occasion celebrated with a good deal of festivity. My friends had all gone off to join in the fun, leaving me alone in the dormitory where I lay on my bed reading. An unattached male such as myself can have difficulty making the time pass with any real sense of enjoyment. Bachelors seem doomed to lives of perpetual loneliness. The fact was that I did not like being on my own, and had devised my own ways of whiling away the time, one of which was to read. Otherwise, I could:

go out alone at dusk and take a look at the streets strewn with smashed earthenware pots and bowls; or watch the shaggy dogs chase each other; or go and sit in a teahouse for an hour and spend the last few coins I had in my pocket on tea; or else I could wend my way down to the southern slopes of the Yao Wang hills and see what the

Buddhist pilgrims to this sacred site had left behind. Small clay
Buddhas, possibly? Or prayer flags bearing images of Sakyamuni? Or
pieces of stone carved with sacred inscriptions?
 or I could simply draw the curtain
 (which was actually my other single-bed sheet, the one with the
famous blue-check pattern on it),
 close the door, switch on the lamp and sit down at my desk with
its three drawers and fabricate a story for you;
 (something interesting, of course – or so I hope).
 In moments such as this, my imagination runs riot, and I am
capable of dreaming up everything that has ever happened or is likely
to happen in the future. Before writing a story, I always rack my
brains over the old questions of what to write and how to go about
it. If Gesang Junior hadn't showed up and told me about his crime-
investigation squad God knows where my imagination might have
led me.
 The first thing he asked me was whether I remembered the man
who sold *songer* stones. Of course I remembered. Last year Gesang
was transferred to the Public Security Bureau. Since he was new to
the game, he was feeling a trifle anxious about the case. Take it easy,
I told him. He undid the buttons of his jacket and took off his wide-
brimmed police hat. I poured him a cup of tea.
 Let me say a few words about the Barkhor. The Barkhor is an
octagonal thoroughfare encircling the famous Jokhang Temple, with
alleys and side streets running off it in all directions. Here you can
see people from almost every corner of the globe. According to esti-
mates, not less than thirty thousand people come here each day for
business and to worship the Buddha, with twice as many on Sundays.
The Barkhor is a huge bazaar and the variety of items on sale here
would surpass even the most extravagant expectations. China's largest
antique and gem market operates here, and deals involving thousands,
if not tens of thousands, of dollars are made daily. People of indeterminate nationality with cool calculating faces surreptitiously extract items
of merchandise from sleeves to show to foreign tourists and, with
perfect equanimity, proceed with the aid of gestures to negotiate their
price.
 It was here that I first made my acquaintance with the world-
renowned cat's-eye gems. At a stall located in the second corner of
the octagon, I bought an emerald green *songer* stone of reasonable
quality. It was the size of a large, double peanut with the shell still

on and weighed fifty-two grams. I know nothing about gems, and only decided to buy it because its shape and colour appealed to me. He began by asking sixty yuan for it; I offered him thirty. He had always had a stall in this spot but there was no way of telling how old he was – he could have been anywhere between thirty-five and seventy. We had presumably got to know each other by sight from my occasional visits to the Barkhor. From his features I guessed him to be from some part of the Indian sub-continent, possibly Nepal. Or perhaps India or Pakistan. I had no problem understanding his Chinese and we agreed on a price of thirty-eight yuan. All this happened on the twelfth of August last year. A detailed account of the event is recorded in my diary.

2

I'm sure you know the side street that runs south-west off from the Barkhor.

To tell you the truth, I don't. I lose all sense of direction as soon as I get anywhere near it.

At the end nearest the Barkhor they're repairing the road surface with blocks of prefabricated cement. You know what a mud-heap that road is in summer.

I nod my head. It doesn't mean I remember. It means I'm listening.

The repairs have been completed.

I still don't understand.

The street is now slightly wider than it used to be. When the repairs were being carried out, the compound walls of the houses, which originally ran right up to the road, were rebuilt inside where they used to stand. The City Construction Bureau demolished and rebuilt them. While they were pulling down the wall of a house occupied by an old woman living on her own, they dug up the body of a man not yet completely decomposed. That's right, it was him. You probably didn't hear about it. His spot on the second corner was taken over by a Khampa woman selling furs.

I won't tell you that I had already noticed. I won't interrupt your story.

This toothless old woman had deeply sunken cheeks. She told us she had no idea why the body was there and didn't know who the man was. Having no children, nor any fixed employment, she used to earn a living by selling second-hand clothes. She had no hobbies apart from snuff. An investigation by the neighbourhood committee

in her area turned up little about her early life. She had come to live
in the Barkhor after the uprising of 1959; about twenty years ago, in
other words. The number of people moving in and out of the Barkhor
area is so huge that keeping tabs on everyone is out of the question;
even long-term neighbours rarely get to know each other. When we
first went around to talk to her, she insisted that she didn't know the
man, but when we got heavy with her, she came clean.

3

She made me think of another old woman I knew. She also lived in
the Barkhor area; a colleague of mine was one of her regular customers. She made her own beer; the taste was reasonable and business
was always brisk. I could never drink *chang* beer. It always gave me
diarrhoea, since most *chang* is made with fresh water. When I went
to see Gesang Senior at home, he tried to make me drink the customary three toasts. I showed him my medical certificate and told him
about my gastro-enteritis. He insisted that his beer had been made
with cooled boiled water and that there was definitely no chance of
my getting diarrhoea. Unable to fob him off any longer, I drank the
beer, and so came to hear about the old woman who made it.

The next time Gesang went out to buy another batch, I went along
with him. I wanted to see how it was made and to find out why it
wasn't made with fresh water like everyone else's.

She was a stout, friendly-looking woman with large puffy hands.
For some reason I had imagined that she would be wizened and
humourless with a deeply wrinkled face concealing countless secrets.
She wasn't the least bit like this. I had made a mistake. She could
never be a character in my story. To be honest, I was a bit disappointed. Never mind. Let's hear Gesang Junior tell us about *his* old
woman.

4

She told us he was a close acquaintance and that he had left all his
things at her house for safe-keeping. She was a dealer in anything
and everything. She said he possessed a nine-eyed cat's-eye stone. A
five-eyed stone in perfect condition is worth over a thousand yuan.
It was his treasure, and he always wore it round his neck. She said
that she had asked him for it several times but he had always refused,

giving her a small number of rather ordinary *songer* stones instead. So one night she got him drunk and, with the help of a couple of Khampa men – itinerant hustlers by trade – strangled him with a rope and buried the body. But after all this she still hadn't got her hands on his cat's eye; the two Khampa men made off with it. She had no way of tracing them, and was left – a defenceless old woman – to suffer the consequences. She also told us that her father was of the Hui nationality, and that she had once dealt in jewellery.

We asked her on three separate occasions for a description of the two Khampa men; each time she gave us three different descriptions, insisting they had fled immediately after the murder. We asked her where they were from and what their names were. She replied that people in business together don't ask such questions; no one enquires about where the goods have come from, nor how they are to be disposed of. Nevertheless, she said that, judging from certain things they had said, they were headed for the Tibetan-speaking part of Sichuan. It was impossible to know how reliable this piece of information was. She had lived here for twenty years, but strangely, no one knew anything about her. With her shrivelled, toothless mouth, she was the very image of suffering. In my opinion, there wasn't a word of truth in anything she said.

Then what happened?

We analysed her statement. It was highly likely that she had invented the story of the two Khampa men just to put us off the track. You can imagine how difficult it would have been to pursue the case with thousands of Khampa people engaged in all kinds of business in the Barkhor, and no accurate description of the men to go on. And on top of that she claimed that the men had left the Barkhor and were no longer in Lhasa! However, we made arrangements to send a couple of our people to Sichuan to see what they could turn up.

5

Gesang was one of the two people going to Sichuan to track down the men. He said he would be setting off in the next four or five days. I made him promise to let me know the results of his trip when he got back. He laughed and asked me whether I was thinking of writing another piece of fiction. I couldn't give him a straight answer. What he had already told me was hardly enough for a story but who could tell what interesting developments might come to light? I placed all my hope in this trip of his.

Another question suddenly occurred to me. I asked Gesang whether the old woman was a Buddhist. He said that they had found several bronze statues of the Buddha in her house together with other religious paraphernalia, but there was no way of telling whether she used them for the purposes of worship or whether she sold them as part of her business. And this is where Gesang's story comes to an end.

I trust you will forgive me. I cannot tell this story to its conclusion. I'm tired, and when I get tired I like to light up a cigarette, even though normally I don't smoke. I leaned back against my folded quilt and closed my eyes. I thought about why it was that all old women caught up in underhand dealings are so wrinkled and wizened; and why the story of a murderous old woman had made me think of the woman who made and sold beer. The funny thing was that the mental image I formed of the beer-seller before I met her matched the description of the murderer perfectly.

6

There was a knock at the door.

"Ma Yuan! Ma Yuan!"

It was Xinjian.

"Is there anyone home? Heavens! What happened to you?"

"Skin ulcer. It must be retribution for some past misdeed or other."

"Must be. Eaten yet?"

"I've got some instant food and a few tins of something."

"Let's go back to my place. Come and stay with me for a few days."

Xinjian was a painter and the overall design co-ordinator at the art gallery. So I took up temporary residence in the gallery.

His place was quite roomy. The minute I set foot in the door I noticed the paper kites on his work bench. He had come to Tibet the year before last and was originally an arts and crafts student. I had seen photographs of his murals, sculptures and oil paintings.

Both single men, we got on well and had some good times together. His place was cleaner than mine, the reason being, of course, because a certain young woman visited him occasionally. She was very beautiful; her white teeth flashed when she laughed. Her name was Nimu. She was nineteen years old. She liked to do her washing in the Lhasa River.

Xinjian also liked the Lhasa River. He went there to sketch from nature, in search of creativity and inspiration for his work. The Lhasa River was very tempting in summer. He succumbed on one occasion and went swimming, cutting the sole of his foot on a piece of broken glass. The wound was two inches long and half an inch deep. Clutching his foot, he yelled out in pain, attracting the attention of Nimu who was washing clothes some distance away.

Afterwards, the usual chain of events: she managed to get him to the hospital and then she came to visit him. Other visits followed.

She found out that he was a painter, and that when he shaved his beard off he was really quite youthful-looking (he was only twenty-nine). She also found out that he lived in a mess of a studio, and became his student. She had been interested in art ever since she could remember; now they sometimes spent the whole day talking about it. He had modelled an abstract bust of her. It is evident that they held an overly romantic view of what my staying there would mean. I was a bit more practical, and so although I ate and slept here, I would go out whenever she came over, using the time to take a walk down to the Barkhor.

The image of Sakyamuni is possibly archetypal. I spent long periods of time just standing in front of the Jokhang Temple. I had no way of understanding those people prostrating themselves, although I was filled with respect for them. What struck me was their fervour and single-mindedness. I came across her unexpectedly in the main temple; even side-on, she looked healthy and good-natured. She wouldn't have remembered me, but I watched her devoutly place four ten-yuan notes into a niche containing a yak-butter lamp. I remembered the time I drank her beer at Gesang's place. As it turned out, it hadn't given me diarrhoea.

Spring was the season to go kite-flying. Another word for kite is *fengzheng*.

There is nothing especially noteworthy about the kites flown in Lhasa, but there is the sky behind them! I would even stick my neck out and say that the sky in Lhasa is without parallel. In the most magnificent blue sky on this earth, it is a most delightful thing to fly – no, pardon me – to watch other people flying their kites.

At this very moment, three eye-catching kites soared over Lhasa, and off in the distance three falcons were flying together. I guessed that Nimu would have left by now. It was time I headed back.

By the time I got back, Nimu had indeed left, but two other guests had arrived. Zhuang Xiaoxiao had studied with Xinjian and required no introduction.

"This is Liu Yu of the China News Agency."

"And this is Ma Yuan. He works at the radio station."

We acknowledged one another with a nod of the head. Liu Yu told me that a friend of his in Beijing had given him a book to give to me, and asked me to come over and get it when I had a spare moment. This friend was a writer. Inside the book was a letter. In the letter it explained that Liu Yu was also a writer.

When a brilliant portrait by Zhuang Xiaoxiao was put on show, a certain high-ranking official in cultural circles had called the picture an offence against the Tibetan people. This got Zhuang Xiaoxiao into serious trouble. As it happened, the portrait was based on Nimu's grandmother, who lived in a remote pastoral area. Nimu was introduced to Zhuang Xiaoxiao by Xinjian, and was struck speechless when she saw the picture in Zhuang's studio. The deep-etched wrinkles on the old woman's face looked like scars in a cracked, ancient elm. After a lifetime's weariness, time had left its mark on this face. The painting was entitled *Time*.

Nimu asked Zhuang Xiaoxiao how he knew her grandmother. He told her that when he visited the area to do some sketching he had stayed in her home. The old woman had made buttered tea for him every day with fresh milk and had told him many of the myths and stories of the grasslands. When he asked if he could paint her portrait, she assented. At first she laughed and chatted away; later, as he became more absorbed in his work, the two fell silent. Although she was very patient, she was obviously concerned about her sheep and her yaks, and as she sat there, her thoughts drifted away. It was then he noticed the underlying weariness in her expression. He seized this moment to bring the painting into focus.

Nimu told Zhuang Xiaoxiao that her father had invited the old woman down to Lhasa several times, but she had always refused, saying that she had her animals to look after. She was over seventy, and had once confided to Nimu that she didn't expect to live much longer and that she had no wish to die anywhere other than on the grasslands. She had grown accustomed to it, as well as to the sheep, the yaks and the eagles.

Zhuang Xiaoxiao was about to send the portrait off to the National Oil Painting Exhibition to be held in Shenyang in October. What would Xinjian submit? Nimu played a part in Xinjians's artistic conceptions.

7

Liu Yu had dropped in to see Xinjian. I took advantage of the occasion to bring up the subject of fiction. Liu Yu was not terribly interested.

He made some comments of a technical nature about Zhuang Xiaoxiao's painting *Time*, saying that he didn't like the way it had been executed. He preferred to talk about the work of several young artists in Beijing, in the same way that the Shanghaiese always harp on about returning to Shanghai.

Later, when Liu Yu asked Xinjian about his rough sketches for the National Oil Painting Exhibition, he wanted to know why he had chosen the Holy Mother for his subject. He replied that painters throughout the ages had painted the Holy Mother, so there was nothing unusual about his decision to paint Her. As well as being a Christian theme, the Holy Mother also symbolized motherhood and maternal love. Even though he was a Chinese living in the twentieth century, Raphael's Madonna could nevertheless inspire religious feelings in him. Xinjian's sketch was of a woman holding a child, her eyes downcast. There were another two children pressing against her, one of them at her feet. It was apparently the portrait of a Tibetan woman and her three children. Visible in the background were the vague outlines of snow-capped mountains, the Potala Palace, the Great Wall and flocks of sheep. He had, rather oddly, painted the flock of sheep against the sky, and for a moment I wasn't sure whether they were sheep or clouds.

The topic of conversation turned to the selection of paintings for the exhibition, a matter which greatly concerned Zhuang Xiaoxiao. The selectors' rejection of several of what he believed to be his best works had taught him a thing or two. He said that he had already made up his mind to collaborate with a native Tibetan next time; the Tibetan's name would appear before his own, in this way improving their chances with both the selectors and the judges. Both committees would be looking to encourage artists from ethnic minorities, and so their chances of making their mark would be greatly enhanced. He said what he did because he had faith in his own work and trusted his feelings. He was completely sincere.

Since Nimu had served as the model for Xinjian's portrait of a Tibetan mother, it occurred to me that he was also thinking along the same lines as Zhuang Xiaoxiao. Maybe. A writer friend of mine, Hu Daguang thinks the same way. Although his mother is Tibetan, his father is a Han Chinese with Mongol and Manchu ancestry. Hu Daguang writes under the pseudonym Pingtso. He grew up outside Tibet, speaking Chinese and living a typical Chinese life. He doesn't speak Tibetan. Nevertheless, he is counted as a young *Tibetan* writer.

But that's beside the point. Back to the story.

I asked Liu Yu whether he had come to Tibet for the purposes of writing something. He said they had come to make a documentary and that they would be staying for several months. He said he was planning to write a piece of fiction in the near future about an old woman who once lived at the base of the Potala Palace.

8

I was told that for the past two years there has been a campaign in Lhasa to reduce the number dogs. There are really far too many dogs in Lhasa. They say there were even more before. They say that Tibetan dogs are of a special breed and that they fetch a high price in London.

The old woman was dead now. She used to live at the base of the Potala Palace, not far from your radio station. They say that it has already been several years since she died, but I would still like to see the house in which she lived.

She was a devout Buddhist and lived alone all her life. From the time she was a young woman, she would circumambulate the outer wall of the Potala three times every day. You know, once round the Potala is nearly two thousand metres. She made three circuits every day. All the worshippers at the Potala knew her. She made Buddhist figurines out of clay for a living.

Everyday, she would sit in the Barkhor on some steps where the sun shone and painstakingly make her small clay Buddhas with a few bronze moulds and a fine yellow clay she obtained from somewhere on the outskirts of Lhasa. Her figures came in various forms: there was the thousand-armed, thousand-eyed laughing Buddha, the sitting Tsong Khapa, and, in greater quantities than the others, radiant Sakyamunis.

Whenever worshippers from farming and pastoral districts passed her way, they would always squat down, choose a few figures, and leave one or two yuan in a cardboard box she put out for money. People from overseas wishing to buy souvenirs of their visit to Lhasa also numbered amongst her customers. She never responded when they asked her the price, but they soon learned what to do by watching the locals. They in turn would pick out several statues and put their Foreign Exchange Certificates in her box. She never even looked up at the people who bought her figures, preferring to immerse herself in the task of removing a new Sakyamuni from its mould.

She worked even when it rained, watching the merchants and ped-lars hurriedly packing up their stalls and scrambling under shelter while the yellow clay she bought out of town dissolved in the rain and trickled away at her feet.

She probably made a reasonable income from her trade, but she gave all of it away in donations. At set times she visited the Jokhang Temple, Xiaozhao Temple, Sera Monastery, Drepung Monastery and the Potala Palace to worship the Buddha. Her donations included Foreign Exchange Certificates, Overseas Remittance Certificates, *renminbi* of various denominations and worthless old Tibetan coins. On each visit, she gave away all the money she had in what could be called wholehearted devotion to the Boddhisattvas. She wore nothing but rags.

*

This is not the kind of story I'd want to tell.

9

This story doesn't quite ring true, but I believe it's authentic. It raises a lot of issues for me. In the two weeks I've been here, two people have already told it to me.

Just now I mentioned the large number of dogs in Lhasa during the last few years, a time before any of you had been to Tibet. Dogs circulated freely in and out of public places such as shops and res-taurants in what might be described as plague proportions. You know how fond the Tibetans are of animals, and how reluctant they are to destroy them, but there really were so many of them in Lhasa at that time – as well as cases of rabies and numerous other diseases which, according to tests, may have been carried by dogs. Furthermore, there were only about a hundred thousand people living in Lhasa then, and the excessive number of dogs put a strain on food supplies. Vicious fights frequently broke out between packs of dogs, and this added to the general unease.

As a result, the government of Lhasa called for a cull of dogs and established a canine extermination squad which operated outside work hours. No employee of any public office was permitted to keep a dog on the premises.

Most people were reluctant to take part in the slaughter, but got rid of their own dogs by chasing them out into the streets. These domestic dogs joined the packs of wild dogs roaming the city, making the overall number of animals even greater than before. Youths with shotguns and small-bore rifles went out hunting them.

This old woman began taking care of the dogs. Those which had been shot she took home and fed. There, they could lie around in the sun, free from the threat of further harassment.

Dogs presumably have their own language and other canines soon learned of their good fortune. As a result, others sought refuge in her home. The newcomers would mingle with the old-timers, slinking warily in through the gate of her courtyard and always keeping a close eye on every move the woman made. If by chance she had a stick in her hand, the new dogs would flee at once, tails between their legs. To a dog there's not much difference between a stick and a gun, especially in such chaotic times.

Subsequently, this small courtyard became something of a haven for the canine species. Each day she would go out and do her three circuits of the Potala and make her clay Buddhas in the Barkhor. She spent less time visiting temples and monasteries, however, and she no longer remained indifferent when someone buying her figures failed to leave sufficient cash. She would look up at her customer with a mournful look on her face until an additional amount was produced.

A short-legged dog with shaggy yellow fur gave birth to a golden yellow puppy. When she went out to make her circuits of the Potala, she would tuck the puppy inside her coat. Its mother would plod along behind swaying to the rhythm of the prayer drums.

People who knew her noticed how thin she had become. Her eyes had sunk into her face while her nose and cheekbones had become more prominent. She had started to buy milk every day.

The children who sold her the milk knew she wasn't interested in haggling over the price. The city price for a bottle of undiluted milk was four *jiao*; the children would dilute the milk with water and sell it to her for five. Every day she would buy four or five bottles, sometimes even more. According to her neighbours, all the milk was given to the dogs; she never swallowed a drop of it herself. She had never drunk milk of any kind in her life. And now she had four puppies to look after.

There were over twenty dogs living in her cramped courtyard, coming and going along a dark, gloomy lane. It was very narrow, with barely enough room for two people approaching from opposite ends to pass comfortably. The old woman's place was on the darkest part of the lane. Every evening at dusk the dogs filed out of her courtyard and disappeared down the lane in single file. If you shot the scene from above with a zoom lens, I think the effect would be quite extraordinary.

I laughed at the way the film-maker in him got the upper hand. But to give him his due, Liu Yu was very competent as a film-maker and I was interested to hear how he thought in terms of film.

The whole affair began to upset the neighbours. The barking and yelping of all those dogs crammed into such a small space was bound to disturb the neighbourhood sooner or later. When the neighbours confronted her, she said little and laughed in embarrassment. I am sure her laughter was tinged with bitterness. As a result, she began spending even more of her time with the dogs, getting to know them better in order to teach them to be quieter and not to disturb the neighbours. They did in fact become more docile, but she spent even less of her time down in the Barkhor.

Her favourite was still the puppy with the golden fur. It was the only dog born in her compound and she treated it as if it were her own child. It had already grown and she no longer tucked it inside her coat when she circumambulated. Instead, she tied a piece of string round its neck and it followed her in the same fashion its mother once had, swaying to the rhythm of the prayer drums as it plodded. At night, when everyone was asleep, it would creep on to the *khaden* and curl up at her breast.

Throughout this time, she was a frequent visitor to the grain market. Lhasa was a high-level consumer city. Since the entire Tibetan region had not achieved self-sufficiency in grain production, the price was always high. As a resident of the city, she was only entitled to a fixed amount, but a lot more than that was needed to feed over twenty

starving dogs. What could she do? As far as everyone could see, she
was getting thinner and more feeble. She was occasionally seen pushing a handcart loaded up with two full bags of flour. It was clear that
her grip on the cart was the only thing that kept her from falling; the
handlebars helped her stay upright. In fact, it was only with the aid
of the cart that she was able to walk at all.

She stopped making buttered tea for herself, and rarely ate *tsampa*.
Tsampa barley was even more expensive than wheat. To everyone's
surprise, she took to drinking *chang*. I don't remember whether or
not I mentioned that she had never touched alcohol or snuff. Now,
every day around noon, she would go and sit inside one of the roadside beer tents and happily down a couple of cups of the stuff. Later,
groggy and bleary-eyed, she would gaze down at the small yellow
dog at her feet and babble to it in a language that only they could
understand. She was an absolute wreck, but every day she went off
as usual to the Potala and then down to the Barkhor to make her clay
Buddhas – Look, Xinjian's fallen asleep. Sorry to have stayed so late.
We'll continue this conversation some other time.

10

At that time, we often went down to the Lhasa River. Where the
river flows through Lhasa there is a large island. Not long ago, I
wrote a story about this island entitled *The Goddess of Lhasa River*.

When I say *we*, I mean Xinjian, Luo Hao and myself. Luo Hao
was a professional photographer, no more than a kid of nineteen. It
was Xinjian's idea to visit the Lhasa River to do his washing. I
wouldn't mind betting that he was trying to recapture a certain special
memory; it was only while we were washing clothes on the island in
the river that he told us the story about Nimu.

I started chatting about Liu Yu's story, and told Xinjian that he
had fallen asleep before the story had come to an end. To my surprise,
Xinjian gave a bored yawn and told me that Luo had told him the
same story ages ago. Luo Hao had lived in Lhasa since he was small,
and naturally knew more of the local gossip.

On that particular occasion we had brought a large bundle of
washing, plus sheets and quilts, as well as plenty to eat, including
tinned food among other things. Luo Hao had slaughtered one of
his younger brother's Leghorn chickens and had made up a delicious
plate of cold chicken spiced with chillis. We had some beer as well.

In Lhasa, tender chicken and beer are two of the greatest luxuries imaginable.

There were two young Tibetan women washing clothes not far from us.

Perhaps because Luo and I had not prepared ourselves for any unexpected encounters we paid no attention to them for a long time. The water of the Lhasa River was clear and one could see right to the bottom. First of all, we put the clothes in the river, weighting down one end with pebbles; after letting them soak for a while, we would remove an item, lay it out flat on the pebbly shore, sprinkle it evenly with washing powder, then rub it with our hands or tread all over it. Then we would do the same with the next item, and so on.

It was the young women who first began laughing. They were beside themselves. They were laughing at us. No doubt they found our clumsy washing technique highly amusing. When we thought about it, we found it pretty funny too.

We were standing in the river rinsing out the soap. We were up to our knees in bone-numbing water with the dancing ripples sparkling on the pebbly river-bed below. When we smoothed out the pieces of washing and placed them in the river, the clear flowing water immediately rinsed them clean, gurgling pleasantly. The high point came when rinsing the quilts and single-bed sheets. There was something very decorative about the checked sheets spread out over the water, rippling like twitching muscles. It brought to mind some rather odd associations. Luo Hao, in a fit of inspiration, went ashore and set up his tripod near the water, then, setting the self-timer, ran back through the foaming water to where we were standing. He had just managed to hold up his sheet in the same way as Xinjian and I were doing when the shutter clicked. A souvenir of the boys out washing their bedlinen in the Lhasa River, with the Potala Palace in the background.

Luo Hao had his next round of inspiration when the two young women undid their thick braids and began washing their hair in the river. They had to be sisters with such black luxuriant hair. As the younger of the two immersed her long tresses in the water, she turned her head to speak to her sister, and it was this rare photographic opportunity that Luo captured on film. He submitted it to "Water/Life", a Japanese photography exhibition.

They weren't at all shy, and Xinjian and I asked them in Chinese to come and have their picture taken with us. This delighted them no end; they spoke excellent Chinese. They told us their names and gave us an address in the hope that we would send them a photograph. They were strong-looking girls and I still remember their cheerful banter.

Looking at them made me think of Liu Yu's story for some reason, about the dogs who had found a refuge, and that old woman. They invited us to share the *chang* they had brought with them. Faced with the threat of diarrhoea but uncomfortable about explaining our fears to them, we politely declined and asked them to share our meal with us. They clearly relished the prospect of spicy cold chicken. We enjoyed a large pot of buttered tea with them after they had finished the beer.

It was the younger of the two sisters who first noticed the kite hanging up in the bushes. She clicked her tongue in admiration, pleasantly surprised. After asking Xinjian's permission, she got the kite up and flying with a practised ease.

She told us they had always had a couple of paper kites in the house; her father had made them – he was an excellent kite-maker. In the spring, neighbours would come round asking him to fold kites for them. He knew two completely different designs. I recalled then that when the older sister had given us her address she had said that they lived at the foot of the Potala Palace. I thought I should ask them whether they knew the story of the old woman and her dogs. They were locals, and they lived in the same area; perhaps they knew a few more details.

What a shame. They hadn't heard of her. As it turned out, it was Luo Hao who had some additional information. He said that the dogs were not something she'd taken to towards the end of her life. She had always had dogs, and there really were at least twenty of them. She had never made Buddhas out of clay, and she had no relatives; she had been dead for quite some time. She had been dead long enough now that even the two young women living in the same area had not heard of her. She had made a habit of feeding her own grain rations to the dogs and had become terribly emaciated. A few years back a lot of people in Lhasa knew her, and some, taking pity on her, gave her some of their own grain, but she went on giving it all to her dogs. It was even reported that the government provided her with extra grain beyond her entitlement, but to no avail. She was stubborn and paid no heed to what anybody else thought. Some say she starved to death. Others say she died of an illness. Anyway, she lived a solitary life and had no dealings with her neighbours; when they found her dead and saw how thin she was, the rumour got around that she had died of starvation. But no one knew for sure. Since she had spent all her time with the dogs which roamed the streets, it was possible that she had picked up some disease passed on by generations of dogs and had died that way.

The younger sister was absorbed in her kite-flying. I happened to notice her older sister turn abruptly aside and wipe her eyes with her hand. I nudged Luo Hao and he stopped talking. Xinjian ended up giving the kite to the young woman who loved it so much.

What had upset her sister? Perhaps . . .

11

Liu Yu finished his story before he left Lhasa. When he did, I made no comment. I knew that Luo Hao's version was probably closer to the truth, but Liu Yu's story was undoubtedly more enticing. He planned to write a fictional account; using his version as a basis naturally gave him more flexibility. Luo Hao's version left too little scope for the imagination.

I guessed that Liu Yu would place more emphasis on the Buddhism and the influences specific to it; he was interested in more than just a bare-bones account of the story. I realized by this stage that I was looking forward to reading Liu Yu's story. I wanted to know what kind of response this story would trigger in another writer's mind. The triggering – that's what I'm interested in.

Three days after Liu Yu's departure, I went to visit the two sisters. I discovered that the small lane they lived in was narrow and gloomy. As it happened, the younger sister was out. When I asked after her, the other sister told me:

"She's gone kite-flying."

Translated from the Chinese by Simon Patton

HARRY MULISCH

The Boundary

To Her Majesty the Queen,
Soestdijk Palace
Your Majesty!
It is only after much hesitation that I have conquered my scruples and make so bold as to write to Your Majesty. Were any other course of action open to me, I would have taken it. Since I have exhausted all other ways, nothing remains for me but to address myself to You, albeit in the knowledge that my personal cares must of necessity pale into insignificance beside Yours which concern the whole nation.

My name is Joachim Lichtbeelt, I am sixty years of age, domiciled in Amstelveen, "Blijstein" A-14, no. 234.

On Saturday 4 May last, I departed from my home at approximately 8.45 a.m. in my motor vehicle, a DAF, registration number HS-47-26. I was accompanied by my wife, Mrs A. F. Lichtbeelt née Da Polenta, aged fifty-nine. We were travelling towards "Zonnehelm", a home for the elderly at Oosterbeek, where my mother-in-law has been residing for several years.

At approximately ten minutes past ten o'clock, in the vicinity of Elspijk, my vehicle went into a skid, probably as a result of oil on the road which, owing to the early morning mist, I had failed to notice. I first ran into the crash barrier and subsequently landed on the soft shoulder, where I overturned.

I must have remained unconscious for several seconds or minutes. When I recovered I perceived that there was ditchwater up against the windscreen; my legs were also standing in water up to the knees. I felt pain in one or two places and had sustained a few minor scratches. Then I discovered that my wife was no longer with me. The door on her side was open. I hurried out of the car and found her lying at a few metres' distance in the field, but in a strange, I might almost say in an impossible posture, which immediately aroused the greatest anxiety in me. She did not react to any question of mine, however urgently I pressed her to answer. At an estimated one hundred and fifty metres away, there was a large farmhouse backed by tall trees, but in the circumstances I considered it inadvisable to leave my wife alone. However, I thought I could descry someone watching us from the gate. In spite of myself I waded through the ditch, climbed the bank and, standing by the roadside, endeavoured to draw the attention of passing motorists. Unfortunately no one was able to stop in order to come to my aid, which indeed it would have been perilous to do and which is in fact forbidden. However, after a quarter of an hour it transpired that someone had had the extraordinary kindness to alert a doctor in Elspijk, Dr K. J. M. Maurits, a most helpful person, who diagnosed a fracture of the base of the skull and suspected serious internal bleeding.

"I strongly advise you," he told me, "not to move your wife. I shall immediately contact the local Health Department in Elspijk, as your wife must be taken to hospital without delay. In view of the fee, may I have your address?"

When I had told him, he sped from the scene.

The ambulance arrived after about twenty minutes. Then an unfortunate state of affairs came to light. It appeared that my wife was lying just outside the confines of the rural district of Elspijk and was in fact lying within the commune of Vrijburg.

"The situation," so the ambulance men explained to me, "is that the boundary between the two communes is formed by the high-tension cables which pass overhead at this point." I looked up and saw that we were indeed standing exactly underneath a line of high-tension cables. From the north-east, the towering pylons advanced with outspread arms over the fields, crossed the road diagonally, and disappeared over the horizon in the other direction. "Or, to put it more accurately," said the ambulance men, "these cables run exactly above the boundary between the two communes. They are our guidelines whenever an accident has occurred in this area."

"But my wife is lying exactly underneath the cables," I remarked.

"Quite so," they said. "But these few metres belong to the district of Vrijburg."

I hasten to add that the men were exceedingly pleasant and

explained the situation to me with much patience; but this could not remedy the fact that the accident was outside their jurisdiction. They had no choice, therefore, but to depart without anything having been achieved.

"We hope," they said, "that you appreciate the delicacy of the situation. You understand, two adjacent authorities . . ."

"Certainly," I agreed. "In my own work I am sometimes faced with this very problem. In such cases a little delay is preferable to a great deal of time being spent subsequently on trying to thrash out questions of competency."

"We promise that as soon as we arrive back in Elspijk we shall alert the Health Department in Vrijburg."

"I should be most obliged if you would."

I must stress here that the Vrijburg ambulance was on the scene in less than half an hour. To my surprise, however, I was informed that the strip of land under the cables belonged to the district of Elspijk.

"But according to the Health Department of Elspijk," I said, "the strip under the cables forms part of the district of Vrijburg."

After a quick glance at each other, their mouths curving down questioningly, they said: "This will have to be looked into at once at the town hall. But naturally, pending the investigation, we cannot take any action."

"I quite understand," I reassured them. "You are perfectly right, it is better if such matters are settled in strict accordance with the rules."

They took their leave with a handshake.

Meanwhile the police had arrived on the scene and made a report. While the gentlemen were conducting their examination, I wondered whether it would be permissible to pursue, through them, a different line of action. I was not unaware that by doing so I would cut across the investigation at the town hall in Vrijburg, after the conclusion of which either the ambulance of Vrijburg or of Elspijk would reappear, only to discover that my wife had already been removed by another authority. All their trouble would have been in vain. Was this morally justified? Or, to formulate it less grandly, was it decent? However, as the care for my wife's welfare was more important to me than any other consideration – and I hope and trust, Your Majesty, that You will sympathize with my point of view – I took a decision.

"Gentlemen," I asked, "does there perhaps exist something like a National Public Health Authority which could take pity on my wife?"

"Alas," they answered, "we must disappoint you. But we appreciate your predicament and advise you to address yourself to the Provincial Public Health Department."

"Thank you very much, gentlemen," I said delightedly. "That seems a most sensible suggestion, considering that the province embraces all the different communes with their mutual boundary problems."

Now I was forced to leave my wife alone for a short time. There had been no change in her condition. She was lying face-down; fortunately, there was no blood to be seen, but somehow it looked as if her left and right leg had changed places. I smoothed down her clothes a little and walked across the field to the farm. The person I had seen standing by the gate from the first turned out to be the farmer himself, Mr P. van Amerongen.

"That was quite a tumble you made there," he smiled. "Come in, come in. I daresay you wouldn't say no to a cup of coffee."

"You can say that again," I replied.

In the living room he introduced me to his wife, Mrs M. van Amerongen. She said with a laugh: "I was already expecting you. Coffee is ready."

When I had informed them of my circumstances they offered me of their own accord the use of their telephone. I asked them which province we were in; it turned out to be just within Utrecht. However, as it was a Saturday, there was no reply at the Provincial Health Department. After some deliberation I decided to phone the town hall in the City of Utrecht. Only a porter was there. When I had explained the urgency of my case to him, he said: "Sir, I can tell you straightaway that such enquiries are dealt with only in writing."

When I told Mr van Amerongen this discouraging news, he placed, without a word, pen and paper on the table, as well as an envelope and a stamp. Equally silently I put pen to paper, but as the table was covered with a high-pile Smyrna rug, the nib went, to my dismay, right through the paper. Hereupon Mr van Amerongen handed me a copy of the weekly journal *Farmer and Market Gardener*, Mrs van Amerongen smilingly gave me a fresh sheet of paper and I was able to write my letter, in which

I gave a detailed account of all the events that had occurred, and urgently requested transport for my wife, in view of the pressing nature of her case. As I closed the envelope, Mr van Amerongen offered of his own volition to post the letter for me, so that I could stay with my wife.

It is only at moments such as these that one gains a true insight into one's fellow human beings. Farmers! How had I looked upon farmers in the past? Being a native of Amsterdam, I had always regarded them as creatures with wooden heads filled with manure, who in times of war were capable of but a single thought, namely how to do the starving city-dweller out of his wedding ring in exchange for a glass of milk. Mr and Mrs van Amerongen cured me forever of this misguided notion.

As I could not expect a reply from Utrecht before Tuesday at the earliest, I realized that the matter was going to take a considerably longer time than I had initially hoped and expected. After having settled with my kind hosts for the phone calls and the coffee, I arranged that in the next few days I would take my evening meal with them while for the remaining part of that day they would provide me with bread and fruit and possibly an egg or two. The price we agreed upon lay well below that which obtained at most restaurants in Amsterdam.

I shall not burden You, Your Majesty, with my ruminations at the side of my wife's helpless, prostrate body, in the subsequent lonely hours of that ill-starred Saturday, as they are of no direct relevance to my request. Most of the time I spent in my car. The badly damaged vehicle was stuck with its bonnet under the water, but inside I experimented with the seats until I had procured a more or less horizontal seating and sleeping arrangement for myself. Out of some wood which Mr van Amerongen had put at my disposal, in return for a small consideration, I made a gangplank so that henceforth wet feet were a thing of the past. I settled down for the night – though not without first having pressed a kiss on my dear wife's forehead.

When I woke up the next morning, stiff with cold, it was raining. My wife was already completely drenched and since I did not consider this to be conducive to her well being, I decided to construct a shelter which would at least provide some protection from the weather. Mr van Amerongen kindly showed me to his shed where I found tools and materials. After ample deliberation I opted for the classical house-shape with gabled roof; perhaps my decision was influenced by the farm of the van Amerongens. The rest of the day I spent sawing and hammering. The roof, side walls and rear I made out of planks; the front I closed off with jute sacking.

When my work was completed, Mr van Amerongen smilingly came to inspect my creation. After supper that evening he charged me an insignificant sum for the materials I had used, as well as a few trifling guilders for the hire of the tools, which I judged to be no more than reasonable. Fortunately, it is my custom never to leave money unattended in an empty house and as this was the beginning of the month, I had a not inconsiderable sum at my disposal, sufficient to keep me going for quite a time.

The next day, Monday 6 May, promptly at 8.30 a.m., I made a phone call to INTEROP Ltd in Amsterdam, where I had been employed for twenty-three years, first as a storeman, later as store manager. My employer, Mr H. J. Groeneveld, proved to be abroad. I was put through to his son, Mr H. J. Groeneveld Junior, who is also his partner. I described my deplorable situation to him and asked whether, in view of the circumstances beyond my control in which I found myself, he would allow me a few more days' leave.

"I see," he said. "Well now. Hold the line a moment, Lichtbeelt." It was a fairly costly long distance call and after keeping me waiting no longer than a few minutes, kindly enough, he said: "Yes, Lichtbeelt, you have still got four occasional days due to you. By way of exception I'll let you take them all in a row."

I thanked him sincerely for his ready agreement. I had never found him a very sympathetic person, I have to admit; in fact, I suspected him of that heartlessness which so often characterizes second generations in the business world, and I was genuinely pleased at having misjudged him.

Next I rang our daughter, Mrs G. J. Hofman née Lichtbeelt, in Middelburg. She sounded most shocked when she heard of the unhappy accident. Although we rarely saw her now that she was married, because of the great distance, there had always been that unique bond between us which exists only between parents and their children. When she asked in which hospital

Mother was being treated, I was obliged once again to tell my sad tale. It therefore seemed as if a light suddenly began to shine in my heart when she said: "I shall come as soon as I can."

When I enquired when this would be, it turned out that, regrettably, she was unable to come before the following Sunday. The little ones had to go to school and she had to fulfil her various social duties. My son-in-law, Mr J. A. M. Hofman, is employed by a prominent publicity firm which relies totally on the successful furthering of relations. Even the occasional absence from the weekly game of bridge can easily be misinterpreted and thus have detrimental financial consequences from which the other employees would suffer too.

After some deliberation I rejected the idea of informing my mother-in-law in Oosterbeek of what had happened. The old lady would probably be greatly distressed and the shock might be too much for her. Our visit planned for the Saturday had been unannounced, so that she could have no suspicions. It seemed better to wait until everything was settled and my wife had completely recovered. Then, over a cup of tea and a cinnamon biscuit, we could tell her all about our adventure.

The next morning I was woken up by Mrs van Amerongen calling out: "Mr Lichtbeelt! Post!"

She was standing under the chestnut trees in the farmyard, in her snowy white apron, waving a letter above her head. I climbed out of my car at once and ran across the field as fast as my old legs could carry me.

And indeed, it was a special delivery from the Department of Public Health in the Province of Utrecht. Full of anticipation I opened the envelope, but what did I find? The boundary between Elspijk and Vrijburg was at the same time the boundary between the provinces of Utrecht and Gelderland. According to the maps, the area under the cables where my wife lay belonged to the province of Gelderland, so that, regrettably, Utrecht could do nothing for me. I was advised to contact the department of Public Health in the Province of Gelderland, in writing. Dejectedly, I let the letter drop.

"Bad news?" asked Mrs van Amerongen.

"I cannot help," I answered, "being agreeably surprised by the promptness of their reply, but in the meanwhile I seem to be no further than I was before. Although: perhaps a little further. The question of the boundary between the two communes has now become an issue between two provinces. If this continues, I must inevitably reach some all-embracing authority which is capable of taking a decision. No, Mrs van Amerongen, it is not bad news. It is good news."

To my shame, Your Majesty, I must confess that I am not much at home in constitutional matters – theoretically speaking, of course, for in practice I am quite well at home in them, one could say I live in them – but I assumed that this one all-embracing authority would be the Council of State, which I believe is sometimes called The Crown. However, Your Majesty, I must refrain from supplying such particulars at Your Esteemed Address.

Once again I sat down by the table with the high-pile Smyrna rug. Mrs van Amerongen handed me *Farmer and Market Gardener* and I wrote to Gelderland. I knew the answer in advance, but in view of further steps I obviously needed to have it in black and white. I was suddenly full of confidence.

"Only one thing still troubles me now," I said to Mrs van Amerongen as I licked the envelope, "and that is the fear that all these delays may have an adverse effect on my wife's condition. Fortunately she has always had an iron constitution, I cannot remember her ever being ill and I trust therefore that she will successfully pull through this ordeal as well."

I decided that from now on I would no longer lift up the jute cloth to take a quick look at her, as I had done at regular intervals. The sudden influx of light might disturb her. Complete rest would surely be better.

The following day, which was Wednesday 8 May, saw warm spring weather at last. Even so, an unpleasant surprise awaited me. I had washed myself under the pump in the yard and was just enjoying my breakfast consisting of an apple and a glass of water, when I observed a Police breakdown van approaching on the road. To my alarm it started making preparations to remove my car, that is to say, my home. After hurrying to the scene, I succeeded in dissuading the gentlemen, who wore police caps but were otherwise clad in beige overalls, from carrying out their intentions. While I informed them of the events of the past few days, it suddenly occurred to me how curious it was that my wife could not be removed at short notice whereas my car could, even though both were situated in no man's land under the high-tension cables.

Lay there not a strange, nay, Your Majesty, I will not hesitate to use the words: an almost inhuman way of thinking at the root of this?

"Gentlemen," I said, keeping my composure, "may I ask to which police force you belong?"

"Elspijk," they said in a tone which made it clear that I should regard it as an extraordinary honour that they were willing to divulge this information to me.

"Exactly, Elspijk. No doubt you are aware that according to influential opinion my car is located within the commune of Vrijburg?"

Shielding their eyes from the sun they looked up at the high-tension cables and shrugged their shoulders.

"That may be," they nodded. "But we are here now anyway and we mean to tow this wreck away. It's an eyesore, so close to the main road."

"Yes," I exclaimed, "I suppose you would think that! But I will tell you this: I shall take steps against you, for exceeding the bounds of your authority, and that means ignominious dismissal from the force, you can be sure of that!"

They looked at each other for a moment and, muttering something like: "We were only doing as we were told," they slunk away.

I believe that this was the only time at which, very briefly, I lost my patience. When a few hours later the breakdown van of the Vrijburg police arrived, my indignation had already become studied.

In retrospect I ask myself whether I did not commit a tactical error here. Perhaps it would have been better if I had simply allowed the car to be towed away, because then I would have had a precedent. But that might have created the impression that I was trying to set traps, which would not have helped to strengthen the benevolence of the bureaucratic machine towards me.

Moreover, I doubt very much whether any incident concerning the police can ever serve as a precedent for the Department of Public Health. At all events I was glad to have saved my bedroom, for if I had been forced to rent a bed in the farmhouse, to which Mr van Amerongen would, without a shadow of doubt, have agreed with pleasure, this would once again have made serious inroads upon my resources. As a result of recent poor harvests the price of apples and pears also appeared to have risen sharply and suddenly.

On Thursday, spring had definitely arrived. But on that day I was for the first time troubled by a most unpleasant smell. I suspected that there must be a refuse processing plant some-where in the vicinity and I hoped that the wind would soon change direction. Meanwhile I would not allow myself to be driven away. I had put the car seat out on the grass and sat quietly in the sunshine beside the little house in which my wife was enjoying her much-needed rest. Mr van Amerongen's cows were grazing peacefully in the meadow, the traffic roared past on the road behind me, and there were sparrows chirping on the high-tension cables. It might almost seem as if I was on holiday. Holiday! Mine was not due until July, and by that time I hoped my wife would have recovered sufficiently for us to go to the Isle of Terschelling again. Or should we go further afield this year? The Ardennes perhaps? Or a trip along the Rhine? Thus musing, I dozed off and was awakened by the voice of Mrs van Amerongen: "Mr Lichtbeelt! Post!"

It was the reply from Gelderland. I cannot have enough praise for the promptness with which official bodies in our country deal with their correspondence – perhaps it does no harm, Your Majesty, if You hear this from the mouth of a humble subject.

The letter said what I had expected: according to the maps, the area underneath the cables belonged to the province of Utrecht; but there was more. I was informed that in view of the pressing nature of my case a request had been sent to the Provincial Deputies of both Utrecht and Gelderland for a com-bined inquiry, to be undertaken by the cartographic services of the two provinces. At short notice the exact boundary between Utrecht and Gelderland and therefore between Elspijk and Vrijburg would have to be determined once and for all, starting from the topographical point where my wife lay. I could expect the officials concerned to arrive at the beginning of the following week and it was hoped that the matter would then shortly be resolved to everyone's satisfaction.

I do not mind admitting that at this news I danced for joy

in the shade of the chestnut trees. Mrs van Amerongen watched me, smiling and shaking her head, but I did not feel in the least embarrassed. I had hardly dared to hope that everything would be settled so soon. Now that the matter had advanced thus far, it goes without saying that I could not abandon it at this stage. Even so, I had now used up all my occasional holidays and the next morning I made another telephone call to INTEROP Ltd. Old Mr Groeneveld was still absent. Mr Groeneveld Junior, even when I had explained everything to him in strict conformance with the truth, could find no grounds to justify keeping me in his employ any longer.

"Now look here, Lichtbeelt, we simply can't have this sort of thing, you can see that yourself."

"Certainly, Mr Groeneveld, I quite understand."

"I have to consider the other employees. If they find out that I have been giving you extra days off, they will all start inventing excuses."

"Mr Groeneveld," I said with admiration, "your insight into human nature is truly astonishing."

"Yes, yes, you learn plenty about that in business. Just think where it would lead, Lichtbeelt, it would end up with no one in the Netherlands doing any more work."

"Ha ha," I laughed, "I would certainly never approve of that."

"Quite."

"But if you will permit me, Mr Groeneveld, and please do not regard it as a lack of trust on my part if I ask . . . but what is going to happen about my sickness insurance and my pension?"

"Well now, there you ask me something. I'll have to check up on that, I am not sure. Have you got a phone number where you are?"

"Certainly, Mr Groeneveld. I am receiving hospitality at the house of Mr and Mrs van Amerongen, whose number is Elspijk 346."

"Elspijk 346. All right then, Lichtbeelt, that is all. I now feel the desire to thank you for . . . how long were you with us?"

"Twenty-three years, Mr Groeneveld."

"For twenty-three years of faithful service to INTEROP. Twenty-three years, that is a lifetime. My lifetime, to be exact. At the time of my birth you came to work for us as a storeman and I remember my father saying, when I was a boy, that with your arrival the stores had at last been put into order.

"Through unwearying industry you succeeded in raising yourself, within the space of sixteen years, to the position of store manager, an achievement which few will be able to emulate. INTEROP is inconceivable without you. You *are* INTEROP. Your departure will leave a great emptiness, Lichtbeelt," he said, and hung up.

Tears had sprung to my eyes. There is probably not one man in the whole world who is not sensitive to praise.

That was on Friday. The fine weather continued. So did the smell, alas, and on the Saturday I did little else but write a letter to the Social Security Board in Amstelveen, explaining my situation and lodging a claim for unemployment benefit.

In shrill contrast to this sombre day on which for the first time in my life I was obliged to beg, the next day became a truly festive one. Towards midday I suddenly heard excited cheers on the main road which I had left so unexpectedly a week ago, and I just caught a glimpse of my son-in-law's car as it zoomed past, children's arms waving out of all the windows. A little further on he took the turn-off for Elspijk and arrived at the farm a few minutes later.

I shall never forget the sight of my dear ones as they came running towards me across the field: the little ones shouting "Grandad! Grandad!", my daughter with a wicker picnic-basket covered with a white napkin and my son-in-law, sporty as always, in tight trousers and with a camera slung over his shoulder.

After the greetings, during which my beard was the object of much comment and had to endure a great deal of pulling and tugging, my grandchildren, crowing with delight, started climbing on the low structure which I had built for their injured grandmama. My daughter wanted to stop them but I said that for this once she should let the little rascals do as they pleased. I knew of course that the sick are often distressed at the slightest sound, but I was convinced that my wife would be only too happy to bear with *this* noise. In any case, the children soon came away from the little house of their own accord. The stench of the refuse plant, to which I had become quite accustomed, appeared to hinder them in their play. My son-in-law took a few photographs which will no doubt form a happy souvenir of the day's events, not least for my wife herself. At lunchtime I tucked into the meal provided by my daughter: French bread, pâté and even wine appeared on the outspread napkin, and a few sips were enough to change this spring day for me into a fairy-tale summer's day.

Unfortunately, my son-in-law was suddenly sick, shortly after which they all said their goodbyes and departed.

You Yourself, Your Majesty, have been blessed with a large family, yes, with a family that increases in size year by year, and You too possess a lawn on which You may take a picnic with Your grandchildren from time to time. There is therefore no necessity to tell You, of all people, how much this means to a someone of our age. I have not seen them again since that day, alas, but then, what purpose would it have served? They could not help me anyway – they helped me most by being happy themselves, wherever they might be.

As expected, on Monday 13 May the land-surveyors and cartographers arrived, no fewer than eight men in all. Of their complicated activities, involving red-and-white striped poles at which they peered through small telescopes on tripods, I understood very little, as I have had no education beyond the Lower School Certificate. But it is always enjoyable to watch a task being carried out expertly, whether it is land-surveying or painting a window sill, sawing a plank, drawing beer, counting banknotes or closing a bag of sugar. One of the maladies of our time is, I believe, that many people no longer know how to do their work properly. And this is a malady not only because they produce poor work but especially because they themselves become dissatisfied as a result, so that their inadequate work breeds inadequate people. One often hears complaints about the disastrous influence which impersonal factory work has on man, but the situation is no better in the case of personal work, so the cause must lie deeper. With these officials, however, there was no question of this – and it is remarkable that even when one does not understand the task one can still tell whether or not it is being performed expertly. It seems as if there is in man a kind of general artistic awareness of elegance and economy, which can be recognized in everything by everyone.

But I digress, Your Majesty, and this is unwise, since this

letter already threatens to make too great a demand on Your Majesty's precious time.

The outcome of the survey was disappointing. The engineer in charge, whose name, to my regret, has escaped me, was kind enough to explain the problem to me afterwards. He showed me a detailed map of the area and ran his little finger along a line marked on it.

"This is the boundary between the provinces," he said, "and therefore also that between Elspijk and Vrijburg. It is exactly correct, we have checked it. The only difficulty is that this is the largest-scale map used in cartography in the Netherlands. Unfortunately, this means that the boundary line as it is printed here is precisely as thick as the distance between the two outer high-tension cables running overhead. In a sense, therefore, the area between the cables where your wife lies does not exist, at least not cartographically. It is the boundary, it separates Utrecht from Gelderland, but it is not itself that which it separates, it is merely that which separates."

At these words, a feeling of great unease took possession of me.

"Then what am I to do?"

"Well," said the engineer as he folded the map and put it away in a small flat case, "the best thing would obviously be for you to press urgently for larger-scale maps to be produced. Preferably at actual size, I would suggest in this case. Scale 1:1. If the boundary was then found to run across your wife's body, one would have to be advised by experts whether her identity is located in her head or in her heart, or even in her little toe, as long as it is in a part of her body which lies altogether in either Gelderland or Utrecht. But I fear this would be a lengthy process."

"So do I," I said.

He looked at me.

"May I make a suggestion? Why don't you simply continue using the official channels."

"Yes, but who is there left for me to turn to?"

"The Inspector General for Public Health in The Hague. If you explain everything to him, including the difficulty about the boundary, he will undoubtedly do whatever is in his power. I would not be surprised if the matter were to come before the

Medical Disciplinary Board, or at the very least before the Civil Service Tribunal. But this will remain between ourselves, I trust."

Again, I regret it more than I can say, the name of this most helpful expert has escaped my memory. However, I followed his advice and wrote to the Inspector General that same evening.

The next morning at ten o'clock Mr van Amerongen shouted across the field: "Lichtbeelt! Telephone!"

I hurried to the farm: it proved to be the familiar voice of Mr H. J. Groeneveld Senior.

"I say, what's this I hear, Lichtbeelt, I've just come back from abroad; has my son given you the sack?"

"It is so, Mr Groeneveld."

"Has he gone mad? Give you the sack after twenty-three years' service, just because you wanted a few more days off in connection with your wife!"

"There was no other choice open to him, I fear."

"No other choice? Are you crazy! I've just given him such a clip round the ear that he's walked out of the room crying."

"Was that not a little too harsh, sir? I am convinced that your son was only acting in the best interests of . . ."

"Nonsense! The snot-nosed brat. I'll teach him. People aren't like old gloves which you throw away when you don't want them any longer."

"Well, yes, if you put it that way, sir . . . there is a germ of truth in that."

"All the same, Lichtbeelt, what's done is done and there is little I can do about it now. I should like to take you back, but then I might as well sack my own son at the same time. He would no longer have any authority with the work force."

"Just so," I said, "there is no doubt about that. You need not say another word, Mr Groeneveld, sir. If it was anyone else but myself who was sacked by H. J. Groeneveld Junior and then taken back by H. J. Groeneveld Senior, I am sure I would laugh my head off."

"Yes, that's the truth of it, isn't it, Lichtbeelt."

I had the impression that Mr Groeneveld was relieved at what I said and I was glad, because I knew that the prevailing unfavourable climate in the business world was causing him sleepless nights.

"There is just one thing, Mr Groeneveld, the question of my sickness insurance and pension; I would like to know what my position is."

"Yes, of course, good thing you mentioned it. I am sorry I have to tell you this, but it seems that the position isn't very good."

"Well then, I had better wait and see and not count on anything, then I can't be disappointed. Please do not worry yourself about it, sir, I am sure it will all be resolved correctly."

"All right then, Lichtbeelt. Wish your wife a speedy recovery."

"Thank you very much, sir. Goodbye, sir."

This most pleasant conversation had made my day. After all, there had been no need for him to phone me at all. Once again it was brought home to me that we Dutch people ought to be *with* each other, not against each other.

I had expected that Wednesday 15 May would be a day of waiting for a reply from The Hague, but quite early in the morning two members of the motorized police arrived. They parked their machines one behind the other on the hard shoulder and came down the bank.

"Your building permit, please," they asked without further introduction.

"Building permit?" As I looked at them uncomprehendingly they pointed in silence at the temporary shelter I had constructed for my wife. I asked, surprised: "Do I need a building permit for that?"

"It has been built, hasn't it?"

"Well, yes," I said. "That cannot be denied. But I have no permit, I am sorry. The point is, you see, that on Saturday 4 May at approximately ten minutes past ten . . ."

"Yes," they interrupted sternly, "we know all that by now. But where would we be if everyone was allowed to build just as he pleased? In a small country like ours, so built-up already, we have to guard every bit of countryside we have left."

"I am the first person to agree with that," I replied. "As a boy I used to roam about the woods and moors for hours without meeting a living soul; bird-watching and botanizing were meat and drink to me; there is no need to tell me anything about that. But this modest shelter for my wife," I said, pointing at it, "I am sure no one has even noticed it from the road."

"That may be so," they admitted, "but that is how it always goes. It starts with a harmless little shed and before you know where you are you've got a bungalow with a swimming-pool."

"I take your word for it, gentlemen," I said. "You have experience in these matters. On the other hand," I added, raising my voice, "if my wife cannot be transported to a hospital because this strip of land does not come under a, b, or c's jurisdiction, you must not come here and bother me about building permits either."

They looked at each other and burst out laughing.

"Perhaps you also think," they said, "that you are allowed to commit a murder under these cables?"

"That would seem to be taking things a little too far."

"Look here," they said, "an accident is not the same as a contravention. If the law has been contravened, and certainly when an offence has been committed, every citizen has the authority to make an arrest, irrespective of which commune he lives in or in which province the law has been contravened."

I bowed my head. I realized that no protests would be of any avail.

"Your camping permit, please," they said curtly.

I no longer had a leg to stand on. When they had written out their report and were putting their notebooks back into their breast pockets, they said: "There is probably no need to worry about the latter infringement, but you can be sure that this illegal building of yours will be pulled down one of these days."

It did not escape me that my affairs were taking an ever graver turn. Mr van Amerongen, too, noticed that it was having an effect on me. When we rose after supper that evening, he silently laid his honest countryman's hand on my shoulder for a moment.

The next day brought two letters. The first contained the reply from the Social Security Board to which I had made a request for unemployment benefit. I was not eligible because I had not called in person within the prescribed twenty-four hours at the local labour exchange in my town of residence. I could not deny having been negligent in this respect. I was advised to appeal under the terms of the Special Sickness Benefits Act, a piece of advice which I decided to act upon. The second letter was from the Inspector General of Public Health. It said that the boundary incident constituted an altogether new problem ("an almost metaphysical problem") in which a decision could be taken only by the minister himself, who unfortunately was at present in Zambia, after which he would pay visits to Nigeria and Uganda. Pending his return, I was advised to write to the Commission for Petitions of the Second Chamber of the States General.

Your Majesty! I realize that, if I continue my narrative in this manner, I shall make too great a demand on Your precious time. On Your desk there are bound to be important matters of State, concerning the general interest, waiting for Your attention: huge stacks of portfolios, it is as if I can see them before my eyes, here at Mr van Amerongen's table. The small problems of the individual must take second place, of that there can be no doubt. It is probably superfluous, Your Majesty, to bring to Your notice that throughout my entire ordeal I have scarcely suffered a single unkind word from anyone. No one ever lost his patience with me, even though at times I may have given ample cause for this. It is therefore not in order to complain that I am making bold to address myself to Your Majesty in Person. I do so only because I am concerned about my wife. It is not well with her. When her shelter was pulled down on 2 June, I observed that her skeleton was coming through her skin in a number of places. When the mere fact is considered that at that date she had taken neither food nor drink for a month, my concern for her, exaggerated though it may be, is perhaps understandable. And perhaps excessive solicitude is forgivable after thirty-six years of marriage. I myself have for the last two months been in the employment of Mr van Amerongen, who has been so kind as to take pity on me, an old man. During the daytime I clean out the stables and see to the pig swill, and in the evening I peel potatoes and wash up the dishes, in return for which my benefactor provides me with board and lodging. So as far as this is concerned, I have nothing to complain of. Meanwhile, however, it is the beginning of September, and during the storm which has been howling through the high-tension cables this past week and which, it may be hoped, has not caused too much damage in the Crown

Domains, my wife was partly blown away. If help is not soon
forthcoming, I fear it may be too late.

My last hope is therefore that You, Your Majesty, will Personally transport my wife to hospital in Your State Limousine
which, if I am correctly informed, bears the registration number
AA1. For truly, in the last instance, Your Majesty Alone is above
all parties and boundaries.

In the sincere hope not to have imposed unduly upon Your
Esteemed Attention, I remain, Your Majesty,

Your humble and obedient servant,

J. Lichtbeelt

Translated from the Dutch by Adrienne Dixon

BORISLAV PEKIĆ

Resistance and Comforts

In 1948 Borislav Pekić was sentenced to fifteen years in prison for his activity in the Union of Democratic Youth of Yugoslavia. He served two years before being pardoned. This experience left him permanently disaffected, but with an enduring concern with the shaping power of ideology and myth. He describes this process of political maturing in his two-volume work The Years the Locusts Devoured, *from which the following extract is taken.*

With a thrill I read *The Colditz Story*,[1]* about a German full-security prison during the Second World War from which it was impossible to escape, and yet people regularly did so; French prisoners longing to go home, the English for the sport of it, and then there were those, of course, still eager for the front. I have watched movies on spectacular escapes, particularly escapes from German camps, which invariably succeed with the tangible aid of patriotic regimes, caricaturing the myth of the meticulous German national character.[2] I have learned of real escapes. From the Ile du Diable (French Guiana), from Boer, Cambodian, Vietnamese, Soviet concentration camps,[3] from jails of all shapes and sizes: American Alcatraz to the Parisian Santé. I have listened to tales of Yugoslav prisoners' escapes, and I once personally assisted, when a friend, M., in May of 1949 hopped a wall before his trial during the exercise session in the prison yard at the Zemun detention centre with the help of a garden rake, and went off to a nearby cinema, only to return, at his parents' prompting, to serve his eighteen-year sentence. I have, therefore, become acquainted with many modes and motives for escape, with all the forms of resistance one can muster in jail – *of which a successful escape is always the best escape* – without adding my personal experience to that list . . .

* See end of chapter for all numbered footnotes.

Of all the attempts at escaping from prison, I was most deeply impressed by the famous tunnel dug by the Count of Monte Cristo;[4] for years he worked on it only to have it take him to the cell of another prisoner whose sentence was even longer than his. Remembrance of this *human-destiny-like* tunnel has inspired me to this memoir in which there will be no mention of something that did happen but rather what did not, and the reasons why.

In *The Gulag Archipelago*, Solzhenitsyn writes: "At what exact point, then, should one resist? When one's belt is taken away? When one is ordered to face into a corner? When one crosses the threshold of one's home?"[5]

The list of questions could continue. On the way to jail? Outdoors, before they take you in? At the registration desk before they enter your name? When they first raise their voice or a fist at you? When they first tell you the lie you will be required to swear to in court as the truth? Or only later, after a few years, when you can no longer bear it?

"Arrest consists of a series of incidental irrelevancies, of a multitude of things that do not matter, and there seems no point in arguing about any one of them individually – especially at a time when the thoughts of the person arrested are wrapped tightly about the big question: 'What for?' – and yet all these incidental irrelevancies taken together implacably constitute the arrest."[6]

It is arguable whether or not all these are truly incidental, although, indeed, they do not matter – in proportion to what will happen to you later on – but it is true that, incidental or deliberate, softening you at the beginning of the interrogation procedure, they do indeed constitute the arrest.

If, on the other hand, one considers escape to be the most effectual, and not merely *effective*, sort of resistance, possible at any phase of prison life, the opportunities for it decrease in proportion to one's proximity to jail. It is obviously easier to break away while still at one's own house or on the way to the police station than it is from inside the station. Later the chances increase again while serving the prison term – during transport, forced labour off prison grounds, medical treatment in a civilian hospital, etc. (There are cases where prisoners have intentionally committed another crime while in jail in order to secure a new trial that might facilitate escape.) The chances for escape during a prison term resemble a *sinusoid*, a curve, the base of which designates the greatest, and the peaks the least likelihood of flight. The actual act of escaping will depend in equal measure or perhaps even more on the sinusoid representing one's *will to escape*. When these two overlap, one flees. By some strange circumstance, which when considered from the psychological point of view is not so strange, the two sinusoids rarely coincide, making a graph on which the best chances for escape overlap with the least will to do so, while the worst likelihood inevitably overlaps with the greatest will. When they arrest us, regardless of animal instinct, one's will to run is either distracted by other things or suffers from an ignorance of what is to come, but the opportunities here are certainly far greater than they will be later on. When in prison, we grasp what we are in for and the will to escape is ferocious but the chances have, generally, evaporated or are coupled with a risk so great they are no longer worth it. By the time chances do arise during the prison term, the will is usually gone.

From this one could conclude that I spent a good deal of my time in prison plotting my escape. But I never, *never once*, so much as considered it. Least of all on the night of my arrest.

For resistance, against one's will, physical readiness, boldness, agility and skill, are advantages which have been lacking, to a notable degree, in me. From that perspective my parents' advice that I should do more gymnastics was appropriate. There are also two essential givens: the chance or the weapon. I say "or" because the presence of one excludes the need for the other. Either you have a chance which makes a weapon unnecessary, or you have the weapon and can create the chance.

Though I had neither one nor the other (a chance *at hand* or a weapon *in hand*), this explains nothing. For where there is a will, it waits not for a chance but forges its own. In the most spectacular of escapes – as I have learned from books and movies – the chance is created, one finds a weapon and slips off, leaving behind the requisite number of corpses, the last of which might easily be one's own. Among the most remarkable of escape stories is one I heard while in jail. Twin brothers shared counter-revolutionary convictions and a striking similarity. The only difference was that the first was innocent, while the second was guilty. Their fraternal pact was that should the police come to arrest the guilty one, the innocent twin would claim to be the other, allowing the guilty one to escape. (They hadn't considered what action to undertake in case the police came for the innocent brother. They weren't Russians.) And so it happened. The police

came, carted off the innocent one and the guilty brother made hastily
for an underground hiding place they had prepared in advance. Meanwhile the police discovered they were holding the innocent party –
formerly innocent, since *from then on* he, too, was guilty – and under-
took to remedy their failure. Failure, mind you, not *oversight*. They
had failed to arrest *both* guilty parties. It would only have been an
oversight or error had they apprehended someone innocent, which
they, evidently, had not. When the police make an oversight they
come to resemble, in psychological state and pessimism, a hunter who
has come home with an empty sack after hours of thrashing around
in the underbrush. (This is perhaps why hunters go to the butcher's
to buy game, and some police forces – formerly the Soviets, now the
South Americans – pick up anyone who happens to be there when
they fail to find the person they are looking for. This is also the reason
why the British police when clashing with strikers arrest random
onlookers if they can't snatch a rioter.) In that mood it didn't take
the police long to reach an agreement with the ex-innocent. He led
them to the hiding place of the ex-wise and guilty one, and the police
took the two of them to the Sremska Mitrovka prison, where they
told me this instructive tale. (The moral is not that you shouldn't
have a brother or that you shouldn't let him go in your stead to jail,
but that *you should never be hiding where you promised you'd be.*)

I know of other escape stories but it hardly seems appropriate to
tell them at a moment when I should be explaining why I, myself,
did not escape. I have said that the fact that I had no chance or weapon
explains nothing, and I stick to that. For even the best opportunity in
the world requires the will to make the best of it, and this always
assumes that the person in question must have contemplated this as
an alternative. At least a little. Even in the form of a passing thought
illuminating the dark horizon of the future with a gleam of hope,
only to vanish just as suddenly, leaving him in even greater darkness.

I never once contemplated resistance in any form – except a "cool
and collected" demeanour and a "decent upbringing" which was,
according to the competent opinion of my mother, all that was left
– "at the demise of the world as we know it" – though I did not have
the same justification that Solzhenitsyn permitted his fancied prisoner.
I spent no energy wondering why they had come to get me. My mind
was an utter *blank* – with the exception of my observations of the
mirror in "a red frame, stained with lead splotches from age", and
"stains on the leather jacket roughly the size of a fist",[7] all of it descrip-

tive gibberish free of thoughts of resistance, or escape. For in all fairness, in such a situation escape is the only *genuine* resistance. Not one's indignant complaint at the agents' rough handling or a polite request for them to be a little more circumspect with their language just as they *happened* to smash your leg with their boot . . .[8]

If, in my defence, I say that I did not, technically,[9] have a real opportunity, I would not be lying. But that would assume that I had considered resistance and then rationally forsaken it when I saw that I hadn't a chance. Which wasn't so. I could claim that surprise paralyses the will to resist, but this is not so. I wasn't surprised. Though I'd hoped that despite M.'s arrest they would somehow – how, I don't know! – neglect to arrest the remainder of us, I had been expecting it deep in my soul and nerves for several days at that point . . . I could also claim that I forsook all thoughts of resistance for the sake of my parents to save them from trouble, but the explanation would be not only untrue, it would be offensive: if I had been thinking of them, I wouldn't have been up to what I'd been doing. I wasn't thinking of them. How could I have been? At the time I hardly knew I had parents; in return for the lovely childhood they'd given me I gave them a lovely old age: an endless vigil at jail gates, doing without for my sake ("the boy must, after all, have only the best"), humiliation before those authorized to issue pardons, correspondence with hostile institutions, trepidation day and night, and an unending uncertainty.

There is no answer. I have no answer because the question has not been precisely posed. The true question is not *why didn't I escape*, but *why did I never so much as contemplate escaping.*

I knew I would be arrested, I merely didn't know – when. It is no good trying to fool myself as far as that's concerned. Perhaps I didn't dwell on it – my resolve not to consult my *Diaries* from the period does not, in this case, obstruct the truth, for in them I was careful enough not to write anything that might betray my underground activities, though they can be sensed, probably, as a sub-text to the many otherwise inexplicable moods; undoubtedly apparent, however, is the fact that I must have been afraid. (Yet, again, that fear, diluted by immaturity and moral-ideological fanaticism is not, presumably, what I would feel today, diluted, again, by other factors such as maturity and indifference.) An authentic undergrounder would have disappeared, or at least tried to disappear, before they came to fetch him.[10] After all, underground organizations are not formed for the express purpose of having their members arrested, are they?[11] My indifferent demeanour would only have been worth something if we had indeed conspired to speed our arrest.

The reasons I propose may seem a bit incredible, perhaps even ludicrous to some, but this by no means diminishes their psychological credibility when I am in question . . .

The reasons lie in . . . *comfort*.

In comfort, in our instinct for comfort – one more part of the legacy of my mother's "decent upbringing". The title of this essay, "Resistances and Comforts", sums up the matter as I see it. And goes further yet in explaining instances when I chose not to resist while in jail, especially those less related to the goal and more related to so-called dignity – vanity, arrogance, as you like – a form of resistance that costs a great deal and brings little in return.[12]

Immediately following 1944 until the "thaw of the socialist chill" in the late 1950s, if one lived and suffered on the outer hostile fringes of reality, stripped of security, rights, outlook and hopes, then the illusion of security and rights, outlook and hopes was not only sustained, but paradoxically, as the external class pressure rose, it swelled, at least in the inner realm of parents, relatives (not all relatives, of course, not those who had adapted, or as we put it "sold out"), friends, compatriots; in other words, *like-minded people*.

This paradox does not point to the particular vigour of one social stratum or the vitality of the Serbian middle class – which would be difficult, after all, to prove despite the inimical geographical and historical circumstances, in light of the relatively easily lost government – it is rather the natural consequence of the *state of being an outcast*. A process of growing cohesion is noted in each community that is made hermetic by force, each social, spiritual, racial ghetto exposed to pressure, persecution, extermination. The vision of reality is disproportionate – and luckily so, I might add – to the reality, thanks to the gradual and spontaneous emergence of the special *self-protective givens of the ghetto*, utterly unreal in terms of external and internal *genuine* realities, but, as I said, really quite vital and sustaining. Regardless of the fact that one in principle knows what a ghetto is, who belongs there and why and what the ultimate fate is to be, a marked man on the inside feels safer, more protected, stronger, than he does on the outside. And not only does he feel safer, he *is* safer, protected, stronger. What starts as an illusion becomes reality. What was escape and retreat becomes concentration and entrenchment. The haven becomes a stronghold. The bourgeoisie in our post-revolutionary period was, I presume, much like all former social élites when they learn overnight that a bit more than egocentrism and a few bayonets are needed to maintain an enduring government and its historical justification (at which a cynic, of course, would comment that though any egocentrism would suffice, many more bayonets are needed and with them the wisdom of when and how they should be used). When faced with the reality of socialism, which seemed like full-fledged communism to us and therefore all the more nightmarish, this bourgeoisie of ours felt more or less like the Jews in wartime Warsaw.[13] Completely exposed, insecure, powerless outside the ghetto when in direct contact with the Germans and the realities of the New Order; much less exposed, more secure, perhaps even powerful within its walls. Yes, *within its illusions*, but illusions which, thanks to the growing cohesion, acquired the strength, resilience, the imperviousness of real walls.

Our bourgeois ghetto differed from the Warsaw Ghetto in its invisibility. Its walls were built not of stone but of class hatred. The stones of the Warsaw wall were, of course, preceded by hatred, but that was racial hatred – in which revolutionary rhetoric was merely in greater disproportion to the traditional class measures of the eradication of freedom, rights, property than it was in this other socialist country of the same period. But more important is the fact that the strongest and most impenetrable parts of that wall were raised not by the class hatred of the victors, but by the class hatred of the vanquished, *not so much by the revolutionary authority around us and against us, as by us around ourselves, against them*. Those who did not live through this or who lived at the time but not with us can hardly imagine, or ever understand, the force, the uncompromising quality and extent of this intolerance, nor can they grasp its unifying role, the defiance it lent the members of the class ghetto.[14]

The illusion of relative safety – which was, in effect, real – *the basis of homogeneity*, was ensured by a spiritual, and to a considerable extent a physical, sense of comfort, freedom where least expected, rights where there are no rights, an outlook and hope where they otherwise seemed impossible. And this made it easier to bear, even with a certain superiority, the spontaneous and select unpleasantries that a person was exposed to outside our circle.[15]

In jail one was exposed, there can be no doubt, to a greater amount of intense external harassment, but this did not remove me spiritually, or even physically, considering the profile of the prison population at the time, from the circle of *illusions with the power of the reality in which I felt secure*, and in which, before and after prison, I spent the finest and purest years of my life . . . I found a part of this circle in jail, where, by the very logic of things, there were more of those who thought as I did than there were on the outside, but it is not to them that I refer. I am thinking, instead, of those remaining outside confinement, *my own circle* from which I was wrenched on the night between 6 and 7 November. That circle, it is true, was now outside prison – with the exception of a few of my friends – but by penetrating the prison walls with their solidarity, loyalty, concern, aid, moral support, these people remained a firm foundation for my sense of invulnerability, and, I believe, for whatever genuine resistance I did offer.

Where would escape have taken me? Under conditions difficult to imagine and even more difficult to realize – ideally to foreign lands.[16] Ideally, perhaps, from that perspective, but far less ideal from this, the perspective of those same foreign lands where I now live as I write these memoirs. In any case, escape would have tossed me into a vacuum, beyond my circle, beyond the ghetto and its shelter.

There would have been people, presumably, to hide me – for what is the purpose of a circle if it cannot provide them? – but no spiritual comfort and certainly no physical comfort, something I have always highly valued. Once the investigation was over I no longer had anything to fear in prison; in flight I would have lived in chronic terror of being apprehended.[17] In jail I received packages: out there a person had to scrounge for his sustenance (as far as life in the jungle was concerned I had no experience whatsoever, and the picture of my father eating acorns in 1917 as a guerrilla fighter was hardly inspiring). There were times in prison – particularly in the biting cold weather – when I would bathe and then dry in the wind; on the run the frost and wind would have been the same, but one had to bathe in rivers. In prison there was no heat but we warmed one another; on the run even on the hottest days the chill of loneliness and fear would be freezing. In jail we met policemen who were people; out there in every person you saw a policeman. In jail I thought freely on all manner of things; in flight I would have thought of nothing but jail and how to keep away . . .

And if I were to wander around like a wild dog, wouldn't I be in a jail anyway, a jail more terrible than all others – *the prison of fear and uncertainty*? And even if I weren't wandering aimlessly, if I were in a safe bunker with someone to watch over me – wouldn't that be a jail, too? *Then why try to escape someone else's jail only to flee to my own?* From a jail that one could, at least, despise because it was some-one else's, to a jail that could not be loved, even though it was – my own?

Every form of incarceration is a waste of time, though some end up being worth something to someone in some other way. Time spent escaping is wasted in all ways. The constant trepidation and hiding, the unending struggle to survive, may well restore the atrophied proto-human jungle instincts. But – to what end? These instincts are useful only if one intends to spend the rest of one's days in the jungle.

I may, of course, be spending my days in the jungle even now without being aware of it, but that is, nonetheless, all the difference for which it was worth doing nothing while they took away my belt . . .

Translated by Ellen Elias-Bursać

1 Reid, *The Colditz Story*, Hodder & Stoughton, London, 1952.
2 Ana Segers, *The Seventh Cross*, etc. In contrast to escapes by British pris-oners of war, this one was rather convincing. The more so with the passage of time: as the real war is forgotten, the bolder and more incredible the escape scenes become, as if the German camps existed only so that Anglo-Saxon wit, skill and initiative could prove their superiority over German dullness and lack of imagination.
3 Henri Charrière, *Papillon*, Granada, 1980; the book and film on Chur-chill's escape from Boer imprisonment; *The Deer Hunter*, and films on Rambo, the incarnation of post-Vietnam American martial spirit beaten in Vietnam, or the spirit whose lack led to defeat; *The Killing Fields*, a film on flight from a concentration camp run by the Pol Pot in Cambodia; countless reports on escapes from Siberia and the camps of the polar circle.
4 A. Dumas, *The Count of Monte Cristo*.
5 A. Solzhenitsyn, *The Gulag Archipelago*, Harvill, 1986.
6 *Ibid.*
7 Comments Pekić found later in his diary from the period, *op. trans.*
8 When, one early May dawn in the year 1970, the organs of Internal Affairs – several! – came to confiscate my passport, thereby preventing my move to England, I protested sharply! Because they were confiscating my pass-port? No! Because I was thrust into dreadful financial and other incon-venience since I had already fully packed my belongings and leased the flat? No! Because this would separate me for months from my wife and

daughter who were free to leave? Not at all! I was protesting because they had come so early, because they woke me up at an *indecent hour*! (As if, in the meantime the confiscation of a passport without a word of explanation except that of discretional law is by definition something not to be explained, something civilized, and moreover, in my case, somehow nearly *natural*. It is natural, you see – the more so, perhaps, for the groggy circumstances – that without a trial I was injured in one of my fundamental civil rights; the only outrageous aspect being that this was done at five o'clock in the morning.) And again, my father was lost, my mother frightened yet practical, my wife upset and miserable. Only I remained above the situation – at least until the agents departed with my passport. I had fallen into a sort of chilly, witty banter, and again, as if being witty were a fitting exchange for my civil rights, as if a few cynical jabs were adequate remuneration for the inflicted injury! Nothing helped! Not my years in jail, the experience of others, my mature age – I was already forty – absolutely nothing: "decent upbringing", my mother's universal weapon against all of life's ailments, was my only defence. My sole consolation in the case of my passport is that far bolder defence tactics fared no better. My lawyer and friend, the late Joro Barovic, felt that the proper channels were the best and most expedient. He sued the police. The channel was a good one, though hardly expedient. The court passed a curt judgment, the only legible part of which was that the police had been right. Even now I maintain that the suit was magnificent, though little was said in it about me and much more of Joro's criticism of the order of things here and elsewhere in the world. When we lost, Joro said, "It doesn't matter. What matters is that they know where we stand on this question." I knew – I stood for nearly a full year in Belgrade instead of London.

9 Even in the case of the open window on the staircase in *Levitan* (Vitomil Zupan, *Levitan*, Cankarjeva zalozba, Lubyanka 1982): "So we left. They had me walk in front of them. From the room into the corridor, on to the landing and then down the stairs. Then a moment of temptation struck . . . The window on the landing was open wide . . . Down below was firmly packed sand. The third floor. High ceilings. Success assured . . ." (p. 13). It is not entirely clear what sort of success was assured. For the jump, perhaps, but for survival, probably not. Yet he does not jump. Why? "The Devil only knows whether I was saved from jumping by a deeply inbred trait that had already cost me much in my lifetime: my curiosity for what would happen next." (*Ibid.* p. 14). The logic sounds crazy, but I believe him. A person might even go before a firing squad out of curiosity. But then comes the thought that proves both *his and their* reputation. "Through my head flashed a demonic thought: if I were to jump, no one in our city would have believed that they hadn't thrown me out themselves, such was their reputation at the time." He doesn't tell us why he didn't jump but it no longer matters.

10 So a certain KM attempted to do, arrested as a member of NKOJ (The

Yugoslav National Committee). I know this for a fact; he told me so himself. But he told me in the Sremska Mitrovka jail, so apparently my lack and his wealth of experience in underground activities landed us in the same place.

11 There are instances, though admittedly rare, where such is precisely the case. At moments of political crisis when rebellious spirits spark a need to organize, it is simpler for a government to instigate such organizations itself. Only then can they control resistance, and discover, along the way, who truly supports the regime. A character of mine, Steinbrecher, said as much: "Only weak police forces limit themselves to suppressing rebellion. Good police are catalysers, fermenters, instigators. And the best? – They organize and lead them." (B. Pekić, *How to Tame a Vampire*, p. 37.)

12 Would you defy the supervisor of a prison hospital where you work as an administrator, thus losing the option of stealing medicine before his very eyes for the needy who are not being given it for whatever reason? Would you refuse to scrub the floor of your cell because you fear catching a cold, only to end up in solitary confinement in a cell sitting in several inches of water on a floor you won't have to scrub but which is guaranteed to give you pneumonia? Would you refuse, in the name of human dignity – your personal dignity, in fact, not the dignity of the human race – to do questionable things that might save the lives of others? Would you, for instance, refuse to lie to the administration of the jail because your decent upbringing, your morals, forbid you to lie, thus placing a fellow sufferer in grave danger, as if endangering someone else *is* permitted by this upbringing and these morals?

13 John Hersey, *The Wall*.

14 There will be other opportunities to describe further this radical state of our consciousness – no less reconcilable than the awareness that surrounded us then – and to explain it in greater detail, but here it will suffice to say that no one ever set foot in my home or the homes of my friends from my classroom or school who was suspected of being a member of the communist youth organization. No one who was even from the indifferent and uncommitted *middleground* on the clearly delineated zone between "open reaction" and "open revolution" (the revolution being, in fact, less open than the reaction) was ever invited to our parties, held with the secrecy and fanaticism of the Early Christian Agapes of pagan times. And on that score I have no regrets. Just as those, on the other side, now claim that *"such were the times"*, so do I. And they were. These were not the times, nor did we have the will, and certainly not the reasons, to contemplate finding those among the communists who might be friends *despite everything*. The reasons were sometimes lacking, of course, because there was no will for such a thing; and where the will might have been found, the reasons were lacking. Such *were* the times. I do regret something that could not be justified no matter what the intolerance – something that was class intolerance in the ugliest sense of the

word, having no "political" alibi: our distrust of everyone whom we considered rural, peasants, from the provinces. These included honest lads who roomed with their city relatives, and others living in lonely cramped rented rooms, and those quartered in dormitories – though they were generally "politically organized" by the powers-that-be – and even those whom no one knew for certain where or how they lived, or rather where they lived, for we could have seen *how* they lived had we looked. Well, we didn't. Such were the times.

15 Just a few notorious illustrations of the revolutionary atmosphere from the period of Reconstruction and Society-Building later portrayed by former activists as so *idyllic*. My mother was chased out of line in front of a store for wearing a fur coat; she wore the coat because most of the rest of her wardrobe had been *re-distributed*. My father – a high-ranking official even then – was practically swept to every city event by neighbourhood women comrades, always muscular and unsightly, if he was not already being borne in the same fashion by his equally masculine and unsightly women comrades from his job, where he was supposed to be fervently thrilled by the country's new destiny and the prospects of its lasting forever. Authorities chopped the legs off our trousers if they were the slightest bit too narrow for the progressive intolerance and their followers in the National Youth. Pupils were sent to Gortanovac, to forced labour hoeing turnips as *vagrants and hooligans* if they didn't sign up for voluntary labour, as were those who listened to jazz records at the American reading room, newspaper vendors for Grol's paper *Demokratija*, the organ of a legal political party (the paper was burnt), those who attended Sunday school, etc. Second cousins of people who had never returned from the camps were chased out of high school and university. Work brigades for laying the youth railway tracks were manned using threats and coercion. After cries for *de-fascization* at public political rallies, to the glum silence of the intimidated majority, the harangues of the minority and the humiliation of being caned by a row of one's peers, all those pupils who could not adapt were expelled from high school and university long before China's "cultural" revolution and Yugoslavia's 1948 came along, though they had, it's true, been able to enroll in the first place – not the case in Czechoslovakia in the heartland of Middle European civilization, a fact that casts a surprisingly favourable light on our Balkan inconsistency and slovenliness. Ah, *such were the times!*

16 In as much as I would not end, as my friend LJ did, dangling from a Triglav cliff only a few years before the Yugoslav borders completely opened up to the world.

17 One of the escapees who came back from the *jail outside* to the *jail inside* told me: "Now at last I can sleep in peace. Out there they were after me every night in my dreams. I would wake up a free man and spend the day trying to elude capture, always fearful I'd be caught. But no matter what I did, when night fell they would be after me again in my dreams.

And besides, when you're on the run your sentence grows, instead of shrinking the way it does with each passing day behind bars." "How so?" I asked him. "It's simple," he told me. "Here your sentence passes, while on the run it doesn't. When they catch you, you start to serve your time all over again, but now you've got three instead of one: the sentence you fled from, the sentence of fear while you were free, and the third one they nail you with for attempting escape."

FRANS POINTL

The Chicken that Flew
over the Soup

That Sunday afternoon we were going to pay a visit to Mother's old girlhood friend, Estella Hamburger, a dentist. Mother said her former friend had been lucky – all the members of her family had survived the war.

Estella had got through the time when she had "gone underground" in a nonchalant way. That little woman had had her black hair peroxided. Now and then she'd gone out of an evening for a walk. Dead cool. She'd not got herself a false identity card. She couldn't see the use in it. If she was stopped, she'd throw an angry fit, saying she'd left that rotten thing at home. For years she walked through the eye of the needle, not caring a damn.

Mother told how Estella carried her shares around on her person all the time, sewn inside her corset. As she was telling me these details, she sat stitching a new lace collar on to a blouse. She wanted to look neat and tidy when she went to visit this rich friend of her youth.

"She's managed to catch a goldfish too in her old age," she remarked as she stuck a new thread through her needle.

In December nineteen-forty-seven, Estella H., who was Mother's age, had married Alex Goudvis, ten years her senior and also a dentist by profession.

When Mother had finished sewing the collar on the blouse, she seated herself at the old piano and played *Poissons d'or*. She had once told me that Debussy had been inspired by a goldfish, inlaid in mosaic, in an imitation pool. All the time she was playing it I saw quivering, live goldfish darting, all a-gleam, through moving water lit by sunlight.

I asked if she was playing that now because she had the name "Goudvis" in her mind.

She shook her head. "I was just playing what came to me, without thinking," she said.

She went on nattering about her girlhood friend. She was now filthy rich. She and her husband lived in a splendid house along Minerva Avenue and were the possessors of a car, a refrigerator and a vacuum cleaner.

Mother would always strew tea-leaves over our cord carpeting and then go to work on it with a dustpan and brush. For us a vacuum cleaner was an unthinkable luxury.

"Are they members of the Jewish Spiritualists Association too?" I asked.

She looked up, scared. "For goodness' sake, don't mention that! Stella would probably make fun of it."

If only *she* had met Mr Goudvis, I reflected. I wasn't exactly waiting for a stepfather, but I could do with the things I would surely get from him.

Lots of my classmates had model forts that had come from America and were all the rage, with little metal soldiers and little cannons from which you could shoot bullets at the enemy. They had boxes of Meccano, clockwork and electric model trains, steam engines. I had my scrapbook, with pictures of toy cars and now and then I'd get a cardboard sheet with cut-outs.

Mother had had her hair waved for this important visit. It lay in flat, shiny waves underneath an invisible hair-net. Before we left she gave herself a striking pair of soft rosy lips. I hadn't even known she possessed a lipstick.

I tried to get out of the visit and asked if I really had to come, complaining that I was always surrounded by old people.

I am seven. A sunny Sunday in the middle of July, nineteen-forty. We ride from Haarlem to Zandvoort-on-Sea on the blue tram. When we finally get there Mother says: "Look at that lovely blue sky!"

On the promenade a man is standing who has as many as a hundred coloured windmills on the end of a long stick. They make one big rattling noise, the lot of them, in the balmy sea breeze. I stand staring at them, as though bewitched. I get one.

She hobbles awkwardly in her shoes of white linen down the flight of broad steps made of tree trunks that leads to the beach. There's a big lump sticking out on the left side of her right shoe, caused by her bunion.

Once on the beach, she takes off her shoes and shakes the sand out

of them. I shove the little windmill into her hand, tear off my shoes
and socks, drop them and run towards the sea.

How fine it is, up to your knees in all that swirling, lukewarm water!

Annoyed, she runs after me, her dress yanked up in an odd manner.
She gives my arm a violent tug and shouts in a piercing voice, "Do
you want to get drowned?" She pulls me roughly out of that glorious
water.

Suddenly my day has been spoilt. I have to make sand-pies with
the metal moulds she's brought with her, sitting next to her wicker-
work beach chair. I scrape out a hole, stick the moulds into it as deep
as I can, cover them up and smooth over the surface.

"Where have your nice little moulds got to?"

I look about me, surprised.

"Stupid! Keep your eyes on your things and don't sit there dreaming all the time!"

She gets up and starts searching. I watch her, delighted.

She returns, empty-handed.

"They've been stolen," she grumbles.

I see children of my own age splashing about together in the sea
and hear their shrieks of joy. What am I to do with such an elderly
mother? Everyone thinks she's my grandma.

Soon we'll be going to see Grandpa, who lives here. He always
smells of fresh soap and has a splendid white moustache, ingeniously
curled up at each end.

After that, we shall go to the nursing home where Grandma is.
She's had a shock in her head, Mother says. Grandma's mouth is
pulled crooked, you can hardly understand what she's saying. She
dribbles. Her one eye looks as though it's sagging. Mother always
tells her mother that it's sure to come right again.

ALEX GOUDVIS
ESTELLA GOUDVIS-HAMBURGER
DENTISTS
BY APPOINTMENT ONLY

the shiny brass nameplate reads.

Mother rings the bell. Meneer Goudvis comes to the door. How
tall he is. I put him at six foot at least. His grey hair is thin and curly.

Has he got protruding eyes or is it those thick lenses that make them look like that?

In the hallway the walls are of white marble, with thin grey veins running through it. There is a tall table of oakwood with a big vase on it containing a many-coloured bouquet of flowers. This is what a palace looks like in my imagination.

I catch sight of the three of us for a moment in a large pier-glass surrounded by an ornate frame of gilt and plaster. We look like a painting. Meneer Goudvis takes Mother's coat, all courtesy, and then mine.

Their room isn't a room, it's a hall. It is much lighter than our place. They have a suite of furniture in beige, with tassels hanging down from it. The carpet is multicoloured, its warm colours becoming lighter or darker as the sun shines on it and disappears again. Against the wall stands an old-fashioned bureau, the wood of which is inlaid with twigs and leaves and flowers in a lighter kind of wood. Grandpa and Grandma used to have just such a writing-desk. I was allowed to look in all the little drawers.

On a blanket chest there stands a radio finished in French polish, one of the kind with a cat's-eye in it that turns a smooth green when the set is tuned in properly. A lid on top of it stands open and, yes, there's a gramophone inside.

Mevrouw Goudvis storms into the room. Mother and she embrace and kiss each other vigorously and protractedly. Then she cautiously pushes Mother away from her. They examine each other's faces minutely. They are speechless. Their eyes have filled with tears, their lips and chins are trembling.

"Now, now, girls," says Meneer Goudvis, "don't make a drama of it." Mevrouw Goudvis is small, at most five foot two. Would she be strong enough to pull teeth, molars?

There is a long, rectangular painting hanging on the wall above the settee. It portrays a recumbent woman, naked. Her one hand lies elegantly low down on her stomach. "A genuine Breitner," Meneer Goudvis informs us.

We drink coffee out of tiny, almost transparent white cups with a gold line along the rims. I don't understand why Mevrouw only pours them half-full. I've a terrible thirst and would be glad of a glass of orangeade. Meneer takes a little dish from the table and presents us each with a large chocolate.

"Splendid porcelain," Mother remarks, examining the cup closely.

"What did you think?" Mevrouw responds. "Genuine Rosenthal."

Mother nods, impressed.

They speak about people I have never known. Now and then I catch a name: Blumenthal, Menist, De Jong. Not come back.

Only he came back, with one son. She came back, but not her husband and three children . . .

Mother asks to be excused and goes to the toilet. Meneer goes with her to show her where it is and returns a moment later. With a touch of inquisitive sensationalism in her voice, Mevrouw asks me how my Uncle Simon is getting on now. "Is he still on drink – I don't like to ask your mother, it's such a painful subject."

I feel a sudden impulse to shock these rich, self-satisfied people.

"Drink, ma'am?" I reply. "Like a fish. Recently they found him in the terminus of the blue tram in Haarlem at dead of night. He was lying in his own vomit, on a bench covered in lovely plush, sleeping off his hangover and snoring away. At first they thought it was some tramp, but then . . ."

Mother comes back in and I shut up quickly. The incident in the tram terminus was pure fantasy.

Meneer has raised his eyebrows and gives his wife a look.

"Dégoûtant," he remarks.

I shall be asking Mother what that word means later on.

"Such a first-class doctor," Mevrouw adds to his remark, shaking her head with sympathy.

It is the first time I have heard Uncle Simon was once a good doctor.

Mother looks at the couple questioningly and Mevrouw skilfully changes the subject.

"It's not an easy task, keeping up a big house like this, Rebecca," she rattles on, as she pours coffee once more into our little cups, parsimoniously.

Meneer passes round the little dish of chocolates again.

"I'm always having to see the servant-girl keeps at it," she goes on, "not to mention the cleaning woman. And don't forget our practice either. You've no idea how many people have neglected their teeth in the last few years – a question of having to, you understand. Luckily, there's gold again now for the bridges and inlays and crowns. And that's not to speak of my difficult, demanding husband."

She looks at him lovingly with a mocking little laugh.

"I wish I had your troubles," Mother responds, in German, and lets out a sigh.

I think of her teeth. She needs dentures too. That costs money. Lots. Why doesn't she ask her girlhood friend to see to it? No, she won't do a thing like that. Mother never asks favours.

"You go and take a look round our house," Mevrouw suggests to me. "Then your mother and I can talk of old times."

Old people often say that. They want to get you out of the room, because they don't think their talk fit for your ears.

I leave the room and stroll towards the kitchen, where the door is open.

This kitchen is half as big again as our living room. It has a tall refrigerator with a rounded door. I read BENDIX on it in big gold-coloured letters. I open the door inquisitively. What a lot of food they have in the house! After all, rich people can eat as much as they want, even the dearest of the dear.

I walk into the hallway and open the door with "Surgery" on it. Oof, what a nasty smell. It's like lysol. There's that drill, too, that instrument of torture that spins round slowly in your teeth. The bowl is of white porcelain, decorated with soft-pink little flowers. Why little flowers? It's only for spitting in, isn't it?

I go and sit in the leather patient's chair, cheekily adjusting the head-rest, which has a roll of paper affixed to it.

There is a narrow brown chest with a lot of drawers in it. I pull one open and see masses of nasty, shiny instruments. The little mirrors are fun. The panel patient dentist holds a mirror like that above a little flame from a spirit-lamp before he puts it inside your mouth – in that way it can't cloud over from your breath.

Another apparatus for drilling is standing in a corner. Its foot looks like the foot of a sewing-machine. It's an ancient pedal drill with a driving belt. Handy, if ever the electricity should be cut off. They must have used that during the war. No, that's impossible. In those days they probably didn't even know each other and didn't live here. Where would Meneer Goudvis have been then?

I go into the hall and walk up the broad stairs. I open a door. Their bedroom. There's a faint odour of some sweet perfume. Everything here is white. The bed, the curtains, cupboards, table-lamps, the enormous linen chest. Even the ornaments. On one of the little cupboards next to the bed there's a small, white Philips radio set. If only it were mine. We can get just three stations on our cable radio and then we have to pay a riksdaalder a month for the hire of the ugly metal loudspeaker.

The bed is enormous. There's room for three people in it. On the one pillow lies an all but transparent pale blue nightdress, on the other a shiny pair of men's pyjamas in peacock blue. I stroke my hand over it. Yes, real silk.

On the cupboard on Meneer's side lies a book. It's called *David Golder*, written by Irene Nemirovsky. It is a German book. What Jew still wants to read and speak German now?

Over a chair next to the window hangs a lonely, flesh-coloured corset with steels and laces on the back. What a piece of machinery! Would this be the same garment Mevrouw hid her shares in during the war?

I lift it up carefully. How heavy a thing like this is. Would Meneer undo the laces of this corset at night-time and would it make them excited? Wouldn't all that paper have rustled when she went out a walk round the block during the war? Why doesn't Mother wear a corset?

One day I would own a bedroom like this, but then in green. I should place the big radio with the built-in gramophone next to my bed and listen to my favourite music as I lay smoking one of those flat Egyptian cigarettes with a gold tip.

I look again at Mevrouw's nightdress. Would she be stark naked underneath it?

For a moment I see myself lying there, smoking. The gramophone is playing Debussy's *D'un cahier d'esquisses* and at my side I discern . . . Mother.

I stare out of the window. There's an elderberry in bloom. Behind it I see the red crown of an oak.

Mother is far better-looking than Mevrouw Goudvis. Mevrouw is small, her legs and arms are too short and too fat. She has a long, hooked nose that ends in a bobble. I must be honest – she does have beautiful eyes, of a clear, hard blue. Her hair is dark-brown – that's dyed, of course.

Mother has black hair that is speckled a silver-grey. I think her eyes are her most beautiful feature: dark-brown, with splinters of beige and green.

At times there's a look of crystallized terror in them. For days.

I turn round and look at the big bed again. I'm still lying there, smoking in perfect comfort. The gramophone is now playing *Reflets dans l'eau*. Something has changed. Hans Heveling is lying next to me. Someone else too is lying in the broad bed. Lying at Hans's side, asleep, is Hannah. To which, then, do I belong?

Hans had had a film projector, with cartoon films included, as a present from his parents. Everyone in the class was bursting with impatience to be invited to his home. To my surprise, he asked me first. I deliberately acted lumpishly, saying that those childish films didn't interest me one bit. But he kept on insisting in a friendly fashion, at the same time giving me a penetrating look, as though I ought to guess something he couldn't say.

Jealousy prevented me from accepting what was a clear offer of friendship.

I go and stand in front of the dressing-table. It looks like a perfumery shop. I stare into the big mirror, take out the miniature mirror from my comb-case and examine my face and profile, full of dislike.

Had my real father such a hooked nose? At home, I often stand manoeuvring like this in front of the mirror above the fixed washbasin. It's compulsive behaviour, Mother says. She thinks I have a handsome nose, a ruler's nose, she says. What can I rule over? I think with envy of Hans. His forehead that flows smoothly over into his handsome, straight nose, his dark, elegantly curling eyelashes. I detect the beginning of another blister on my right eyelid.

I pick up a small, cobalt-blue phial from the dressing-table. The shape of the oversized gold-coloured stopper makes me think of the headdress worn by Queen Nefertiti. There's a picture of the Eiffel Tower on the label, with *Soir de Paris* in gold letters underneath it.

I screw the cap off. Ooh! What a lovely smell, a rich people's smell. I sprinkle a few drops on my hair. It is not until I am screwing the cap on again that I realize that when I get downstairs again in a few minutes, everyone will detect my little theft.

Once again Mother will go on about the need for me to read her book called *Etiquette* by Amy Groskamp-ten Have.

They smell it immediately. Mevrouw Goudvis laughs. "You've been at my *Soir de Paris*!" she cries.

"You can't do such a thing," Mother comments with a sigh.

Mevrouw tells her not to fuss so much about such trifles.

We go home. In the vestibule Meneer helps Mother into her coat with an exaggerated show of politeness. He searches for something in the inside pocket of his jacket, pulls out a ten-guilder note and hands it to me.

"Buy something nice with this."

I stutter my thanks, all confusion.

On the way to the tram I tell Mother that I want to have such a house later on, with beautiful white furniture like that and especially with so much light.

She nods her head. "Then you'll have to learn a lot and work hard."

I wave the ten-guilder note. "Shall we have hotpot at Heck's Lunchroom? I'll treat us."

She shakes her head and says the hole in my palm is bigger than my hand itself. She doesn't understand that I want to cling on a bit longer to the feeling of luxury that I have just experienced.

We get off at Mint Square. A moment or two later we're sitting next to the window at Heck's, watching the passers-by in Rembrandt Square. An orchestra is playing in the restaurant.

I order two plates of chicken soup and hotpot for two. The soup is yellow. A few strands of vermicelli are floating around in it.

"Do they call this chicken soup?" Mother complains.

She calls the waitress, a girl with long, blonde hair with a funny little white cap on top of it. Mother asks her severely if the soup has really been made with chicken. The little waitress goes and asks the cook.

"Madam, the soup has been made from real chicken."

Mother gives a scornful laugh. "I think the chicken just flew over this soup," she says.

The hotpot is full of meat and beautifully flavoured with herbs.

I settle the bill like a man of the world and get two guilders change. With that I plan to buy a cut-out model of a Buick Eight tomorrow. The coins dance in my pocket.

"Things will soon be going much better for us," I assert, optimistically. "After seven lean years will come seven years of plenty."

Mother shrugs her shoulders. "Don't count on it," she says. "Perhaps an angel will appear to you tonight and tell you these last seven years *were* our years of plenty."

"In that case, we'd do better to get off the bus," I mumble to myself.

We walk slowly home through the twilight. A policeman on a horse rides past.

"A grey horse in the evening means good luck," Mother says dreamily.

When we get home the miserable way we live hits me for the first time good and proper. We shall never be able to invite the Goudvis couple here.

I'm lying in bed. Tomorrow the monotony of a new week begins. I set the alarm clock for six o'clock: tomorrow practice French. So far I've done practically nothing about it. I can't get to sleep. All the luxury of the day just passed is still spinning round in my head.

I imagine myself in the future. I have a house outside town. My car – an ancient Pierce-Arrow – is parked in front of the garage. I get into it. Then along come Hannah and Hans. How goodlooking they are, and gay. Hannah goes and stands in front of the car, admiring the emblem, a silvery bow and arrow. Hans is walking round the car, inspecting it, stroking the wire spokes of the spare tyre.

I open the door. Hannah moves up beside me, with next to her Hans, who closes the door.

We roll down the drive. "Beige," says Hannah, dreamily. "A beautiful colour for so distinguished a car."

I see Hans has put his arm round her. She presses her head against his. I don't like that.

I stop and say he must get out.

As he gets out he casts me a tender, meditative glance.

When we drive further I have the feeling of having lost something.

Hannah presses up against me and kisses me lightly on the lips. "It wasn't really serious with him," she murmurs.

The alarm goes off with a deafening rattle. I stretch and immediately grab my textbook. "A shining example," the head-teacher calls me. In our class I am SOMEBODY, but I pay for it with immense effort.

Mother – free of illusions about herself – is waiting for me to get my Lower Certificate and be able to keep myself. Then her existence will become superfluous. Time after time she reminds me that the only weapons I possess are my little grey cells.

I am prepared to join the tough, protracted fight against an enemy under whose yoke I don't intend to bend my neck in the future: poverty.

Translated from the Dutch by James Brockway

JEAN ROUAUD

Of Illustrious Men

Three successive generations of Frenchmen were born to suffer the invasion of their homeland by their neighbours the Germans. The traumas of the generation that fought in the 1914–18 war were evoked in Jean Rouaud's prizewinning first novel, Fields of Glory. *In this new novel,* Of Illustrious Men, *we see the nation's wounds reopened, in 1940, before they ever had a chance to heal. It is not long before Frenchmen in their twenties are rounded up for forced labour in Germany. One of them is the narrator's father . . .*

The young men were herded together on the station platform, surrounded by soldiers, waiting for the train that was to transport them to Germany. In spite of the mildness of this steely-blue March morning, tempered by a chilly little wind enfilading the tracks, they were warmly equipped in preparation for the harsh climate they had been told to expect. Each man was dressed according to his condition in life, his overcoat more or less well fitting, more or less threadbare; the more humble of them had piled on as many clothes as possible under a tight little jacket whose buttons were feeling the strain. At their feet was a suitcase containing everything they had been ordered to bring with them: a change of clothes, of shoes, either "heavy duty" or "best" (depending on which pair they had put on that morning), and enough provisions to last over a long two-day journey. Some of them had added a haversack which revealed the neck of a bottle of wine with its cork sticking out – a miraculous commodity in these difficult times. When they extracted their bottle and took a swig, the most swashbuckling among them would first belch, and then boast: "That's another one the Germans won't get", or "Like in nineteen-fourteen, it's wine that'll win the war", which in the circumstances raised no more than a half-hearted smile. Most of them remained silent, like on your first day in a new class at school when you don't yet know each other, when you're sizing each other up, hoping to see some signs of fellow feeling. When a distant hissing sound announced the arrival of a train, they turned their resigned faces towards the wide curve in the track round which the expected locomotive would suddenly appear in a cloud of steam.

The most ardent desire of the man who was a head taller than all the rest was to escape attention. This was the moment of truth. When the letter arrived he had known at once that this was not going to be the way he would discover Germany. And as he had had his call-up papers duly stamped, and therefore felt he no longer needed to worry about his aunt, what he had to do now was find some way of giving his companions the slip. Would he wait until he was on board, and then jump from the moving train? Or could he manage to escape by unobtrusively sliding under the carriages? He was bending over to glance under the train standing at the other platform when a suspicious soldier came up and pushed him back into the ranks with the barrel of his submachine gun. "Cigarette," he said, pointing to a fag-end opportunely thrown on to the ballast, and he jumped down on to the track, retrieved it, and immediately started smoking it with relish, to prove his good faith. At least he had seen what he wanted to see. It was possible to creep under a carriage with his suitcase, and later emerge on the opposite platform. In the hope of avoiding any unpleasant surprises on that side. All he had to do now was wait for an auspicious moment, and he stepped back a few paces to try to merge into the crowd of his companions in adversity, coming to terms with his mounting fear, and answering one of the men who suggested making a dash for it by raising his eyebrows questioningly.

When, in a cacophony of connecting rods, pistons, brake shoes and bursts of steam, the train slowly drew up at the platform, there was a mad rush for the doors in the search for seats, since the young men leaning against the windows, having got in at Saint-Nazaire, had announced that there wouldn't be enough for everyone. While the sentries were fully occupied in restoring discipline by giving gruff orders, he slid down with his suitcase between two carriages, worked his way beneath the buffers and crept under the other train. Lying flat on his stomach across the sleepers, his heart beating frantically, for an eternity of seconds he awaited the shouts and hysterical activity that would certainly have ensued had his escape been noticed. Every time a whistle blew to signal the departure of a convoy, he tightened his grip on his suitcase, ready to spring, reproaching himself for having loaded it down with so many books, although not for a single moment

did it occur to him to abandon it. As the minutes passed and the
normal frenzy of the occupants didn't sound any more alarming than
usual, he began to crawl forward a few metres, all the time keeping
a watch on the feet clomping along the platform above him. Even
more than a pair of boots, what he dreaded to see were the four paws
of an Alsatian, whose nose would certainly have condemned him,
whose fangs would have torn him to pieces. But neither boots nor
dog appeared. All that was to be seen through the narrow gap between
the bottom of the carriage and the edge of the platform was the
heart-rending procession of miserable substitutes for shoes. Old,
worn-out, patched-up shoes, complete with wooden or cork-
agglomerate soles, or even with a bit of carpet. He himself, in preparation for his get away, had done a deal with the postman, who got
preferential treatment, and he had acquired a pair of sturdy leather
shoes. He had remembered a remark made by a prisoner who had
escaped from a Stalag: "The secret of an escape is shoes."

For the time being, though, a blacksmith's apron would probably
have served his purpose better, as he made his way along under the
train, bumping his suitcase over the sleepers in front of him. Another
thing he feared was that the train above him would pull out. He could
imagine the tragi-comedy of the scene, with him on all fours in the
middle of the rails, his pathetic surrender and its terrible consequences.
What could he pretend to be looking for? The fag-end story wouldn't
work a second time. But anyway, this is it, this is the end of his
disappearing act: a slight jolt, an imperceptible gliding movement –
no, though, his temporary shelter hasn't budged. A comparison of
the position of the wheels with a fixed point is enough to reassure
him: it's the convoy taking the forced labourers that is pulling out on
the other track. And he aims a relieved little smile at the sleepers and
axles: the train for Germany is leaving without him.

By now he has reached the end of the train and, flat on his stomach,
he takes stock of the situation: wagons waiting or abandoned on a
siding, a railwayman pulling up a lever at the points, some workmen
chatting by a shed, a contemplative seagull perched on a rail, sparrows
hopping up and down. The railway line on this side crosses the west
of the town. If he were to walk along it, with that wire fence between
the station and the avenue, he could hardly escape notice. Should he
cut through the marshalling yard and get down to the river? Too
many pitfalls, and he would be almost certain to come across a patrol.
Wait until it gets dark? Without a secure hiding place, he wouldn't

like to bet on his chances until then. All that remains is the station. And he leaves his cover, bending double as he crosses the rails, as if his great height made him too conspicuous, pausing, crouched down under the end of the platforms, risking a glance, but still squatting there on the lookout for the arrival of a train which would allow him to melt into the crowd of passengers. Dusting off his overcoat, to improve his appearance, he notices that it has lost a couple of buttons, one of which has taken a bit of cloth with it on to the ballast. There are greasy patches which refuse to come off, and he even adds a bit of blood to them which, to his great surprise, comes from his hand. While he is examining his wound, a few drops of rain fall on to his open palm. He looks up. The sky has taken advantage of his sojourn under cover to muster up some dark, heavy rain clouds, which precipitate a splendid deluge. The master of the elements is generous: the rain, which reduces people's ardour, will be an invaluable ally. The watchdogs aren't going to look twice, being more interested in finding somewhere to shelter.

The rain is now pelting down on all sides, creating a halo of vapour above the steaming locomotive which has just appeared round the wide curve. It seems to be trying to find its way among the points, and then passes within a few centimetres of him, spitting sparks. He nimbly hoists himself up on to the platform and is soon just one of a group of passengers. In spite of his fears, he doesn't stand out too much in his shabby get-up. War doesn't make it any easier for people to buy new clothes, and some have great difficulty in disguising their destitution. He is even amused at the way the women have drawn a thin pencil line over their tea-tanned calves to simulate the seam of imaginary silk stockings. But his anxiety grows when he notices several people staring at him, as if his new condition of a man on the run had branded a star on his forehead. "I've had it," he says to himself, and he feels an icy liquid piercing his heart. He walks more slowly and, to keep up his courage, lights a cigarette. When the flame reflects his face in a carriage window, he realizes that what had caught their attention was the streak of black oil covering his nose. The very thing for daylight camouflage.

The exit towards which the crowds of passengers are moving is under strict surveillance. In view of the increasing number of assassination attempts and acts of sabotage, the German police, backed up by the recently created Militia who, so it is rumoured, are even more to be feared, have intensified their controls with the frenzy of lost causes.

For the tide is beginning to turn against the upholders of the new order. He can see them barring the exit, suspicious, touchy, irritable, impatient, checking papers, opening bags and suitcases, and for no apparent reason picking on one man, who casts a fearful glance around him, and pulling him to one side. Should he cut across to the buffet? He has to be on his guard against plain-clothes policemen, and informers who lean on the bar pretending to be unconcerned but then suddenly abandon their drinks and start following you. Arrests of this type, muttered conversations have reported, are the most pernicious, because they also affect the friend who is hiding you, and sometimes lead them to pick up a whole Resistance network. As he catches sight of the departure hall, he remembers a Latin translation from his school years where a crafty shepherd spirits away some oxen by pushing them out of a cave backwards, which causes some incredulity in their owner, Hercules maybe, who is misled by their footprints. But that would mean passing the ticket collector in the opposite direction. So he goes up to him and, covered in confusion, putting on his Planchet act, explains that he doesn't know the time of his connection at Angers for Sablé, changing at, that's just it, he's forgotten where: could he possibly go back to the information office? "Make it quick, then," grumbles the official, irritated that he doesn't know the answers by heart.

In the waiting hall, apart from the passengers actually waiting, there are quite a few passers-by, caught in the shower, who have hurried in to the dry, still out of breath from their little sprint, wringing out their hair and shaking their overcoats. Others, crowding round the doorway, are waiting for the sky to clear and indulging in inspired comments: "The English are at it again," someone hazards, while the rain buckets down even harder on to the cobblestones.

The tall young man with the suitcase has worked his way into the front row, deaf to the protesters standing on tiptoe watching the vagaries of the sky over his shoulder. He shivers in the moist breeze brought by the shower, and pulls his coat collar tighter round his neck. The stream flowing in front of him, a former branch of the Loire recently filled in to prevent the spring floods, seems to have reverted to its original state. The running water glistens like a great river, froths up in the gutters, and rushes down the gratings into the drains. It is as if the rain has the deserted town at its mercy, and has brought it to a standstill. The comments become rare, more laconic, everyone is plunged in pleasant contemplation. A kind of inner peace is achieved. The tall young man has taken off his glasses and is rubbing the top of his nose. He can be seen to be in two minds about whether to put them on again, but then to slip them into his pocket. Why does he need to see clearly in this murky atmosphere? The haze that now surrounds him seems to keep danger at arm's length, to attenuate it, like the massive towers of Anne of Brittany's castle which he can see in the distance through the mists. And, benefiting from what might be taken for blind confidence, the ultimate negligence, he suddenly dives out into the cover of the liquid canopy.

The kindly rain even makes it possible for him to walk more quickly without his haste appearing suspicious: after all, he is merely a simple pedestrian who refuses to submit to the diktats of the heavens. He is getting further away from the danger zone, but he still doesn't allow himself to look over his shoulder, or give way to the delirium of joy overwhelming his final reservations. His sturdy shoes make a mockery of the puddles and seem like seven-league boots, his suitcase no longer weighs his arm down. He will have plenty of time to read, now, and he no longer regrets having filled it so full. At last he looks behind him. No one is following him. And, under the protection of the mighty ramparts of the ducal castle, he allows himself to take his first deep breath as a free man.

His friends would probably not be expecting him so soon. He was already savouring the moment when he would knock at their door, they would open it, and, with a mischievous grin, casually adjusting his glasses behind his ears, he would simply say to his astonished hosts: "I missed the train."

Translated from the French by Barbara Wright

JOSÉ SARAMAGO

Reflux

First of all, since everything must have a beginning, even if that beginning is the final point from which it cannot be separated, and to say *cannot* is not to say *wishes not*, or *must not*, it is simply *impossible*, for if such a separation were feasible, we all know that the entire universe would collapse, inasmuch as the universe is a fragile construction incapable of withstanding permanent solutions – first of all, the four routes were opened up. Four wide roads divided the country, starting from their cardinal points in a straight line or ever so slightly bent to follow the earth's curvature, and therefore as rigorously as possible tunnelling through mountains, dividing plains, and overcoming, supported on pillars, passing over rivers and valleys. Five kilometres from the place where they would intersect, if this were the builders' intention or rather the order received from the royal personage at the appropriate moment, the roads divided off into a network of major and secondary routes, like enormous arteries which had to transform themselves into veins and capillaries in order to proceed, and this self-same network found itself confined within a perfect square which clearly measured ten kilometres on each side. This square which also had started out, bearing in mind the universal observation that opened the story, as four rows of trig points set out on the ground, subsequently became – once the machines that opened, levelled and paved the four roads appeared on the horizon, coming, as we said, from the four cardinal points – subsequently became a high wall, four curtain-walls which could soon be seen, as was already clear from the drawing-boards, delimiting a hundred square kilometres of flat or levelled ground, because a certain amount of clearing had to be done. Land chosen to meet the basic need of equidistance from that place to the frontiers, a relative advantage, which was fortunately confirmed later by a high lime content which not even the most optimistic had the courage to forecast in their plans when asked for their opinion: all of this simply brought greater glory to the royal personage, as might have been predicted from the outset if greater attention had been paid to the dynasty's history: all its monarchs had always been right, and others less so, according to the accounts of events which were officially recorded. Such a project could never have been carried out without a strong will and the money that permits one to have a will and the hope of seeing it fulfilled, the reason why the nation's coffers paid for this gigantic enterprise on a per capita basis, which naturally meant levying a general tax on the entire population, not according to income but in the inverse order of life expectancy, since this was considered to be just and readily understood by everyone: the older the person, the higher the tax.

There were some remarkable feats in carrying out a project of this magnitude; endless problems arose, and workers who had been sent ahead met their death even before the cemetery was finished, many were buried in a landslide, some fell from great heights, calling out in vain, others were struck down by sunstroke, or suddenly froze on the spot, lymph, urine and blood having turned to cold stone. All of them victims of being in the vanguard. But the accolade of genius, provisional immortality, excepting that inherent in the King which was guaranteed to last longer, was bestowed by luck and merit on the discreet civil servant who argued that the gates in the walls on the original plan were unnecessary. He was right. It would have been absurd to make and install gates which had to remain open at all hours of day and night. Thanks to this diligent civil servant, some savings were made: the money it would have cost to make four main gates and sixteen secondary gates, twenty gates in all, distributed equally along the four sides of the square and strategically placed along each wall: the main gate in the middle of each wall and two secondary gates on each side. Therefore there were no gates but only openings where the roads ended. The walls did not need gates to support them. They were solid, thick from the base to a height of three metres, then narrowing progressively to the top, nine metres from the ground. Needless to say, the side entrances were served by roads forking from the main road at a convenient distance. And as one might expect, this simple geometrical lay-out was linked by means of suitable junctions to the general network of roads throughout the country. If everything ends up everywhere, everything would end up there.

The structure, four walls served by four roads, was a cemetery. And this cemetery was to be the only one in the land. This had been decided by the royal personage. When supreme greatness and supreme sensibility are united in a king, a single cemetery is possible. All kings are great, by definition and birth: any king who might wish otherwise will wish in vain (even the exceptions of other dynasties are great amongst their peers). But they may or may not be sensitive, and here one is not speaking of that common, plebeian sensibility, which expresses itself with a tear in the corner of an eye or by an irrepressible tremor on the lip, but of another sensibility, unprecedented to such a degree in the history of this nation and perhaps even of the universe: a sensibility incapable of confronting death or any of the paraphernalia and rituals associated with death, whether it be the mourning of relatives or the commercial manifestations of bereavement. Such was this King. Like all kings and presidents, he had to travel and visit his domains, to caress little children selected by protocol beforehand, to receive bouquets of flowers already inspected by the secret police in case they might have poison or a bomb concealed inside, to cut ribbons in fast, non-toxic colours. All this and more the King carried out with good grace. But each visit caused him endless suffering: death, nothing but death wherever one looked, signs of death everywhere, the pointed tip of a cypress tree, a widow's black shawl and, more than once, the unbearable sight of some funeral procession the master of ceremonies had inexcusably overlooked, or which, setting out late or early, unexpectedly appeared at the most solemn moment of all, just as the King was passing or about to pass. After these visits the King would return to his palace in a state of distress, convinced he was about to die. And the sorrows of others and his own fear of death caused him so much anguish that, one day when he was relaxing on the highest terrace in the palace and looking into the distance (this being the clearest day ever recorded not only throughout the history of that dynasty but throughout its entire civilization), he saw four resplendent white walls and these gave him the idea of building one central cemetery to be used by everyone.

For a nation accustomed for thousands of years to burying its dead in public for all to see, this provoked the most awful revolution. But those who feared revolution began to fear chaos, when the King's idea, with that resolute and rapid progress ideas make, especially when thought up by kings, went further and became what evil tongues described as delirium: all the cemeteries in the land had to be cleared of bones and remains, whatever their degree of decomposition, and put into new coffins which would be transported for burial in the new cemetery. Not even the royal ashes of the sovereign's ancestors were exempt from this mandate: a new pantheon would be built in a style probably inspired by the ancient Egyptian pyramids, and there, in due course, once calm was restored, their remains would be carried with all pomp and ceremony along the main northern road lined on either side with loyal subjects, until they eventually reached the final resting-place for the venerable bones of all those who had been crowned since the time when one man managed to persuade the others by means of words and force, saying: "I want a crown on my head, make me one." Some claim that this egalitarian decision helped more than anything to pacify those who saw themselves deprived of the remains of their dear departed. Another factor of some weight must have been the tacit satisfaction of all those who took the opposite view and were tired of the rules and traditions which turn the dead, because of the demands they make, into transitional beings between what is no longer life and a death that is not yet real. Suddenly everyone decided the King's idea was the best thing any man had ever conceived and no other nation could boast of having such a king, and since fate had decreed that the King should be born and reign there, it was up to the people to obey him gladly, also for the solace of the dead who were no less deserving. The history of nations knows moments of utter bliss: this was such a moment and this nation rejoiced.

When the cemetery was finally completed, the enormous task of disinterment began. At first it was easy: the thousands of existing cemeteries, large, medium and small, were also surrounded by walls, and, so to speak, within their perimeter, it was enough to excavate to the stipulated depth of three metres for greater safety, and remove everything, cubic metre upon cubic metre of bones, rotten planks of wood, dismembered bodies shaken out of their coffins by the excavators; then the rubble had to be transferred into coffins of different sizes, for new-born babes as well as for the very old, emptying some bones or flesh into each of them at random, two skulls and four hands, odd bits of rib, a breast that was still firm along with a withered belly, a simple bone or hip, or one of Buddha's teeth, even the shoulder-blade of some saint or the blood missing from the miraculous phial of St Januarius. It was decided that each part of a corpse would count as a whole corpse, and they lined up the participants in this infinite funeral which came from every corner of the nation, carefully wending its way from villages, towns and cities, along routes which became increasingly wider as far as the main road network and from there, by means of junctions specially built, on to roads subsequently known as the roads of the dead.

In the beginning, as stated earlier, there were no problems. But then someone remembered, unless the idea came from the country's precious monarch, that before this ruling about cemeteries had been enforced, the dead had been buried everywhere, on mountains and in the valleys, in churchyards, under the shade of trees, beneath the floorboards of the very houses in which they had lived, in any convenient spot, and only a little deeper than the depth, for example, of a ploughshare. Not to mention the wars, the vast trenches for thousands of corpses, all over the world, from Asia and Europe and other continents, even though probably with fewer corpses, for naturally there had also been wars in this King's realm and therefore bodies had been buried at random. There was, it had to be confessed, a moment of great perplexity. The King himself, had this latest idea been his, would not have kept it to himself for that would have been impossible. New orders were given and, since the country could not be turned over from end to end, as the cemeteries had been turned over, wise men were summoned before the King to hear this injunction from his royal lips: with all possible haste they must invent instruments capable of detecting the presence of buried remains, just as instruments had been invented to find water or metal. It would be no mean feat, the wise men acknowledged, once gathered together. They spent three days in discussion and then each of them locked himself away in his own laboratory. The State coffers were opened once more, and a new general tax was imposed. The problem was finally resolved but, as always happens in such cases, not all at once. To give an example, the case of that wise man could be cited who invented an instrument which lit up and made a noise whenever it encountered a body, but it had one serious drawback in so far as it could not distinguish between live or dead bodies. As a result, this instrument, handled of course by living people, behaved like someone possessed, screeching and flashing its indicators in a frenzy, torn between all the reactions from both the living and the dead surrounding it and, in the end, incapable of providing any reliable information. The entire nation mocked this unfortunate scientist, then lavished tributes and honours on him several months later, when he found the solution by introducing into the instrument a kind of memory or fixed idea. If one listened attentively, it was possible to detect a constant sound coming from inside the mechanism which went on repeating: "I must only find dead bodies or remains, I must only find dead bodies, or remains, dead bodies, or remains, or remains . . ."

Fortunately, there was one remaining drawback, as we shall see. No sooner did the instrument begin to function than people realized that, this time, it could not tell the difference between human and non-human bodies, but this new flaw, which explains why I earlier used the word fortunately, turned out to be an advantage: when the King understood the danger he had escaped, he had the shivers: in fact, all death is death, even the non-human kind, and there would be no purpose in removing dead men from sight, when dogs, horses and birds go on dropping before our eyes. And all other creatures, with the possible exception of insects which are only half-animal (as was firmly believed by the nation's scientists at that time). Then a full-scale investigation was ordered, a Cyclopean task which went on for years. Not so much as a hand-breadth of land remained to be examined, even in places which had been uninhabited for as long as anyone could remember: not even the highest mountains escaped or the deepest rivers, where thousands of dead bodies were discovered; the deepest roots did not escape, sometimes entangled around the remains of someone higher up who had been trying, out of desire or necessity, to reach the sap of some tree. Nor did the roads escape, which had to be lifted in many places and rebuilt. Finally, the kingdom found itself released from death. One day, when the King himself formally announced that the country was cleansed of death (his words), he declared a public holiday and national rejoicing. On such days it is customary for more people than usual to die, because of accidents, muggings, etc., but the National Life Service (as it was called) employed rapid, up-to-date methods: once death had been confirmed, the corpse followed the shortest route to the great highway of corpses, which had inevitably come to be known as no man's land. Having got rid of the dead, the King could be happy. As for the people, they would have to get used to it.

The first thing to be restored was a sense of tranquillity, that calm of natural mortality which allows families to be spared bereavement for years on end, and sometimes for many years if these families are not numerous. It could be said without exaggeration that the removal period was a time of national mourning in the strictest sense of that expression, a mourning which came from the depths of the earth. To smile during those years of sorrow would have been, for anyone who dared, an act of moral degradation: it is unseemly to smile when a relative, however distant, is being carried to the grave, intact or in pieces, and is tipped out from the bucket of an excavator on high into a new coffin, so much for each coffin, like filling moulds for sweets or bricks. After that lengthy period when people went around with an expression of noble and serene sorrow, smiles returned, then laughter, even guffaws and outbursts of derision and mockery, preceded by irony and humour; all of this regained some sign of life or renewed its hidden struggle against death.

But this tranquillity was not merely that of a soul back on the same old rails after a grand collision, but also that of the body, because words cannot express what all that effort, sustained over such a long period of time, meant for those who were still alive. It was not only the public works, the opening up of roads, the building of bridges, tunnels, viaducts, it was not only the scientific research, of which a pale and fragmentary idea has already been given; it was also the industry in timber, from the felling of trees (forest upon forest) to the sawing of planks, the drying out by means of accelerated processes, to the fittings for urns and coffins which required the installation of huge mechanical assembly lines for mass production; it also meant, as previously stated, the temporary reconversion of the metal industry in order to meet the demand for machinery and other material, starting with nails and hinges; then textiles and braidings for linings and decorations; then the quarrying for marble and stonework which, in its turn, suddenly began disembowelling the earth in order to supply so many tombstones and headstones ornately carved or plain; and those minority occupations almost akin to crafts, such as painting letters in black and gold, touching up photographs, panel-beating and glazing, that of artificial flowers, the making of candles and tapers, etc., etc., etc. But perhaps the greatest contribution of all, without which none of the work could have gone ahead, was that of the transport industry. No words could express the amount of effort put into the manufacturing of trucks and other heavy vehicles, an industry obliged in its turn to reconvert itself, to modify its production plans, to organize new sequences of assembly before delivering the coffins to the new cemetery: try to imagine the complications involved in planning integrated time-tables, the periods of disruption and convergence, the continuous flow of incoming traffic with ever increasing loads, and all this having to harmonize with the normal circulation of the living, whether on working days or public holidays, whether travelling to work or for pleasure, without forgetting the infrastructure: restaurants and inns all along the route so that lorry-drivers might be able to eat and sleep, car parks for the larger vehicles, some distractions to relieve the pressures of mind and body, telephone lines, the installations for emergencies and first-aid, workshops for electrical and mechanical repairs, garages for petrol, oil, diesel, tyres, spare parts, etc. And this in turn clearly boosted other industries in a cycle of mutual regeneration, producing wealth to the extent of maximum output and full employment. As was only to be expected, this revival was followed by a depression, and no one was surprised because it had been foreseen by the economic pundits. The negative effect of this depression was generously compensated, as the social psychologists had forecast, because of the irrepressible desire for respite which began to manifest itself among the people once their output had reached the point of saturation. They were embarking on a new phase of normality.

In the geometrical centre of the country, open to the four winds, stands the cemetery. Much less than a quarter of its hundred square kilometres was occupied by transferred corpses, and this prompted a group of mathematicians to try to demonstrate, with the figures to hand, that the land needed for these reburials would have to be much bigger, taking into consideration the likely number of deaths since the country was first populated and the average amount of space needed for each corpse, even discounting those who, reduced to dust and ashes, were beyond recovery. The enigma, if it could be called that, was to exercise the minds of future generations, like the squaring of the circle or the duplication of the cube, because the wise devotees of disciplines related to biology proved in the presence of the King that not a single corpse worthy of the name remained to be disinterred throughout the entire country. After some deep reflection, the King, torn between trust and scepticism, passed a decree which declared the matter closed; the decisive argument for him was the sense of relief he experienced when he returned from his travels and visits; if he no longer saw death it was because death had finally withdrawn.

The occupation of the cemetery, although the initial plan conformed to more rational criteria, went from the periphery to the centre. First near the gates and up against the walls, then following a curve which began almost perfectly radial and gradually became cycloid, this, too, being a transitional phase whose future plays no part in our story. But this internal moulding, as it were, undulating along the walls and isolated by them, was reflected almost symmetrically, even during the removal, in a form that matched faithfully on the outside. No one had suspected that this might happen, but there were those who asserted that only a fool could have failed to foresee the outcome.

The first sign, like the tiniest of spores about to sprout into a plant, then into a tuft, then into a thick cluster, and finally impenetrable scrub, was an improvised stall for the sale of soft drinks and spirits beside one of the secondary openings on the south wall. Even though revived for the journey, the transport workers felt they would find even greater refreshment there. Then other tiny shops sprang up nearby at the other openings, and began selling identical or similar goods, and those who ran them soon felt the need to set up house there, primitive huts on stilts to begin with, then using more durable materials, such as bricks, stones and tiles. It is worth observing in passing that from the moment these first buildings appeared, one could distinguish a) almost imperceptibly, b) from the evidence before one's eyes, the social status, as it were, of the four sides of the square. As with all countries, this one, too, was not uniformly populated, nor, despite His Majesty's extraordinary complacency, were his subjects socially equal: some were rich and others poor, and the distribution of the former and the latter conformed to universal criteria: the poor man attracts the rich man at a distance that suits the rich man; in his turn, the rich man attracts the poor man, but that is not to say that the outcome (the constant factor in the process) will operate in the poor man's favour. If, because of the criteria applied to the living, the cemetery, after this general transfer, began to divide up internally, it also became noticeable on the outside. There is scarcely any need to explain why. Since the northern region had the highest concentration of the country's wealthy people, that side of the cemetery, with its imposing outlay, assumed a social status opposed, for example, to that of the south, which happened to service the poorest region. And the same thing occurred, in general, when it came to the other sides. Like attracts like. Although in a much less clearly defined manner, the outside reflected the inside. For example, the florists who soon began appearing on all four sides of the square, did not all sell the same quality of goods: some displayed and sold the most exquisite blooms cultivated in gardens and hothouses at great expense, others were more modest and sold flowers gathered from the surrounding countryside. The same could be said about all the other goods displayed there, and as one might have expected, the civil servants complained, on finding themselves weighed down with petitions and complaints. One must not forget that the cemetery had a complicated system of administration, controlled its own budget, employed thousands of grave-diggers. In the early days, the different categories of civil servants lived inside the square, in the central part, and well out of sight of any burials. But soon there were problems regarding hierarchy, provisions, schools for the children, hospitals, maternity care. What was to be done? Build a city within the cemetery? That would mean going back to the beginning, not to mention that with the passage of time the city and the cemetery would overlap, the tombs penetrating gaps in the streets or actually bordering the pavements, the streets circling the tombs in search of land for the houses. It would mean returning to the same old promiscuity, now aggravated by the fact that things happened within a square of ten kilometres on each side with few exits to the outside. So now it was a question of choosing between a city of living human beings surrounded by a city of the dead, or the only alternative, a city of the dead surrounded by four cities of living human beings. Once the choice was formalized, and it also became clear that those accompanying the funeral processions could not make the long, exhausting return journey immediately, either because they did not have the strength or because incapable of sudden separation from their loved ones, the four external cities grew apace in haphazard fashion. There were boarding-houses of every category in every street, hotels with one, two, three, four, five stars or more, numerous brothels, churches for every legally recognized cult and several secret sects, little corner shops and enormous department stores, countless houses, office buildings, public offices and various municipal bodies. Then came public transport, the police, restricted circulation and the problem of traffic. And a certain amount of delinquency. One fiction alone was preserved: to keep the dead out of sight of the living; therefore no building could be more than nine metres high. But this matter was solved later, when an imaginative architect reinvented Columbus's egg: walls higher than nine metres for buildings higher than nine metres.

In the fullness of time the cemetery wall became unrecognizable: instead of the initial smooth uniformity extending for forty kilometres, what appeared was an irregular denticulation, also variable in width and height, according to the side of the wall. No one can any longer remember when it was decided that the time had come to install the cemetery gates. The civil servant who had pressed for this economy

had already passed on to the other side and could no longer defend
a theory that was sound at the time but no longer tenable, as he
himself would have had the good sense to acknowledge: stories began
circulating about souls from the other world, about ghosts and apparitions – so what else could be done but to install gates?

And so four great cities rose up between the kingdom and the
cemetery, each one facing its cardinal point, four unexpected cities
which came to be known as Northern Cemetery, Southern Cemetery,
Eastern Cemetery and Western Cemetery, but which were later simply
referred to as Cemeteries Number One, Two, Three and Four, inasmuch as all attempts to give them more poetic or commemorative
names had failed. These four cities acted as four barriers, four living
walls which surrounded and protected the cemetery. The cemetery
represented one hundred square kilometres of almost total silence and
solitude, surrounded by the outer ant hill of the living, by the sound
of people shouting, hooters, outbursts of laughter and snatches of
conversation, the rumbling of engines, by the interminable murmuring of nerve-cells. To arrive at the cemetery was already something
of an adventure. Eventually nobody could retrace the rectilinear plan
of the old roads within the cities. It was easy to say where they had
passed: you had only to stand in front of one of the main gates. But
leaving aside some of the longer stretches of recognizable paving, the
rest had got lost in the confusion of buildings and roads, improvised
to begin with and then superimposed on the original plan. Only in
the open countryside was the road still the highway of the dead.

And now the inevitable happened, although we do not know who
started it or when. A summary investigation, carried out afterwards,
verified cases on the outer periphery of City Number Two, the poorest
city of all, and facing south, as we stated earlier: corpses buried in
small private backyards beneath flowering plants which reappeared
each spring. About this same time, like those great inventions which
erupt in various minds simultaneously because the time has come for
them to mature, in sparsely populated parts of the realm certain
persons decided, for many different and sometimes contradictory
reasons, to bury their dead near, or inside caves, at the side of forest
paths or on some sheltered mountain slope. There were fewer pros-
ecutions in those days and many civil servants were prepared to accept
bribes. The statistics bureau announced that, according to the official
registers, a lower mortality rate could be safely predicted, and this
was naturally attributed to the government's health programme, under

the direct supervision of His Majesty the King. The four cities of the
cemetery felt the consequences of the decline in the number of deaths.
Certain businesses suffered serious losses, there were a fair number
of bankruptcies, some of them fraudulent, and when it was finally
recognized that, however laudable, the royal strategy for the nation's
welfare was not likely to concede immortality, a thoroughly repressive
law was introduced to enforce the obedience of the masses. To no
avail: after a short-lived outburst of enthusiasm, the cities stagnated
and became dilapidated. Ever so slowly, the kingdom began to be
re-populated with the dead. In the end, the vast central cemetery
only received corpses from the four surrounding cities, which became
increasingly deserted and silent. But the King was no longer there to
see it.

The King was now very old. One day, looking down from the
highest terrace of the palace, he saw, despite failing eyesight, the
pointed tip of a cypress tree rising above four white walls, in all
probability indicating the presence of a courtyard rather than death.
But one divines certain things without difficulty, especially as one gets
older. The King stored every item of news and every rumour in his
head, what they told him and what they kept from him, and he realized
the hour of understanding had come. Followed by a guard, as protocol
demanded, he descended into the palace gardens. Dragging his royal
cloak, he slowly made his way along an avenue leading to the concealed heart of the forest. There he lay down in a clearing and stretched
out on the dry leaves; then summoning the guard who had fallen to
his knees, he told him before dying: "Here."

Translated from the Portuguese by Giovanni Pontiero

JOSÉ SARAMAGO

Revenge

The boy was coming up from the river. Barefoot, with his trousers rolled above his knees, his legs covered in mud. He wore a red shirt, open in front where the first hairs of puberty on his chest were beginning to blacken. He had dark hair, damp with the sweat that was trickling down his slender neck. He was bent slightly forward under the weight of the long oars, from which dangling strands of green water-weeds were still dripping. The boat kept swaying in the murky water, and nearby, as if spying, the globulous eyes of a frog suddenly appeared. Then the frog twitched and vanished. A minute later the surface of the river was smooth and tranquil and shining like the boy's eyes. The exhalation of the mud released slow, flaccid bubbles of gas which were swept away by the current. Under the oppressive heat of the afternoon, the tall poplars swayed gently, and, in a flurry, like a flower suddenly blossoming in mid-air, a blue bird flew past skimming the water. The boy raised his head. Across the river, a girl was watching him, motionless. The boy raised his free hand and his entire body traced out some inaudible word. The river flowed slowly.

The boy climbed the slope without looking back. Right here the grass ended. Above and beyond, the sun burnt the clods of untilled soil and ashen olive-groves. In the distance, the atmosphere shimmered.

It was a squat, single-storey house, its whitewashed wall edged with bright yellow paint. A stark wall without windows, a door with an open peephole. Inside, the earthen floor was cool underfoot. The boy rested his oars and wiped away the perspiration with his forearm. He remained still, listening to his heartbeat, the sweat slowly resurfacing on his skin. He stopped there for several minutes, oblivious to the sounds coming from behind the house and which suddenly turned into a deafening outburst of squealing: the protestations of an imprisoned pig. When he finally began to stir, the animal's cry, now wounded and outraged, deafened him. Other cries followed, piercing and wrathful, a desperate plea, a cry expecting no help.

He ran to the yard, but did not cross the threshold. Two men and a woman were holding down the pig. Another man with a knife covered in blood was making a vertical slit in the scrotum. Glistening on the straw was a squashed crimson ovule. The pig was trembling all over, squeals coming from the jaws secured with a rope. The wound opened up, the testis appeared, milky and streaked with blood, the man inserted his fingers into the opening, pulled, twisted and plucked inside. The woman's face twitched and turned pale. They untied the pig, removed the cord round its snout, and one of the men bent down and grabbed the two thick, soft testicles. Perplexed, the animal swerved round and, panting, stood there with its head lowered. Then the man threw the testicles to the ground. The pig caught them in its mouth, avidly chewed and swallowed. The woman said something and the men shrugged their shoulders. One of them started laughing. And at that moment they saw the boy in the doorway. Taken unawares, they fell silent and, at a loss, they began staring at the animal which had lain down on the straw, breathing heavily, its lips stained with its own blood.

The boy went back inside. He filled a mug and drank, allowing the water to trickle down the corners of his mouth, then down his neck on to the hairs on his chest which seemed darker. As he drank, he stared outside at those two red stains on the straw. Then he stepped wearily out of the house, crossed the olive-grove once more beneath the scorching sun. The dust burned his feet but, pretending not to notice, he walked on tiptoe to avoid that burning sensation. The same cicada was screeching in a lower key. Then down the slope, the grass smelling of warm sap, the inebriating coolness beneath the branches, the mud getting between his toes until it covered them.

The boy remained there, watching the river. Settled on the sprouting mosses, a frog as brown as the previous one, with round eyes under bulging arches, appeared to be lying in wait. The white skin of its gullet was palpitating. Its closed mouth creased scornfully. Time passed and neither the frog nor the boy moved. Then, averting his eyes with difficulty as if fleeing some evil spell, he saw the girl reappear on the other side of the river, amidst the lower branches of the willows. And once again, silent and unexpected, a blue streak passed over the water.

Slowly the boy removed his shirt. Slowly he finished undressing and it was only when he no longer had any clothes on that his nakedness was slowly revealed. As if he were healing his own blindness. The girl was watching from afar. Then, with the same slow gestures, she removed her dress and everything else she was wearing. Naked against the green backcloth of trees.

The boy again looked at the river. Silence descended on the liquid skin of that interminable body. Circles widened and disappeared on the calm surface, marking the spot where the frog had plunged in. Then the boy entered the water and swam to the other bank as the white, naked form of the girl withdrew into the shadow of the branches.

Translated from the Portuguese by Giovanni Pontiero

ZINOVY ZINIK

Hooks

In America I would never run across people like him; they fly in circles too lofty for me to reach. And the Soviets are still reluctant to let such a person visit Tel Aviv. As an émigré, I'd only encounter them in Europe, here in London or in Paris. But somehow I can never get used to them – it is either their casual familiarity, as if nothing untoward had occurred, or the reverse, the long, tragic face, as if you were attending your own funeral. That Moscow was, for me, irrecoverable was never discussed, as if the two of us just happened to be in London for a while and, whereas he had to get back shortly, certain urgent business compelled me to stay on. At least he didn't launch into the predictable discourse on the destiny of the West as seen through Russian eyes, the standard counterblast to émigré ideas on the destiny of Russia as seen through Western eyes. His own eyes were semi-transparent, dangerous-feeling, as though if you peered deeply into them myopia would set in and you'd never find your way out.

But he kept those eyes averted; he wasn't at ease either. He didn't know how to behave with me. I flattered myself that he might be feeling some shame in my presence. But perhaps I was merely assigning him noble feelings to put myself in a good light. Or it may have been an effect of the difference in our status: he was, after all, an industrial expert on an official exchange visit, the holder of a great state prize, the honoured representative of Soviet history, whereas I, a wandering émigré, had been consigned by that same state to the blacklist with the dubious label of "rootless cosmopolite". Even that term belonged to his vocabulary, not mine – the vocabulary of the old wartime Stalinist generation. But, like most exiles, I was given to striking up acquaintance with strangers, and in hopes of being understood and accepted I would slavishly accommodate myself to their speech.

For someone like me, our meeting had the air of an ideological duel; he, on the other hand, must have found my agitation fascinating.

He would keep his eyes averted; then suddenly, seemingly offhand, he would touch my shoulder lightly, or nudge my elbow, till I began to think that I had been wide of the mark in imagining any kind of official arrogance in his actions, or calculated condescension in his conversation.

Not that there was any real conversation. Actually, I couldn't understand why we were meeting at all. He had introduced himself as the uncle of my wife's high-school sweetheart back in Moscow. To that I found little to say; I thought of Yesenin's line: "I am your nephew, you are all my uncles," and Eichenvald's: "All men are brothers; me, I'm a cousin." But poetry was not one of his interests. On the other hand, he wasn't taking the occasion to make the usual Soviet visitor's request for either of the naked truths that Moscow banned: Solzhenitsyn's books or Soho's porn displays.

We were sitting in his seedy hotel room looking at one another with the simulated amicability of the dentist's waiting room. I couldn't make out why he said nothing – was it fear, plain indifference, or some inherent inability to start up a conversation? I repeated to myself my wife's admonitions on similar occasions: Don't worry about him, he's been in this situation before; he'll tell you what he wants soon enough. He was clearly not at all discomfited by the protracted pause, and like anyone accustomed to an iron curtain of silence he transferred to his companion the sense of guilt for the break in communication. It is in the nature of words to abhor silence; forgetting my wife's injunctions, I filled the air with overexcited and largely inconsequential talk:

"What really amazes me is my indifference. Actually, when I do feel drawn to Moscow it's the earlier Moscow I picture. What goes on there now, in fact, doesn't really interest me much. I mean, even the old notion that it's the people who stayed behind who betrayed *us*, and we émigrés are the heroes carrying on the battle without them – even that seductive old idea has lost its savour; those who betrayed us are no longer crucial to our happiness. If we get homesick, it's not for our actual home but the home of memory."

"As to life in Moscow" – he finally resolved to interrupt my rambling meditations – "I would quote from a poem I prize highly – Mezhirov: 'The acts we put on may be sham, but you have to remember we're working without a safety net – one false step and we're smashed to smithereens.'" I was silent. Well, of course. To hear them talk, their only concern is Absolute Truth, unlike the materialistic

West, with its relativism and hypocrisy; prophetic fire, the endless task, all that. They might lie to each other, but it's always about great matters, for noble purposes; perhaps superficially, to the outsider's eye, things don't look right, but deep down inside it's all real and true. "Smashed to smithereens" – the danger justifying the ends *and* the means. Yes indeed. I just hoped he wasn't going to start discoursing about "inner freedom". It seemed it was business as usual back there.

"The day they acknowledge what they did in the Hitler-Stalin Pact, that's the day I'll . . ." I began, but I dried up. I recognized that look. My father, a Communist and a Jew, who lost a leg in the war, used to look at me that way when, in the heat of argument, I would blurt that if Hitler hadn't stirred up Russian patriotism Stalin and the whole Soviet system would have gone into the dustbin of history long ago. I wasn't afraid of my father's belt, much less his raised voice, but his tears made me feel terrible. It was with those same eyes, those pink-tinged lids, that the Muscovite visitor looked at me now. That was the worst thing, that defenceless look of a person who suddenly realizes he is being viewed critically. I shouldn't have mentioned the war. That glance had betrayed a bitter nostalgia for those days. For him, the war must have been a unique period of freedom, when fate had granted his spirit the gift of a genuine patriotism; when it had been possible to defend the fatherland without orders from above or a pistol in the back of the neck: when he was issued a gun of his own and bullets to strike down what were enemies of the people in the true sense of the term, not in Stalin's. He might have been my own father – and I had absolutely nothing to say to him.

"Could you possibly help me find a certain little thing I want in London?" he asked in a pleading tone, and I sighed with relief. So – he, too, was after some piece of scarce merchandise; he was no exception after all. It just might have been conceivable that a man who'd worked his way up to responsible posts, titles, and decorations could remain a decent human even over there – well, it's nice to have one's scepticism validated, I said to myself. The old motherland can always come through with a fresh example of Darwinian principle – the evolution of the worthy idealistic Bolshevik model into an ape of material greed in response to his environment. Determinism shaping subspecies *Homo sovieticus* – an animal with a highly spiritual ideological mask over a primitive avaricious grimace. Yes, squirm as you like, you grow the way conditions ordain. It's pitiable, I suppose. But somehow my own spirit wasn't up to purging its revulsion.

"You couldn't take me to Oxford Street, could you?" asked the Soviet gent when I, despite my interior harangue, spoke aloud of my readiness to help.

"What part of Oxford Street?"

"Where the shops are."

"It's all shops."

"Fine, let's go there, then." He added in a confidential whisper, "I want some hooks."

"Hooks? What sort of hooks?" I asked, somewhat flabbergasted.

"Fish-hooks," he explained imperturbably and, rising slightly from his chair, poked two fingers into an inconspicuous watch pocket in his trousers; there was something tucked away in there, deep down, that refused to be brought to light. At last he withdrew a cellophane packet about the size of a matchbox. It, in turn, contained a piece of paper torn from a school exercise book and folded into four. I followed all these operations as if watching a conjurer at work. He proffered the folded note. On it enigmatic English words and names had been written with calligraphic exactitude; to the left of these was a no less puzzling column of figures with hieroglyphic curlicues – or were they drawings? It all looked like some spy cipher to me, and only served to intensify the false atmosphere of intimacy between us. Could he possibly have been sent by Moscow to recruit me into the KGB's Russian Literature Service, as we called it – to ask me to add my reports on London émigré activity to the files stacked inside the world's biggest humanities collection, the Lubyanka security headquarters? I looked up in alarm.

"It's a list. English fish-hooks with sizes. Can you give me a hand?" He moved his finger about the paper. Once again I began to flounder in that translucent gaze, trying to swim out of turbid water, keeping clear of whirlpools and shoals. They'd obviously gone off their heads over there, perched with their élite salaries beside the well-stocked ponds at their Politburo country dachas. Couldn't they manage with Soviet hooks? They must figure that even the cunning old pike of Russian folklore could never resist an elegant, unbreakable English hook. Maybe they heard of them in the handbook by Aksakov, our nineteenth-century Compleat Angler; for all his Slavophile outlook he might have gone Anglophile himself when it came to recommending fish-hooks.

"I can't go back to Moscow without hooks," whimpered this man,

this apparent adult. There it was again: Soviet civilization turns everybody into a child where *things* are concerned; *things* are the toys of
civilization and the citizen of a vast country that hasn't many of them
acts like a deprived child. You feel sorry for him, and irritated, and
you know you can't shake him off. Ridiculing their puritanism as
sham, though, is like calling a hungry man a hypocrite for taking a
job advertising meat on a sandwich board. Like children everywhere,
they simply must have material proof of their own idealism; thus
Soviet people are materialistic idealists. Children have to be indulged,
life won't give them a chance like this again – so we strode out of the
door in search of English fish-hooks.

London was deluged in one of those spinning storms of rain and light
you find only on this island, where the wind blows from four directions at once and you never know which way to turn to shield your
eyes from the blinding droplets. We hung, as it were, in the timeless-
ness of streaming rain, detached from the earth, pressed against one
another, heads bent together like a pair of lovers: he'd left his umbrella
in the hotel. We couldn't be bothered to go back for it, so the hurricane of rain and wind bore us along the side streets under one
umbrella. The closer we became welded by the weather, the more
alien I sensed his body to be, pressed against my shoulder in his smelly
gabardine macintosh and the sort of tartan cap that unversed tourists
take to be typically English. He grated on me because of the absence
of physical distance between us; I couldn't get free of him. To do
that I would have to snag him with those special hooks, and we simply
could not find any. These hooks turned out to be most rare and
intricate, and the salesmen startlingly ignorant and rude. As we
trudged for mile after mile along shopping streets, I subsided into a
despairing resentment. I shook feverishly, either because of the penetrating wind or because of the intense exasperation I felt at the whole
enterprise I'd been dragged into by that old business between my
wife and the nephew of this Soviet fisherman.
     One umbrella was clearly inadequate: my companion was wearing
a decent raincoat at least, whereas I had casually donned a corduroy
jacket, which, as it absorbed the moisture, grew heavier and heavier,
like an old soak under the Charing Cross arches. My back ached, my
shoes squished, my throat was raw, and I cursed the Soviet regime for
its false liberalism in letting perverts with English-fish-hook fetishisms

loose on London. We advanced in rushes, dashing through one glassy curtain of rain only to run into another, and as we halted to catch our breath in this jerky course we seemed to be on different landings of the same flight of stairs. No, it was as if two glass-cabined elevators had stopped for a second in a dark shaft and we gazed at each other through their walls: was it even conceivable we both lived under the same roof? Bound together, kin forever? That was all I needed of hell.

"Don't worry, I'm not trying to persuade you to go back," said my Soviet gent. He didn't mean to the Old Country, he meant to Oxford Street, which we had left further and further behind – a mistake, in his view, since all shops that could possibly exist must be there. I could have no objection: I really didn't know where to go next. I'd got well off my planned route.

"I know what this rain reminds me of," he said, wiping his face with a handkerchief as we were waiting out the next squall under an arch at Piccadilly Circus. "This London rain reminds me of mosquito netting and the evening mist after a hot day at the dacha. It's just come back to me: your wife used to visit my nephew at the dacha. That was where I first saw her, maybe the last time, too. A slim schoolgirl she was, like a dandelion. They were walking together arm in arm, towards the terrace. Through a sort of haze like this rain. I was sitting with my sister on the terrace. Mist all round, you know, makes distances hard to judge. Mosquitoes and moths were flying around the lamp, and there was a sweet smell of paraffin. I remember that so well."

He stopped as if hoping for an answering burst of lyricism. As it was, this nephew, whoever he might be, was getting on my nerves; "Poor boy," my companion would say whenever he mentioned my wife's adolescent admirer. I resolved to curtail these nostalgic evocations of dacha life at least.

"After three emigrations, from one country to another," said I, "my yearning for the Old Country long ago lost any geographical dimension. It's not connected physically with any one point on the earth's surface. My normal state of mind, generally speaking, is rather like the indisposition of middle age: it's a kind of equilibrium, when one agonizing pain is balanced by another, newer one, which we know perfectly well we'll ignore as a third one looms up."

"But where on earth is Eros?" he broke in, as if rebuking me for excessive intellectualism in my reflections. He was pointing, however, at the wooden hoarding in the centre of the square. Black Eros – the winged messenger with his arrow of love, balanced on one foot on the top of the fountain in the centre of Piccadilly Circus, that symbol of gay old London – was gone from behind the planking. I had to explain that Eros had been sent off for restoration. Eros was under repair, the fountain of the soul was dry, only intellect sparkled in neon signs through the shrouding rain. Britannia was poor and stingy; everyone was on his own.

"Won't I see Eros at all this time, then?" He shook a mournful head. Like all Soviet tourists, he further annoyed me with his rustic raptures over cliché London – the red buses, the black taxis, the bobbies in their crested helmets. I felt an imbecile urgency to maintain the reputation of my émigré life in those alien Russian eyes, as if to say, "We have everything here, there's nothing you can't get. Especially rare and intricate fish-hooks." With a heavy sigh, I darted into the swirling rain.

It enveloped us in a dense, wavering veil, solidly separating off the rest of the world, which might have been anywhere: England, Russia, ancient Rome. I calculated that we were on Pall Mall, where that Jules Verne novel starts – what was it, "Twenty Thousand Days Under the Sea" or "Eighty Thousand Leagues Around the World"? The snowy-white columns of the club buildings gleamed through the bathysphere of rain as they loomed over us like Arctic icebergs, mist-enshrouded, and, as Captain Nemo might have done, I wanted to cry, "To hell with this mercantile civilization!" Retreating from the elements, we found ourselves in an arcade, where the window of another tackle shop floated before our eyes like the porthole of an aquarium. The salesman luring us inside could have been Captain Nemo himself, or a Russian bog monster. He seemed to be expecting us. He put on his tortoiseshell glasses and spent a long time chewing his lip over our crumpled list of magic figures and markings. Finally he informed us, with the solemnity of an oracle, that he did have these hooks but that "they bend the other way."

"That doesn't matter." I hastened to explain this enigmatic phrase to my companion. "It's like driving on the left – it's all relative. From the Russian viewpoint, they bend the way you want, you see what I mean?" By way of visual illustration, I absurdly twisted my head around nearly backward. I just wanted to make clear that the problem was resolved and I would go no further. In the little shop it was dry, rather dark, and deserted as we sat down to wait at a table in the corner. There was something in that interior reminiscent of the Ark, pitching under the lashing assault of the storm. Around us were gleaming glass cases of mounted fish; nets and harpoons hung in the corners, fishing poles sprouted everywhere like exotic bamboo, and, most important, gigantic show cases held hooks of all sizes, shapes, and tints overlapping like metallic scales. My companion in his sodden raincoat reminded me of a shivering *dachnik*, stranded on a suburban station platform after missing the electric train.

And I remembered where I'd seen exactly the same suffering expression, reproach mixed with hope. Those same grimaces had been displayed by the old repairman in the typewriter shop on Kuznetskiy Most, when I brought my Olympia to him for the last time before I left the country. The very same heavy rain, Muscovite variety, had beset his premises, too, replete as it was with objects no less exotic than those in this tackle shop. How he'd fussed about, sighing and shaking his head when he found out what far lands I was quitting Moscow for. How he'd started unscrewing the casing with excessive roughness to conceal his trembling fingers as they tugged out the accumulated dirt, hair, and assorted rubbish.

"You've got a cat at home, then," he'd grumbled. "I can tell what any household is like by the stuff in the typewriter."

We had no cats at home – it was me going bald, not a cat – but never mind; he was just filling up a tense silence with his mutterings. Then he got out a jug of alcohol, but instead of using it to clean the keys he ran some tap water into it and banged down two glasses. I remember the light, acrid smell of the spirits and the mustiness of the basement shop, his tear-filled eyes and the network of blood vessels on his flaccid, alcoholic cheeks. And the dim gleam of the part in his brilliantined hair. An hour later, his hair sticking up wildly by now, he was recounting for the nth time his exploits as an air ace.

But finally he couldn't hold back, he burst the net of restraint: he had, he said, a Tartar friend – the carriage on the man's typewriter even went backwards, the Muslim way – but *he* had no plans to leave, even though Stalin had moved *him* to Siberia for a while. What was wrong with me, couldn't I sit still? He and the Tartar used to go fishing at a reservoir a mere hundred kilometres from Moscow, and he'd feel homesick even there; on the way back, the very mention of Moscow made his heart beat faster. How could anybody leave – forever? He just couldn't see that. He'd be glad to take me to that reservoir with a net, to get some big fish. Or in winter maybe, to sit out all night with a line through the ice. He'd found *yeriki* there, spots where the ice seals off the water and all the fish are caught inside as in a bucket: you could take them out with your bare hands.

I remember his oddly intent stare – and mine, shifty, though it should have been the other way round. I remember us sitting there for a long time, like now: close kin and at the same time totally alien. I couldn't argue with him because the only ideas he could comprehend were foreign to me, and I can't convey alien thoughts in my own words.

The exotic word *yeriki* had taken me aback considerably – was it the resonance with "eureka"? I even took the trouble to consult Dal's dictionary. I felt like that old gudgeon (or whatever inhabits Moscow reservoirs), gasping under the ice in those *yeriki*. Meanwhile outside, the yellow houses on Kuznetskiy Most were wet with rain. Yellow houses – Moscow isn't a fairy-tale snow-white city, it's a city of yellow houses. It was grim hauling my typewriter home past those sodden yellow façades; what sort of people was it who could construe your longing for peace of mind and for freedom as treachery? I remembered my fear, not of treason, or prison, but of becoming one of them myself, the fear of being defined, my fate ordained, by others. But how I longed to be back under the lowering Moscow skies at this moment; for any fear contains the hope of release from that fear, and the memory of that feeling of hope, which accompanied all the years I spent there, overcame the memory of fear. That insistent sense of a hope lost forever is in itself punishment for my decision to free myself permanently from fear. And lost along with that hope was the avidity of eye and finger, the pleasure with which this stranger from my Soviet past was now picking over the shining fish-hooks on the table. It was for the sake of this scene then – to witness another's appetite for my new life when I myself had grown blasé – that I had dragged along with this venerable Soviet official under an English cloudburst. It was for the joy of recognition in the eyes of the other – a perverse sense of nearness, no matter whether with friend or enemy. (No one is closer to being a sworn enemy than your best friend; the two can be almost the same.)

"You've saved a man's life, you should know," said the Soviet fellow, looking up at me as if guessing my thoughts about him. "You've saved a human being. Thank you."

"No need to exaggerate," I managed to bring out with affected nonchalance. "You'd have survived somehow without English hooks."

"Me? I would, of course. But what about my nephew? Poor boy." And his chin began to quiver. He reached for his handkerchief. The shopkeeper, off behind his counter, gazed through his tortoiseshell glasses at the vast window spattered with raindrops, pretending not to notice our corner mutterings in some incomprehensible and unreal tongue: for me, this heightened the sense of conspiracy, of the confessional, that surrounded the words of this elderly man, who had suddenly lost all traits of the Soviet. All that remained was his bewilderment at the perversity of fate and a mute plea for sympathy, nothing more. The mention of the nephew, again, annoyed me so much that at first I didn't take in what he was saying – about cards and billiards, about Dostoyevsky's "Gambler", a woman, and underworld Moscow, and the odd idea of escaping from a politicized world into some sort of casino where stakes were high and payment was not in cash but in kind – and what an effort it had taken to get that list of English fish-hooks out of prison. In jail they keep accounts their own way, he was saying: you don't pay up, your throat gets slit.

At length it began to dawn on me what my former countryman was talking about: these double-damned hooks were not destined for privileged bureaucrats to go catch sturgeon in Kremlin ponds, no. Lord knows *who* would be fishing with them, in what troubled waters. These hooks were the equivalent of beads for savages; they were treasury notes, legal tender, hard currency in the jailhouse banking system of incorrigible gamblers. The nephew was such a gambler, and he was in jail. "If I hadn't looked you up in London, the poor boy . . .", and he made a gesture near his throat.

"You know," he went on, "I'd have washed my hands of that boy long since; he's a hopeless case." My companion snorted into his handkerchief. "But not long before he was arrested he took me to one of those awful restaurants I can't stand – people filling their faces, champing, belching, the orchestra hammering out some execrable stuff . . . I looked around at it all, and I quoted a line from I think it's Heinrich Heine: 'To think the Redeemer died on the cross for these swine – what a waste!' My nephew smiled a little, and said, 'No, my dear uncle, your Heine was wrong. Decent folk can take care of their own salvation; it was precisely to save such miserable worms as these that the Fisherman got himself on the hook.' Imagine! And I'd

taken that good-for-nothing for a fool. How wrong can a man be?"
He began stowing the English fish-hooks about his person.

Translated from the Russian by Alan Myers

ZBIGNIEW HERBERT

Reconstruction of a Poet

VOICES:
Professor
Homer
Elpenor
A woman's voice

PROFESSOR: [*starts always in the same manner, like a gramophone record in mid-track*] . . .eece. Fragments were dug up . . . In the lower section . . . Artemis of Miletus.

Discovered at the beginning of the twentieth century by Evans, it hadn't been explored fully. Evans was misled by a layer of petrified rubble beneath which he did not expect to find anything else. We have taken into account sources – admittedly late ones dating from the Persian wars – I have in mind Apollodorus of Dioros, and especially Eutyphron the Elder, a second-rate historian, but reliable, who . . .

[*water drips from a tap*]

. . . expectations and represents a break-through for scholarship. In the sector we call the Third City we have discovered the earliest inscriptions by the Homeridae. These undoubtedly constitute fragments of *The Iliad* and pre-date the final official version in which it has reached us by at least two centuries. The team working contemporaneously with us on the island of Milos has also discovered written sources which, however, are artistically worthless – I will refer to them in passing at the end – important only in the sense that they confirm our thesis that an artistic centre flourished in Asia Minor and not on the peninsula which . . .

[*water drips from a tap*]

. . . who then was that Anon? We know only that he was a Greek, but from the fragments he has left we can recreate his portrait.

So first of all a man at the peak of his career and happy (valuable remarks about the art of gilding), a powerful personality displaying great self-control and calm. No sign of nervousness, a total absence of exaggeration which regrettably is such a great blemish on contemporary art. And above all – one is tempted to cry out – the voice is never raised, the emotions and the speech under control. Even the cruelties of war he sees with the cool eye of a true epic poet. A noble restraint and a dignified seriousness cover these fragments in simple yet noble garments.

A deep understanding of life enables him to cover a wide range of themes which we can classify under seven headings:
1   War themes
2   Mythologico-genealogical themes
3   Love themes
4   Pastoral themes (a valuable reference to sheep grazing)
5   Metallurgical themes (bronze, copper, iron)
6   Themes of daily life
7   Other

[*water drips from a tap*]

. . . and for example this fragment testifies to the power of Anon's poetic imagination:

> *Light-footed Hermes hastens to Gorgias's bed*
> *while he supports the tent's awning with his snores;*
> *in his ear he whispers calling him to stand by Gymedes*
> *whose father ruled Lemnos rich in harvests,*
> *while his elder brother, the strong-fisted Atarchus,*
> *drew the ire of Apollo when sailing the Hellespont*
> *for snatching Bryseis against her will*
> *and she gave birth to Castor, the cause of evil,*
> *who overly confident forsook his father,*
> *white-bearded Nicos . . .*

[*sound of shattering glass*]

HOMER: [*shouting*] Enough! I can't bear these parodies. First Virgil, then the translators, philologists, archaeologists . . . I am reduced to a handbook of mythology and a model for stylistic analyses.

I am forty-five. I live in Miletus. A wife, a son, a house and garden.

I am very fond of Miletus. A busy town. Just enough noise for a pleasant life. A healthy climate. A willing and prosperous public.

At first I worked on a ship. But I had an accident. I fell on deck and lost my sight; the medics said it was a shock, that it will pass. But things aren't quite right. I wasn't fit any more for a job at sea so I worked in the docks as a guard. I always did have a good voice; as powerful as a storm. Friends said I should give a concert. I did and the idea caught on. I changed my profession. The new job was easier and more interesting. I would have been completely happy if it weren't for the eyes. Doctors say I must stay in the dark for as long as possible and avoid the sun. The wife locks me up in the house. I have to sneak out. It's a bit demeaning.

I can't break off now when I am most successful. I'll be able to retire in a couple of years. I'll buy a large inn in the centre of town. It will be noisy and teeming with life – from the cellars where they roll the barrels to lovers whispering in the cheapest little rooms in the attic. I'll take care of my eyes then. I'll screw up my eyes to examine the world entering the front door. I'd also like to work on the theory of the epic. I do think I've made something of a contribution there.

My predecessors saw the epic as a plain. They droned about battles, marches, ruined cities and fire. Everything seen from a distance and therefore very flat. I got right in there. I turned the epic into a mountain, heavy matter, which pulls itself up from the earth to the sky and reaches the gods.

My predecessors controlled emotions by controlling the voice. A silly ploy and a lie against nature. I discovered the need to shout. So long as fear dwells in man he needs to shout.

Now it's noon. The town is white with heat. Everything is covered in quiet dust but a cry lurks beneath.

A WOMAN'S VOICE: Where are you off to, Homer?

HOMER: I'm off for a walk.

A WOMAN'S VOICE: You know surely . . .

HOMER: I know, I know.

A WOMAN'S VOICE: They were hurting you again yesterday.

HOMER: But today they are better.

A WOMAN'S VOICE: Don't go to the market-place. Promise.

HOMER: I promise.

A WOMAN'S VOICE:

And keep out of the sun. Keep an eye on Father, Elpenor.

ELPENOR: We are being naughty again.

HOMER: Can't help it, my boy; I can't stay at home all the time.

ELPENOR: Why?

HOMER: As noon approaches, the silence becomes unbearable. You can hear the wasps swarming in the attic. My flesh creeps.

ELPENOR: You have peace, you can compose verses.

HOMER: I don't think about verses then.

ELPENOR: About what then?

HOMER: About the market – like the sea; plunging up to the neck.

ELPENOR: You like the market that much?

HOMER: There's nothing more beautiful, son. Onion bread smells better than marble. I'd exchange an Ionic capital for a cabbage.

ELPENOR: What's beautiful in that?

HOMER: Everything, you silly boy. The colour, the smell, the noise. All the voices of life: the mumbling beggars, the shrieks of girls pressed in a crowd, the guardsman's drum, the calls of vegetable sellers and the roar of animals tied by their horns. Then the poet arrives and the battle begins.

ELPENOR: Battle?

HOMER: Yes, I have to shout louder than them, deafen them, deprive them of voice, swallow it and then pull it out of myself.

ELPENOR: That's a great pain.

HOMER: And joy. I become a plenitude like the world.

ELPENOR: That precisely is what I dislike, when towards the end . . . your voice rises and you begin to shout.

HOMER: Why?

ELPENOR: It's as if you were afraid and calling for help. Are you afraid then?

HOMER: No. Then I fight.

ELPENOR: With whom?

HOMER: With fear.

[*sounds of the market-place*]

HOMER: We've arrived. Let's start to work.

ELPENOR: Citizens! The poet Homer, renowned on the continent and on the islands, has succumbed to your pleas and despite

pressure of work has consented to give a concert. This will be the
first presentation of "The Seventh Battle at Troy". The work was
completed today at dawn and has not been published anywhere.
A portion of his receipts will be donated to a religious cause: the
purchase of glass eyes for the statue of Hera.

HOMER: [*against the sound of welling music*]

At first light. A pink rain is falling on a tin sky.
The first rustle in the bay. A bird choked in sleep.
Pale mists, intolerably quiet like the dead, rise from the marsh.
Now voices and metal against metal are heard in leather tents
Combed by the wind and bring the full day, the day unwrapped
Out of night like a screaming baby having its nappy changed
And drinking the fine air. Agamemnon is ready first, inspects
The lines, exhorts; Piramedes and Castor, Pandarus
With Pindarus and Archimedes follow. Hooves, the cracking of
    whips,
Cries, the creaking carts. I wake the Trojans, the gates open
Loudly. Two regiments of cavalry and foot, now rolled up
Like a fist, stand in the milky mist, resembling a forest.
Agamemnon draws his sword. Cools it in the air,
And then warms it up, with a mighty swing touching
The sun, the metal sizzles, soldiers stifle a gasp.
They start. A mighty roar as if a giant's sandal
Were moving over the rocks: stone against stone,
Metal against metal and thongs, the wondrous
Noise of things, but people are still numb, entwined
In speed and thoughts about the dead waters of Erebus.
Eurylocus next to Ajax. Ajax gives him advice
(mindful of the dream and prophecy, a broken column
of smoke): "Be mindful my friend to avoid Demetrius
The Trojans' bowman"; a spear shatters the speech.
Ajax's charioteer falls, his cry cut short as if
Torn reins dragged by maddened horses. Fear shared
By men and beast, hair rising inside the helmets,
Sweat and knees trembling. To overcome fear the Greeks
Raise a huge shield of cries. The battle is huge
And wonderful. The din, which the gods love,
As they love the fattened meat in sacrifice,
Rises and reaches divine ears pink with sleep

And joy; the gods descend to earth. Thus begins
The poem. For what is an epic if not a thick knot
Of people, metal and gods, linked together
Convulsed, with a red cock on the top. The cock
Which sings the terror, the cock, the cock . . .

[a sudden pause]

HOMER: Elpenor!
ELPENOR: I'm here, Father.
HOMER: Let's go home.
ELPENOR: What's the matter, Father?
HOMER: Lead me home.
ELPENOR: But you must finish. They're all waiting.
HOMER: Home.

[they leave the hubbub, pause]

HOMER: Walk slowly, my boy. Something's happened to my eyes.
ELPENOR: They hurt?
HOMER: No.

[pause]

HOMER: Come closer, Son, and look me in the eyes. What do you see?
ELPENOR: Me in the middle. Also trees and the town.
HOMER: But I don't. Nothing. Nothing.
ELPENOR: You just see a mist? Just like in the past when you had these spells?
HOMER: I don't even see the mist. There's nothing.

[pause]

ELPENOR: You're tired, Father. A white glare comes off the stones.
HOMER: White, you say?
ELPENOR: Yes, is that strange?
HOMER: No, it's normal. It's what I now have in my eyes that's strange. It's not even blackness. It's the colour of emptiness.

[pause]

HOMER: I don't understand at all what's happened. What do you think?
ELPENOR: You'll get home and rest.
HOMER: But I haven't gone blind.

[pause]

HOMER: When I sang the death of the charioteer, I could still see quite well. I noticed how Sephar left the slaughtered ram, wiped the blood off his hands against his apron and walked towards us. At that moment I had them all in my hand. I was happy.

ELPENOR: You'd better close your eyes, Father. I'll lead you. With eyes shut you'll relax better.

HOMER: Yes, you are right. I am calm.

ELPENOR: There you are.

HOMER: You feel very stupid not seeing anything with your eyes open.

[pause]

HOMER: Do you think I will see when I open my eyes?

ELPENOR: Of course. But don't do it yet. There's no hurry.

HOMER: Yes, there's no hurry.

ELPENOR: Do you want to sit down?

HOMER: Gladly, but let's get out of town first. Now the walls close above me like water.

[pause]

ELPENOR: You sang beautifully.

HOMER: Out of fear. I've been haunted by fear since morning. I tried to kill it with a cry.

ELPENOR: You killed it with poetry.

HOMER: Poetry is a cry. Do you know what remains of a poem when you remove the din?

ELPENOR: I don't.

HOMER: Nothing.

[pause]

HOMER: Do you think it will pass?

ELPENOR: I'm sure it will pass. Don't you feel better?

HOMER: Better. But I'd rather not open my eyes yet.

ELPENOR: Certainly.

HOMER: Let's sit here. Where are we?

ELPENOR: Near Pan's fountain.

HOMER: Of course, I can hear. So we are almost home.

ELPENOR: No need to hurry.

HOMER: You're right, Son. Let's take it easy.

[pause]

HOMER: When my eyes are closed I calm down. But I'll have to open them eventually.

ELPENOR: We'll try just outside the house.

HOMER: Let's.

ELPENOR: What are you doing, Father?

HOMER: I'm inspecting my face. Everything's in place. The eyes too. A terrible sensation when something which is intimately yours suddenly leaves you.

ELPENOR: It's nice here.

HOMER: Yes, it is. Peace. Shade.

ELPENOR: Lie on the bench. I'll cover your face with your coat.

HOMER: You look after me the way Antigone looked after Oedipus. But Oedipus really did go blind. Say something, Son.

ELPENOR: When we buy the inn you won't need to leave the house. The sun harms you.

HOMER: Yes, very much.

ELPENOR: The inn will be among trees. In the shade.

HOMER: We'll have to give it a name.

ELPENOR: *The Snoring Merchant.* That'll draw merchants and thieves.

HOMER: Or *The Eye of Zeus.* That'll draw pilgrims and moderate atheists.

ELPENOR: We'll have lots of servants.

HOMER: And good wines. Just the two of us will carry the cellar key.

[*pause*]

ELPENOR: Let's go, Father.

HOMER: Let's. It isn't far?

ELPENOR: Just round this corner.

HOMER: I can tell by the gravel: I see with my feet now.

ELPENOR: Here we are. Our home, Father. Look.

[*Homer shouts*]

THE PROFESSOR: . . . eece. As I have already observed, this second discovery is in fact of no great significance. In comparison with Anon of Miletus, a giant, Anon of Milo is a dwarf.

[*water drips from a tap*]

. . . trivial and vulgar themes. Anon doesn't hesitate to devote a poem to a tamarisk, a common, fertile and useless plant.

HOMER:

> I sang of battles
> towers and ships
> of slaughtered heroes
> and slaughtering heroes
> but forgot this one thing

I sang of the sea-storm
of crumbling walls
of wheat in flames
and flattened hills
but forgot the tamarisk

when he lies
pierced with a spear
and the lips of his wound
close
he sees
neither the sea
nor the city
nor his comrade
next to his face
he sees
a tamarisk
he climbs
on the highest
dry branch of the tamarisk
and avoiding
green and brown leaves
he tries
to fly up
without wings
without blood
without thought
without –

THE PROFESSOR: The poverty of the subject is a match for
atrophied form, which . . .

[*water drips from a tap*]

HOMER: Well, I must confess. It was me writing about the tamarisk.
And how did it come about?

On the third day after that incident at the market-place I left
Miletus. Alone. A sort of pilgrimage to a holy place. That was on
the island of Milo. A spring and the temple of Zeus the
Miracle-Maker.

There was a terrible crush at the spring. According to the

instructions from the priests you had to splash yourself with the holy water and loudly proclaim your petition. The din was indescribable. "Hippias wants his missing leg back." "Anticlea begs for fertility and the return of her husband." I cried the loudest in a dark voice heavy with tears: "Homer demands the return of his sight!" Three days passed and no miracle.

I went to the temple at night and repeated my plea. My voice curled round the columns, bounced off the ceiling and fell flat at my feet.

I climbed the altar and touched the god's face. His lips were shut like a clam. He was as blind as me.

I felt sorry for him and composed an ode to cheer him up.

> I kept thrusting up
> the thick rope of my cries
> to pull you to earth
> the noose fell empty
>
> now I know
> that neither in the blood
> nor in the bones
> nor even
> in the flesh of thought
>
> but only in the great silence
> can we feel
> the pulse of your being
> constant and vanishing
> like a wave of light
>
> you attract
> like all non-being
> I pay you homage
> by touching the flesh
> of your absence.

I didn't have much time for the god. More important things were happening. My body was ripening in darkness and silence. It was like the earth in spring, full of unpresaged possibilities. My skin was growing a sensitivity. I began to discover myself, I examined and described myself.

First I will describe myself
starting with the head
or better with the leg
the left leg to be precise
or from the hand
from the little finger of the left hand

my little finger
is warm
bent slightly inwards
a nail at the top
consists of three segments
grows straight out of the palm
separated from it
it would be a large worm

it's a special finger
the only little finger of a left hand in the world
given me directly

other little fingers of the left hand
are a cold abstraction

with mine
we share a birthdate
we share a death date
we share a loneliness

only the blood
scanning dark tautologies
ties distant shores
with a thread of understanding

    I began to examine the world very cautiously. Everything I knew about it was useless. Like sets from another play. One had to come to know afresh, starting not with Troy or with Achilles, but from a sandal, a buckle of a sandal, from a stone kicked casually on the road.

A stone is a perfect
being

equal to itself
confined to its borders
filled precisely
with a stony sleep
with a smell which recalls nothing
disturbs nothing and rouses no desire

its fieriness and cold
are proper and full of dignity

I feel very guilty
when I handle it
and a false warmth
penetrates
its noble flesh

stones can't be tamed
to the very end they'll watch us
with a calm and very bright eye.

I will never return to Miletus. That's where I left my cry. It
could assault me in an alleyway and kill me.

Between the cry of birth
and the cry of death
examine your fingernails
the sunset
the fish-tail
and whatever you see
don't take it to the market-place
don't sell it cut-price
don't cry

the gods like lovers
like a huge silence

between the cry of the beginning
and the cry of the end

        be like an unfingered lyre
        which has no voice
        yet has them all

This is only the beginning. The beginning is always funny. I'm sitting on the lowest step of the temple of Zeus, the Miracle-Maker, praising the little finger, the tamarisk, the stone.

I have no disciples, no listeners. They are all standing still, gazing at the great conflagration of the epic. But the fires are dying down. Soon there will only be smoky ruins which grass will conquer. I am grass.

Sometimes I imagine that out of my new poems I will succeed in drawing new men who will not be adding iron to iron, cries to cries, fear to fear.

Surely one can add seed to seed, leaf to leaf, emotion to emotion.

And word to silence.

THE PROFESSOR: . . . eece. The poverty of the poetic world of Anon from Milo enables us to assume that he had no successors and that . . .

Translated from the Polish by Adam Czerniawski

NOTES ON THE AUTHORS

BENNO BARNARD was born in Amsterdam in 1954 and now lives in Antwerp. He has published a number of collections of poetry but is better known for his autobiographical novel *Uitgesteld paradijs* (*Postponed Paradise*) to which *Het gat in de wereld* (*The Hole in the World*) is the sequel. He is presently editor of the *Nieuw Wereld Tijdschrift* and also works as a translator.

PAOLA CAPRIOLO was born in Milan in 1962. In addition to the collection of stories from which the two here published are drawn, she has written two novels, *Il Nocchiero* (*The Helmsman*) and *Il Doppio Regno* (*The Double Kingdom*). She has been published in several European languages and is considered one of the most creatively original of Italy's younger writers.

DERMOT HEALY was born in Finea, Co. Westmeath, in 1947. He is the author of the story collection, *Banished Misfortune* (1982), of a novel, *Fighting with Shadows* (1984), and the poetry collection, *The Ballyconnell Colours* (1992). He wrote the screenplay for Cathal Black's acclaimed film about the Christian Brothers, *Our Boys*, and his plays include *The Long Swim* and *On Broken Wings*. He is the editor of *Force 10*, which has been acclaimed as Ireland's best community arts journal. His most recent publication is the novel, *A Goat's Song* (1994). He is a member of Aosdána and lives near Sligo.

ZBIGNIEW HERBERT is one of the best-known living Polish poets. English translations of his poetry and essays have been appearing during the last three decades. These include: *Selected Poems* (1968), *A Barbarian in the Garden* (1985), *Report from the Besieged City and Other Poems* (1987), and *Still Life with a Bridle, Essays & Apocryphas* (1993). Hardly known outside Poland are his miniatures for radio, of which *Reconstruction of a Poet* is one.

PETER HØEG was born in 1957 and followed various callings – dancer, actor, fencer, sailor, mountaineer – before he turned seriously to writing. He published his first novel in 1988, and it earned him the description of "the foremost storyteller of his generation" from *Information* magazine. Two years later he published his first collection of short stories, including the one reproduced in this anthology. Then came his novel *Miss Smilla's Feeling for Snow*, which brought him an international readership; it is a novel of detection which wholly transcends the genre, for it enriches the imagination and stretches the mind.

JAAN KAPLINSKI was born in Tartu, Estonia in 1941. His mother was Estonian, and his father, who disappeared into a Stalinist labour camp while the poet was still a child, was Polish. A professor at the State University in Tartu, he has translated from the Spanish, French, English, Polish and Chinese, and co-translated two collections of his own poems, *The Same Sea in Us All* and *The Wandering Border*, for English publication. He is a member of the Estonian Parliament.

GIUSEPPE TOMASI DI LAMPEDUSA (1896–1957), Prince of Lampedusa and a notable survivor into our own day of the great Sicilian landed aristocracy, is best remembered as the author of *The Leopard*, "perhaps the greatest novel of the century" (L. P. Hartley). A man of broad culture, his acquaintance with English literature surpassed that of many a well-read Englishman. He is also the author of one of the best appreciations of Stendhal ever written. His essays on Izaak Walton and Samuel Johnson are taken from a selection of his writings to be published by Harvill in 1995 under the title *The Siren and Selected Writings*.

SVEN LINDQVIST was born in Stockholm in 1932 and received his PhD from Stockholm University in 1966. In the early sixties he lived in China for two years, studying Chinese, and has since travelled extensively in Asia, Africa and Latin America. Several of his books on Third World problems have appeared in English: *China in Crisis* (1963), *The Shadow* (1972), *Land and Power in South America* (1979). In Sweden Sven Lindqvist is better known as the author of such autobiographical essays as *The Myth of Wu Tao-tzu* (1967), *Diary of a Lover* (1981) and *Exterminate All the Brutes* (1992). As a major Swedish writer he was awarded an honorary professorship in 1990.

CLAUDIO MAGRIS was born in 1939 in Trieste. After graduating from the University of Turin, he lectured there in German Language and Literature from 1970 to 1978, before moving to the faculty of Literature and Philosophy at the University of Trieste. He has translated works by Ibsen, Kleist and Schnitzler and written many works of literary criticism. He is internationally recognized as the author of *Danube*, and more recently, of a novel, *A Different Sea* – which has pertinent things to say about shifting frontiers. Since the 1994 elections he has been an independent Senator in the Italian parliament.

MA YUAN was born in Liaoning Province. After the Cultural Revolution, he studied machine construction at technical school and then went on to university. Losing interest in study, he applied to go to Tibet upon graduation. It was during his time in Lhasa that he first achieved acclaim as a writer of "post-modernist" fiction. He has published one collection of his work, and currently lives on the island of Hainan, off the south coast of China, where he makes films for television.

HARRY MULISCH was born in Haarlem in 1927 and published his first novel in 1952. Mulisch's oeuvre comprises novels, poetry, short stories, plays, contemporary histories and studies. He has received many awards, including the Anne Frank Literary Prize (1957), the Vijverberg Prize (1963), the Constantijn Huygens Prize (1977), the P. C. Hooft Prize (1977) and the Multatuli Prize (1993). The film adaptation of his best-seller *De Aanslag* (*The Assault*) won an Academy Award.

CEES NOOTEBOOM was born in The Hague in 1933. He is a poet, the author of seven novels and ten travel books. An experienced hitchhiker and traveller, he has journeyed through much of the world, making his first voyage as a sailor to earn his passage to South America; he has been travelling ever since. His first international success was the Pegasus Prize for *Rituals*. More recently, for *A Berlin Notebook*, he was awarded the German Order of Merit. His novel *The Following Story*, published by Harvill, won the 1993 Aristeion European Literary Prize, confirming Nooteboom's stature as a prominent and popular figure in contemporary European and World literature.

MALACHI O'DOHERTY is a freelance journalist living and working in Belfast. He is forty-three years old and has made a number of television documentaries on Northern Ireland for the BBC and Independent Television. He is a regular contributor on Northern Ireland affairs to the *New Statesman, Fortnight*, and BBC Radio Ulster.

ANDREW O'HAGAN was born in Glasgow in 1968, made his First Holy Communion in 1975 and smoked his first full cigarette – a Rothman's Royal – in the toilet of a cinema in 1979. He now works at the *London Review of Books*.

BORISLAV PEKIĆ was born in the Montenegrin capital Podgorica in 1930 and educated in Belgrade. In 1948 he was sentenced to fifteen years in prison for his activity in the Union of Democratic Youth of Yugoslavia. He served two years before being pardoned. In 1970 he moved to London but returned frequently to Yugoslavia, where he was a member of the Serbian Academy of Sciences and Art, later becoming vice-president of the Democratic Party of which he was a founding member. Author of a vast opus which encompassed novels, stage, television and radio plays, film scripts, essays and articles, Borislav Pekić was awarded all the most prestigious Yugoslav literary prizes and was vice-president of the Serbian PEN. He died in 1992.

FRANS POINTL, born in Amsterdam in 1933, did not turn to the writing of short stories until his forty-eighth year. His first collection, *The Chicken that Flew over the Soup*, was published in 1989 and two years later had run into nineteen impressions. It has appeared in German in Switzerland and has been followed by two more collections, *The Touch* and *The Rich Are Harder to Fit*. Frans Pointl survived the Holocaust but underwent all the rigours of its aftermath about which he writes.

JONATHAN RABAN was born in Norfolk, England, in 1942. After spending four years as a university lecturer, he became a professional writer in 1969. He is the author of *Soft City* (1974), *Arabia* (1979), *Old Glory* (1982), which won the Royal Society of Literature's Heinemann Award and the Thomas Cook Travel Book Award, *Coasting* (1986) and *Hunting Mister Heartbreak* (1990), which also won the Thomas Cook Travel Book Award, making him the only writer ever to have won that prestigious award twice. He is author of the novel *Foreign Land* (1985), the collection *For Love and Money* (1987) and the pamphlet *God, Man and Mrs Thatcher* (1990). His anthology, *The Oxford Book of the Sea*, has recently been published in Britain and America. A Fellow of the Royal Society of Literature, he is a well-known book reviewer and broadcaster; his recent journalism has appeared in *Harper's*, *New York Review of Books*, *New Republic*, *Granta*, *Esquire* and other magazines in Britain and the USA. He lives in Seattle with his American wife, Jean; their daughter, Julia, was born on Thanksgiving Day, 1992.

JEAN ROUAUD won the Prix Goncourt, France's most prestigious literary prize, for his first novel, published by Harvill as *Fields of Glory* in a translation by Ralph Manheim. He was thirty-eight when he published it, after a varied career as a nightwatchman, stagehand, philosophy teacher and newsvendor in a kiosk in northern Paris. He now lives in the south of France. *Of Illustrious Men* is published by Harvill in 1995.

JOSÉ SARAMAGO was born in Portugal in 1922, and has been a full-time writer since 1979. His opus embraces plays, poetry, short stories, works of non-fiction and several novels, which have been translated into more than twenty languages and established him as Portugal's most influential living writer. It was the publication in 1988 of *Baltasar and Blimunda* that first brought him to the attention of an English-speaking readership. *The Year of the Death of Ricardo Reis* won the *Independent* Foreign Fiction Award for 1992. And his novel *The Gospel According to Jesus Christ* has won him new readers all round the world.

JEAN-PAUL SARTRE (1905–80): Philosopher, novelist, playwright, critic. A leading light of the existentialist movement, Sartre's influence on intellectual life in the post-war years was considerable. His doctrines are best expressed in *L'Etre et le Néant* (1943). With Simone de Beauvoir, he founded the review *Les Temps Modernes* (1945) and became an active supporter of numerous moral and political causes. His most celebrated novel is *La Nausée* (1938), while his plays include *Les Mouches* (1943) and *Huis Clos* (1944). He was awarded but declined to accept the Nobel Prize for Literature in 1964.

ZINOVY ZINIK was born in Moscow in 1945. He emigrated in 1975 and spent one year in Jerusalem as director of a Russian student theatre group. Invited by the BBC, he settled with his family in London, becoming a British citizen in 1988. His short stories and essays have appeared in the *New Yorker*, the *Times Literary Supplement*, the *Spectator* and other periodicals. Since his arrival in the West, his six novels, along with various novellas and short stories, have been published in a number of European languages. Zinik's most famous novel, *The Mushroom Picker*, was adapted for television by BBC2 and his most recent novel, *The Lord and the Gamekeeper*, was nominated for the 1992 Russian Booker Prize.

NOTES ON THE TRANSLATORS

ANNE BORN [*Compassion for the Children of Vaden Town* by Peter Høeg] is a veteran translator from Danish, Swedish and Norwegian, including works by Karen Blixen, Bo Carpelan and Stig Dagerman, as well as being a prizewinning poet of considerable stature. She has taught at St Clare's Hall, Oxford, and in the University of Cambridge, and has served as Chairwoman of the Translators' Association.

BARBARA BRAY [*Walking in Venice* by Jean-Paul Sartre] studied English at Cambridge, lectured in Egypt, was Radio Drama Script Editor at the BBC, and is now a freelance writer and theatre director living in Paris. Her translations include plays and novels by Marguerite Duras and works by numerous other French authors, classical and contemporary.

JAMES BROCKWAY [*The Chicken that Flew over the Soup* by Frans Pointl] went to Holland after the War, during which he flew with the RAF, and besides his own writing soon took to translating in many fields, particularly Dutch fiction, poetry, art and academic work. The Dutch awarded him their Martinus Nijhoff Prize for services to Dutch Literature as early as 1966. His most recent titles are *A World Beyond Myself* (translations of the poetry of Rutger Kopland) (1991) and *Singers Behind Glass – Eight Dutch Poets* (due in 1994).

DAVID COLMER [*An Autumn Day in Bohemia* by Benno Barnard] has published short stories in Britain and Australia. He translates from German and Dutch, and has lived in Amsterdam for the last three years.

ADAM CZERNIAWSKI [*Reconstruction of a Poet* by Zbigniew Herbert], a Polish writer and translator living in England, recently retired as Assistant Director of the British Centre for Literary Translation at the University of East Anglia. His latest publications include: *Poezje zebrane* (*Collected Poems*) (1993), a memoir, *Scenes from a Disturbed Childhood* (1991), and translations of the poetry of Tadeusz Różewicz (*They Came to See a Poet*) (1991) and Wisława Szymborska (*People on a Bridge*) (1990).

ADRIENNE DIXON [*The Boundary* by Harry Mulisch] was born in 1932 in the Dutch province of Drenthe and moved to England in 1957 where she married a year later and lived with her English husband, teaching English and French at secondary school. Her translations of Dutch and Flemish fiction won her two distinguished prizes: The Martinus Nijhoff

Prize in 1974 and the Translation Centre of Columbia University's Translation Prize from the Dutch for her rendering of Cees Nooteboom's novel *Rituals*. Her translations include the works of Cees Nooteboom (*Rituals*, *In the Dutch Mountains* and *A Song of Truth and Semblance*), Harry Mulisch (*The Stone Bridal Bed* and *Last Call*) and J. Bernlef (*Out of Mind*). Adrienne Dixon died in 1990.

ELLEN ELIAS-BURSAĆ [*Resistance and Comforts* by Borislav Pekić] is a literary translator and South Slavic scholar with degrees from Macalester College and Zagreb University. Her translations include the novel *Holograms of Fear* by Slavenka Drakulic, published by Norton, Hutchinson and the Women's Press in 1992 and 1993, and shorter pieces in the *Cimarron*, Stanford Humanities and Colorado Reviews and the North Dakota Quarterly.

DAVID GILMOUR [*Izaak Walton* and *Doctor Johnson* by Giuseppe Tomasi di Lampedusa] is the author of *Lebanon: The Fractured Country*, *The Transformation of Spain: From Franco to the Constitutional Monarchy*, a biography of Lord Curzon, and *The Last Leopard: A Life of Giuseppe Tomasi di Lampedusa*.

SAM HAMILL ["The East-West Border" and "Once I Got a Postcard" by Jaan Kaplinski] is co-publisher with Tree Swenson at Copper Canyon Press, Washington, USA. He is the author of seven collections of poetry, and has translated several volumes of poetry from the Chinese, and also selected poems of Catullus from the Latin. Riina Tamm is, in Sam Hamill's words, his "patient and generous correspondent in all matters Estonian".

ALAN MYERS [*Hooks* by Zinovy Zinik] has translated a wide variety of Russian prose and verse, including Dostoyevsky's *The Idiot* and Joseph Brodsky's plays *Marble* and *Democracy*, as well as *An Age Ago*, an anthology of facsimile translations of nineteenth-century Russian poetry.

SIMON PATTON [*Three Ways to Fold a Paper Kite* by Ma Yuan] is completing a PhD thesis on the poetry of Gu Cheng at the University of Melbourne, Australia. He is president of the Australian Literary Translator's Association (ALiTrA).

GIOVANNI PONTIERO [*Reflux* and *Revenge* by José Saramago] is Reader in Latin-American Literature in the University of Manchester. Among his many publications are *An Anthology of Brazilian Modernist Poetry* and *Eleanora Duse: In Life and Art*. He is the principal English translator of the works of Clarice Lispector and José Saramago. His translation of Saramago's *The Year of the Death of Ricardo Reis* won the 1992 *Independent* Foreign Fiction Award.

INA RILKE [*Gateway to China* by Cees Nooteboom] has translated a wide variety of essays and art-historical literature; she teaches at the Department of Translation Studies at Amsterdam University. She is the translator of Cees Nooteboom's *The Following Story* (Harvill, London, 1994), which won the Aristeion European Literary Prize. Her translation of Nooteboom's *Long Road to Santiago* is to be published by Harvill in 1995.

JOAN TATE [*The Desert Divers* by Sven Lindqvist] has been writing, translating and reading for publishers full time for more than thirty-five years. Her translations for Harvill include Ingmar Bergman's *The Best Intentions* (1993) and *Sunday's Child* (1994).

GUIDO WALDMAN [*Who Is on the Other Side* by Claudio Magris and *The Giant* and *Letters to Luisa* by Paola Capriolo] has translated Italian writers as early as the thirteenth-century Anonimo Toscano and as recent as Italo Calvino and Giuseppe Tomasi di Lampedusa. He was editor of *The Penguin Book of Italian Short Stories*. His translations of Ariosto's *Orlando Furioso* and Boccaccio's *The Decameron* are published in Oxford University Press World Classics.

BARBARA WRIGHT [*Of Illustrious Men* by Jean Rouaud] has brought her creative fantasy and encyclopaedic knowledge of the English language to a wide variety of French writers, including Raymond Queneau, Robert Pinget, Nathalie Sarraute, Pierre Albert-Birot and Michel Tournier. She has been three times winner of the Scott Moncrieff Prize, and has been recognized in France with the award of Officier de l'Ordre des Arts et des Lettres.